K.I.S.S

DK

The Only Guides You'll Ever Need!

THIS SERIES IS YOUR TRUSTED GUIDE through all of life's stages and situations. Want to learn how to surf the Internet or care for your new dog? Or maybe you'd like to become a wine connoisseur or an expert gardener? The solution is simple: Just pick up a K.I.S.S. Guide and turn to the first page.

Expert authors will walk you through the subject from start to finish, using simple blocks of knowledge to build your skills one step at a time. Build upon these learning blocks and by the end of the book, you'll be an expert yourself! Or, if you are familiar with the topic but want to learn more, it's easy to dive in and pick up where you left off.

The K.I.S.S. Guides deliver what they promise: simple access to all the information you'll need on one subject. Other titles you might want to check out include: Playing Guitar, Living With a Dog, the Internet, Microsoft Windows, Astrology, and many more to come.

K·I·S·S

GUIDE TO

Gardening

L. PATRICIA KITE

Foreword by H. Marc Cathey
President Emeritus, American Horticultural Society

A Dorling Kindersley Book

LONDON, NEW YORK,
MUNICH, MELBOURNE, DELHI

DK Publishing, Inc.

Editorial Director: LaVonne Carlson
Series Editors: Beth Adelman, Jennifer Williams

Dorling Kindersley Limited

Project Editor: Caroline Hunt
Managing Editor: Maxine Lewis
Managing Art Editor: Heather McCarry

Production: Michelle Thomas
Editorial Director: Valerie Buckingham

Produced for Dorling Kindersley
by **Cooling Brown**
9–11 High Street, Hampton, Middlesex TW12 2SA

Senior Designer: Tish Mills **Designers:** Pauline Clarke, Hilary Krag
Senior Editor: Amanda Lebentz **Editors:** Clare Hill, Helen Ridge

Published in the United States by
DK Publishing, Inc., 95 Madison Avenue, New York, New York 10016
A Penguin Company

Library of Congress Cataloging-in-Publication Data

Kite, L. Patricia.
    KISS guide to gardening / L. Patricia Kite -- 1st American ed.
        p. cm. -- (Keep it simple series)
    Includes bibliographical references (p.) and index.
        ISBN 0-7894-6141-2 (alk. paper)
        1. Gardening. I. Title. II. Series.
SB453 . K64 2000
635--dc21

                                                    00-009321

Color reproduction by ColourScan, Singapore
Printed and bound by Printer Industria Grafica, S.A., Barcelona, Spain

For our complete catalog visit

www.dk.com

Contents at a Glance

 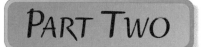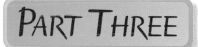

CONTENTS

PART ONE Begin With the Basics

CHAPTER 1 Planning Ahead   22

CHAPTER 2 Be a Soil Detective   38

PART FOUR Exploring Edibles

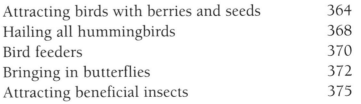

Foreword

I REMEMBER WHEN I FIRST REALIZED that growing plants could lead to a lifetime experience. I had no idea what would be involved. I knew, however, that marvelous things happened to gardeners. They always seemed to have interesting things to do, good vegetables and fruits to share with friends, and all sorts of fun places to visit. Along the way I learned to identify plants brought back to our North Carolina gardens from all parts of the world. I grew to appreciate the twisting and bending involved in every gardening act. I also thoroughly enjoyed giving plants away as tokens of my regards.

Gardening is the number one hobby in the United States. All you need is an open space in your yard, or a spot on the terrace in your home for container plants. This K.I.S.S. Guide encourages you to experience the joys of gardening and its many benefits to your home, your community, and our shared environment.

The book has been created to start you on your journey as a gardener. You begin by analyzing your microclimates and how preparation of your soil is critical to your success. You find out what your obligations are in terms of time and resources, then you visualize your space to understand its limitations for safety and easy care. Next you prepare your site by planning for paths, beds, trees, screening, and fencing. Then you select your plants.

The plants suggested in the K.I.S.S. Guide to Gardening are the ones most frequently recognized as tough plants for tough times. They are readily available from your garden center and catalogs. Like children, plants can be very different in their "personalities" and the ease with which they prosper in your environment. This guide will help you make the best matches. Along the way it will add new words to your vocabulary and guide you to many plants that you will nurture as Steward of the Garden.

This K.I.S.S. Guide will help turn your idle spaces into gardens. Every day will involve learning, achievement, and failure – and you will vow never to let it happen again. It will also teach you how to observe, record, analyze, and plan for alternative actions.

Gardening has many languages to teach. Once you have success with the plants recommended in this book, you can trade up to growing more demanding plants. There are more than 250,000 kinds of plants to learn about, grow, and enjoy. And there is always a neighbor, extension technician, Master Gardener, garden center, and the American Horticultural Society (1-800-777-7931) to supplement what you'll learn in this book.

Remember, you are in control of what you grow. Avoid reckless shopping for plants, supplies, and equipment. Focus on what will help you achieve your goals. Consider the creative solutions, designs, plants, and management tips you'll find here. Then go where your garden and knowledge have never gone before.

H. MARC CATHEY
PRESIDENT EMERITUS
AMERICAN HORTICULTURAL SOCIETY

Introduction

IT SEEMS AS IF EVERYBODY these days is gardening, or wants to garden, "as soon as they have the time." There is something quite spiritual about working as a companion to the Earth, helping to provide flowers, trees, and scented herbs, as well as offering our families the practicality and health of fresh fruits and vegetables. It's a pleasurable option for most of us today, but it is an option that has evolved over time.

ENCOURAGING GROWTH

The garden of our ancestors was a transient place. The men searched for meat with primitive weapons. The fallback against hunger was the grains and fruits found in the forests and open lands. Groups didn't stay long enough in one place to develop their own controllable plot of land. When humans finally did band and settle, land was the common property of the group. There was more than enough for everybody.

Gradually, this changed too. As groups or tribes discovered the comforts of staying on one site for a long time, certain lands became parts of tribal domain. While the men hunted, women and children could go out into the surrounding acreage and bring back grain seeds and edible roots for eating and also for planting. These early gardens would ensure there was food for the coming year, even if no game was brought in that day, that week, or even that month. For in some hidden corner of the village, each woman had a well-concealed stash of edibles to tide her family through the leanest days.

It was a lot of work, with sharpened sticks and strong branches, to prepare the ground for planting. When the grains and early vegetables emerged, they had to be protected. Materials were certainly at hand. Early fences were thorny hedges or tree branches thrust into the ground and woven into sturdy barriers with thick vines.

The gardens became more polished, through increasingly effective equipment and greater knowledge. And so, in accordance with a hierarchy of needs, there was a tad of leisure. The garden provided foodstuffs, as well as a friendly, safe haven and the opportunity to create beauty and order in a disorderly world.

Many of the earliest pleasure gardens contained a versatile assortment of herbs. Some were grown for energy, others purportedly cured or ameliorated disease and distress. Anthropologists have found papyrus records dating back to about 1550 BC that include prescriptions containing garlic, peppermint, anise, and other heartily fragrant herbs. Eventually, various plants became a necessary import. Spices, medicinal plants, fruits, and plants used for dye were carried long, dangerous distances for commercial profit.

All so different from today – or is it? Perhaps only the outward facade has changed. New foodstuffs are constantly under development and herbs have undergone a tremendous resurgence, not only in tea bags, but also in modern pharmacopoeia. As our places of escape become more crowded, a little personal plot of land takes on increasing importance.

I wrote this book to help you with the practical aspects as well as the pleasure of gardening. Not everything you plant will grow, but even the tiniest success will spur you onward. To put a seed or plant in the soil and tempt it to flowering is, to me, the essence of creativity, even if the plant is doing most of the work.

L. PATRICIA KITE

Dedication
This book is dedicated to
Sarah Rose Raney.
Happy sunshine and many roses.

A PRIVATE REFUGE FROM THE OUTSIDE WORLD

What's Inside?

THE INFORMATION IN THE K.I.S.S. Guide to Gardening *is arranged so that you learn the basics, then swiftly progress to the rewarding challenges of creating the garden you've always wanted – and keeping it that way.*

PART ONE

In Part One I'll start with the basics: planning your garden, assessing and improving the soil, choosing and using the right tools, and how and when to water.

PART TWO

In Part Two I'll introduce you to some of my favorite annuals, perennials, and bulbs, and show you how to make the most of their unique characteristics.

PART THREE

In Part Three I'll reveal how big woody plants – ornamental trees, shrubs, roses, and vines – can make a real statement in the garden.

PART FOUR

In Part Four I'll whet your appetite with tempting fruit and vegetables as well as berries and herbs, and show how easy they are to grow, whatever the size of your garden.

PART FIVE

In Part Five I'll show you how to use the unifying elements of a garden – groundcovers, lawns, and container plants – to create a beautiful and harmonious environment.

PART SIX

In Part Six I'll encourage you to experiment and learn some new techniques. I'll explain how to make your own plants, attract wildlife, and deal with weeds, pests, and diseases. I'll also suggest various projects and activities for different times of the year.

The Extras

I KNOW THAT YOU'RE BUSY, so this book has special tidbits, marked with little pictures, to help you along.

Very Important Point
This symbol indicates directives to perform a task in a particular way.

Complete No-No
When you see this symbol, just don't do it!

Getting Technical
For you very thorough sorts, I've included these technical pointers to keep you happy.

Inside Scoop
These are special hints from me and other gardening gurus.

Throughout the book, you'll also find little boxes – some for facts, some just for fun.

Trivia...
My favorite boxes share minutiae about gardening, which is, above all, joy, and a link to the past and present.

DEFINITION
Here I'll **explain** *fancy gardening words and terms. You'll also find a simple Glossary at the back of the book with all the gardening lingo.*

INTERNET
www.internet.com

Boxes marked www send you to informative Web sites pertinent to gardening and related subjects. The Internet is a great resource for gardeners.

PART ONE

RICH, CRUMBLY LOAM, THE IDEAL SOIL FOR PLANTING

BEGIN WITH THE BASICS

EVERY GARDEN requires some planning, even if you prefer an "unplanned" garden. That's because what goes in your garden is determined by the space itself (How big is it? Is it windy or hilly?), the type of soil it contains, and the amount of light and water it gets. With these factors in mind, *it's a simple matter* to start planning what you want to plant, and where.

In this part I'll walk you through the planning stages of your garden. My idea is to help you start off on the right foot, so that your first efforts are *successful*. And the greater your success, the more you'll want to know about creating a *gorgeous* garden. So before you start to dig, read.

Chapter 1

Planning Ahead

BEFORE YOU CAN MAKE a garden, you have to plan. It's the same with any kind of journey: you must start with a map. There are many ways to approach the planning and basic landscaping. This should take into account the interests and needs of your entire family, including pets.

In this chapter...

✓ Who should do the planning?

✓ Landscape components

✓ The front of the house

✓ The flower garden

✓ The four seasons

✓ Some questions to ask yourself

✓ Climates and microclimates

✓ Dealing with difficult sites

Who should do the planning?

MAYBE YOU BOUGHT YOUR HOUSE *just for the big garden and have been looking forward to planning everything out yourself. Perhaps you already have some garden ideas in mind and can't wait to start work on implementing them. This is going to be fun! However, not everyone feels comfortable making all the decisions. Perhaps you wish you could get a little advice. Perhaps you wish you could just turn the whole project over to someone else. All kinds of help is available.*

Call in the professionals

A landscape architect has a degree in landscape architecture and should be able to show you a specific degree from an accredited school. Budget constraints may deter you from considering a landscape architect or a landscape consultant, but do think about it before you automatically say no. A licensed professional with many years of experience can save you from making expensive mistakes – not only immediate ones, but those that come later when you have to pay several hundred dollars to take down a tree that simply shouldn't have been there in the first place. A professional will not only help you plan, but also may be able to recommend contractors and nurseries that will do the best job.

Nurseries

Some nurseries employ a specialist who can help customers plan their landscapes. You are not going to find these people at hardware stores or general store garden departments. I am talking here about nurseries that are independent of other businesses. What do they get for providing this service? Usually, in exchange for a plan, you agree to buy all the necessary materials from that nursery, and perhaps let their staff do the labor.

Before you make any definitive arrangements with a nursery, it is wise to review their plans thoroughly. The landscaping should meet your needs, which you have wisely listed on a piece of paper and kept a copy of. You do not want the same plan as everybody else in your neighborhood, either.

And, of course, you have selected a reliable nursery by chatting with your neighbors, looking at landscaping done elsewhere by the same folks, and even making a phone call to the Better Business Bureau, just in case.

Simply plan it yourself

There's no reason why you can't draw up your own plan. Just remember to think of your garden as a whole, and not as the patch behind the house, the area by the fence and so on. Don't create a hodge-podge.

Before you sit down with drawing paper and pencil, study the neighborhood. Look for houses that are similar to yours. This includes the house size, one or two stories, which way the front of the house faces, doorways, windows, the entry walkway, and distance from the street.

I like to look around rich neighborhoods and see what their landscape architects have accomplished. It gives me lots of great ideas for free.

When you're walking around a neighborhood, try chatting with people who are outside gardening. Ask them what grows well "around here." What doesn't? How about local weather? Gardeners are often quite willing to share information on plants, especially if you admire their pretty yard. They may even give you a cutting or two.

■ **Having a look** *at other people's gardens may give you some useful ideas. For example, if you want your patio to receive maximum sunshine, why not site it away from the house?*

Making a scale drawing

How does an amateur plan? First, roughly measure your front and back yards. Then buy some graph paper, the kind with little squares on it that perhaps you may remember from high school. Paper with 10 squares per inch is a good size. Figure out the scale you will use to measure your garden.

An easy scale to remember is one square on the paper equals one foot of your site. If you're using paper with 10 squares per inch, 1 inch on your graph paper will equal 10 feet of your garden.

Sketch your yard on the graph paper according to your scale. Draw your house, walkways, existing trees, and any other permanent fixtures on the paper in approximate scale.

Now spend a few days in spring or summer observing sun and shade patterns in your garden. Mark these on the graph paper with a line that shows the sunny and shady portions. In the margins, write down when the sun strikes: "morning sun from 7 a.m. until 10 a.m." or "no sun due to shadows from neighbor's trees." This will give you some guidance in selecting your plants.

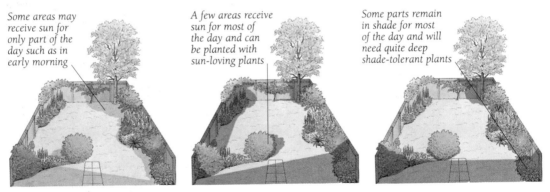

Some areas may receive sun for only part of the day such as in early morning

A few areas receive sun for most of the day and can be planted with sun-loving plants

Some parts remain in shade for most of the day and will need quite deep shade-tolerant plants

EARLY MORNING   NOON   EARLY EVENING

■ **When moving to a new house** *you'll probably have a good idea of whether the garden is quite sunny or shaded. Before you start to plan in earnest, though, take time to fully assess your site. For example, a north-facing garden (shown above in summer) will be colder all year round than a south-facing one. Plants will therefore grow more slowly because the soil will take longer to warm up.*

Now start searching the Sunday newspaper advertising sections for plant advertisements. Collect catalogs. Start cutting out those little bitty pictures and placing them on your graph. It helps if you also have in front of you a few pictures of your home's exterior. Even if you are not artistically inclined, concepts seem to form themselves when you've got pictures to shuffle around.

Landscape components

NOVICES TEND TO THINK ABOUT GENERIC green plants when they're planning a garden. But there's a great deal more to be considered. Landscaping components can include fencing, trees, shrubs, privacy hedges and walls, walkways, steps, patios and porches, a pool or pond, and lawns.

You also have to decide whether you want a formal, informal, or deliberately wild garden. Should there be a special place for roses? Vegetables? Herbs? Fruit trees? Standard trees or dwarf varieties? What about a rock garden? Do you want a lot of flowers, which require some fussing, or a cool panorama of green? If that sounds like a lot to consider, there's more.

Where will you put the garbage can? Unless you like to stare at it (I don't), you will need a screened corner next to the back or front of the house. Do you want to build something? Plant something? Where will you put your tools, including the lawn mower? If you need a tool house, where will it go? Tool houses are not the most attractive items, so you have to conceal them someplace or plant to enhance their appearance.

Will you eventually want a greenhouse? You may say no now, but as you get into the many pleasures of gardening you may change your mind. And if you live in a place where the winters are cold, a greenhouse may almost become a necessity. Even a

■ **In a smaller garden** *you don't want to be restricted by too many landscaping components, so keep them to a minimum. Rather than building a permanent barbecue, for example, you might do better to purchase a portable one that you can move out of sight when it's not being used.*

child's sandbox or wading pool should be planned for. And then there's the barbecue, hot tub, and gazebo. No matter what you ultimately decide about any of these items, you should at least consider them when you're in the planning stage.

The front of the house

PLAY A LITTLE NEIGHBORHOOD GAME. Try guessing the personality of the home owners just by looking at the front of their houses. How many times do you think "blah?" Which homes just look so interesting that you want to meet the people living there?

■ **For a smart impression,** *a carefully chosen tree that won't overshadow the house, together with a few key shrubs, are all that's needed.*

In addition to reflecting the taste of its inhabitants, the external appearance of a building can increase or decrease its value.

Foundation plantings, those around the base of the house, are important. Use trees to frame the house like a picture frame, with the house itself clearly visible. Consider the eventual size of a tree when you buy it. A small tree can become a huge tree in 15 years, and do you truly want it in front of your picture window, or its roots doing wonders for your lawn or sidewalk?

Do seriously consider shrubs, rather than a plethora of flowering plants, for your home's exterior. Not that flowers shouldn't be included, but lots of them festooning the spring and summer months aren't quite as elegant as shrubs that change color with the season and provide fruit and flowers too. There's a temptation here to buy one of every type of shrub to give variety. Do that in the back yard if you like. In the front, repetition using just a few carefully selected shrub varieties is the key to an organized and tidy appearance. Start with smaller ones toward the street and grade upward so the eye follows the plantings. Again, remember that plants grow. Use a reference book to determine the eventual height and width before you buy a shrub or bush.

The flower garden

YOU CAN HAVE ALL PERENNIALS, *all annuals, or a kaleidoscope that includes some of each plus flowering vines and bulbs. (I'll talk about all these kinds of plants in Part Two.) A mixed garden has many advantages, including design flexibility, longer-lasting color, and easier maintenance.*

Styles change. Right now, cottage gardens full of heirloom-type varieties are fashionable. So are tropical gardens. But that can alter almost overnight. You must plan for what you like best, after doing your homework via neighborhood scouting, reading catalogs, and checking out the local nurseries. If you can visit some public gardens as well, that's a real plus.

Tall and short

As a general rule, taller plants go in the back of a garden, medium ones (those between 18 and 36 inches high) in the middle, and shorties up front. That way you can see everything. If you use a lot of bulbs, you need to consider ways to camouflage their browning foliage with other plants, rocks, or other landscape features.

When considering garden design, make sure you can get to the plants in the back without having to tromp on others in passing. Consider placing a stepping stone pathway for large areas, to make meandering easier. Stepping stones can be very inexpensive, but give a polished look to the garden.

■ **Colorful flowering perennials** *can be combined with a variety of shrubs and bushes to great effect. As well as planting with height and size in mind, think about choosing textures and different hues of foliage to create added interest.*

> ### Trivia...
> *The earliest gardens were strictly practical and were used to grow food and medicinal herbs. But in Egypt, by 1500 BC the first decorative gardens appeared. They had walls, pools, trees, and plants grown just for their beautiful flowers.*

The four seasons

WHEN YOU'RE PICKING *flowering plants, think how you can have flowers for most of the year. If you pick plants that flower in each season, you'll have color almost year round. Here's a list of some popular flowering plants. Note that some plants flower through more than one season. Removing faded flowers can prolong the blooming period.*

■ **Colorful canna** *flowers from mid-summer to early fall.*

Spring

- Alyssum (*Aurinia*)
- Bergenia (*Bergenia*)
- Bugleweed (*Ajuga*)
- Columbine (*Aquilegia*)
- Crocus (*Crocus*)
- Daffodil (*Narcissus*)
- Evening primrose (*Oenothera*)
- Fleabane (*Erigeron*)
- Forget-me-not (*Myosotis*)
- Grape hyacinth (*Muscari*)
- Honeysuckle (*Lonicera*)
- Lily-of-the-valley (*Convallaria*)
- Phlox (*Phlox*)
- Primrose (*Primula*)
- Rose (*Rosa*)
- Speedwell (*Veronica*)
- Thrift (*Armeria*)
- Violet (*Viola*)
- Sweet woodruff (*Asperula*)
- Tulip (*Tulipa*)

Summer

- Amaryllis (*Lycoris*)
- Baby's breath (*Gypsophila*)
- Bachelor button (*Centaurea*)
- Bee balm (*Monarda*)
- Calla (*Zantesdeschia*)
- Canna (*Canna*)
- Clematis (*Clematis*)
- Dahlia (*Dahlia*)
- Dame's rocket (*Hesperis*)
- Daylily (*Hemerocallis*)
- Gladiolus (*Gladiolus*)
- Honeysuckle (*Lonicera*)
- Iris (*Iris*)
- Jasmine (*Jasminum*)
- Joe Pye weed (*Eupatorium*)
- Lantana (*Lantana*)
- Lavender (*Lavandula*)
- Lily (*Lilium*)
- Montbretia (*Crocosmia*)
- Pinks (*Dianthus*)
- Purple coneflower (*Echinacea*)
- Rose (*Rosa*)
- Sage (*Salvia*)
- Sea lavender (*Limomium*)
- Snow-in-summer (*Cerastium*)
- Spurge (*Euphorbia*)
- Stonecrop (*Sedum*)
- Tiger lily (*Lilium*)
- Trumpet vine (*Campsis*)
- Tuberose (*Polianthes*)
- Verbena (*Verbena*)
- Yarrow (*Achillea*)

Fall

- Aster (*Aster*)
- Boltonia (*Boltonia*)
- Cardinal flower (*Lobelia*)
- Catmint (*Nepeta*)
- Chrysanthemum (*Chrysanthemum*)
- Japanese anemone (*Anemone*)
- Purple coneflower (*Echinacea*)
- Rose (*Rosa*)
- Sneezeweed (*Helenium*)
- Stonecrop (*Sedum*)
- Trumpet vine (*Campsis*)
- Verbena (*Verbena*)

■ **Sneezeweed's daisy-like** *flowers bloom over a long period until fall.*

Winter

- Christmas rose (*Helleborus*)
- Snowdrop (*Galanthus*)
- Snowflake (*Leucojum*)

- Winter-blooming bergenia (*Bergenia*)
- Winter jasmine (*Jasminum*)
- Witch hazel (*Hamamelis*)

Some questions to ask yourself

IT'S ALMOST IMPOSSIBLE, *when you're visiting a colorful garden center in springtime, to resist buying plants. However, if you can restrain yourself, here are some things to consider before you make a purchase:*

1. Is the plant an annual or perennial?

2. Does it need sun or shade?

3. What are the water and soil requirements?

4. How high and wide will it grow, and how fast?

5. Is it *invasive*?

6. When does it flower, and for how long?

7. Is it bothered by a plethora of diseases or insects and is it hardy in my climate zone?

> **DEFINITION**
>
> *An invasive plant, also known as an aggressive or a rampant grower, is one that tends to gradually take over the surrounding territory. Some bamboos, for example, will crowd out everything in their path. Some ivies can cover buildings. The kudzu vine creates its own forest. If you want a rampant grower, confine it to a container.*

Climates and microclimates

TO SAVE MONEY AND TIME, and to avoid disappointment, you should know what garden plants suit your growing area. The United States is a huge country, and it has many and varied growing regions. As temperature and rainfall change, so does plant life. Additional modifying factors include the soil's ability to retain and distribute water, proximity to the ocean, wind, mountain barriers, frost, and the length of the growing season. It's easy to see climate zones when you're traveling by car. Look how the trees and shrubs change as you drive up a mountain road or traverse a state by highway or back road.

Climate zone maps of one type or another can be found in many garden books. They often give a general idea of temperature extremes in specific regions. However, while climate zone maps may give you a general idea of what your area weather is, these maps don't account for microclimates.

What is a microclimate?

Simply put, microclimates are changes in climate that may occur only a few miles, or even feet, apart. As an example, suppose one portion of your yard is very shady and another is in full sun. The general climate zone is the same, but the microclimate will vary even though the sections of the yard are just a few feet apart.

Here's another example: You live at the foot of a hill and another house is near the fog-shrouded hill top. The microclimate may be different in each site. A third example: If you live on a beach front, the sun and wind may be different than if you live a half-mile away, where the wind is blocked by buildings. And finally, suppose the city adjacent to yours gets 2 inches more rainfall per year than your home town. Or the city 10 miles away has average summer temperatures that are 10 degrees higher. All these situations, and many others, create different plant-growing conditions that must be considered when making your plans and purchases.

Why are microclimates important?

While there are many plants native to the United States, many more have been imported from all over the world. They may come from tropical humid forests. They may come from mountainous areas or deserts. The innate structure of a specific plant is based on its origin. Although modern hybridization has provided some leeway, you still can't plant a desert cactus in a bog, and you still can't put a water lily into a temporary puddle in the Mojave Desert.

■ **You can create** *different microclimates, or growing environments, in even the smallest gardens. Simply exploit or manipulate your garden features, as necessary, to provide the kind of conditions that plants from many different regions enjoy.*

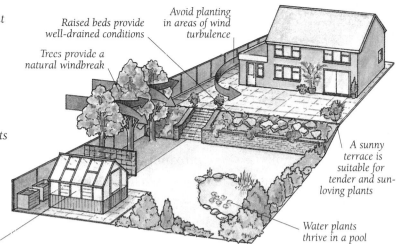

Raised beds provide well-drained conditions

Avoid planting in areas of wind turbulence

Trees provide a natural windbreak

A sunny terrace is suitable for tender and sun-loving plants

A greenhouse provides a suitable environment for tender plants

Water plants thrive in a pool

THE PROS AND CONS OF CLIMATE ZONES

Many, if not most, of the references you see about gardening will provide a climate zone map. You find the climate zone you live in and look to see if every plant you like is right for your climate zone. If it is, great! If it's not, too bad. You'll have to choose a different plant. The idea is that if you follow the recommendations for your climate zone, you'll have a green thumb after all.

I have found, however, that using climate zones to plan your garden often isn't quite as simple as it seems. It's not that your climate is unimportant; it's just that the maps can't really tell the whole story. To be honest, it seems to me that every map is different, so I'm never really sure which zone is which, anyway. And the recommended plants for particular zones vary from reference to reference. Who's right?

In my years of gardening, I've discovered that a plant's specific needs – for a certain type of soil, to be in a sunny spot, or to be located where there is good drainage, for example – are more important to success than what climate zone you live in. That's why I prefer to focus on the microclimates that exist in your garden.

One last tip: When in doubt, stop by your local garden center. The retailer wants your business, and it's in his or her best interests to sell you plants that will do well. If the store sells a lot of plants that don't thrive in your area, you and your fellow gardeners won't be shopping there very much.

How microclimates change

Even within an established garden, microclimates don't always remain the same.

If your neighbor builds a second story onto his home, the shadow may change the microclimate on your side of the fence. Another neighbor may install a wide-ranging sprinkling system, affecting drought-tolerant plants on your lot. If your rural area loses a nearby windbreak of tall trees to a shopping center, wind patterns will now need to be considered.

You might change the microclimate yourself, either intentionally or otherwise. If you remove a huge Monterey cypress from your yard, the microclimate in the immediate area will change. Conversely, if the tiny cypress sapling you planted some years ago reaches 30 feet tall, the microclimate around it changes along with the growth. All this affects which plants you will choose and which plants will succeed in your garden.

■ **A solid brick wall** *can provide shelter and shade for non sun-worshippers, or if it's exposed to the sun, can create a haven for heat-loving plants.*

Modern gardening is really wonderful, because you can create a specific microclimate for a plant that you really want to grow. A greenhouse is a microclimate. Fencing built to deter prevailing winds also creates a microclimate. Planting against a sun-reflecting white stucco wall increases heat reflection, and so that's another microclimate. Even putting container plants outside on the porch in spring and summer, and then moving them indoors in the fall to help protect them from the cold, is a managed microclimate.

■ **Fencing acts** *as an effective windbreak, providing a protected environment for more vulnerable plants.*

Dealing with difficult sites

YOU WILL SOON RECOGNIZE DIFFICULT sites because plants may have a tough time growing there. However, it's a lot easier on your wallet to recognize difficult sites before you begin buying your garden plants. Then you can buy plants that will thrive in the face of horticultural adversity.

Slopes

It may not look like much of an incline to you, but slopes of any kind can be water wasters. Not only are some difficult to water adequately, but when you do water it runs downhill, taking good topsoil with it. Mowing is also difficult, sometimes impossible, on a slope. Nor do you want to chase weeds at a 45-degree collection angle. How much extra work your slope demands depends on how steep the slope is. Many homes have yards that are literally carved out of hillsides, with the hill remaining as part of the yard.

What to do? If you have a minimal maintenance mentality, put in ground cover. Plant it during the rainy season so you don't have to fuss about watering while the plants are in the fragile get-started phase. On steep slopes you will need a fast and thorough ground cover.

If your slope is very sharply angled, you may wish to create a terrace arrangement. Terracing means creating narrow, flat shelves of land (terraces), and then bordering the terraces with wood or brick to keep the soil from sliding downhill – making what are basically large containers. Terracing is a lot of work, but once it's done you have made ample room for a selection of lovely plants and a food garden, too.

Trivia...
One of the oldest garden plans, that of the St. Gall monastery in Switzerland, dates back to 820 AD.

Of course, even with terraces the yard is still sloped. Sprinklers will encourage water runoff. The best solution, if you put in any plant that needs regular watering, is to use a drip irrigation system. (You'll find more about irrigation in Chapter 4.) Slow watering allows water to soak in before it gathers enough weight to start running downhill. If sprinklers are already in place, create a basin around each plant by digging a shallow trench around it. The water will pool in this basin and seep in more slowly.

Wind

Wind spreads airborne diseases, tears plant leaves, turns their edges brown, and speeds up water evaporation, causing drought stress in plants that are regularly watered. Strong winds can uproot plants and snap branches. While you cannot stop the wind, you may be able to alleviate some of its harmful effects. For example, prune trees regularly and fewer branches will break off.

Wind in combination with steady rain will cause big trees to topple. If you live in a windy area, look around the neighborhood and see what trees are thriving. To protect smaller plants, place them where the house blocks the wind, or create a windbreak. A windbreak can be a hedgerow of shrubs or a fence. If it's a fence, it needs to be constructed so some wind can pass through. Slats will do, or lattice. With a solid fence, the wind goes over the fence and then drops to the ground, creating a disturbance on the other side.

Shade

It may not be so obvious where the shady parts of your garden are. A neighbor's tree or two-story home may create shade part of the day. Your own home may create shade part of the day, and so may a fence. Plants that need full sun won't thrive here.

When thinking "shade," one tends to think "cool." But that's not always true. Shaded areas adjacent to concrete may actually receive quite a bit of heat. However, there are many plants that thrive in shade, warm or cool.

■ **Tall plants that are susceptible** *to damage from strong winds, or small plants that need more protection, can benefit from the shelter afforded by the side of a house or enclosed fencing.*

Soggy soil ✗

Another name for this is waterlogged soil. By any name, very little will grow due to a lack of oxygen available to the plant. There are only a few trees, such as willows, that will grow in soil that is always wet. So you will have to take action. Action means correcting the water drainage so the soil has the chance to dry out. Either that or install a bog or water garden. If there are just a few plants you're concerned about, create a mound of drier soil and plant within this for better drainage.

A simple summary

✔ To plan your garden, you can hire a landscape architect, consult a specialist at your local nursery, or tackle the job yourself.

✔ In addition to the plants, think about fencing, trees, shrubs, privacy hedges, walls, walkways, steps, patios, porches, lawns, a barbecue, a greenhouse, and anything else that might appear in a yard when you're planning your garden.

✔ Plantings in front of your home will increase its value. Consider using a few key shrubs rather than a plethora of flowers at the front of the house. To get an idea of what will look nice, why not drive around and see what the neighbors have done?

✔ When you're choosing flowering plants, try to pick some that will bloom in each season so you have color in your garden for as long as possible.

✔ Consider both your local climate and the microclimate when planning your garden. Microclimates are localized areas where climate may vary, such as a very shady spot in a yard, a house near the ocean, or an area that's protected by a wall.

✔ Slopes, windy areas, shady spots, and patches that are always wet can create problems in your garden. Make sure you plan for plants and other garden features that can withstand these difficult conditions.

Chapter 2

Be a Soil Detective

IT WOULD BE WONDERFUL if all gardeners had perfect soil that didn't need anything added to it for perfect plant growth. However, very few garden sites do. Depending on where you live, clay or sand may be a main soil ingredient. The pH may be a little too acid, or too alkaline. But you can always improve on what nature gave you.

In this chapter...

✓ The particle particulars

✓ Analyzing your pH

✓ The constitution of amendments

✓ Comprehending composting

✓ Deducing drainage woes

✓ Masterminding mulch

✓ Fertilizer finesse

WELL-ROTTED COMPOST, A GREAT SOIL CONDITIONER

The particle particulars

SAYING A SOIL HAS A LOT OF CLAY, or calling it silty or sandy, refers to the size and proportion of certain mineral particles present in the soil. These mineral particles can determine how well your plant survives – a factor that can be quite frustrating to the long-time gardener as well as the novice. But don't despair. Horticultural scientists and dedicated amateurs continue to locate, and *hybridize*, plants suited to specific sites in all but the most extreme terrain. Or, if you are willing to put in a bit of extra work, you can alter most soil types to fit your needs.

Clay

Clay, also called heavy soil, has a significant proportion of very, very tiny mineral particles.

Each clay mineral particle measures only about $1/12,500$ of an inch. To see a single particle you'd need a special microscope. Because clay particles are so minute, they tend to stick together when wet.

If you pick up a handful of moist clay soil and squeeze it, you get a sticky, heavy, hard lump. However, when clay soil dries out, as in hot weather, the particle groups separate. The soil then cracks and more moisture evaporates, making the situation even worse. Many gardeners who have predominantly clay soil will grumble that it's very difficult to grow plants in it.

CLAY SOIL

When the minute clay particles stick together, they can become dense enough to prevent full water and air movement. Instead of reaching roots, water puddles above or below the soil surface. If it puddles above the surface, little water reaches the plant roots. If it puddles below the soil surface, the roots may drown. Air does not circulate through dense, compacted soil, either. Air, sunlight, and the right amount of water are essential requirements for plant survival and healthy growth.

Plant roots, which can be as thin as threads, have difficulty reaching down through hard clay soil. And since clay soil does not absorb sunlight easily, in spring when new plants need light and warmth, clay soil is slower to meet their needs.

Clay does have advantages, when you know how to work with it.

Nutrients, whether natural or added with fertilizer, often leach quickly out of other soil types. But the heavy density of clay tends to hold nutrients in place.

Many well-selected plants simply thrive in clay soil. But you must fuss with the soil a bit. That's where organic matter comes in. This crumbly material keeps the clay particles from sticking together. With it, air, water, and plant roots can easily make their way throughout the soil surrounding the plants.

Sandy soil

Sandy soil is also called light soil. Sand particles are visible to the naked eye. They vary in size, from quarter-inch coarse sand particles to microscopic sand particles. When rubbed between your fingers, sand particles feel gritty. They don't stick together the way clay soil particles do. While soil containing ample sand warms up quickly in spring, drains well, and is easy to work with, it does have drawbacks.

SANDY SOIL

A matter of air

The major drawback of sandy soil is limited water retention. Sandy soils have large air spaces between the particles. Water tends to run quickly through these air spaces, dispersing beyond the reach of the plant's roots. Fertilizers leach or strain quickly out of sandy soil along with the water, so plants don't get their full benefit. And very sandy soil may not contain sufficient organic matter to sustain healthy plant growth.

You need to fill up those air spaces between sand particles. How? By adding plenty of organic matter.

Organic matter improves a sandy soil's ability to retain moisture and nutrients in the root zone. It acts like a sponge to hold water.

Many homes on beach fronts manage to have beautiful gardens because the gardeners have added organic matter to their soil. However, because organic material tends to wash away, it must be supplemented every few years. If you live in an area like this, always add organic matter to the soil when you are putting in new plants.

Silty soil

Silt particles are between clay and sand in size. When a sample of silt is held in your hand, it feels like flour.

Silty soil is subject to a problem called capping, where a crust or cap forms on the soil when soil crumbs on the surface are damaged by heavy rain or watering, or by walking on the soil when it is wet.

If your soil tends to crust, it will keep air from reaching the plant's roots, and also prevent seeds from germinating.

Silty soil can be improved by adding small amounts of clay to improve the soil structure and incorporating organic materials to encourage the soil to form crumbs.

SILTY SOIL

Loam

Loam is a rich, dark soil that feels crumbly. It is a balanced mixture of about 40 percent clay, 40 percent sand, and 20 percent silt particles, in combination with ample organic material. Loam is porous, providing good drainage. It retains moisture. It has humus, which provides good growing conditions for soil bacteria essential to plant nutrition. Loam is the soil type you want to try to create.

TESTING YOUR SOIL TYPE

For an accurate soil type test, ask your County Agricultural Agent if they do texture testing. There is also a test you can do yourself, but it's not always accurate. Fill a quart jar ⅔ full of water and add a teaspoon of a water softener. Add dry soil, no lumps, almost to the top of the jar. Cover tightly and shake to mix well. Then set the jar on a level surface and observe.

Sand particles will sink to the bottom. The smaller silt and clay particles will remain suspended in the water. Within 2 hours, the silt particles will settle but the clay particles may take two weeks to settle. You will then see the layers: sand on the bottom, silt next, then clay on top. If you see ¾ sand, you have sandy soil. If you see more than ¾ silt, that's the answer. If you see ⅔ clay on top, you have clay soil. Use soil samples from different areas of your garden.

Analyzing your pH

THE MEASURE OF ACIDITY OR ALKALINITY *is the pH. You will see the term pH used in many gardening books. (You'll also see it in aquarium and chemistry books, and on some shampoo bottles.) It is used because some plants grow best in an alkaline soil, others in an acidic soil, and still others in a neutral soil that is somewhere between acidic and alkaline.*

pH is measured on a scale from 0 to 14. Zero is the most acidic, 7 is neutral, and 14 is most alkaline. This is a logarithmic scale, which means that each numeral on the pH scale actually represents a tenfold change. That is, a pH of 7 is ten times more alkaline than a pH of 6.

I know these chemical terms can be intimidating to some people, but all it means for a gardener is that pH determines what organisms in the soil will thrive and what types of nutrients contained in the soil will be available to resident plants. The pH numbers depend, basically, on the amount of calcium (lime) present in the soil. In general, plants prefer a pH between 6.1 and 7.8.

pH tests

Most plants prefer to maintain their neutrality, but there are those that like life a little on the acidic side, and those that prefer things a bit more alkaline. If pH is very important to a specific plant's success, you will want to test it.

There are two kinds of tests available. The first is the do-it-yourself kit available at most garden centers, or through garden mail order catalogs. They are easy to use, and generally indicate pH by changing color. The second test is more accurate and requires sending soil samples to a private soil-testing laboratory, County Cooperative Extension Agent, or County Agricultural Extension Agent. Ask at a local nursery for a list of laboratories or look in the telephone book under "Laboratories—Testing."

After settlement, a yellow or orange color indicates an acidic soil

A green solution indicates a neutral soil

Dark olive green solution indicates an alkaline soil

■ **Soil acidity or alkalinity** *is measured on the pH scale, which runs from 0 to 14: above 7 is alkaline; below 7 is acidic. You can buy an easy-to-use kit to test your own soil: colors are matched against a chart to give you a numerical reading.*

pHiddling with your pH

What if you find out your soil is not what your plant prefers? Additives are available at most garden centers that can change the pH. You must follow the specific instructions on each container.

In general, to lower soil pH (that is, make alkaline soil more acidic), use soil sulfur, iron sulfate, or aluminum sulfate. Or you can fertilize with acid-type fertilizers. You can also make the soil pH more acidic organically by working in peat moss, oak leaf mold, sawdust, ground bark, or decayed pine needles. Plants that prefer very acidic soil (pH 4 to 6) include azalea, blueberry, camellia, cranberry, ferns, heather, lily, marigold, pine, radish, rhododendron, and yew.

If there's a lot of rain where you live, chances are you have acid soil. The calcium in the soil, which would make it more alkaline, has probably been washed away by the rain. Areas where the soil is very high in organic material, or sandy soils, also tend to be acidic. In some regions, acidic soil is called sour soil.

■ **Rhododendrons** *prefer acidic soil (pH 4 to 6)*

To raise soil pH (that is, make it more alkaline) for your vegetable garden, add lime – which is a form of calcium.

Be careful when adding lime to the soil, because too much can harm instead of help.

Follow the directions on the container precisely. You can add wood ashes instead, but just a little bit at a time. Plants that prefer a somewhat neutral to alkaline soil (pH 6.8 to 7.5) include asparagus, carrots, cole crops such as broccoli and cabbage, cucumbers, lettuce, onions, peas, pumpkins, spinach, sweet corn, and zucchini.

Flowers such as carnations and irises also prefer soil that tends to be more alkaline. However, if your soil is quite alkaline, sometimes it's easier to garden in raised beds, where you can bring in better soil.

INTERNET

homeharvest.com/plant phpreference.htm

If you want to determine your soil's pH, try this Home Harvest Garden Supply site – it offers a wide range of tester kits.

SALTY SOIL

A variety of minerals form salts that can build up in your garden soil. Many plants will not grow well, or grow at all, if the soil is salty. There may be one or several causes, including animal manures, chemical fertilizers, soft water from a home water softener, and salty irrigation water. Coastal areas often get buffeted by winds that bring a lot of salt with them from the ocean. It's also possible that the soil in your home area is naturally high in salts. In high rainfall areas this salt would pass through the soil. But in low rainfall areas salt concentrates in the upper soil layer.

Testing for salty soil

Soil salt causes several problems. It slows or stops seed germination. It also harms plant roots, which, in turn, results in slow growth. Salt burn may also occur, where leaf edges looked burnt. Saline soil may also harm beneficial organisms in the soil. Testing for soil salt levels requires special equipment. Ask your County Agricultural Agent for advice. If you have salty soil, always use fertilizers that have a low salt content and water well with salt-free water. But when you're giving lots of water, make certain your soil drainage is good. Puddles of salt-laden water are not an improvement.

The constitution of amendments

A VARIETY OF SOIL AMENDMENTS ARE AVAILABLE. Your choice will depend on the type you can find nearby and the needs of your soil. In general, you combine the amendment with soil in a 50-50 mix. That means you have half soil and half additive. That can add up to a lot of additives.

Agricultural food products

If you live near a winery or an apple-processing area, you may be able to get leftover grape or apple seeds and skins. These are called pomace. Like any decaying product, they may smell for a week or two, but they are an excellent soil amendment, especially for clay soils. Other leftovers include bagasse (ground sugarcane leftovers), cocoa bean hulls, cottonseed meal, ground corncobs, peanut hulls, rice hulls, or soybean meal.

Manure

Animal waste, or manure, is a good source of nitrogen. If you buy it already bagged at a garden center, the bag should be labeled "dried" or "dehydrated." This means it has been pasteurized, or heat-treated, to destroy any harmful elements, including weed seeds. There are various types of animal manure. Fresh manures, whether horse, sheep, chicken, pig, pigeon, or rabbit, must be very well composted for at least a year before using. That's because fresh manure releases heat as it decomposes, and will burn adjacent plant roots. It may contain a great deal of salt, depending on the animal's diet, and it probably carries weed seeds.

Some commercially produced manures have been treated with chemicals to reduce odor. These chemicals are not good for plant roots. It's better to put up with the smell and go with manure au naturel.

In some areas, sewage sludge is offered. This is usually safe if it is packaged commercially. If you are not confident about the product's safety and want to use dried sewage sludge, compost it correctly first (I'll tell you how a little later in this chapter). However, home composting may not eliminate metallic and other chemical substances that end up in sewage.

Always wear protective gloves when touching human or animal waste products, and clean your hands thoroughly with soap and warm water afterward.

If you are dealing with animal waste products, make certain your tetanus booster shots are up to date.

Wood byproducts

Wood byproducts include sawdust and ground bark. Because all wood byproducts decompose, they take necessary nitrogen from the soil, sawdust more so than other products. Wood byproducts purchased at nurseries have usually been fortified with nitrogen, but if you get wood byproducts directly from a lumber yard, you will have to add nitrogen fertilizer.

If the byproduct is mostly sawdust, you must let it decompose first before you add it to the soil. If you don't, it will form a solid mass that doesn't let rainwater penetrate.

> **Trivia...**
>
> *In 1529 author Thomas Hill, in* The Gardener's Labyrinth *from Oxford University Press, wrote that of all the animal dung, or manure, doves' dung was the best. After that he recommended the dung of hens and other "foules," excepting water "foules." He also gave commendations to asses' dung, "goates" dung, then "oxe," cow and swine, in that order. Horse dung was "the vilest and the worst." Mr. Hill did not recommend the use of human dung.*

Compost

Compost can be made up of fallen leaves, grass clippings, fallen fruit, aged flowers, manures, commercial leftovers, and kitchen organic leftovers. It makes an excellent soil amendment, and some gardeners also use it as a mulch.

Leaf mold

Leaves should be composted, shredded, or at least left to rot before using them as a soil amendment. If you contemplate collecting leaves from places other than in your yard, be careful your collection doesn't include poison oak or poison ivy leaves. You can also buy leaf mold by the cubic yard (or by the truckful) in a few nurseries. Leaf mold especially benefits acid-loving plants and vegetable gardens.

Peat moss

Peat moss is more expensive than the other soil amendments, because it must be gathered from long-ago wetlands. Peat moss is basically decayed sphagnum moss that has been compacting for hundreds of years. It is often used with indoor or container plants that demand a true acidic soil environment. Peat moss is lightweight, holds moisture well, and drains well.

However, peat moss has its drawbacks as an outdoor conditioner. First, it does not contain any nutrients. In the yard, you may want to mix it with other amendments, particularly those containing nitrogen. Moreover, peat moss sheds water when it's dry, rather than letting water soak in.

■ **Perlite and vermiculite** *are very useful if you have a lot of container plants, as they help with soil drainage and allow air to reach into the plant roots more easily.*

Perlite and vermiculite

These inorganic, porous, mineral, white or gray granules are often used for indoor plants. The granules are sterile, lightweight, and constructed so that air passes easily to plant roots. If you use perlite or vermiculite outdoors, mix it with compost and peat moss to provide essential nutrients. Do not use vermiculite to break up clay soil outdoors or indoors. The clay conjoins with vermiculite, making it sturdier than before. Although attractive, perlite and vermiculite contain little in the way of beneficial elements.

Sand

If you just need a little bit of sand for potted plants such as cacti, it can be purchased in two-quart bags at most garden centers. If you want larger amounts, check out "builder's sand," sometimes available at hardware stores catering to the construction crowd.

Do not obtain sand from a beach. Legalities aside, beach sand is unscreened and contains a mixture of sand particle sizes as well as salt.

Commercially purchased sand is usually quartz sand that has been washed and sifted through a screen, so you get larger particles. Sand is most often used to help aerate clay soil, and larger particles are the best for this. However, you must use a mixture of 80 percent sand to 20 percent clay soil, or you will create concrete soil, which is worse than the clay you started with.

Comprehending composting

COMPOSTING IS QUITE THE TREND TODAY. Many gardeners have purchased inexpensive composting bins. Bins are designed for both large and small gardens and instructions come with each bin. If you have an out-of-the-way corner in your yard, you don't need a special bin to start composting.

Composting basically takes leftover organic material and leaves it to rot or decompose. This decaying organic material turns it into a great soil conditioner. It's the ultimate in recycling. Use a mix of wet materials, such as leafy material and grass clippings, with dry, such as shredded paper, bark, or straw.

■ **Compost bins** *should start with a layer of twiggy materials, building up with waste matter. When the contents reach a height of about 4–5 inches, add a little manure to the top and leave to decay. Use when well rotted.*

How does composting work?

Although leftover organic material just looks like leftovers, it contains microorganisms such as bacteria and fungi. Give these minute creatures some fresh air in a compost pile and they quickly go to work.

Earthworms

Earthworms soon enter the picture. As earthworms eat their way through the compost, the tunnels they make create spaces for air to enter, further aiding the bacteria and fungi. The byproducts of all this activity are extremely beneficial to plants. So are earthworm waste products, called castings. Some people purchase earthworm bins and raise earthworms just for the castings they generate.

The free-standing compost pile

If you have a large yard and can create a free-standing compost heap in an out-of-sight corner, try the following:

Make a flattened pile of green material such as weeds, leaves, small twigs, rotted sawdust, shredded branches, straw, kitchen vegetable and fruit leavings, eggshells, coffee grounds, alfalfa meal, farm animal manure, and cut grass. You can add some garden soil too.

Do not pile a whole batch of grass in the compost pile without mixing it with some other compost ingredients first, because grass tends to clump up and turn into smelly slime if it's put into the compost pile in heaps. Slimy grass encourages flies to lay eggs in your compost pile. Do not put herbicide-treated weeds in the compost pile, either, because they will just recycle the herbicide back into your plants.

About once a month, sprinkle a small amount of all-purpose fertilizer over the pile. Water afterward, and keep the pile moist. The leftovers in the compost pile must be moist to decompose properly. Moist does not mean soggy, though. A soggy compost pile doesn't let air through, and the bacteria, fungi, and earthworms can't grow without air. A compost pile without air gets smelly, like rotten eggs. If this happens to you, stir and turn the pile, adding some dry leftovers as you do.

INTERNET

wildhorses.com

You'll find frequently asked questions on compost here.

Piled high and deep

The minimum height for a free-standing compost pile is 3 feet, with a maximum of about 5 feet high. You can make it as wide as you want. If you can, use a shovel or pitchfork to turn the material so the bottom stuff moves near the top and the top stuff goes underneath. That encourages everything to heat up properly (heat is a byproduct of decomposition), which will kill weed seeds and young insects. If everything is done correctly, in about 3 months in warmer climates (6 months where the winters are cool) you should have wonderfully aromatic, brown, crumbly, usable compost.

Some gardeners cover their compost heap with black plastic film, canvas, or garden soil to encourage it to heat up faster. If you do, don't forget to pull the covering back occasionally to add the necessary water.

If you don't like turning the compost pile, you don't have to. It just takes longer to decompose all the materials.

Some folks, concerned with appearances, build a gated fence around their free-standing compost pile. Others like the look of leftovers rotting in the sun. It's all a matter of perspective.

The container compost pile

A container compost pile is ideal for the smaller garden, because you can hide it behind some pretty 4-foot-high perennial plants. The ingredients for a container pile are the same as for a free-standing one: a little of this, a little of that. The easiest way is to use a ready-made bin, available at most large garden centers and hardware stores for about $25 to $50. They hold about 3 cubic feet of compost and have ventilation holes in the sides and a removable cover.

You can use a large plastic garbage can. Drill holes in its sides, from bottom to top to provide the air necessary for decomposition. It's hard to stir a big garbage can, so some people tuck in a long piece of sturdy plastic pipe right in the middle before they start adding leftovers. Then they use this as a stirring spoon.

Uninvited guests?

Some people worry that a compost pile will attract pests. However, insects will not meander to your compost pile if it is properly constructed. A good compost pile generates heat as it decomposes. Insects are not usually crazy about this.

Rodents, dogs, and other invaders will not bother your pile unless you tuck in meat products or bones.

Deducing drainage woes

IF WATER PUDDLES AROUND YOUR PLANTS, *you need to improve the drainage. Plant roots, unless they have adapted to live in marshes, will not survive in soil that's usually soggy. Sometimes it takes awhile to figure out that your plant's bedraggled look is due to poor drainage, but here's a clue: poor drainage seldom occurs in sandy soils; if you have clay soil, suspect this problem. Other things can also cause this problem. Let's take a look at the symptoms and possible causes of poor drainage.*

Early clues

The earliest clue of poor drainage is water puddles that remain visible for some time after rain or watering stops. Simple, right? Another clue is which type of plants survive and which don't. If mint, mosses, spruce, and willow thrive and normal grasses disappear as if by magic, you probably have a moisture problem. Trees that do well when they're small but die as they get older and larger are another symptom, as are any size trees or shrubs that die seemingly without any reason after a wet winter.

Do not underestimate the damage and expense that poor drainage can cause.

Plant roots need oxygen. When soil is waterlogged, oxygen is not fully available. Wet soil tends to be low in vital plant nutrients, such as nitrogen. Soil that is constantly wet or damp is colder than dry soil. This slows plant growth in spring, when growth is all important. Wet soil encourages the proliferation of fungus diseases that attack plant roots.

Investigating hardpan

Hardpan is a condition of some clay and silt soils in which the particles are so tightly packed that water cannot drain through. A layer of hardpan below the surface can be the sole cause, or a major contributing cause, of drainage problems. To find out if you have a hardpan problem, take a shovel and try to dig a hole about 18 inches deep in your garden. That should be pretty easy, but sometimes it isn't. If, by 6 or 8 inches down, you start scraping at the earth instead of digging, and if it's become a lot of slow, hard work, you've hit hardpan.

Trivia...

Hundreds of years ago, local legends abounded about why some areas just wouldn't grow anything. Some bad deed was said to have taken place at the site. There is, for example, a hill in Great Britain where St. George is said to have slain the Dragon. Known as Dragon Hill, it was said grass never grew where the dragon's blood was spilled. Other barren sites included those where fatal duels had taken place.

You can eventually get pretty far down with hardpan, particularly if you put some muscle into it. Gardeners who want plants to put down deep roots or who want to put in a tree but don't want to dig and scrape for what seems like forever can rent a power post-hole digger or hire a professional to do this sweaty job.

INTERNET

gardenweb.com/glossary

This is the Garden Web Glossary of Botanical Terms, where you can look up more than 2,500 terms relating to botany, gardening, horticulture, and landscape architecture.

B is for bedrock

In some areas, not even scraping the soil gets the hole deeper. It is possible that you have bedrock – a layer of some type of rock underneath the soil.

It is tempting to try to plant in the softer soil above hardpan or bedrock. But it's not wise. When water comes in – hose water or rain – it sits above the hardpan or bedrock almost as if it's contained in a bowl. The roots reach down until they are blocked by the hardpan or bedrock. Then they become waterlogged, and if the situation continues the roots will eventually rot.

In warm weather, hardpan and bedrock cause additional problems. Plant roots, instead of reaching deep into the soil, are confined above the hard layer, in a shallow layer of soil. Being shallow, the soil dries out very quickly and plants wilt very soon after being watered.

How high is the water table?

Natural water under the earth can be very deep down or almost just below the surface. When it rises above the surface, as in streams or floods, you can easily see it. But if the water is just below the surface you don't notice it or even think about it. That is, until you start digging a planting hole. In addition to other drainage problems, you may see water seeping into your hole. You will either have to plant in another way (in a pot or a sunken container, for example) or consider installing some type of drain line.

Basically, a drain line is a downhill trench with the high point at your targeted planting area and the low point where you want the water to emerge. The trench will have to be lined and pipes installed. You may prefer to use a professional landscaper for this job.

Dealing with drainage problems

Dealing with drainage problems depends on what you want to plant. If you have hardpan, dig down to a minimum of 12 inches for a small plant and 36 inches for a small tree. Replace all soil with good topsoil. For a deep-rooted plant such as a tree, you may want to dig down as far as possible, fill the hole with good soil, and then create a raised mound about 2 feet high. An alternative is to use containers and/or raised beds.

Masterminding mulch

MULCH IS ANYTHING *that can be put on the surface of the soil without injuring the plants. Mulch reduces topsoil erosion, helps keep soil from baking in the sun and drying in the wind, and discourages the sprouting and growth of many weeds. Mulch also helps limit soil movement during the winter. Sudden frosts, alternating with sudden thaws, make the soil shift, disturbing plants. In the vegetable patch, mulch scattered underneath such plants as cucumbers, squash, or unstaked tomatoes acts as a cushion. This cushion decreases vegetable contact with damp ground, a situation that encourages rot.*

When to mulch

To deter weeds, apply mulches in early spring before seeds sprout, or germinate. To control water loss during hot summer months, apply mulches after the ground warms up in spring. If you place a mulch too early, the soil stays cool and plant growth slows. This particularly affects vegetables such as corn, cucumbers, melons, and early-ripening tomatoes, which need warmth for a good start. To prevent more delicate plants from winter frosts, apply mulch right after the first hard frost of the season.

Do not apply mulch on seeded areas or around emerging seedlings. This will encourage damping off, eliminating your tiny new plant growth almost overnight.

If you're growing seedlings, wait until they have become reasonably sturdy before you start mulching around them.

> **DEFINITION**
>
> **Damping off** *is the collapse of a young plant as a result of fungal disease that destroys the plant's roots.*

Picking the perfect mulch

As with soil amendments, lots of different substances might be used as a mulch. Some are organic and some are not. The best mulches are inexpensive, easy to get, and easy to use. Organic mulches disintegrate over time, but you can then dig them into the soil, which is quite beneficial.

Mulches can be made from all manner of substances, such as spent mushroom compost, rotted garden compost, granulated bark, shredded bark, and coconut shells. There are even decorative mulches, such as gravel, pebbles or glass beads. I'm going to go into a bit more detail about mulches on the next few pages.

Pebbles

Gravel, pebbles, or crushed rock make an elegant mulch, and they are often used for the front of the house, where looks are everything. Colors include white, gray, shades of beige-brown, and a dark auburn for volcanic rock. These colors can be selected to blend with your home, porch, or patio.

Be careful when putting stone mulches close to a lawn, because mowers can pick up and throw the pieces. This can cause very serious injury to the person mowing and to passers-by. Rock mulches don't integrate into soil over time, the way organic materials will. They tend to scatter onto adjacent pathways, so put down more rock about every 5 years.

■ **The muted shades** *and smooth texture of pebbles look particularly attractive next to plants of different hues of green, such as golden creeping jenny and bugle. The effect looks very natural.*

Black polyethylene film

PLASTIC MULCH

I call this black plastic film, which, to me, describes it better. Sold in rolls from about 12 inches to 48 inches wide, black plastic film makes a functional, if unattractive, mulch. Sunlight doesn't penetrate the plastic film, so weed sprouting (and thus weed survival) is minimal. An added benefit is its heat-holding capacity.

Planting within black plastic film is simple. You carefully cut a hole in the plastic where you want your plant to grow. Then you dig a planting hole, backfilling with a mixture of native soil and good organic soil. Plants sited within a plastic mulch stay about 10 degrees warmer than their film-free neighbors. Those few degrees can mean the survival of tender plants when the weather fluctuates.

Many gardeners use black plastic film covered with a layer of bark chunks or gravel. The covering enhances the film's appearance, endurance, and safety. Plastic without a covering can be slippery when wet. Covered, it is less exposed to the elements and to damage caused by foot traffic. If you do decide to use this lightweight material alone, you will have to weight it down. You can do this with either soil or rocks.

Plastic film will shred after a few years. If unprotected, plan on replacing it in 2 to 3 years. Note that plastic films are not great on poorly drained areas, because they hold the moisture in the ground.

Wood products

Bark chunks, usually brown or reddish-brown, often come from pine, cedar, fir, or redwood trees. Quite natural looking, bark chunks make a very attractive mulch. Some gardeners put a layer of black plastic beneath the bark to help keep weeds away. Bark chunks, available in various sizes, tend to scatter or thin after a while. Plan on augmenting them every 2 to 3 years. The larger the size initially, the longer bark chunks last and the less they tend to scatter.

BARK CHUNKS

Another option is to use chipper material – wood chunks in small pieces of various sizes. Lay them down in a layer about 3 inches thick. If chipper material is used continually and not mixed with anything else, you may need to add a bit of extra nitrogen fertilizer.

If you're considering sawdust, only use well-composted sawdust. If you simply can't wait, you can mix it with shredded fallen leaves or straw bits to break it up. As with chipper material, some gardeners like to add some extra nitrogen fertilizer to their sawdust mulch.

In some areas there are a plethora of pines, and therefore pine needles. They are quite useful as a mulch if you have acid-loving plants, such as azaleas, blueberries, camellias, chrysanthemums, and rhododendrons. Never smoke a cigarette or use a match around dry pine needles. They are extremely flammable. Old, shredded, oak leaves are also useful around acid-loving plants.

■ **Bark chunks and chips** *help to control weeds by blocking out the light. The mulch will need augmenting, but should last for several years.*

Your recycled yard

Fallen leaves and dried lawn clippings must be used as a team in order to make an effective mulch. Using just leaves, or just lawn clippings, will eventually result in a matted, smelly, damp blanket.

Straw

Many years ago, straw was commonly available and in some areas, especially if you live near farmland, you may still be able to get it. It usually makes a good, clean mulch that eventually decomposes to benefit the soil internally as well as externally. When using straw as a mulch, aim to spread it about 6 inches deep, where practical. Make sure the straw you buy doesn't contain any weed seeds or grain, however, or you'll live to regret it. And, of course, never smoke a cigarette or use a match around straw. It is extremely flammable.

■ **A straw mulch** *provides a thick layer of light and airy protection around delicate flowering strawberry plants. It also helps improve the soil when it decomposes.*

How much mulch?

Mulch depth depends a lot on what type of mulch you are using. If you are using chipper wood, shredded leaves, or grass clippings, your mulch should not be more than 2 inches thick after it settles down. Any thicker than that, especially around shallow-rooted plants, and you may suffocate the roots. If you are using coarser materials, such as bark chunks, you can mulch up to about 4 inches thick. The open texture allows for good air movement. When mulching around young trees, make a mulch circle that is at least 2 feet wide. You should then continue enlarging the area as the tree grows.

Regardless of plant type, keep all organic mulches about 1 to 2 inches away from the trunks of trees, shrubs, and other plants. And mulch perennials at the end, not at the beginning, of the rainy season.

Mulches hold moisture when they're next to the base of a plant and this can lead to crown rot, which is caused by bacterial and fungal organisms.

INTERNET

nhq.nrcs.usda.gov/ccs/ mulching.html

This site has tips on how to mulch, what to use, and the benefits of each type of mulch.

Fertilizer finesse

FERTILIZERS BRING *nutrients to your plants, keeping them strong and healthy. The fundamentals of fertilizing follow.*

Even if chemistry was your worst subject in school, you must understand that successful plant growth requires the presence of certain elements.

To grow successfully, plants need boron, calcium, carbon, chlorine, copper, hydrogen, iron, magnesium, manganese, molybdenum, nitrogen, phosphorus, potassium, sulfur, and zinc. They also require these key elements in specific amounts. It's just like the measuring you do when you're baking a cake: so much flour, so much sugar, so much salt, so much vanilla.

Take heart. Although all of the elements are required, you really need to know about only three – nitrogen, phosphorus, and potassium. Nitrogen is part of each plant cell. It helps leaves and stems grow, and helps leaves turn green. Phosphorus encourages root growth and is very important for good flower, fruit, and seed production. Potassium helps plants resist disease organisms and balances the actions of nitrogen and phosphorus. Potassium is also sometimes called potash.

Reading the label

Different types of plants need different amounts of nitrogen, phosphorus, and potassium. That's why you must read the container label when making a fertilizer purchase. Generally, nitrogen will be abbreviated as N on a fertilizer label, phosphorus as P, and potassium as K. The amount of each element in the fertilizer is usually expressed as a number. Nitrogen always goes first, then phosphorus, then potassium. So a 10-6-4 fertilizer, for example, has 10 percent N, 6 percent P, and 4 percent K. These numbers usually add up to 20 percent. What's in the other 80 percent? Filler material and small amounts of the other elements, which are needed for various plant growth processes.

In general, lawns require a fertilizer high in N and perennial flowers or fruiting plants require a fertilizer high in P. Annuals often don't require fertilizer if they're planted in enriched soil.

Different fertilizer types

Liquid fertilizers are most often used for container plants, but you can use them in the yard too. Just follow the directions and place the desired amount of liquid into a specific amount of water. Liquid fertilizers in solution can be used in a watering can, sprayed on plant leaves as foliage fertilizer, or applied to garden soil. They are high in nitrogen.

Combined fertilizers are fertilizers combined with weed killers, fungicides, or insecticides. This is stated on the package. If you're a beginning gardener, it is best to purchase each item separately, using each as needed.

Always read labels carefully before you buy a product, and again before you use it in the garden.

Organic fertilizers are, of course, fertilizers that are natural or organic. Because packaged fertilizers are made up of chemicals, they are sometimes called "inorganic" fertilizers. Organic fertilizers include manures, bone meal, and wood ashes. Bone meal is high in phosphorus and doesn't burn seeds the way inorganic fertilizers might. It is often used when planting bulbs, because it releases phosphorus slowly.

Wood ashes are a good organic potassium source, but go lightly, because wood ashes can raise the soil pH. Blood meal, which is powdered blood obtained from slaughterhouses, is high in nitrogen. Use it lightly and always handle with gloves, washing up well with warm water and soap afterward.

Perfect timing

There are two prime times to fertilize. The first is when the yard is full of spring flowers and trees are starting to fruit. The second is after plants have stopped growing in the fall. At this time, the absorbed fertilizer will become available as root growth begins anew in spring. Do not fertilize newly installed plants. They're shocked enough. Wait a few weeks.

And technique

The simplest way to disperse fertilizer for small areas is with your gloved hand, or with a hand-held *broadcast spreader*. For lawns, a *drop spreader* does a more even job. There are also fertilizer attachments for your garden hose, and mechanical spreaders. A good garden nursery department will have a display of tools to choose from.

Fertilizer must reach the roots to be effective. Around plants, try to work in the fertilizer 1 to 2 inches deep, and water well after fertilizing. For big trees and shrubs, root feeder spikes are available at most nurseries. Avoid fertilizing seedlings until they have at least three true leaves – the leaves that form above the two baby leaves. Remember, a little fertilizer goes a long way – too much can burn and over-stimulate plants.

Trivia...

Many years ago, farmers thought rotting leather was a great fertilizer for peach trees. They would travel for long distances seeking discarded boots and other leather items, which they would then bury as close as possible to their peach trees. You can try it if you like, but it will probably just give your dog something to dig up.

DEFINITION

Broadcast spreaders *consist of a container, a disk, and a crank. You put the fertilizer in the container and turn the crank, which turns the disk to disperse fertilizer evenly.*
Drop spreaders *have the container mounted on wheels and no disk. As you push the container along, the fertilizer falls from holes in the bottom. You can adjust the size of the openings on the holes.*

A simple summary

✓ Clay and silt soil particles stick together, preventing full air and water movement. Sandy soils have problems holding water.

✓ You can alter most soil types to fit your needs. If possible, you want to create a balanced soil mixture of clay, sand, and silt with lots of organic matter.

✓ Some areas of the garden may have drainage problems. This can be caused by clay soil, hardpan, bedrock, or a high water table. Drainage problems should be fixed.

✓ The pH and salinity of your soil will greatly affect the health of your plants.

✓ If possible, do a soil analysis of various garden sections to determine what type of soil you have. You can then choose plants accordingly, or do what you can to improve the soil quality.

✓ Ingredients that can be dug into soil as improvements include agricultural leftovers, manure, sewage sludge, compost, wood byproducts, leaf mold, peat moss, and sand.

✓ Composting means taking organic material and letting it decompose to form a soil amendment or a mulch. This can be done in an open pile or in a container.

✓ Mulches are placed on top of the soil to protect nearby plants. They include bark chunks, chipper material, sawdust, pine needles, gravel, crushed rock, black plastic film, and straw.

✓ Most soils aren't perfect. Adding proper amounts of fertilizer at the right time is very beneficial to plants. Nitrogen (N), potassium (K), and phosphorus (P) are the most common ingredients in fertilizers.

✓ Fertilization adds important nutrients for good plant health. It is best done in the early spring, and then again in the fall.

Chapter 3

Tool Talk

THE VARIETY OF TOOLS offered at a large nursery, hardware store, or garden show can make your head spin! When it comes to tools, you really can keep it simple, or you can go all out and buy a whole range of fancy tools. But plan ahead so you know what you're likely to need.

In this chapter...

✓ Hand-held tools

✓ Long-handled cutters and pruners

✓ Digging big holes

✓ Raking it in

✓ Hoe ho

✓ Lawn mowers

✓ Gardening extras

✓ Where to put the tools?

Hand-held tools

EVERY GARDENER NEEDS *some simple hand-held tools. Get ready for some grass stains on your knees!*

In my suburban garden, I use hand-held pruning shears, a garden trowel, curved-blade lopping shears, and a long-handled shovel with a pointy blade. These are my basics, and I don't need more. You may.

The size and type of garden you have should determine what type of tools you buy. However, some people are gadget-happy, and if that's your thing you may end up with an entire garage full of special tools. You may even buy a huge tool shed to store your collection. That's OK too. Gardening can be fun and fancy!

Dig those trowels

One of the most important tools is a hand, or garden, trowel. The garden trowel is shaped like a long, narrow scooper, and is used to dig and to place small plants. It may be made entirely of metal, or have a metal scoop with a plastic or wooden handle. Usually the handle is about 5 inches long. However, if you search, you can find garden trowels with 24-inch (or even longer) handles. These are designed for people who can't easily bend or kneel.

A bulb trowel, also known as a planting trowel or bulb planter, is quite useful. It is used to move seedlings as well as dig and place bulbs. The trowel is narrower than the garden trowel, and tapers to a rounded point. Unless it's very inexpensively made, it will have markings on the blade telling you how deep into the soil you've dug.

BULB
TROWEL

Highly recommended by a friend is a dibble, or dibbler, a little metal or plastic cone with a handle. You stick it in the earth and give a little twist, and you've got a planting hole. Simple!

Trivia...

The original dibble was a cow's horn. But I recommend you stick with the metal ones.

Trowel tips

Buy the sturdiest steel trowel you can afford. Don't skimp here. A cheap trowel may bend the first time you dig into hard earth and break by the third time you use it. It is neither cost effective nor effective.

There are inexpensive trowels, in the $4 range, and trowels priced as high as $25.

If you have a choice, buy one narrow and one wide trowel. There are also ergonomic designs for people with hand problems such as arthritis. You may have to search a bit for the unusual, but in today's innovative market you can usually find what you want. Keep your trowels clean and oiled for maximum efficiency.

Hand-held pruners

Also known as pruning shears, these are another necessity. Hand-held pruners are used to cut small branches, such as those on roses. They come in an amazing variety of styles and a wide range of prices, from about $8 to $30. Note that the price often reflects the tool's cutting efficiency.

Pruning shears are designed to cut things that are about the thickness of a pencil. They should open easily after each closing, and have a firm closing latch to store them safely when not in use. Test the several varieties to see how each fits in your hand. For lefties, there are left-handed models available if you look hard enough.

Picking a pruner

For the general-needs gardener, the best pruner to buy is the curved bypass shears. It has two somewhat curved blades that work the way scissor blades do. Get the best you can afford. Inexpensive hand pruners have a tendency to fall apart at the connecting mechanism, especially if you use them on too large a branch – and you will. They also dull easily.

Sharp steel blade makes clean, precise cuts

Brightly colored handles are easy to spot

Safety catch may be moved with the thumb

BYPASS SHEARS

For more delicate pruning tasks, you might want grape shears, also known as straight bypass pruning shears. These have straight, narrow blades that come to a point, quite resembling sewing scissors. Grape shears are handy if you need to get between stems or some other very narrow space – for example to clip just one flower without disturbing other leaves or flowers nearby.

Flower shears are a nice gift to get from someone. They look like sturdy, short-bladed scissors with relatively wide finger loops. If you bring a lot of small to medium perennial and annual flowers indoors, these shears come in handy for a quick, sharp cut.

I was always losing my pruning shears and trowels in the garden, until I started tying red ribbons around the handles.

Some gardeners paint the handles of their shears red or bright yellow to make them stand out amidst garden green.

Cultivators

A hand cultivator has three curved tines, and it looks a little like the foot of a bird. It's useful for scratching soil to loosen the upper layers. It also is convenient for scratching in fertilizer, particularly in areas such as raised beds. Make certain the tines are sharp enough to dig into soil.

A hand fork, also called a flower fork, has straight tines. It is designed to turn over soil in a small area.

Weeders

A hand-held weeder helps you dig weeds all the way out, including the roots. There are many types on the market, including a fishtail weeder, a dandelion digger, and a pronghoe.

HAND FORK

Long-handled cutters and pruners

NO DOUBT ABOUT IT, gardeners tend to spend a lot of time on their knees. But when you're tired of bending, you get a chance to stretch. And every real gardener knows that stretching without the right tool in hand is nothing but a warm-up wasted. So make sure you're prepared.

Lopping shears

Lopping shears resemble hand-held pruning shears, but have 2- to 3-foot long handles and either a curved or an *anvil-type* cutting head. Some have expandable, or telescoping, handles. You'll use lopping shears to cut branches and to trim rose or other thorny bushes safely from a distance.

DEFINITION

Anvil-type *shears have a single cutting blade and a solid, non-cutting opposing part. They produce a slicing action.*

Since you may be working with your arms straight out or over your head, take the time to heft the shears and make sure you can handle them comfortably. It's quite possible that you'll be using these shears for a long period, and they seem to get heavier by the second.

LOPPING SHEARS

Hedge shears

If you have a hedge, you'll eventually need hedge shears. While their length varies, the most common hedge shears are about 2 feet long and usually have straight blades.

HEDGE SHEARS

Hedge shears are for soft-stemmed hedges and those people who enjoy a *topiary* hobby. Gardeners who like perfect lawn edges may use them to get at otherwise inaccessible areas.

> **DEFINITION**
>
> *Clipping trees or shrubs into ornamental shapes, such as squares or animal figures, is called* topiary. *This is an art form practiced since early Roman times. You'll find good examples in many formal gardens, and also in Disney theme parks.*

Hedge shears should not be used for pruning branches. This will break the hedge shears, and will not do a very good job on the branches either.

Saws

A saw is used to cut branches that are too thick to be cut with lopping shears. Saw blades may be straight or rounded. A tremendous variety of saws may tempt you, but if you want to keep things very simple, the general-purpose pruning saw is a good choice. It's lightweight and easy to manipulate at awkward angles. A nice second saw to have around is the double-edged pruning saw. While somewhat unwieldy and requiring some arm strength, it works well on branches that are close to the ground.

For upper branches, and/or treasured trees, call a certified arborist to do your pruning. Large branches are heavy and may not fall where you want them to. Cutting randomly can decimate a tree, preventing flowering, fruiting, and growth, and can slowly kill your tree. Look under "Tree Service" in the telephone book business section for an arborist and get a few different price quotes before you commit. Estimates are usually free, but do get them in writing.

Your tree service should be licensed and fully insured, and willing to show you written proof of both.

Digging big holes

THE RIGHT TOOLS FOR SERIOUS DIGGING *will do a lot to make your gardening experience a pleasure. Make sure you test-drive each piece of equipment so you know you'll be happy with it when you get it home.*

Shovels

A good-quality shovel will last for a decade or longer. I'm still using my father's wood-handle shovel 30 years after he bought it. Get a shovel with a blade of forged steel, even though it costs a bit more than the other kinds. An inexpensive shovel may bend, or even snap, with hard use.

Shovel handles come in various sizes, as do people. A long handle may prove easier on your back, but test before you buy to best suit your height. The handles can be long, medium, or short, and the blades can be wide, narrow, rounded, pointed, or square. A narrow blade penetrates the ground more easily when you're digging. The wider blade is best for moving earth from one place to another. The square one is best used for construction projects. Whichever you use, don't try to lift an entire mountain with one shovel-load. After use, clean and oil the shovel for premium performance.

INTERNET

builderscentral.com/
rakesshovels.html

Builders Central's home and garden site displays a wide range of garden shovels, spades, and diggers that you can order and have delivered.

Spades

Although they are quite similar in appearance to shovels, you'll want to call a spade a spade. What's the difference? A spade is generally rectangular and is most useful for digging holes and lifting soil. Spades are usually lighter than shovels but test for weight when you buy. There are several sizes available.

■ **Make your legs** *do the work when you are digging. Keeping your back straight will avoid back strain.*

When digging, use the ball of your foot to drive in the shovel or spade. Don't press down with the arch of your foot on the blade top. You can injure your foot, as well as slip and fall.

Raking it in

SPRING-TINED LAWN RAKE

IF YOU DON'T *have a grass catcher on your lawn mower, you will need a lawn rake, also called a leaf rake. Come October, you may need one anyway. Lawn rakes are also handy for keeping mulch evenly spread. There are large ones for the lawns and leaves, and smaller ones to help you get behind bushes.*

Garden rakes have many short tines set on a square or curved back. Some gardeners never buy one. Others like them for leveling and breaking up soil while preparing a seedbed. A garden rake can be useful for spreading compost and cleaning up general garden debris. If you have a large area, a rake with 16 tines is preferable.

INTERNET

guild.bham.ac.uk/ bucv/tools.html

The Birmingham University Conservation Volunteers in the U.K. offer practical tips on all kinds of garden tools.

Garden forks

A garden fork is a long-handled fork with four long tines. It looks like a pitchfork, but the tines are flat and are shorter. It comes in a variety of sizes. Garden forks are used for extracting and lifting vegetables that a spade might damage. Obviously, you won't have any vegetables to extract when you first start your garden, so this tool might be added to your collection later. Garden forks are also helpful in turning compost piles.

Hoe ho

GARDEN HOES ARE AVAILABLE *with a wide variety of bases. The standard draw hoe, or common garden hoe, is quite adequate for most garden needs. This type of hoe is used to chip away at weed patches, as well as general cultivating. Make certain the handle is appropriate for your height and body type, so you don't have to bend over awkwardly to work.*

DUTCH HOE

Other hoes include the triangular, digging, combination, and Dutch hoe. If you want two hoes, the Dutch hoe is good for removing surface weeds without damaging plant roots. There are also hoes for specific purposes, such as the onion hoe and the eye hoe.

TAKE CARE

Always hang up hoes, rakes, and shovels. When you take a rest while gardening, do your best to prevent passersby from tripping on, or stepping on, your tools. Place them upright, out of the way, with blade or tines facing away from passersby. Should it be absolutely necessary to temporarily put a garden tool down flat, place tines, rake, or blades face down. This makes it less likely that an unsuspecting neighbor will inadvertently step on the face-up blade and get clobbered by the handle. This was really funny on *The Three Stooges*, but in real life it's not.

Lawn mowers

IF YOU HAVE A LAWN, you are going to need a lawn mower. Some mowers run on gas, some on electric power. You can still find manual push mowers, too, especially at garage sales. Because your needs and those of your lawn are quite specific, it would be imprudent for me to try to advise you on what type of mower to get.

INTERNET

dspace.dial.pipex.com/town/square/gf86/

The site of the Lawn Mower Museum in Southport, England. It displays the largest collection of vintage lawn mowers in the world, as well as toy lawn mowers and lawn mowers of the rich and famous.

If you buy a gas-powered lawn mower, you'll need to have gasoline on hand when you want to use it. These mowers can be difficult to start unless they have an electric ignition. Electric mowers require an outlet and the dexterity to avoid running over the cord when you're mowing (although there are battery-powered ones available). All are designed for ease of use on flat surfaces. You cannot use electric mowers on wet grass, and, like all mowers, you must keep them away from children and pets.

ELECTRIC
MOWER

In addition to testing for pushing ease, starting efficiency, and safety, you may want to check out a recent Consumer Reports lawn mower rating. Mowers require regular maintenance, including professional servicing once a year.

Gardening extras

IN ADDITION TO MOWERS, *there are many mechanical devices, such as hand trimmers, lawn sweepers, leaf blowers, rotary edgers, and string trimmers. There are hand tools in every shape and size. Should you buy any of these things? You may decide you should. Just wait until you know your precise needs. Until then, keep it simple. However, there are a few items you truly should have.*

Gloves

Unless you like hands pricked by rose-thorns and fingernails with dirt under them, gloves are a garden must. They're also useful if you have a problem picking up worms and bugs with your bare hands. There are all sorts of gardening gloves. Some are made specifically for dealing with thorny branches. A pair of these heavy-duty gloves, which have long arm extensions, is great if you intend to do a lot of pruning. If you buy roses, pyracantha, or bougainvillea, you will need them.

Soft cotton gloves are suitable for many ordinary garden tasks. They're inexpensive enough (about $2 a pair) to replace as needed.

If you're handling chemicals, you must use heavy-duty rubber or vinyl gloves. Read the package to see if they are suitable for the job.

Gardening gloves basically come in small, medium, and large. Make sure you buy the right size.

Padding

If you're going to be kneeling or sitting on the ground while gardening, spend $5 and get a soft, rectangular sitting and kneeling pad made specifically for garden use. That means you can hose it off with no harm done.

Wheelbarrow

Eventually, you'll need a wheelbarrow. It is helpful when you're transporting large plants or moving earth, rocks, or compost. You can push the kids around in it, too. Get a good one. You will have it for many years.

■ **A sturdy wheelbarrow** *with long handles will make light work of shifting heavy loads around the garden.*

Push broom

For general yard cleaning, these horizontal, heavy-duty brooms are indispensable. Make certain your broom is reinforced where the handle fits into the broom head. If you don't, you will find that the handle keeps coming out as you sweep – a constant nuisance.

Garden hat

You shouldn't have to think twice about wearing a garden hat or sun visor. You'll avoid skin cancer, and also keep your skin looking younger and healthier. If you're outdoors during prime sunburn hours, consider using a sunscreen too.

Where to put the tools?

YOU CERTAINLY DON'T WANT YOUR *tool collection to get wet, pilfered, or misused. Although a special corner of the garage is fine for storing tools, as you amass merchandise you may want to consider a tool shed. Sheds come in vinyl, aluminum, steel, or wood. Some tool sheds are quite large and come equipped with windows and doors. Others are quite small. Unless you like stooping over and peering around in the dark, get a shed where the tallest adult in the family can stand upright.*

Some assembly may be required, or you can buy tool sheds ready-made. If you have young children, the tool shed should have a secure lock.

Vinyl resin panels are the least expensive. They're simple to put together, and can be cleaned with a hose. Aluminum sheds are also a thrifty buy. Usually small and requiring minimal maintenance, they may have a door and even a window.

■ **A wood tool shed** *has a certain rustic charm, as well as being useful for storing your precious garden tools safely.*

Stainless steel sheds are bit more expensive, partly because they must be plastic-coated to deter rust. Here again, the quality of what you get is reflected in the price.

The premium, in terms of visual appeal, are the wood sheds. As with the steel sheds, quality usually improves with price. But shop around. Prevent deterioration by buying a shed made of hardwood, such as cedar, which is rot resistant. If that's too pricey, look for pressure-treated softwood. Paint the shed with a preservative as soon as you get it, and line it with waterproof building paper from a hardware or building supply store. Add gutters to keep the rain off the sides. Get the highest quality roofing material you can afford.

A simple summary

✓ Always buy the best quality garden tool you can afford. It really is cost-effective. Cheap tools break easily.

✓ For small areas of hand digging, a hand trowel is a necessity. Buy both a slim and a wide version, and tie a red bow to the handle so you can easily find it when you leave it in the garden.

✓ Pruning shears are useful for general duty, such as cutting roses or other flowers, as well as trimming wide stems.

✓ Lopping shears have long handles, and some stretch even longer with expandable handles. Loppers are used for cutting relatively small branches.

✓ There are power saws and people-power saws for larger branches. For major pruning on large limbs or old cherished trees, consult a certified arborist. Find one under "Tree Service" in the telephone book business section.

✓ Consult Consumer Reports before purchasing a power mower.

✓ Don't leave garden tools lying around. Someone could trip on them or step on them and be severely injured.

✓ Consider a tool shed to keep your equipment clean, safe, and dry. Make sure there's a lock on it if you have children. You don't want them playing with the shears and saws.

Chapter 4

Water Wisdom

ALL PLANTS NEED WATER, even a cactus in the middle of the desert. But different plants need different amounts of water. Some thrive on just a teensy bit every once in a while. Others practically insist on swimming. And you don't want to drown a dry-loving plant, or deprive one that thrives in damp soil. You have to add water somehow, but how and how much are not always clear. That's what I'll talk about in this chapter.

In this chapter...

✓ Watering methods

✓ When to water?

✓ Meeting the watering needs of every plant

✓ What's in the water?

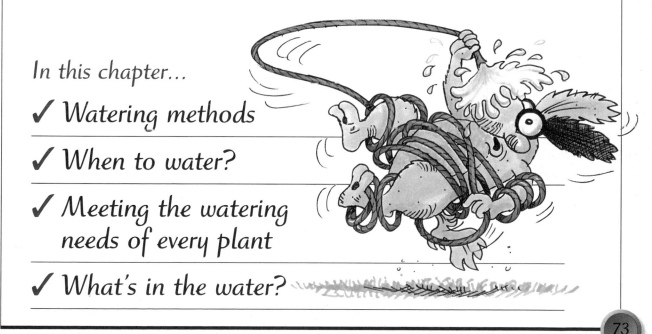

Watering Methods

HOW TO WATER YOUR PLANTS sounds so simple that it's not even worth discussing. But in fact, there are lots of ways to get water into your garden, and your plants will appreciate a little knowledge on your part.

Watering can

Watering cans are your simplest option, and they're great for adding water to container plants and even to raised beds. Some are highly decorative and are used more for ornament than function. Others are made from plain plastic or metal, and either material is fine. A long spout comes in handy when you have to reach into corners at home or in the garden.

■ **A strong watering can** *will give you many years of service, watering plants both in beds and in containers. The long spout gives extra flexibility.*

Trivia...

Five hundred years ago, clay jars with little holes poked all over them were used as watering pots. The jar had a handle and a top opening with a removable cover.

If you have overhead plants, try a hanging plant waterer. This is a plastic bottle with a very long tube attached. You put the open end of the tube into the soil around the plant. A few squeezes and your job is done. It beats standing on a chair to water, and is ideal for people with limited mobility.

When selecting a watering can, keep in mind that small containers require many trips to the faucet. However, if you choose a larger can, it may be difficult to fit under a faucet, and it's heavy when filled. Overfilled, it tends to slosh.

Watering can tips

When hand watering, remember that you must give the plant enough water to wet its roots, not just the top layer of soil. Sprinkle slowly so that the water has time to soak into the soil. Look for a can with a strainer at the base of the spout, as the flow from these cans is more even and more gentle.

Never use a watering can to distribute weed killer. The potent chemicals can leach into the can material or remain in seams. If you have no other way to get weed killer into your garden, get a special can in a bright color, mark it distinctively, and place it away from the can you use to water.

Hoses

Buy the best hose possible. It's cheaper in the long run, and a leaky hose will be a tremendous annoyance.

There are several lengths and widths of hose available. The length you need depends on how many faucets you have in your garden, where they are located, and how big your garden is. While it's a nuisance to drag a super long hose across an entire garden, it's more of a nuisance to be a few feet short of your orange tree. Yes, you can get a hose extender that can be screwed onto the original, but it's easier to get the right length to begin with. Measure the distance from your faucet to the farthest spot in your garden, then add ten feet. This gives you some slack, and also compensates for when the hose wraps itself around garden furniture, corners, and bushes.

Hoses tend to come in a standard width, but you can get extra-wide ones. While they cost a lot more, the wider ones don't kink as easily as their skinnier counterparts. If the rubber hoses sold at your hardware store or garden center aren't too pricey, this should be your choice. The more common nylon or vinyl hoses won't last as long as a rubber hose. A good hose has a great life span and is cost effective. Should you actually have a choice of colors, green goes best with plants, black is a basic, and red makes it easier to see, thus hopefully avoiding the trip-and-fall phenomenon.

The hose connection

If you don't have a lot of faucets, you'll want to consider buying a double hose connector, also called a Y-connector. A Y-connector enables you to put two hoses on one faucet. You can then drag one hose to the left and another to the right, covering the whole garden. Little switches on the connector allow you to control each hose individually.

Hoses shouldn't be left lying around, because sunlight damages the material. If you can't roll yours up and tuck it in a corner, consider buying a hose reel so you can roll and unroll the hose. Some hose reels are designed to be attached to a wall. Others come equipped with wheels, so you can take them for a walk around the garden. Look at quite a few in a major garden center before you make any purchase.

■ **A hose reel** *keeps your hose tidy and conveniently rolled up. Two lengths of hose may be joined with a connector to extend its range.*

INTERNET

happygardener.com/
text/chap8/
ch8doc10.htm

Click here and you'll be taken straight to a site that provides step-by-step information on repairing your garden hose.

Nozzles and sprinklers

If you like to stand and water your domain, an adjustable general-purpose nozzle is the single best device you can buy for your hand-held hose. Just keep it simple. Get one for each hose, plus a spare. Use the finer spray for seedlings, the moderate spray for most other jobs, and the really strong spray to hose down your car.

I like nozzles that you twist to adjust the spray. After a while, the trigger types tend to stick or break.

Other types of nozzles are available, including an overhead extension for watering hanging baskets and a root irrigator that is ideal for watering trees.

If you also want to use your hose as a sprinkler, hose sprinkler heads are available in a multitude of designs. Some rotate, some swing left then right, and others spout straight up, then out, like a fountain. Most heads screw onto the end of your garden hose and are placed on the ground, but a spike sprinkler has a base you stick into the soil. I've tried all kinds of sprinkler heads, and now just get the $5 size with little holes that shoot the water up fountain style. They don't jam or rotate the wrong way, and are inexpensive to replace. Keep it simple, right?

SPIKE SPRINKLER

■ **A soaker hose** *runs along your garden delivering water across its entire length. Some are made of a porous material that lets water seep through; others have teeny holes in them.*

Soaker hoses

If you can leave a flat hose in place, consider using a soaker hose. Water seeps out slowly and isn't wasted into the air or deposited on leaves to encourage fungus growth; instead it goes straight down to the roots. It's necessary to leave soaker hoses in place, because pulling them along or moving tends to twist them, and then the water doesn't go where you want it to.

For cosmetic reasons, some gardeners bury the soaker hose under a light layer of soil. If you do this, cover the far end with a small plastic bag to prevent dirt from entering and clogging the system. Should you later install an automated system, soaker hoses can then be integrated.

Sprinkler systems

Many home-owners have sprinkler systems professionally installed. Others tackle this intricate installation job with the aid of how-to books, relatives, and neighborly advice. Sprinkler systems are great if you have large expanses of garden to cover, or don't want to be tied to regular lawn or garden watering. Depending on the sprinkler system, you can set it on an automatic timer, or turn it on and off by hand.

It's very important that the sprinkler systems be arranged to water the targeted area evenly. Remember that on a windy day, sprinklers deliver water in the direction that the wind is blowing.

Keep in mind that they wet plant leaves as well as the ground, which may encourage mildew and fungus growth on some plants.

■ **Sprinklers are ideal** *for lawns or large borders – but they do use a lot of water, so an automatic timer may be a good investment if you are likely to forget to turn yours off! Water early in the morning or in the evening for maximum benefit.*

Drip irrigation

Drip irrigation systems are above-ground pipes placed around the perimeter of the garden and adjusted by a central faucet. They deliver water just a drop at a time. Some can be adjusted for misting and other special needs. They are excellent for most garden areas, and the preferred choice for slopes that have been planted with plants that really need substantial water. Drip systems require about 30 percent less water than other systems, and so are especially valuable for drought-prone areas. They do require some maintenance to keep the tiny holes open.

Some gardeners employ a professional to install drip irrigation, others do it themselves. It helps to be handy or to have the advice of someone who has accomplished the job successfully.

INTERNET

garden.com

This on-line magazine offers information about drip irrigation and soaker hoses, plus a whole lot more. There's also great shopping here.

When to water?

SEVENTY TO NINETY PERCENT *of a healthy plant is composed of water. This water evaporates through a plant's leaves, and does so quickly in warm weather. All plants need to replenish this lost water in order to survive. Some plants need a lot of water and some, such as cacti, need less. You'll want to pay a lot of attention to water demands when you purchase plants for your garden. This is especially true if you have a very busy schedule and tend to be forgetful about watering, or if you are away from home a lot. In that case, buy plants that won't wither if they get a little dry.*

In general, early morning is the best watering time. As the day progresses, light and sunshine will help dry the leaves. Why do you want the leaves to dry?

Overhead or high sprinkler watering can splash fungus spores from one plant to another. If the leaves dry out quickly, the fungus doesn't get a chance to take hold.

If you can't water in the early morning, early evening is the next best choice. Water early enough in the evening so that plants get a chance to dry off before evening damp and dew appear.

How much water?

So many variables come into play when determining how much to water your garden that it's impossible to answer this question simply. You must consider plant type, soil type, soil slope, time of year, length of day, available light at the site, mulching practices, and, of course, the weather. I don't just mean rain, but also the impact of temperature, humidity, and wind. That being said, I'll try to answer the question anyway.

In general, each time you water, soak the soil deeply. In hot weather, of course, you'll need to pay extra attention to your plants. Just looking at their leaves often tells you the story. As temperatures rise, plants lose increasing amounts of water through their leaves. The leaves then start to sag. If garden plant leaves are sagging in the evening, you can wait until morning before taking action. If the leaves haven't perked up, this is the plant's message that it definitely needs more water. Other water deprivation symptoms include flowers that fade rapidly, flowers that fall off, poor plant growth with no other discernible reason, and older leaves turning brown and dropping early in the season.

Meeting the watering needs of every plant

IT SHOULD COME AS NO SURPRISE *that different types of plants have different watering needs. I'll give you more detailed advice about specific plants in later chapters about the plants. For now, you should have a basic understanding of how to address the needs of every member of your garden.*

Plants in pots

Pay extra attention to the needs of any plant in a container. Don't wait overnight to water a thirsty potted plant. If it looks like it needs water, it does — now!

Unlike plants in open garden soil, container plants have no way of sending out roots to find more water. They rely solely on what you give them.

Flowers

How frequently you need to water your flowers will depend, in large part, on your type of soil. Your goal is to have the water reach the plant's roots, not just slide over the surface or run downhill. If you have good loamy soil, it will absorb and distribute water well. So perhaps you can just water once a week. If you have sandy soil, water tends to pass right through. The soil therefore dries out quickly and you'll probably need to water more often. Clay soil tends to let water enter slowly, retains water due to poor drainage, and has a tendency to puddle if over-watered. Depending on the amount of clay, you may want to let the soil dry out a bit before watering again.

Poke a stick down about 2 inches a few days after you have watered, and see what the soil moisture looks like at that level.

■ **A wilting** *potted plant or hanging basket needs prompt first aid. Immerse it temporarily in a bowl of water so that it can absorb moisture from the roots.*

Trivia...

If you like cut flowers to display in your home, avoid watering your flowering plants from above. This can bend the flower stalks and damage the blossoms.

Lawns

Water lawns before they look dried out.

Water-stressed lawns change color, taking on odd shades of blue-green or green-brown. When you water, make certain the water reaches down 6 inches into the soil. If you're not sure how long that takes with your watering system, put clean, empty 6- to 8-ounce cans at various places on your lawn. When these are filled with water, you've probably accomplished your goal.

Be certain, if you use an attachable sprinkler on your garden hose, to move it so that all parts of the lawn get an equal and sufficient share of the water.

Trees and shrubs

Newly planted trees and shrubs must be watered regularly. Older trees and shrubs can usually withstand some drought, but when the weather is dry for a long period, you'll have to water. The water must reach the tree and shrub roots, which can go quite deep. Rather than sprinkling or hose watering, you can use a root irrigator, or deep root waterer. This is a long steel tube with holes at the end. You push it into the soil at the *drip line*, and attach the top end connector to a hose. Turn on the hose, and water is forced downward into the root zone.

> **DEFINITION**
>
> *A drip line is an imaginary circular area around a tree based on where the tips of the outermost branches end and where rainwater normally drips off the leaves.*

Another method for watering trees is to let the water trickle slowly at the base of the tree. If you really want to do it right, dig a trench around the base to hold the water in. The trench should be about 3 inches deep and 6 inches wide.

■ **To ensure that the water** *stays where you want it to stay – around the roots of the tree or shrub being watered – create a basin at the base of the stem and water into it.*

Seeds and seedlings

Seeds must have water, and you will want to keep the soil slightly moist at all times. If you are sowing seeds in very dry soil, water it very well before placing the seeds. Water reaching a depth of 6 to 8 inches is not too much. After you have placed the seeds and covered them with the recommended amount of soil, water again very lightly. Use the fine spray on your garden hose or a watering can with a strainer on the spout. If the weather is warm, you may want to do this every day, preferably in the morning. Conscientious gardeners put a light mulch over the seed bed to conserve water. Don't worry – the blanketed seeds will grow through this mulch.

Monitor your seedlings closely and never let the soil totally dry out. The roots formed by seedlings are thinner than fine thread. They are extremely delicate and don't have much resilience. Once they dry out, it's unlikely they'll resuscitate even if you water them abundantly.

Be aware that wind is as much a culprit in soil drying as sun. Early morning water, followed by a hot, windy afternoon, can decimate seedlings by evening.

Vegetables

Waving a garden hose several times over the area where your vegetables are planted will not do a bit of good. You really want the water to reach deep into the plants' roots. Shallow watering results in plants that have roots only at the surface. The first dry spell and the plants die. Plants with deep-reaching roots can survive a brief dry spell, because they have more space from which to draw moisture. But they'll only develop deep roots with regular deep watering – going to a depth of about 5 inches. You'll get the best results by letting the water soak in gradually, rather than using overhead sprinkling.

While spring is a favorite sowing time, many vegetables can be planted throughout the summer. These late-planted seeds need special care, as heat causes extremely rapid water evaporation.

When putting out late-seeded vegetables, initially cover them with a light mulch to reduce evaporation. Remove the mulch as the seedlings start to appear.

Trivia...

In ancient Egypt the prime source of water was the Nile River, which rose and fell quite a bit every year. As a result, water shortages were not uncommon. To obtain a steady supply, the Egyptians used a shaduf, or swipe. This is a long pole supported on a pivot. It has a bucket at one end, and an opposing weight, such as a stone, on the other.

The operator dipped the bucket into the water, then pushed just hard enough on the stone to get it to drop – which lifted the bucket. The pivot allowed for a swivel action. This mechanism was invented by the Assyrians some time before 2200 BC and is still in use in some places.

What's in the water?

AS A RULE, the water out of your faucet should be perfectly safe for your plants – you let your kids drink it, don't you? Still, there are some precautions to be taken when watering your gorgeous new garden plants.

Hard water

As water travels through rocks and soil, it picks up particles of calcium, magnesium, iron, lead, and other minerals. Water that is hard contains a fair amount of dissolved minerals. If your tap water is hard, you have to scrub harder to work up a lather in the shower, and you may see mineral deposits on your shower heads or faucets.

Hard water in areas with alkaline or desert-type soil isn't much of a problem, unless you want to grow acid-loving plants such as azaleas, blueberries, camellias, gardenias, and hydrangeas. You can try adding fertilizers that create a more acidic environment, or dig in a substantial amount of peat moss when you're putting plants in place.

If you use a water softener, you should obtain your plant water from another source or find a way to bypass the softener. Continued use of softened water is harmful to all plants, particularly container plants and others with slow drainage. The softener ingredient replaces the normal soil calcium with sodium. This sodium accumulates in the soil. It can cause leaf burn, and also block water transmission through the soil layers.

Distilled water

Distilled water is sold in 1- and 2-gallon containers for $1 to $4 per container. Many gardeners prefer distilled water for indoor plants, raised beds, or salty soil, as it does not have dissolved minerals in it, but it would be too expensive for an outdoor garden.

Rainwater is also distilled water, because it hasn't passed through the earth, picking up minerals along the way. If you live in a rainy area, you may want to collect it in a barrel to save some money. Or, if you live in a drought-prone area, you may want to collect rainwater to save the environment. Either way, make sure the barrel you use has a lid to keep out dirt and bugs. It should also have a tap at the bottom. It helps to put the water barrel on a little platform, so the tap is easily accessible.

Unfortunately, rainwater in some areas is full of impurities from air pollution. If your local forecaster gives frequent warnings about the air quality, you may just want to pass on the rainwater.

Gray water

Gray water is the water from the rinse cycle of washing machines or dishwashers, or water from showers and sinks. Special piping is installed to transfer this water outdoors instead of into the sewer system. Gardeners in water-thrifty areas are often interested in the possibilities for using gray water. But opinions vary. The biggest problem is that gray water has soap residue, which contains sodium, and too much sodium will kill plants.

If you live in an area where water restriction is mandated and you need to use gray water, try adding gypsum to the soil. Gypsum is sold in containers at larger nurseries. Just follow the instructions on the container.

A simple summary

✓ For small jobs you can use a watering can. But even if you have a drought-tolerant garden, you will probably need some other type of watering mechanism.

✓ When selecting watering equipment, buy the best quality you can afford. While hoses aren't expensive, drip irrigation and sprinkler systems can be. It's better to put off the purchase until you can afford a bit better quality.

✓ When putting in a drip irrigation or sprinkler system, consider hiring a professional to do the job. If you want to do it yourself, read how-to books, consult with other do-it-yourselfers, talk to garden center staff, and get some help with the manual labor.

✓ Water early in the morning if at all possible, to give leaves a chance to dry off throughout the day. This helps prevent fungal infections from taking hold of your plants.

✓ Water deeply each time, except if you have hardpan, which requires shallower and more frequent waterings.

✓ Seeds and seedlings require special care. Water them daily, because even a little thirst can quickly kill them.

✓ Plants tolerate most types of water, but avoid the additives in softened water and gray water. If gray water use is unavoidable, add gypsum to the soil.

PART TWO

CHRYSANTHEMUMS FOR SUMMER AND FALL COLOR

FLOWERS FANTASTIC

SPRING ALWAYS SEEMS to begin when you can cut a bouquet of fresh flowers from your garden. It's amazing that, come March in many areas, the ground is already alive with yellows, reds, and purples. Color stretches until fall in the well-planned floral garden.

It may seem a difficult job to plan and place this panorama of color and beauty. But you can *keep it simple*. Selecting the right plant

for the right place is a challenge most gardeners come to enjoy.

Flowering plants are usually divided into three major categories: annuals, which bloom in their first year and then die; perennials, which come back year after year; and bulbs, which are in a class by themselves.

Chapter 5

Ample Annuals

YOU CAN BUY ANNUALS as seed packets, as six-pack youngsters, or in full bloom. Give the requisite amount of water, the proper sunlight or shade, and a little soil assistance, and simple! Success is yours. In this chapter, I'll concentrate on easy-to-grow annuals for general garden use. I'll discuss flowering annuals that grow best in containers in Chapter 18.

In this chapter...

✓ Let's shop!

✓ Lightly shaded annuals

✓ Drought-tolerant annuals

✓ Damp-site annuals

✓ Fragrant annuals

A MAGNIFICENT DISPLAY OF VIOLAS

Let's shop!

YOU MIGHT FIND *your first flowers right outside of a supermarket in the early spring. The store will usually feature the most popular annuals, bulbs, or* perennials *just starting to bloom. The sight of primrose pinks and reds, or pots of early golden daffodils perking up the day, often compels you to buy them on the spot. Go ahead! You'll get weeks of beauty from your purchase.*

It won't be long, however, before you find yourself spending some serious time at a garden center. You'll find a wide selection of the most popular plants that tend to thrive in your area (as well as those that are a bit more challenging). If you look around thoroughly, you'll be amazed at the variety of plants and equipment you'll find. Because these big retailers purchase in quantity from growers and distributors, their prices are usually fair, too.

Once you discover the joys of gardening, you'll start reading garden books and catalogs, too. And sooner or later, you'll make the grand leap to the true garden nursery. Here there may be an acre of plants, many different varieties of the same species, and a bewildering array of choices. Unless you have a gigantic garden (and a gigantic bank account), you won't be able to buy everything that strikes your fancy. So how do you choose?

■ **Pink and white** *spring tulips interplanted with annual bedding plants provide a colorful spring display against a background of burgeoning foliage.*

Selecting sensible plants

The true novice often visits a garden center, sees some attractive blooming plants, brings them home, puts them in the ground, and watches them wilt. Disappointed but not discouraged, the novice returns to the garden center. This time the new gardener asks some questions: "Does this need a lot of water?" "I have a shady yard; what do I plant?" and "Do you have something that smells nice?"

If you recognize yourself in this scenario, back up a little bit to just before you leave home. Stand in the garden, be it large or small, and write down the following: "I need plants that are so many inches or so many feet tall. The place I want to put them is sunny. Or shady. Or semi-shady. I need drought-tolerant plants because I tend to forget to water. I want (or don't want) bees in my yard. I do (or don't) want plants that demand a lot of attention." Take that list with you when you go shopping. (You might want to go in with just a mental list, but how many times have you come back from the supermarket with everything except the milk?)

If you are really serious about getting the correct plant, take a generic garden book with you that has a fairly complete plant identification list and description. Garden center descriptions can be a bit over-enthusiastic, giving scant information on whether a plant will survive in less than ideal conditions, and garden books are often more practical.

Pick a pack of plants

When you're at the garden center, you'll find many plants in 1-gallon cans, usually priced at $3 and up.

Purchase only plants that look healthy.

If they are sickly in the container, they are going to have an extremely difficult time surviving the move from one place to another. Plants in gallon containers and larger should not have dying leaves, roots desperately pushing their way out of the can, or little bugs having a meal.

A popular way to buy plants is to get an inexpensive six-pack. These packs of six little plastic cubicles containing young plants are the best way to purchase annuals – which look best in small groupings. Again, look for healthy plants, just as you look for healthy green vegetables in the supermarket. You don't buy wilted lettuce or parsley, so don't buy a wilting green plant, regardless of its size.

Healthy, green top-growth

Sturdy new shoots

Potting mix just moist

Roots just visible around the root ball, but not congested

A HEALTHY CONTAINER-GROWN PLANT

When you're buying a six-pack, make certain you get all the plants you are paying for. Count them.

And while you're at the garden center, buy a large sack, or two, of soil amendment. Pick the one that's best for your soil (remember, we talked about that in Chapter 2). You're probably going to need it. Keep your shopping simple, too.

Bringing home the blooms

Make your trip to the garden center your last stop. Do not leave your plants in the car while you run other errands. Remove your plants from the car as soon as you get home and place them in a shady, cool site. Give your purchases a drink of water while they are in the container. Plant them promptly. While plants can sit a day or two in gallon containers, those little six-packs will not hold a plant for very long. Hopefully, you have already dug the site and integrated some organic soil. No? Do it now.

INTO THE GROUND

1 **Transplant as gently as possible**

Remove your plant carefully from its container, keeping the roots and soil in one ball. Place in the hole you've made in the ground, and fill in with good organic soil.

2 **Give your new plant extra care**

Gently press down the soil with your fingers and water thoroughly. Over the next 2 weeks, don't let the soil dry out: lack of water, combined with the shock of being moved, can kill new plants.

UNDERSTANDING SCIENTIFIC NAMES

Throughout this book, and in many gardening books, you'll see plants referred to by their scientific names. Although you may not be into learning Latin just to garden, these names are actually quite useful. Common names, such as "pansy," vary greatly from region to region. Even your neighbor may use a different name for a particular plant than you do. To add some uniformity in how we refer to plants, scientists developed a universal naming system using Latin words. Of course, not all scientists agree about what the correct Latin name for a plant is, and plants are often being reclassified. Be that as it may, a basic understanding of how to read the Latin names will help you select the plants you want.

Dividing large groups into smaller ones

Science divides all living things into large groups, which are then divided into smaller and smaller groups. Eventually, each living thing is classified into a genus, and that group is further broken down into specific species. Humans, for example, are classified in the genus *Homo* and the species *sapiens*.

Genera and species

Latin names are written in italic type. The genus name is capitalized but the species name is not. Some genera (plural for genus) include a tremendous number of species, while others include only one. So when you see the name *Myosotis sylvatica* alongside the flower forget-me-not, you're reading the Latin name for a particular flower. The genus *Myosotis* contains over 50 species of flowers, including the species *sylvatica*. A short form for the name would be *M. sylvatica*. So what?

Latin names can help

Well, perhaps you're browsing through a seed catalog, and can't find the forget-me-not *Myosotis sylvatica*. Perhaps you can find another species in the *Myosotis* genus that appeals to you. Or perhaps you only want the *sylvatica* species. Knowing the Latin name will help ensure that you select the right flower. On occasion, I'll give just the genus name for a group of similar plants, because that is enough information to get you on your way. You'll also see that lots of plants are known only by their Latin name – irises, for example, are simply members of the genus *Iris*.

Lightly shaded annuals

THERE AREN'T A SLEW OF ANNUALS *that truly thrive in the sort of shade you get under an established tree, but you can still pick and choose what to plant if your area has light to medium shade.*

Canterbury bells

Most flowers in the genus *Campanula* are perennials – plants that live on year after year – but the Canterbury bell (*Campanula medium*) is a delightful biennial/annual. Blue, lavender, pink, or white flowers have a bell-like appearance, dangling in clusters among slightly hairy leaves from stems that are about 2 feet tall. This plant does like good soil, although it doesn't have to be perfect. Water Canterbury bells regularly. While you can grow them from seed, it's a lot easier to buy a gallon pot at a garden center. Get them started as early in the season as possible for June and July blooms.

Forget-me-nots

Prolific re-seeders, forget-me-nots (*Myosotis sylvatica*) will turn your garden into a sea of blue wherever you plant them. Just about 6 inches tall, they're great toward the front of any area. They do best in light semi-shade, and are one of the few annuals that tolerate fairly consistent moist soil. In addition to the traditional blue flowers, there are pink and white varieties, but you may have to search for these in garden catalogs. Sow seeds in very early spring (you may never need to buy seeds again) for flowers from mid-spring until mid-summer.

Trivia...

In the Victorian era, a codified language of flowers was developed to serve as a guide for appropriate flower use. A flower's symbolic meaning was taken quite seriously, and books were written that explained the language. A gift of a bouquet of forget-me-nots, according to the language of flowers, signified friendship and fidelity.

■ **Dainty forget-me-nots,** *like this variety of Myosotis sylvatica known as Victoria Rose, will cover a bed with tiny pink flowers every spring for years to come.*

Balsams

Many people simply use the Latin name *Impatiens* when referring to this genus of annuals. From the word for "impatience" in Latin, *Impatiens* has the habit of propelling its seeds outward when its seedpods are touched. This is an annual that tends to have a lot of offspring for you to enjoy each summer. I like the balsam variety (*I. balsamina*) and the busy Lizzie (*I. walleriana*), *a perennial that is usually grown as an annual*. Busy Lizzie gets its name from the plant's determination to be the one with the most blooms.

> **DEFINITION**
>
> A perennial usually grown as an annual *is a plant that has a very short life span. Instead of trying to get it to grow from year to year, as a perennial does, most gardeners re-seed or replace it every year.*

Colors include pink, white, orange, salmon, and red, with both single- and double-flowering varieties commonly available. Size ranges from 6 to 36 inches high, depending on the variety. The flowers can reach 2 inches wide, so space the plants accordingly. *Impatiens* likes semi-shade and shade, in that order. You will have to keep the soil slightly moist to maintain *Impatiens*' happiness. If you're going to plant from seed, sow in early spring. Don't put them out in the garden until after the last frost, as they are not frost tolerant.

BUSY LIZZIE
(*Impatiens walleriana*)

Pansies

Although pansies (*Viola* x *wittrockiana*) don't object to some sun, they do best in semi-shade with regular watering. Loamy soil should be provided. Colors, and color combinations, are so striking, especially close-up, that you will want them in masses along walkways as well as in planter boxes closer to eye height.

When you put pansies out depends on where you live. For those in cold winter climates, set out nursery plants in spring, after the last frost, to enjoy summer blooms. For those in mild climates, you can purchase nursery-grown pansies in the fall and have blooms through the winter and into the spring. You'll want to pick these delicate flowers for table decorations. The more you pick, the more new flowers will appear.

PANSIES (*Viola* x *wittrockiana*)

More annuals for shade

Among the other visual delights that will tolerate some shade are flowering tobacco (*Nicotiana*), larkspur (*Consolida*), love-in-a-mist (*Nigella*), mignonette (*Reseda odorata*), and wishbone flower (*Torenia fournieri*). Coleus (*Solenostemon scutellarioides*) have tiny flowers that are not much to look at, but their spectacular patterned leaves, in colors ranging from white to green to red to purple, will brighten your garden from the time you plant them until the first frost.

Drought-tolerant annuals

THERE ARE ANNUALS that will live on less water. But "less" does not mean no water at all. Even if you decide to plant drought-tolerant annuals because of water shortages, water bills, or a dislike for watering, you still must water for a few weeks to get the plants started.

CREEPING ZINNIA (*Sanvitalia procumbens*)

Creeping zinnia

This looks like a miniature zinnia or daisy that happens to be trailing on the ground. Flowers are bright yellow or orange, single or double, with dark purple centers. Plant seeds in mid-spring, or buy young plants in six-packs (but be aware that flowering plants don't transplant well). Place the plants about 5 inches apart to leave room for them to creep outward.

Because they don't grow to more than 6 inches high, place creeping zinnia (*Sanvitalia procumbens*) along a walkway or in another spot where you'll be sure to see it. Once you get creeping zinnia started, it needs very little water. You should see blooms from mid-summer until the first frost.

Four o'clocks

If you have children who would like to have their own little garden, four o'clocks (*Mirabilis jalapa*) are a great choice with their large, easy-to-handle seeds. Flowers can be scarlet, white, yellow, or *variegated*, and they appear in profusion from late spring until the fall.

DEFINITION

When something is variegated, it has streaks or patches of different colors.

The hard, round, black seeds fall to the ground, and if they land in a suitable spot, you'll have new plants next year. Underground tubers may also provide a plant resurgence. I have grown four o'clocks successfully in clay soil and against a white wall. Although they need water to start, they tolerate dryness and just adore heat.

■ **For evening scent** *choose* Mirabilis jalapa's *fragrant, trumpet-shaped flowers that open later in the day, hence its name four o'clock.*

Globe amaranth

When buying globe amaranths (*Gomphrena globosa*), make sure that you get the type that you want. There are dwarf varieties, 6 inches high, that are suitable for edging; and taller ones, up to 18 inches high, that make great cut flowers. The flowers can be white, yellow, scarlet-purple, or rose. Give these flowers full sun and average soil.

Globe amaranths are one of the few flowering annuals that don't mind a bit of wind. In fact, the wind may scatter seed at the season's close, so that you have more amaranths next year.

Trivia...

You can create stunning dried flower arrangements with globe amaranths. Pick the flowers as they begin to open. Hang groupings of five stems upside down in a cool, shady place until they are dry. Unlike many dried flowers, these will keep most of their color.

Sweet alyssum

Sweet alyssum (*Lobularia maritima*) is a low-growing (4 to 8 inches high) edging plant with the most delightful honey-sweet fragrance. This is an easy annual to grow from seed. It thrives in just about any soil if it's given enough water to get it started. Then water a bit from time to time for the most flowers.

Most often seen in white, there are also pinks and purples, but they don't seem to be as hardy or prolific. Some varieties, such as 'Carpet of snow,' will re-seed, cropping up in the oddest garden places, but always lovely. In mild climates, you may have alyssum almost throughout the year. If you like the sight of a roving bumblebee (or three), you'll discover that this hardy annual seems to send out an invitation to visit.

SWEET ALYSSUM (*Lobularia maritima*)

Statice

Not only does this papery-flowered plant do best when in dry soil, but it thrives in seaside gardens. This, no doubt, accounts for its other common name – sea lavender. Colors include blue, lavender, and rose, with lavender being the most common.

Statice (*Limonium sinuatum*) will grow to about 2 feet high. Plant seeds early in the spring for mid-summer blooms, or buy plants in six-packs at the nursery.

Do not put statice near plants that get a lot of water. Over-watering can be quickly fatal.

STATICE (*Limonium sinuatum*)

More drought-tolerant annuals:

- African daisy (*Arctotis*)
- Cape marigold (*Dimorphotheca*)
- Rose moss (*Portulaca*)
- Scarlet sage (*Salvia*)
- Sunflower (*Helianthus*)
- Zinnia (*Zinnia*)

Damp-site annuals

THERE IS A DIFFERENCE, *of course, between damp and soggy. If you have soggy soil, think perennials rather than annuals. There are few annuals that truly thrive in constant moisture. But if things are just a little damp, try the forget-me-not, Madagascar periwinkle* (Catharanthus), *pansy, spider flower* (Cleome hassleriana), *or one of the following annuals.*

Meadow foam

If you can find the seeds, try planting meadow foam (*Limnanthes douglasii*) this way in spring or fall. Once you have it growing and it's happy, it will self-seed. This small annual measures only 6 inches high, at most, but it's quite cute, with the nickname poached-egg plant. From summer until fall, yellow-green leaves are crowned with yellow-centered white flowers.

INTERNET

msue.msu.edu/imp/
mod03/master03.html

This address gets you into the Michigan State University Extension Home Horticulture database.

Monkey flower

This colorful plant is technically a perennial, but is usually grown as an annual. For some, the 2-inch wide flowers resemble a smiling monkey. Colors include browns, yellows, rose, orange, and scarlet, usually with a lot of maroon spotting. Monkey flowers (*Mimulus hybridus*) must have shade, a lot of water, and rich soil with ample organic matter. They are not, in my experience, the easiest plants to grow, but it's not always easy to find plants that enjoy sitting in quite moist soil. They grow to about 2 to 4 feet high. Ferns make nice companion plants.

Snow-on-the-mountain

A member of the extensive spurge family, snow-on-the mountain (*Euphorbia marginata*) is more of a background than a foreground plant, since the light green leaves take precedence over the minute white *bracts*. Use it to frame brightly colored plants, such as some of the vivid dahlias, sages, and zinnias.

DEFINITION

A bract is a group of modified, or changed, leaves. While most are green, bracts are sometimes quite colorful.

In warmer climates this plant does need some shade, but does well in full sun in more temperate areas. The colored bracts appear in summer on plants growing to about 2 feet high.

The sap of all euphorbias is a skin and eye irritant, and is poisonous if swallowed.

Wishbone flower

WISHBONE FLOWER (*Torenia fournieri*)

This delicate yellow and purplish, trumpet-shaped flower gives summer and fall color. It needs lots of water, so put it where you will remember to sprinkle regularly. A short period of drought will kill it quickly. Wishbone flowers (*Torenia fournieri*) do best in light to medium shade. They grow to about 1 foot high, and thus are suitable for quite visible borders. They also look nice in pots. The name "wishbone" derives from the wishbone-shaped pollen-carrying *stamens* nestled in the flower's throat.

> ### DEFINITION
>
> Stamens *are usually located inside the flower petals. They are usually a slim stalk topped by an anther. An anther contains pollen grains, and is usually yellow.*

Fragrant annuals

SOME ANNUALS ARE BEST KNOWN *for their fabulous fragrance. If you really want to engage passersby, try planting some of the following flowers.*

Heliotrope

Trivia...

The leaves and flowers of heliotrope turn toward the sun. The name heliotrope is from the ancient Greek: helios for sun and trepos, which means "turning to go into it."

In their native Peru, heliotrope (*Heliotropium arborescens*) grows year-round, sometimes to enormous size. But here they usually act as annuals, and seldom get over 2 feet tall. The aroma, reminding some of vanilla, is absolutely delicious up close. It is not one of those fragrant plants that grabs you by the nose from quite a distance – a plus for some, a minus for others.

While the scent of heliotrope is world-famous, the entire plant is poisonous if ingested. Contact with leaves may irritate skin and eyes on sensitive folk, so this is a plant to keep away from youngsters.

Heliotrope requires a bright, sheltered site in rich soil full of organic material, and needs regular watering. Even if you can't find a suitable site in your garden, think about putting it in a pot by the front door.

Mignonette

MIGNONETTE (*Reseda odorata*)

This North African native wins accolades as the most fragrant of all garden annuals. Plant it right next to your patio doors, or next to windows that are opened on cool summer evenings. Then sneak some more here and there in the garden, and tuck a few in good-size pots. Mignonette (*Reseda odorata*) needs part shade, good soil, and regular watering. It likes cool summers, and does not bloom well in hot, dry weather. This plant grows about 12 inches tall, and small, drab, greenish-yellow flowers appear in groups about 6 inches long.

Mignonette heartily resents transplanting, so if you can sow seeds in early spring, do it. Otherwise, move from six-pack to garden quite tenderly, and do not move it again.

Stock

This *biennial* is usually grown as an annual. Stock (*Matthiola incana*) has a spicy aroma that's best in the evening and on cool, overcast days. There is also an evening version called night-scented stock (*Matthiola longipetala*), for those who enjoy their gardens after dusk. Native to the Mediterranean coast, stock likes you to reproduce a similar climate – moist, quite well-drained soil that is high in organic matter. It does best in very light shade, and you want it to bloom before the weather gets hot. Colors include ivory, shades of red, and shades of purple. Stock can grow as high as 35 inches, although most plants don't get that tall. You must give stock regular water, but be very careful not to over-water, which often results in rotted roots.

> **DEFINITION**
>
> *A biennial is a plant that takes two years to complete its life cycle. The first year it grows from seed to a leafy plant, but no flowers appear. The second year, the plant flowers, develops seed, and dies. If you buy biennials already started at nurseries, you are buying a plant in its second year. In the garden, they'll behave just like annuals, which also die at season's end.*

■ **The spice-scented stock** – Matthiola incana – *has soft, gray-green foliage that surrounds the fragrant flower spikes.*

Sweet pea

Every old-fashioned garden had sweet peas (*Lathyrus odoratus*), and although they seemed to all but disappear for a while, the trend toward traditional gardening is bringing them back again. There are bush sweet peas that reach to 30 inches tall, and climbing sweet peas, and both are excellent for cutting. If you grow the climbing variety, you will need to provide some type of support. Give them full sun, ample water, plenty of fertilizer, and good soil.

The scent was bred out of many sweet pea hybrids to obtain more flamboyant flowers.

Make certain your sweet pea packet says "scented," or look for this variety in a catalog of heritage-type plants.

Sweet peas are relatively easy to grow from seed, so do try it. Unless you want to wait seemingly forever, soak the hard seeds for 24 to 48 hours before planting.

SWEET PEA (*Lathyrus odoratus*)

Trivia...

There are long-term arguments about where the name "sweet William" came from. Among the purported European namesakes are William the Conqueror, King William III, and William, Duke of Cumberland. Others believe the flower was named after Saint William, whose festival day is June 25th — which is about when sweet Williams first bloom.

Sweet William

Sweetly fragrant, this low-growing annual does best in sun or light shade. Most often seen in the reds and pinks, there are also violet and white flower varieties of sweet William (*Dianthus barbatus*). The flower clusters are about 3 to 5 inches wide, appearing in bouquet-like groups. The leaves are usually grass-like and tinged blue or gray. This charming plant looks best in an informal, natural setting. It will re-seed and then behave as a biennial if conditions are right, including good soil, regular watering, a sunny spot, and occasional fertilizer.

A simple summary

✓ There are lots of places to find plants, from the supermarket to the sophisticated garden nursery. Take a small garden encyclopedia with you to help you pick the best choices for your garden and for unbiased advice.

✓ The least expensive way to grow annuals is to get a six-pack of young plants. These need to be planted in your garden as soon as possible. If you pay more, you can get larger, more established plants in 1-gallon containers. Either way, choose only plants that look healthy.

✓ Very few annuals like shade, but there are a few that enjoy semi-shade. Take a thorough look at your planting site to determine how much sunlight it actually gets – and at what time of day – before you buy your plants.

✓ There are a host of drought-tolerant annuals, most of which also need partial or full sun. If well-treated, many of these plants will re-seed, giving you lots of plants in the same area – which you can move or give away to friends.

✓ Not too many like damp soil, so you might try to correct it, or create raised beds. However, there are some that will do fine in soil that's fairly wet, as long as it's not wet all the time.

✓ Everyone enjoys fragrant flowers, and annuals can help add wonderful aromas to your garden. Put them near windows, doors, and patios, so that you can enjoy the fragrance both inside and out. Plant some near the front door to welcome you home in the evening.

Chapter 6

Perennially Perfect

PERENNIALS WILL APPEAR in your garden year after year, becoming like old friends. Some perennial flowers are short-lived, while others, such as the peony, seem to last forever. Keep in mind that most perennials go dormant, or take several month-long naps, during part of the year. If they don't disappear from sight, they may grow so slowly that you get worried about their health. Wait until spring, or mid-spring if you've had a frosty winter, and see if they revive. In this chapter I'll explore some of the best-known perennials, and explain what grows well in different types of gardens.

In this chapter...

✓ Perennial preliminaries

✓ Perennials for semi-shade

✓ Drought-tolerant perennials

✓ Perennials for moist soil

✓ Fragrant perennials

Perennial preliminaries

Nature doesn't use a ruler when designing a natural garden, and neither should you. On the other hand, you should put some thought into where you plant your flowers. For premium beauty and color, group your perennials according to their blooming times. You'll want sections dedicated to spring, summer, and fall flowers. (Remember, there's a chart in Chapter 1 detailing what blooms when.) The groups should slightly overlap from side to side and from front to back.

It's very important to consider the watering needs of your flowers before you put them in the ground. Regardless of their season and height, plant drought-tolerant plants together, and separate from the water-lovers.

Timing your purchases

The simplest and most successful way to grow perennials, usually, is to buy a six-pack of already started plants. You should do this in late fall or early spring, as soon as the variety appears at the garden center. Put newly purchased young plants in prepared soil as soon as possible, water daily if necessary to keep the ground slightly damp, and let them grow on your home turf.

■ **Planting in groups** *is a highly effective way of using plants to fill a bed or border. The impact of mass plantings cannot be beaten.*

One major reason flowers die soon after you bring them home is that the plant was bought too late in the season, when the bloom is at least halfway finished, or almost done. Your plant will not extend itself because you made a purchase and popped your pretty in a prime garden site. All is not lost, however, if you have some patience. Next year, at the right time, you'll get your flowers.

■ **Bright yellow and deep red**
coneflowers provide a welcome splash of color at the back of a border, especially when planted in groups.

Size and shape matter

Place your taller perennials, such as coneflowers (*Rudbeckia*), delphinium (*Delphinium*), or hollyhocks (*Alcea*), in the rear of your garden, and shorter ones up front so they can be easily seen. An exception would be if you have a very narrow planting site, as is true with many modern homes. You might then want to skip the taller perennials entirely, and instead plant the medium ones and the shorties. If your garden center doesn't have what you need, check out the catalogs. Modern hybridizers have created miniatures of what were formerly only tall perennials.

If you're installing perennials that don't spread wide enough to make a good show, plant three to five of the same variety together. Repeat the variety planting at least once in a nearby area to avoid an artificial appearance. If you can repeat more than once, that's even better.

Considering color

Colors that clash when you wear them, such as oranges and reds, clash in the garden too, so separate bright colored flowers by those with mellow hues. Because flowering is seasonal, you'll want to intersperse your perennials with bulbs and annuals. This will help to fill in blank areas and supply continuing color throughout the warm months. Don't forget tiny flowering bulbs right up front, too.

DELPHINIUM
(*Delphinium*)

Perennials for semi-shade

EACH PERSON'S DEFINITION *of semi-shade varies. No perennial will truly thrive in constant deep shade, such as that created by a large tree. However, if they get some sunlight during the day, and you remember to water them, some perennials have a good chance of doing just fine. What follows is a list of some of the most popular perennials that will tolerate some shade.*

BEAR'S BREECHES (*Acanthus mollis*)

Bear's breeches

This hardy, easy, relatively fast-growing perennial makes an attractive, dark green, stately display under trees that do not have shallow roots. Bear's breeches (*Acanthus mollis*) grows about 3 feet tall and is good as a *specimen plant*, standing alone for show or as part of a border. The underground roots eventually become parents of new plants. If you don't want them, simply pull them out and move them to another site. In late spring to early summer there are tall, dramatic spikes of usually white flowers that gather many admiring glances.

> **DEFINITION**
>
> A specimen plant *is a single plant, usually medium or tall, that is planted individually. It's designed to serve as a focal point in the garden. The phrase is often used to refer to trees or shrubs.*

Bergenia

This is a plant that really knows how to keep it simple. All you really need to do is give the super-sturdy bergenia some water. It will repay you from winter's end to late summer with intermittent pink flowers on little stalks emerging from leathery, lettuce-like, medium green leaves. It is happy in just about any soil, and eventually forms multiple clumps. These are easy to break off, giving you more plants for free. Bergenia (*Bergenia*) is a great plant for the somewhat forgetful gardener, because once you get it started, it tolerates some neglect. There are all sorts of hybrids available in catalogs that have flowers ranging from white to red.

BERGENIA (*Bergenia*)

LILY-OF-THE-VALLEY
(*Convallaria majalis*)

Lily-of-the-valley

Lilies-of-the-valley (*Convallaria majalis*) are super to plant under *deciduous* trees and evergreens that are not overly dense. As you will find out (if you haven't already) it isn't easy to find plants that will grow under trees. Tree roots tend to snatch away water and nutrients, and the foliage often provides too much shade. But lilies-of-the-valley are accommodating. This plant's needs are relatively straightforward – just give it regular water, plus a little extra if you do put it under trees.

> ### DEFINITION
>
> **Deciduous** *trees shed their leaves annually at the end of the growing season. They're a reason why fall is such a lovely season.*

It will multiply cheerfully underground, sending up 8-inch-long green leaves in the spring that disappear in the fall. White, waxy, highly scented bell-like flowers appear in late spring, and red berries sometimes appear in the fall. Lilies-of-the-valley are particularly pretty when potted and set on the patio, and their scent will sweeten an entire room when brought indoors as cut flowers.

If you have young children in the home, or even young visitors on occasion, it's best not to keep lilies-of-the-valley. As lovely as they are, all parts of this plant are poisonous if ingested.

Virginia bluebells

Virginia bluebells (*Mertensia virginica*) are one of the few perennials that will truly grow in almost full shade, although they prefer partial shade. In exchange for their tolerance, these American natives (sometimes also called Virginia cowslip) insist on good soil that is kept damp. They'll get about 15 inches high, and pinkish buds appear in early summer. The buds open to sky blue, bell-like flowers. These plants will multiply and reseed.

Tuck the seedlings here and there if you like to attract bees to pollinate your garden. At season's end, Virginia bluebells die back. Consider accompanying them with plants such as bee balm (*Monarda*), maidenhair fern (*Adiantum*), or tobacco plants (*Nicotiana*).

More perennials for semi-shade:

- Aquilegia (*Aquilegia*)
- Aster (*Aster*)
- Bee balm (*Monarda*)
- Bleeding heart (*Dicentra*)
- Cardinal flower (*Lobelia cardinalis*)
- Japanese anemone (*Anemone japonica*)
- Jacob's ladder (*Polemonium*)
- Joe pye weed (*Eupatorium fistulosum*)
- Loosestrife (*Lythrum*)
- Plantain lily (*Hosta*)
- Primrose (*Primula*)
- Solomon's seal (*Polygonatum*)

Drought-tolerant perennials

IF YOU THINK "drought-tolerant" means you can forget to water altogether, think again. It simply means the plant can survive with less water than many others. If you never want to water your garden again, consider cactus! Bearing the need for some water in mind, here are some less-thirsty perennials.

LAMB'S EAR (*Stachys byzantina*)

Lamb's ears

The temptation is to bend down and pet the leaves, soft like a lamb's ear, from time to time. These are one of the few plants happily placed next to heat-baked concrete, provided you give them some water from time to time. Gray leaves are covered with downy, sun-protecting, silver hairs. The leaves appear on ground-hugging stems about 12 inches long. Come mid-summer, if you peer closely, you'll see tiny pink flowers.

In winter, with the rain, the leaves turn mushy and you're sure the plant is finished. But come spring, there it is again. Lamb's ears (*Stachys byzantina*) grow into clumps that are extremely easy to separate and move elsewhere as needed. Red or pink poppies are good neighbors for the color contrast they provide.

Sage

There are entire books, and entire gardens, devoted to sage (*Salvia*), and I think no garden is complete without at least one sage plant. Sage comes in perennial, annual, and shrub forms – well over 700 species in all – so there's something for everybody.

A super-simple perennial is Mexican bush sage (*Salvia leucantha*), a plant that is particularly popular in the southern United States. Chances are you'll start with just one in a sunny, dryish corner, and soon you'll be picking places to tuck a few more. Mexican bush sage, also called velvet sage, has prolific, velvety, bluish-purple flowers from summer until fall. A pretty, slightly bushy accompaniment might be the perennial pineapple sage (*S. elegans*), which truly does smell like pineapple and is festooned with red flowers in fall.

PINEAPPLE SAGE
(*Salvia elegans*)

Artemisia

Silver, feathery leaves are the main attraction of Artemisia, although it does flower in late summer. Once you get one started and notice how nicely it does in that hot, dry space that most other plants shun, you'll think about filling similar garden niches. And all you have to do is clip off a few of the longer stems, stick them in a water jar for about two weeks until they develop roots, and pop them in the ground, giving a little water until they adapt. That's about as simple as it gets!

Artemisia likes the simple life. Don't add fertilizer to your artemisia's soil.

There are several types of artemisia that you might find attractive. The most common is sometimes called wormwood (*A. absinthium*). It grows up to 2 feet high, but often stays shorter. Since silvery leaves are usually the main visual attraction, place this plant where it makes a nice contrast with a brighter companion – perhaps one with fragrant red or orange flowers.

■ **Silvery artemisia,** *with its delicate foliage, enjoys an open, sunny, well-drained site. Some species have the added attraction of a pungent fragrance.*

Stonecrop

Generally, stonecrop (*Sedum*) perennials need occasional watering to keep them nice and plump, although *S. spathulifolium* is extremely drought tolerant once it gets started. Usually low growing, from about 2 inches to 2 feet high, the various stonecrops are often used as a low-maintenance ground cover.

Use these sun-adoring perennials as border plants in an area where you don't want to fuss. For once, you'll have no soil worries. Flowers are often pink, but there are an abundance of reds, depending on the species. If you want yellow blossoms, they're available too.

To get the colors you want, check the nursery in summer for the stonecrops in bloom.

Many have leaves that turn reddish in fall – a nice perk to finish off the year.

INTERNET

gardenguides.com

Garden Guides' site on annual flowers discusses a very wide range of topics. Other areas of the same website look at perennials, bulbs, herbs, and vegetables.

Yarrow

Ultra-hardy yarrow is a great choice for the person who claims not to be able to grow anything, but yearns for success.

Silvery yarrow leaves are fernlike and dainty. Of the many types of yarrow (*Achillea*), you're most likely to find common yarrow (*A. millefolium*). Common yarrow flowers come in a variety of colors, including red, yellow, white, and cream.

■ **Cerise Queen** *is a common yarrow (*Achillea millefolium*) with a mass of feathery leaves and flat heads of rich reddish pink flowers in summer.*

Trivia...

An old English nickname for common yarrow was "nose-bleed." Young women considering a potential husband would tickle the inside of a nostril with a yarrow leaf. While doing this, they would recite, "Yarrow, yarrow, bear a white bow, if my love loves me, my nose will bleed now."

These plants will usually grow about 24 inches high. If your garden has a sunny background space to fill, try fernleaf yarrow (*A. filipendulina*), which will grow up to 4 feet tall. Yarrow will spread a bit, and sometimes a lot, looking quite nice in compatible color groupings. You can tuck it in among the low-growing lamb's ears (*Stachys byzantina*) for an attractive contrast of leaf textures.

Yarrows are quite nice for flower arrangements, including dried arrangements. This is another plant that you can divide and use elsewhere in the garden.

More drought-tolerant perennials:

- Adam's needle (*Yucca filamentosa*)
- Baby's breath (*Gypsophila paniculata*)
- Butterfly weed (*Asclepias tuberosa*)
- Chamomile (*Anthemis tinctoria*)
- Cinquefoil (*Potentilla*)
- Coneflower (*Rudbeckia*)
- Cranesbill (*Geranium*)
- Globe thistle (*Echinops*)
- Iceland poppy (*Papaver croceum*)
- Maltese cross (*Lychnis chaledonica*)
- Milkwort (*Polygala calcarea*)
- Moss phlox (*Phlox subulata*)
- Sunflower (*Helianthus*)
- Tickseed (*Coreopsis*)

I know you're thinking, "But sunflowers were listed in Chapter 5 as annuals!" Yes, some are. And some are perennials.

Perennials for moist soil

KEEP IN MIND that there are varying interpretations, and degrees, of moist, from slightly damp all the way to soggy. Much depends upon the amount of sunlight, fog, and wind that may accompany a moist area of your garden. Of the plants listed here, some will fit your site better than others. When in doubt, talk to a garden center consultant for informative advice.

Cardinal flower

In the cardinal flower (*Lobelia cardinalis*), dark green leaves surround summer spikes of bright, flame-red flowers. A patch of 3-foot-high cardinal flowers creates a great background for a garden pond, and looks stately at the rear of a mixed border of perennials and annuals. Wherever they're placed, cardinal flowers like boggy conditions, and so must be given great soil and ample water. A sheltered site in light shade is preferred.

Marsh marigold

Full of vim and vigor, marsh marigolds (*Caltha palustris*) do well in those marshy garden places where more finicky plants have refused to thrive. The flowers are bright yellow, and appear in small clusters in spring. Plant them in a semi-shady area for best results, but they'll put up with fair amounts of sun or shade as well.

Also called water cowslip and kingcup, these 1-foot by 1-foot low-growers display best as a splash of color among your ferns. Dot the backdrop with some of the irises that also enjoy constantly moist soil, such as blue flag (*Iris versicolor*).

PRIMROSE (*Primula*)

Primrose

So often found in old-fashioned gardens, primroses (*Primula*) have never lost their popularity. Modern colors include reds, pinks, salmon, white, and purples. There are *double* and *single* forms available, as well as miniatures. Their height ranges from 6 to 12 inches, and each can provide enough flowers for a small bouquet. They are relatively easy to grow, if you water them very regularly.

> **DEFINITION**
>
> *Flowers can be denoted as* single, semi-double, *and* double. *These phrases refer to the arrangement of a flower's petals. A single whorl of two to six petals is found on most wildflowers. A semi-double flower has two or three whorls, and a double flower will have three or more.*

Sweet woodruff

Six-inch-high woodruff (*Galium odoratum*) will survive in barely damp soil. But give it some shade with ample moisture and it gets so enthusiastic that it may eventually spread to cover several feet or more. For the thrifty gardener, this means division in the fall or spring and extra plants to move elsewhere, or to give to friends. (For more on how to divide plants, see Chapter 19.)

This is a true old-fashioned plant, and you may still find it listed as *Asperula odorata*, its old Latin name. In late spring, small white flowers appear in clusters. Interestingly, the "sweet" part of this plant's name derives not from the flowers but from the leaves and stems, which, if dried, have a pleasant, hay-like aroma.

> *Trivia...*
>
> *Long ago, sweet-smelling bunches of woodruff were hung in churches, along with dried lavender and roses, to improve the air quality. Because of its fragrance, woodruff was also used as a mattress stuffing.*

WILLOW GENTIAN (*Gentiana asclepiadea*)

Willow gentian

The color of willow gentian (*Gentiana asclepiadea*) is so intense that the phrase "gentian blue" has come to describe a hue that's blue with a purplish-blue undertone. In bloom from late summer to early fall, gentians are fantastic in the midst of a garden border, by a pond, or in a wildflower garden.

There are about 400 species in the *Gentiana* genus, from very low-growing plants to ones that are several feet tall. Although they need some personal attention, willows are one of the least demanding gentians. In time, they'll spread to 18 inches in width and grow to 2 feet tall, or even more.

Ample water and good drainage are absolute necessities for willow gentian.

More perennials for moist soil:

- Bee balm (*Monarda*)
- Dropwort (*Filipendula*)
- Evening primroses (*Oenothera*)
- Joe pye weed (*Eupatorium fistulosum*)
- Loosestrife (*Lysimachia*)
- Solomon's seal (*Polygonatum*)
- Swamp milkweed (*Asclepias incarnata*)

Fragrant perennials

THE LEAVES, RATHER THAN THE FLOWERS, *are the source of fragrance for some perennials. Of course, "fragrance" is a matter of taste. When in doubt, take a sniff test before you buy. Perfumes that are nasal ambrosia to some are bland or downright stinky to others.*

Carnation

Omitting carnations (*Dianthus*) and pinks (similar flowers in the *Dianthus* genus) from the spotlighted list of fragrant perennials would raise the instant wrath of devotees who love them for their distinctive clove-like aroma. Carnations and pinks come in many, many varieties, and so they are divided into several groups.

These favorite cut flowers are fairly easy to grow if you don't live in areas with very hot, dry weather or very cold, wet weather. They are adaptable to coastal sites, and tolerate some air pollution. They do well in full sun, although they appreciate some light afternoon shade at the height of summer. Give them regular watering and good drainage.

Although many plants like organic mulches, carnations prefer gravel or sand around the base, which keeps soil away from the stems and leaves. To prolong flowering, remove dead blossoms.

There are so many colors and *bicolors* available (and so many shapes) that it's best just to look at them in person and pick what strikes your fancy. When selecting, be sure to do the sniff test to ensure the presence of the famous clove-like fragrance, because it doesn't occur in all Border group flowers.

> **DEFINITION**
>
> **Bicolor** *flowers have two very distinct colors, each appearing in one area on the blossom.*

> **Trivia...**
>
> *If you have young children, grow some white carnations. Cut them with long stems and place in a clear, tall water glass to which some red or blue food coloring has been added. Watch the carnations slowly change color. It's a fun garden lesson on how water and accompanying nutrients travel to parts of a plant.*

CARNATION (*Dianthus*)

Dame's violet

Sun or light shade, good-enough soil, and regular watering are all this exceptionally hardy perennial requires. Also called damask violet and sweet rocket, Dame's violet (*Hesperis matronalis*) usually blooms in early summer with lilac flowers on slim, drooping stems. Flowers are clove-scented at night, attracting pollinating moths.

If your goal is an informal (and oh-so-trendy) cottage garden, Dame's violet is a "must." It was commonly grown in 17th-century English cottage gardens, and single-flowered varieties have been grown in North America since the 1600s. Pretty accompaniments to dame's rocket are columbine (*Aquilegia*), hollyhock (*Alcea*), monkshood (*Aconitum*), and sweet William (*Dianthus barbatus*).

ENGLISH WALLFLOWER (*Erysimum cheiri*)

English wallflower

Often a bright orange-yellow, but also found in cream, red, and burgundy, these sweetly fragrant flowers are late spring visitors. This isn't a plant for hot, dry areas. It likes a cool climate and ample moisture. If you decide to sow seeds, you must do so very early in the season, or you won't get any flowers until the following year. Gardeners who prefer an easier path buy six-packs from the garden center in the late fall or early spring. English wallflowers (*Erysimum cheiri*) are great container plants for seasonal color.

Gas plant

Don't expect a gassy aroma from this ultra-hardy gas plant (*Dictamnus albus*). In fact, the leaves exude an intense, lemony fragrance.

The reason for the unusual name of gas plant is that the plant has glands containing an inflammable oil. If a match is held near the flowers on a warm, calm day or evening, this oil will ignite and burn quite briefly.

GAS PLANT (*Dictamnus albus*)

Not surprisingly, the gas plant's alternative nickname is burning bush. In addition to providing an adult diversion, gas plants are great cut flowers, and are lovely in among garden borders. They are especially long-lived in cool climates, preferring a dry, semi-sunny site. Flowers, appearing in early summer, are usually pink, but if you hunt around you can find purple and white.

Close contact with gas plants is not advised. All plant parts, especially the seedpods, may cause mild to severe stomach upset if ingested. And bare skin coming in contact with the leaves may cause an allergic reaction. So be sure to plant or cut them with your garden gloves on.

And some more:

- Common valerian (*Valeriana officinalis*)
- Evening primrose (*Oenothera*)
- Jupiter's beard (*Centranthus ruber*)
- Phlox (*Phlox*)
- Peony (*Paeonia*)
- Rockcress (*Arabis*)

A simple summary

✓ Always buy the right plant for the conditions in your garden. This requires some knowledge of your garden, and timing your purchases properly.

✓ Although definitions of shade and semi-shade may vary, there are many plants that will grow in some type of semi-shade if given sufficient water.

✓ There are plenty of drought-tolerant perennials, but even these plants need water from time to time. Some need a tad more than others, so do your homework if you don't like to water, or need to regulate water use.

✓ Moist soil doesn't mean soggy soil. If you truly have inches of water, you should think of pond plants instead.

✓ Fragrant plants are sometimes powerfully fragrant, while other plants must be enjoyed with your nose much closer to the blossom. If you want a plant to perfume a room or a garden site, take the sniff test before you buy it.

Chapter 7

Beautiful Bulbs

FLOWERS FROM BULBS are often the first harbingers of spring. Their foliage peeks up through the last melting layer of snow, bringing a bit of color and a promise of your great garden to come. In this chapter I'll explain how to buy bulbs and start them, and make some suggestions for plants that are simple to grow.

In this chapter...

✓ **When is a bulb not a bulb?**

✓ **Bulb basics**

✓ **Spring-flowering bulbs**

✓ **Summer-flowering bulbs**

✓ **Bulbs for fragrance**

SNOWDROPS: THE FIRST SIGNS OF SPRING

When is a bulb not a bulb?

YOU MAY BE CURIOUS as to the difference between bulbs, rhizomes, corms, and tubers, all of which are often just called bulbs. The distinction is not extremely important, because growing methods are pretty much the same. In everyday conversation, you'll undoubtedly refer to all of these flowers as bulbs. That's fine. Still, I like to keep things straight from the beginning. It's so much simpler that way.

DEFINITION
A bulb is basically a plant's food-storage organ. It is a modified shoot, with layers of fleshy leaf bases and roots.

True bulbs

True bulbs are usually rounded, with a pointy tip, a round base, and an interior made of layers, similar to an onion. Mature bulbs – those that have been in the ground for more than a season – reproduce by a dividing process within the parent bulb. True bulbs include the allium (*Allium*), caladium (*Caladium*), daffodil (*Narcissus*), grape hyacinth (*Muscari*), hyacinth (*Hyacinthus orientalis*), iris (*Iris*), lily (*Lilium*), scilla (*Scilla*), snowflake (*Leucojum*), and tulip (*Tulipa*).

Corms

Corms are rounded, and are small to medium size. They're not composed of layers, like true bulbs, but are solid all the way through. After a season, corms may produce baby corms, or cormlets, around the parent corm. These baby corms may be very small – about the size of a pea. Each cormlet contains the ingredients to make a new plant exactly like the parent. The corn lily (*Ixia*), crocus (*Crocus*), freesia (*Freesia*), gladiolus (*Gladiolus*), montbretia (*Crocosmia*), and peacock flower (*Tigridia*) are a few of the common plants springing from corms.

Rhizomes

A rhizome is a swollen section of an underground, horizontal plant stem. Roots grow from the underside of this stem, and plant buds develop on top of the stem. Plants growing from rhizomes include some of the irises, blackberry lilies (*Belamcanda chinensis*), and cannas (*Canna*).

Tubers

Tubers are swollen sections of root. Tubers may be shaped like short sausages or be entirely irregular. Buds grow from the top of each tuber. Begonias (*Begonia*), buttercups (*Ranunculus*), dahlias (*Dahlia*), and daylilies (*Hemerocallis*) are grown from tubers.

Bulb basics

NOW THAT YOU KNOW WHAT A BULB IS, and what it isn't, let's talk about how to start them in your garden. Here again, it's best to avoid just buying, digging, and crossing your fingers. You're much more likely to enjoy success if you make careful purchases and know ahead of time where your flowers will go.

Choosing bulbs

Outer layer (tunic) intact

Undamaged tip, with no signs of growth

Firm base without new root growth

A HEALTHY DAFFODIL BULB

If you plant at the right time, a good-quality bulb will give you flowers the first year. Get the largest bulbs of each kind that you can, from a reputable dealer. Buy only bulbs that feel solid; never take soft ones.

Avoid bargain bulbs, whether half-price at season's end or advertised in magazines at very low prices. Bargain bulbs are inexpensive for a reason. They may be incorrectly labeled, undersize, improperly stored or transported, or diseased. There is no saving when half of what you buy doesn't flower.

Before planting

Bulbs are a lot less picky than many other plants about their surroundings, but you can't expect bulb roots to tunnel through clay. You paid good money for the bulbs, so put a little more into their bedding, and provide them with some fertile, light-textured soil to grow in.

Simply put, bulbs like to be in the ground. Install spring-flowering bulbs in autumn, and summer-flowering bulbs in spring or early summer. Plant as soon as you get the bulbs.

If you're ordering from catalogs, order early. If for some reason you cannot plant your purchases immediately, store them in an open bag in a cool, dry place.

INTERNET

bulb.com

Site of the U.S. Netherlands Flower Bulb Information Center. You'll find plenty of facts about tulips and other bulbs grown commercially in the Netherlands.

PLANTING BULBS OUTDOORS

1 Make a planting hole

Dig a large hole in well-prepared ground and place the bulbs, tips upward, at least twice their own depth and width apart.

2 Cover with soil

Draw soil over the bulbs gently by hand to minimize any risk of displacing or disturbing them. Firm down the soil to remove any air gaps.

After planting

Place little plastic markers or Popsicle sticks by each bulb grouping. Use indelible ink to indicate "daffodil," or "tulip," or whatever you've planted. Push the marker well into the ground so it doesn't fall over. Everybody believes they are going to remember where they put each bulb, even after the leaves die back and there's no aboveground sign of the plant anymore. But nobody ever does. And if you forget, you may slice through a favorite bulb when digging in the area for some other plant. Keep it simple and you'll do fine.

Water deeply just after fall planting, and let spring rains take care of the spring bulbs. For summer-flowering bulbs, you must water regularly unless the package specifically says not to. But never over-water. A thick bulb will rot if it gets soggy. As a general rule, bulbs like dry feet. Fertilize lightly in spring before the plants bloom, and in autumn after the first serious cold spell. Use just a little bit of fertilizer.

After blooming

Remove the spent flowers and let the foliage die back. Spent flowers go to seed, which takes energy away from the bulb.

Foliage dieback is a process that provides food for the bulb underneath, and therefore next year's flowers. Remove leaves only after they have turned brown.

Spring-flowering bulbs

WHEN YOU CAN'T *find a wide variety of bulbs to choose from at your local garden centers, visit a large nursery, or try a catalog. Many specialize in bulbs.*

Bearded iris

There are entire volumes written about the 300-plus species of iris, and there is no way to cover them all in a few paragraphs. Tall bearded iris (*Iris*) rhizomes are most commonly found in garden centers. The "beard" is the little fuzzy moustache on the flower. Colors are gorgeous and the choice bewildering: you may have 50 options. And that's before you've seen the fashion show in catalogs featuring irises.

■ **Magic Man** *is a bearded iris that flowers in early summer. The beards are bright orange.*

Buy and plant bearded iris from July through September. When planting, the tops of the rhizomes must be just visible.

Place the rhizomes about 12 inches apart. Group similar colors together – you may find that some colors look better in your garden than others. These exquisite plants are easy to grow almost anyplace. Most bearded irises insist on lots of sunshine and well-drained soil, preferably just on the dry side. If you don't have good drainage, rhizomes will rot. So create a slight mound and plant there.

Baby irises

Irises multiply by increasing their rhizomes, so you will get more flowers every year. Flowers appear in May and June, and in mild-weather areas you may receive a flower surprise in later months.

INTERNET

irises.org

The home page for the American Iris Society where you can find all you want to know about irises.

When a clump becomes crowded, after 3 or so years, the flowers become smaller. Dig up the rhizomes and divide them in summer through fall. Separate and replant portions that have leaves attached. Your irises should ideally be replanted within a few days. For more details on the technique of dividing rhizomes, turn to Chapter 19.

Trivia...

Iris, the Greek goddess of the rainbow, has given her name to both the multihued iris of the eye, and to the iris flower, which blossoms in just about all colors of the rainbow. This goddess carries messages of love from heaven to earth, using a rainbow as her bridge. Another job is transporting the souls of women to the Elysian fields – a happy place where good souls go after death.

Crocus

Because you may see crocus (*Crocus*) flowers as early as February 14, the crocus is dedicated to St. Valentine. This lovely plant is a true harbinger of spring. While it likes good care, this corm will thrive in just about any soil or situation. The Dutch crocus (*C. vernus*) is the one most commonly found in garden centers. To get the longest lasting display, plant corms at intervals from September through November. Plant them three inches deep, and in clusters – a lot of crocuses just look great together.

Crocuses are available in a wide variety of yellows and purple-blues, and there are variegated, or multi-colored, types. Although an area of mixed crocuses has a quite pleasing appearance, I like distinct groupings of color for maximum impact. A nice plan is yellow at the edges of the group to define boundaries, and purples and whites within. Crocuses, just 3 inches high, should always be at the front of any planting.

■ **The Dutch crocus** (Crocus vernus) *combines rich violet-purple flowers with bright yellow stamens for a colorful display.*

Daffodil

Even a plaid-thumb gardener can grow daffodils (*Narcissus*), as long as excellent drainage is provided. Put them indoors by a sunny window or outdoors in a pot by the front door, scatter them in a flower bed, or plant them *en masse* to create a show stopper for the neighborhood. Purchase bulbs as soon as they appear in the marketplace, and plant them outside from fall through early winter. A succession of plantings will result in a succession of blooms. How deep to plant them depends on the variety, so be sure you read the package carefully. By early spring, pointy leaves start poking their tips above soil line.

Including hybridized varieties, there are now thousands of types of daffodils. Early plants probably came across the ocean to America tucked in settlers' baggage, brightening the doorways of early log cabins and Spanish missions. If you're interested in a particularly fragrant daffodil, try planting the wild jonquil variety, *Narcissus jonquilla*. And if you have deer or gophers chowing down on your plants, take heart: they don't like to eat daffodils.

DAFFODIL
(*Narcissus* Quince)

Trivia...

The daffodil's name stems from the Old English "Affo dyle," or "that which cometh early," from its prompt spring flowering. This original name generated a slew of regional nicknames, such as Daffy, Dilly, Daffadilly, Daffadowndilly, and, for some reason, Churn.

Snowflake

Happy in moist soil and sun or partial shade, this very hardy plant offers a profusion of green-tipped, white, bell-shaped flowers on 10-inch-high stems. In addition to the springtime version, there are snowflakes that appear in summer and autumn – although you may have to chase through bulb catalogs to obtain them.

Snowflakes (*Leucojum*) will grow nicely under high branching deciduous trees, as well as in the open. Since the flower display is better in groups, leave them alone until they seem truly crowded. Then, once the leaves have died back, divide and replant them immediately about 3 inches apart. Bulb tips should be about 3 inches under the soil surface.

SNOWFLAKE (*Leucojum*)

Tulip

Although most gardeners would love to grow tulips (*Tulipa*), these aren't the easiest of bulbs. You need a rich, sandy soil, good drainage, and sun. Don't attempt tulips in clay soil unless you have added plenty of soil amendments. Unimproved clay soil generally results in crooked, dwarfed stems and leaves with sad little flowers. This doesn't mean you can't have tulips – just put them in pots where you can control the growing medium. There's another problem as well: gophers are very fond of tulip bulbs.

TROUBLE WITH TULIPS

Tulips are susceptible to a virus known as the mosaic virus. In infected plants, solid color flowers develop odd, but often beautiful, markings. When these strange tulips appeared in Holland in about 1637, people thought they had discovered a new strain, or type, of plant. A tulip-buying craze developed. People thought they would have instant riches if they could breed just one of these unique bulbs. One of the prices paid for just a single bulb included a load of grain, 1,000 pounds of cheese, 12 sheep, 10 oxen, 5 pigs, 4 barrels of beer, 2 tubs of butter, 2 hogsheads of wine, a suit of clothes, and a silver cup. But nobody was able to breed these flowers.

The mosaic virus is still around. It is contagious to all tulips, and although some thrive despite it, others die quickly. So do not replant virus-infected tulips, or replant tulips in areas where the mosaic virus has appeared in the last 3 years.

There are so many kinds of tulips that the genus has been divided into 15 major groups, including Darwin hybrids, Triumph, Lily-flowered, Double early, Rembrandt, and Parrot. These groupings are based on the characteristics of the flowers. There's a tulip in virtually every color of the rainbow. Plant them in the fall, 10 inches deep and about 6 inches apart, in groups of one type and color. You can even plant as late as December if the ground isn't frozen. Around the tulip clusters, consider planting low, spring-flowering annuals.

TULIP (*Tulipa*)

More spring-flowering bulbs

- Allium (*Allium*)
- Anemone (*Anemone*)
- Glory of the snow (*Chionodoxa*)
- Grape hyacinth (*Muscari*)
- Hyacinth (*Hyacinthus orientalis*)
- Snowdrop (*Galanthus*)
- Star-of-Bethlehem (*Ornithogalum*)
- Striped squill (*Puschkinia scilloides*)
- True squill (*Scilla*)
- Winter aconite (*Eranthis*)

Summer-flowering bulbs

SPRING IS DEFINITELY *the main time for bulbs, but there are some rhizomes, tubers, and bulbs that will bloom for you in the summer. If you do a bit of research before you plant, you'll have better luck.*

BEGONIA (*Begonia*)

Begonia

Unless you live in a frost-free area, start your tuberous begonias (*Begonia*) indoors. Put one tuber in a pot containing rich soil. The pots must be at least 6 inches high and 6 inches wide, and they must have drainage holes or the tubers will rot. The growing site must be semi-shaded and warm. Press the tubers, round side down, into the soil until just their tops show. Water them well, just once, then water just a smidge every now and then until green shoots appear.

Transplant the begonias outside, very carefully, when shoots are about 4 inches high, taking care not to disturb the roots. Some people leave begonias in the pot and just set them outdoors. Give these plants indirect light, ample water without over-watering, and fertilizer every 2 weeks as growth continues. If the weather temporarily gets hot and dry, lightly spray them with water.

Do not put tuberous begonias outdoors until the weather is reliably warm. Depending on where you live, "reliably warm" may be March, but it may also be as late as June.

I recommend planting tuberous begonias of the same color and variety together, because I think this makes for the nicest display. At season's close, usually before the first frost, remove the tubers gently from the soil. Let them sit a few days in a dry spot until they harden. Store the tubers in a cool, dry, frost-free area until next planting time.

Blackberry lily

Flower arrangers love this charming August and September bloomer for its beige seed capsules that split to frame clusters of large black seeds. Another common name, leopard lily, aptly describes the sprays of small, red-spotted orange flowers on 2-foot-high stems. The flowers open daily, one after another, for a period of 3 weeks.

Plant the rhizomes in groups of three, about 1 inch deep, in good soil. Blackberry lilies (*Belamcanda chinensis*) should be placed in sun or light shade and need regular watering. They are related to the iris and can be similarly divided after a while for more plants. Alternatively, they can be propagated by seed in spring.

Canna

Tropical flowers are trendy, and cannas (*Canna*) will make just the right statement. If you've inherited an old garden, you may still have some of the old-time cannas. These plants can reach 6 feet high, and are sometimes dull looking. With minimal attention, they multiply via tuberous roots into a tall, solid wall of large leaves and big, floppy flowers.

But times, courtesy of *hybridizers*, have changed. Now cannas come in an array of pinks, reds, yellows, and stripes, and in a delightful size range. You can find dwarfs only 18 inches high – ideal for the large patio pot, or as part of a small garden. There are mid-size plants at 3 feet tall, and the orchid-flowering varieties can reach over 5 feet.

> **DEFINITION**
>
> Hybridizers *spend their time creating new plants by crossing genetically different parent plants. Some of the most glorious flowers we grow today are hybrids. If you're concerned that there's something "artificial" about growing hybrids, relax. Hybrids occur in nature, too.*

Planting your cannas

The best times to plant canna rhizomes are May or June. Plant them about 5 inches into the soil and 10 to 20 inches apart. They will multiply slowly, so allow enough space between them. Of course, they're easy enough to dig and divide, so if they get a little dense, it's easily remedied.

Cannas like heat and sunlight. If you place them in semi-shade, they may have leaves but they won't flower. As they're tropical plants, you must regularly water them, although they do tolerate short dry periods. At season's end, they'll get raggedy and you should cut them back to about 6 inches high. Cannas will come back amply the next year, unless you live in really cold territory. Then you have to dig up the rhizomes, let them dry, and store upside down in a cool, shaded area.

■ **Rosemond Coles**, *with its yellow-edged orange petals and large decorative leaves, is one of the more spectacular cannas.*

■ **Fragrant daylilies**, *such as this Little Rainbow* Hemerocallis, *demand very little in the way of attention and provide a reliable display every year.*

Daylily

The daylily (*Hemerocallis*) is one of the most popular rhizomes. It is hardy, grows in sun or light shade, and, while preferring organically enriched soil, will tolerate poor soil if given good drainage. You must be careful to avoid areas where the tuberous roots have to compete with ground covers or shallow-rooted trees. Regular watering and occasional fertilizing promote the best-looking plants.

Often fragrant, daylilies come back, increasing in size, year after year. The new hybrids (hundreds are appearing each year) have larger flowers than the originals, and the bloom is more profuse. The traditional yellow-orange daylilies may still be found, but usually in someone's garden – not at the nursery. If you plant early-, mid-, and late-season varieties, your daylilies will flower for about 3 months.

INTERNET

daylilies.org

Visit this site of the American Hemerocallis Society. You'll learn about conventions, sources of daylilies, publications, and regional display gardens.

Montbretia

Plant five corms of this South African native, and unless you live where the weather is really cold, you'll have 25 next year and more the year after that. This plant is simple-simple if you give it mostly sun and occasional water. The most common variety has bright orange-red flowers, about ten per 12-inch stem. Other varieties have yellow or red flowers, although they may not be as hardy. Flowers open one after another, with the first appearing in summer.

Despite their prominence in English gardens, montbretias (*Crocosmia*) are not always offered in American garden centers, so you may have to buy yours from a catalog. Of course, if you know someone who has them, perhaps they would be happy to share. Plant in the fall if possible, although you can safely install montbretias through March.

More summer-flowering bulbs

Some of the hardiest summer blooms include these plants (a few of which may continue blooming into early fall):

- Allium (*Allium*)
- Blazing stars (*Liatris*)
- Fairy wands (*Dierama*)
- Foxtail lilies (*Eremurus*)
- Gladiolus (*Gladiolus*)
- Lilyturf (*Liriope*)
- Magic lilies (*Lycoris*)
- Peruvian lilies (*Alstroemeria*)
- Red-hot poker (*Kniphofia*)

Allium will actually bloom in the spring, summer, or fall, depending on the variety.

■ **The stunning purple flowers** *of* Allium rosenbachianum *are packed together into tight balls that make excellent dried flowers. The leaves, when crushed, smell of onions.*

Bulbs for fragrance

THE NOSE MAY KNOW, but every nose is different. One person will insist a certain flower has a marvelous scent, and another says it has no scent at all. Sometimes you have to put the flowers right under your nostrils to get the scent, sometimes it wafts through the air. The aroma may waft during the daylight hours, or it may do so only at night. The following featured bulbs would be my selections for fragrance, but you may discover others that you like more.

Hyacinth

When first introduced to Europe, hyacinths (*Hyacinthus orientalis*) were only for the wealthy. Now bulbs are only a few dollars, and can be found in myriad colors, including red, white, and blue. Many people enjoy planting them in this "patriotic" combination, especially if there are three of each planted about 6 inches apart. The bulbs should be planted about 5 inches deep. For outdoor success, choose medium-size rather than large bulbs. While many other early-flowering bulbs are short stemmed, the 12-inch-high hyacinth displays its flower-studded stem quite effectively.

Some protection from the wind will help ensure the health of your hyacinths. Planting in groups helps them withstand inclement weather, which can snap the long stems. Stake the stems if you anticipate really bad weather.

Hyacinths need a minimum of half a day's sun, good drainage, and enriched soil. Plant in the fall, when the bulbs appear in local nurseries. If there's no rain, water once a week for a month. After they bloom (in the spring), fertilize, water regularly, and put a light organic mulch on top of the area. With care, each bulb will give 5 years of bloom, and sometimes more. Plant some candytuft (*Iberis*) around your hyacinths to provide a nice cover when the foliage of the bulbs dies back.

Trivia...

In long-ago Greece, bridesmaids wore crowns of hyacinth and parsley. The flower is said to symbolize faith, wisdom, prudence, and resurrection.

HYACINTH (*Hyacinthus orientalis*)

FORCING THE BLOOM

Hyacinths are just as splendid grown indoors in pots, where just one plant can perfume a room. If you want to get sophisticated, you can "force" your hyacinths to bloom in the later winter. Forcing is the practice of inducing an unseasonal growth by manipulating the plant's environment.

1 Cover the bulbs with soil

Plant hyacinth bulbs in some potting soil, leaving just the noses showing, in September. Make sure the soil is moist but not waterlogged.

2 Expose them to light

Keep the bulbs in a cool, dark place until the shoots are about 4 inches high, then gradually bring them into the light for January flowers.

Madonna lily

Madonna lilies (*Lilium candidum*) are known to be a bit finicky, but worth the effort. They require moist, organic, very well-drained soil for their roots. The base of the plants should be kept shaded, but the tops like to be in full sun. (This particular shade and sun combination is the favorite of almost all lilies.)

Plant the bulb in early fall, not more than 2 inches deep. For a truly great effect, plant three at a time, about 10 inches apart. Water well after planting, and repeat if the weather is dry. You'll see leaves quickly, and then the 4-foot-high, white-flowered stem shoots up in August, with fragrant, funnel-shaped blooms. The plant disappears after blooming, with leaves reappearing in the fall. These leaves remain throughout winter but die off in spring.

Often purchased in gift pots, Easter lilies (*Lilium longiflorum*) should be planted outside in an appropriate site after the flowers fade. Plant them about 6 inches deep. You may, or may not, get flowers the following fall, or in the normal midsummer blooming time.

Regardless of lily type, never move a plant if it can be avoided. If you must, handle very carefully and replant immediately.

Freesia

Often purchased by the bag in mixed or single colors, relatively hardy freesias (*Freesia*) will cheerfully self-sow if you don't remove faded flowers. Regardless of the original color – purple, red, pink, white, or gold – the next generation or so tends to come up with cream-colored flowers.

■ **The fragrant white** *trumpets of the Madonna lily* (Lilium candidum) *look so spectacular that it's well worth putting in a bit of extra effort to grow them.*

Purchase corms from August to November. By planting small groups every 2 weeks, you'll get a succession of blooms, since each plant flowers for about 6 weeks. Plant corms 2 inches deep and 2 inches apart, with the pointy end up. Freesias require mostly sun and regular water. You get healthier plants when you fertilize every few weeks. For the adventurous, try planting freesia from seed.

Freesias also make good foot-high potted plants for the patio or balcony. If you have a truly sunny window, try them indoors too on the windowsill. Yellow and white flowers tend to be more fragrant than other hues.

Tuberose

These flower clusters are so aromatic that you'll want to be sure to place them where you can enjoy the scent. In fact, the scent is so exuberant, some folk prefer not to bring tuberoses (*Polianthes tuberosa*) indoors, while others insist.

Tuberoses can be a tad fussy about producing their waxy, white, tubular flowers. You need to have a quite warm site for these Mexican natives, and they find any type of chill quite distressing. But they're certainly worth a try, even in a warm, sunny window if you live in an area with cold weather.

Don't take chances when you buy tuberoses – purchase good-size rhizomes. They go into rich soil, 3 inches deep and about 6 inches apart. Give regular watering in spring and summer, and fertilize every 2 weeks when in growth. Expect one-time flower clusters, on 2- to 3-foot-high stems, from late summer to fall. In warm weather areas, rhizomes left in the soil may reappear the following year. For appealing companions in the garden, I recommend caladium, coleus, and elephant's ear (*Alocasia*).

A simple summary

✓ When buying bulbs, rhizomes, tubers, or corms, get the largest and heaviest you can find. Don't purchase so-called "bargain" bulbs. They usually have more than one flaw, and are not true money-savers.

✓ Although the more common bulbs are found in local garden centers and nurseries, look for others in catalogs. There's a huge variety available.

✓ If you really like a certain type of bulb, such as a daylily or daffodil, and want to learn more about it, join a specific society. There are societies for many of the more popular bulbs.

✓ Plant as soon as you obtain bulbs, as early in the proper season as possible. Plant spring-flowering bulbs in autumn, and summer-flowering bulbs in spring or early summer.

✓ Always mark the place where you've planted your bulbs, so you don't accidentally slice into them later.

✓ Place bulbs at the recommended depth for best performance.

✓ After flowers fade, always let bulb foliage die back naturally. This dieback is part of the bulb's natural life cycle, and it gives it strength for next year's growth.

PART THREE

COLORFUL FOLIAGE OF THE NORWAY MAPLE

WOODY PLANTS

OF COURSE, you'll want to grow more than just flowers in your garden. Big woody plants *make a statement*, as they have hard fibrous stems that remain above ground all year. Included in this group are ornamental trees, shrubs, roses, and vines.

There are so many choices you can make: Do you want flowers, berries, fragrance, foliage, color? Do you want to hide a fence or tool shed with a vine? Do you want enough roses for cutting, or just a few to dot the garden with spring and summer flowers and perhaps fill a vase or two? Sometimes it seems like you want all of everything you see, and just making the choice can be tough. So sit down with this part of the book to get a grip on your options.

Chapter 8

Ornamental Trees

EVERY GARDEN deserves some type of tree. Tree leaves dance in the wind, shade you from the sun, shelter birds. Some provide fall color and spring flowers. If your tree grows big enough, you may even become grandparents to a batch of baby birds. There are evergreen trees that keep their leaves all year around, while deciduous trees lose their leaves in the fall and develop new ones in the spring. The idea is to present trees that will give you the best shade, color, or fragrance possible.

In this chapter...

✓ Arboreal anatomy

✓ Buying your tree

✓ Shade trees

✓ Flowering trees

✓ Instant arbors

✓ Fall color

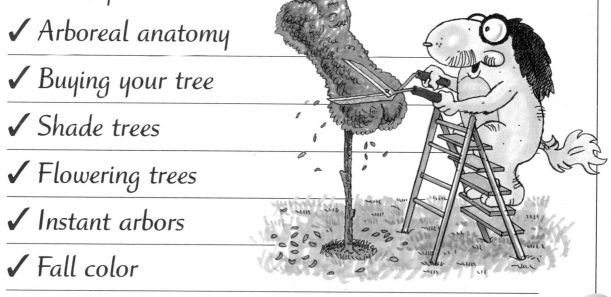

A STRIKING DECIDUOUS HIMALAYAN BIRCH

Arboreal anatomy

THE THREE MAIN PARTS *of a tree are its roots, trunk, and crown or top. There are three types of roots: the big, easily seen ones near the trunk, the* **tap root,** *and the thousands of threadlike* **root hairs** *at the end of rootlets. The complete root system of a full-size tree can reach out 40 feet or more! The big roots anchor the tree within the surrounding soil and help it remain upright. Trees fall over in a flood because the soil turns to mud and the roots can't stay in place.*

A tree's trunk is its food storage mechanism as well as its support. The tree trunk has three parts: bark, wood, and pith. The bark is the outside of the tree that you're familiar with. Beneath the bark is a thin layer called cambium. This is the growing part of wood, having cells that become either bark or new wood. Underneath the cambium is the wood itself. There may be a darker type of wood called heartwood, and a lighter type called sapwood. Underneath all this, in the center, is the pith.

> **DEFINITION**
>
> A **tap root** is a strong center root that grows straight down into the soil. This is a vital root to many trees, and a reason why they don't transplant well as they age. **Root hairs** are little tubular outgrowths from a growing root. They absorb water and nutrients that have dissolved in the water. The root hairs transfer the plant's vital circulating fluid, or sap, through increasingly larger roots into a tree's trunk, and then to branches and leaves.

Buying your tree

Before you buy any tree, find out how large it will get. The size of a tree includes both its height and its width.

Stand and stare at the spot in your garden where you plan to put the tree. Do you have room for a tree that's 100 feet tall with a 50-foot spread? A 50-foot tree with a 25-foot spread? A 25-foot tree? Will your neighbor appreciate your spreading branches? Think now, or possibly pay a tree removal service later. This is expensive! Take it from one who has had her wallet flattened several times.

Even if you want your garden to look well established, it's best to buy trees when they're younger and smaller. Juvenile trees recover much more easily from the shock of being transplanted than do more mature trees. Because of this, younger trees will often catch up with larger trees of the same type planted at the same time.

In the bag or in the can

You can purchase trees "bare root," or "balled-and-burlapped (B&B)," where the roots are surrounded by dirt held in place by burlap. When receiving bare root or B&B trees, do dampen them a bit.

Some gardeners soak the roots in mud. I just plop them in a large pail of water for at least an hour, although some soak them for 1 or 2 days.

BALLED-AND-BURLAPPED
TREE IN GOOD CONDITION

Firm root ball with covering intact

Bare vs. burlapped

Bare-root trees are those you see plunked directly into the dirt at the garden center, usually in groups. When you buy one of these dormant trees, the employee takes it out of the earth and its roots are bare. There will be no soil mass around the roots. The employee will wrap it up in plastic or a similar material, hopefully putting some damp shredded paper or sawdust around it so the roots don't dry out. Bare-root trees must be planted very promptly. Remove any wrapping just before you do.

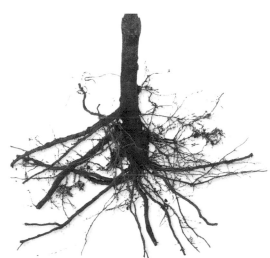

■ **When you buy a bare-root tree** *check that it has well-developed roots that spead out evenly. It should also have small, fine roots. These are a good sign because they indicate that the tree will grow well. The roots should not look dry and withered.*

When you buy some trees, they're dug out of the ground with some original soil around their roots. This is covered and held in place by burlap fabric that is fastened in some way around the trunk. This burlapped area has the appearance of a ball. Hence this type of tree is known as "balled and burlapped." Don't worry about the burlap. Just loosen it at the fastened top and cut a few slits in the side. Then go ahead and plant the tree. The burlap will eventually disintegrate on its own.

More often than not, trees you buy will be sold in cans ranging from 5 to 15 gallons. Have someone at the nursery partially cut the can sides for you, to make removing the tree easier. Add water to the soil in the container as soon as possible after bringing your new tree home.

PLANTING YOUR TREE

The best time to plant most trees is at the beginning of their dormant, or resting period, some time in the fall. The key is to wait until most of the leaves are gone, and complete the job before new leaves appear in spring. There are several trees, however, that prefer to be planted in the spring. These include the birch, dogwood, magnolia, several of the oaks, and the tulip tree, among others.

1 **Dig the hole**

Dig a hole about 50 percent wider than the root ball, and one and a half times its depth.

2 **Check the depth**

Set your tree in the hole. Use a cane to check that the tree is planted at the same depth as it was in its pot, or that the root ball is just covered.

3 **Knock in the stake**

Choose a strong wood stake and knock it firmly into the soil with a mallet, about 4 inches away from the trunk of the tree.

4 **Fill with soil**

Fill in around the root ball and stake with soil, firming it gently as you go with hammer or foot.

5 **Firm the soil**

Check the tree is still upright and finish by treading the soil gently until the surface is level, which also removes air pockets.

6 **Water in**

Fasten your young tree to its stake with a tree tie, then give it a good drink of water to help it recover from planting.

Perfect positioning

After you've dug the planting hole, place your tree, stand back, and see how it looks. Also check it in relation to other plants or trees planted nearby. You do not want to traumatize it by digging it up and moving it elsewhere. If all is satisfactory, plant it.

Feeling hungry?

If you're tempted to fertilize the newcomer in the fall (thinking to speed up its adjustment), don't. Wait until new leaves appear in the spring, and then use a 5-10-5 fertilizer as recommended on the container.

If you plant in spring, you can fertilize appropriately. Always double-check the label to be sure the fertilizer is right for your particular type of tree.

Prudent pruning

Should you prune? Well, to be honest, I've seen some pretty disastrous results when novices start chomping away at deciduous tree limbs. Be kind. You can always prune a little more, but it's tricky to paste the branches back on. I prune for shape, to remove any sickly looking material, and to thin, especially where branches crisscross each other.

Flowering trees should be pruned when the blossoms are just about gone. Evergreens seldom need pruning, although you may have to shape them a bit each year. When pruning evergreens, trim junipers and yews before new growth appears, and pines, firs, and spruces after new growth begins.

If you have purchased a selection of pruning tools and are eager to use them all, take a class on pruning. Some untutored enthusiasm with sharp tools could be disastrous. A local nursery may offer a class, or a staff member might be able to direct you to one. But do yourself a favor: If it's a big tree, or a prized specimen, call a licensed tree service.

CUTTING BACK A STEM

■ **For stems with alternate buds,** *make a slanting cut about ¼ inch above a bud. This sloping cut allows drops of rain, which might cause disease, to drain away from the bud.*

■ **For stems with opposite buds,** *make a straight cut directly above a pair of healthy buds. Keep the pruners as close above them as you can without grazing or damaging the buds.*

Shade trees

WHEN YOU'RE GROWING TREES FOR SHADE *you want to choose trees that spread out a bit, covering a nice wide area with their leafy branches. A tall, thin tree simply won't do the job. Here are some of my favorites.*

Chinese elm

Elm varieties are plentiful, and include Scotch, white, cork, camperdown, Dutch, English, rock, and fluttering. The American elm and the English elm, both once extraordinarily popular in the United States, have had continuing problems with Dutch elm disease, although semi-resistant strains have been developed. Your local nursery can advise you on this, as well as recommend the elm best suited for your climate zone.

CHINESE ELM (*Ulmus parvifolia*)

Chinese elm (*Ulmus parvifolia*), also called Chinese evergreen elm or lacebark elm, is often recommended for its hardiness. It survives nicely in poor, compacted soil, and sustains itself well in both heat and drought. It is also resistant to Dutch elm disease and the hungry elm leaf beetle, making it a super choice for the new gardener.

Do not confuse this sturdy, good-natured shade tree with the brittle Siberian elm, which is not recommended for gardens or street planting. Siberian elm is sometimes – incorrectly – sold as Chinese elm.

The layered look

Chinese elm gets its "lacebark" nickname from its *exfoliating* bark. As the tree matures, the outer layer of brown bark sheds here and there, showing puzzle-piece displays of pale yellow inner bark. The result is quite attractive. The leaves are rather pretty too, with a dark green display in spring and summer, changing to purple and pale yellow in the fall. This tree may keep its leaves throughout the winter, or drop them, depending on how cold it gets in your neighborhood. There are no flowers, but red clusters of inedible fruit appear in late fall.

> **DEFINITION**
>
> *When anything* **exfoliate** *, it comes off in pieces. A tree can exfoliate bark.*

These elms grow big

Chinese elms grow quickly, sometimes 5 feet a year when young, to an eventual height of 40 to 60 feet. (Most elms grow much taller, reaching 100 feet. An exception is the mushroom-shaped camperdown elm, more common in England than here, which reaches 20 to 40 feet.) Elms, in general, are for large, sunny, well-drained yards where the dappled shade they provide is a pleasure during the warm season, yet doesn't impinge on the rights of sun-loving plants nearby. They do need fairly regular watering.

Hackberry

Also called the nettle tree, this native American elm-like tree is useful for both shade and ornament. Tiny flowers appear in May, often followed by ⅓-inch orange-red fruit that later becomes dark purple. Birds love the fruit. Leaves on this 60-foot-high tree are shiny, bright green on top and paler green beneath. The bark is a grayish-brown with prominent warty or bumpy areas.

A lovely relative of the hackberry (*Celtis occidentalis*) is the sugar hackberry or Mississippi hackberry (*C. laevigata*). This tree is native to the southeastern and south-central United States, and is grown primarily as a shade tree. Like the hackberry, its bark has little distinctive bumpy areas. Fruit, which follows rather insignificant May flowers, is tiny and turns from orange to dark purple. All hackberries are tough trees, growing well in city conditions or with their roots in brackish water. They're tolerant of heat, hot dry winds, alkaline soils, and some drought. And insect pests tend to leave these deciduous trees alone.

■ **Wide spreading** *branches, colorful fruit, and a hardy nature make the hackberry (Celtis occidentalis) an excellent shade tree.*

Japanese pagoda tree

Known by some as the Chinese scholar tree (*Sophora japonica*), this moderate-grower will reach a pleasant 20 feet high, then turtle along to 50 feet. Spreading branches provide pleasant, filtered shade. *Pinnate* leaves, divided into numerous leaflets, are dark green, turning yellow in autumn. After the first few years, long clusters of yellowish-white, sweet-smelling, pea-shaped flowers appear in the summer. This lovely flower display can last for up to 2 months, attracting lots of bees.

Here's a deciduous tree where you don't have to worry about soil. It doesn't need much water either, once it gets started, although some protection from the wind may be needed. Best of all, insect pests and diseases tend to go elsewhere.

■ **The hardy Japanese pagoda** *will thrive in most gardens. It is popular for both the shade it provides and its fragrant flowers.*

> **DEFINITION**
>
> A **pinnate** *leaf has little leaflets running along both sides of a main axis. It looks a bit like a feather, and, in fact, the Latin word* pinna *means feather. As a rule, a pinnate leaf will be shed in its entirety, with the leaflets attached.*

Silk tree

From late spring until summer, powder-puff pink flowers jostle to almost hide the silk tree's (*Albizia julibrissin*) light green, ferny-leafed branches. Not fussy about soil, a silk tree still prefers a sunny site, and does best if you give it enough water. If you're forgetful, it will still grow, but not as quickly. A mature silk tree will reach 40 feet high, and about 40 feet wide. Although silk trees will tolerate temperatures as low as 5° F, they may die down in the winter. If so, remove the dead stems to encourage new growth.

Silk trees grow either with multiple trunks, or as a single tree with an umbrella shape. When shopping for one, make sure the tree is large enough to have developed its final shape (unless you want to fuss with it later). Also be aware that some people call a silk tree a Persian acacia, some know it as a pink siris, and yet others as a mimosa.

If you're considering adding a silk tree to your yard, think about placing it where you can really enjoy the blooms. Many people plant it so they can look down at the flowers from a second-story window.

SILK TREE (*Albizia julibrissin*)

More trees for shade:

- Alders (*Alnus*)
- Arborvitae (*Thuja*)
- Ashes (*Fraxinus*)
- Canoe birches (*Betula papyrifera*)
- Dogwoods (*Cornus*)
- Flowering cherries (*Prunus*)
- Flowering crabapples (*Malus*)
- Franklinia (*Franklinia*)

- Hawthorns (*Crataegus*)
- Hemlocks (*Tsuga*)
- Lacebark pine (*Pinus bungeana*)
- Magnolias (*Magnolia*)
- Maples (*Acer*)
- Mountain ashes (*Sorbus*)
- Russian olives (*Elaeagnus angustifolia*)
- Yews (*Taxus*)

Flowering trees

FLOWERING TREES GIVE YOU *two pleasures for the price of one. Blossom in spring or summer complements the new leaves, and if you're lucky you'll get the extra benefit of fall color.*

Flowering dogwood

Noted for its spring color, the flowering dogwood (*Cornus florida*), also called eastern dogwood, brings you ample pink- or white-clustered blossoms, for an extremely showy display that just about covers the entire tree. Then, in the fall, the bright green leaves blaze forth in crimson hues. Bright, shiny red berries appear too, delighting the local birds. The berries may remain even after the leaves of this deciduous tree have fallen for the winter. Look closely, however, and amid the branches you can see flower buds waiting for spring.

If you want to select the flower color, you will have to wait until spring to buy your tree. Many people have several flowering dogwoods, all in differing flower hues. The trees will grow to approximately 20 feet high. Branches will generally take a pyramid or umbrella shape.

FLOWERING DOGWOOD (*Cornus florida*)

143

More dogwoods

Other dogwood trees are extremely beautiful too. I'm partial to the Cornelian cherry dogwood (*Cornus mas*), and the redtwig (also known as the bloodtwig) dogwood (*C. sanguinea*). You might also want to try the pagoda dogwood (*C. alternifolia*), a tree that does particularly well in cold-winter climates. If possible, put dogwoods in a sheltered, wind-free site. And give them plenty of water, especially during the first year.

Southern magnolia

It's difficult to choose which magnolia to spotlight, but I think I'd have to go with this North American native. The southern magnolia (*Magnolia grandiflora*), also called bull bay, is exquisite, with its dinner-plate-size, fragrant white flowers – so popular for floating in a display bowl on the dinner table. Flowering begins in June and continues right

■ **The Cornelian cherry dogwood** *has star-shaped yellow flowers appearing in early spring, followed by bright red fruits.*

through the fall. If the temperature in your growing area doesn't drop below 40° F, you may even see a few flowers all year round. Large leaves that are shiny green on top and pale orange fuzzy underneath provide the flowers with a beautiful framework. Once the flowers drop off, orange-green, 2-inch-long fruit will develop. It really is a spectacular tree and one that will give you a lot of pleasure.

Magnolias like moist, well-drained, rich soil of a slightly acidic nature. They don't do well in compacted soil. Think about their eventual height when you select a spot, and then place them where they are to grow permanently.

Magnolias do not transplant graciously. Because they also quite dislike people puttering around their base, this is not a place to put support plants that you will be digging up for any reason. Put an attractive mulch there instead.

The falling leaves can be somewhat messy, so keep them away from your patio. In general, most magnolias aren't too tolerant of city conditions. Also, do avoid dry and windy sites when planting. Other than that, magnolias are hardy and rarely have serious disease or pest problems.

STAR MAGNOLIA (*Magnolia stellata*)

More magnolias

The southern magnolia is a tall tree. Growing slowly, it will eventually reach 80 feet high or higher, and it can fill up a small yard when it reaches 35 or more feet wide. But if you have the space and live in a warmer climate, it is worth it for sheer magnificence. If you don't have the space, look for the little gem variety, which reaches about 20 feet high. Other fabulous magnolias include the ear-leafed umbrella tree (*M. fraseri*), the willow-leafed magnolia (*M. salicifolia*), the sweet bay (*M. virginiana*), and the star magnolia (*M. stellata*), a hardy specimen plant that averages just 25 feet high. For a lovely tree that blooms nicely at a young age, plant the deciduous saucer magnolia (*M. x soulangeana*). Check out the catalogs if you can't find what you want near you.

Yoshino cherry tree

If you've ever visited Washington D.C. in the spring, you probably were awestruck at the fragrant, light pink or white flowers festooning the hundreds of Yoshino cherry trees (*Prunus yedoensis*) near the Jefferson Memorial and the Washington Monument. As you wandered around town, perhaps you saw other cherry trees as well, including the exquisite ariake, or Japanese cherry tree (*P. serrulata*), with its attractive pink flowers, or *P.* Kwanzan, with clusters of double rosy flowers. You may have even returned home thinking that a flowering cherry tree would look great in your yard. It probably will.

YOSHINO CHERRY (*Prunus yedoensis*)

A tidy tree, the Yoshino grows to just 20 feet tall. Other varieties may reach 40 feet. Some have white flowers, others pink. All are deciduous. Flowering cherry trees require a sunny site, excellent drainage, and good soil. Root rot will occur with poor drainage, so place them on raised mounds if unredeemable clay or the like is a problem.

INTERNET

nps.gov/nacc/cherry

Visit this site to learn all about the cherry trees in Washington D.C., including the date of the annual Cherry Blossom Festival.

Eastern redbud

Clusters of pink, purple, reddish, or white flowers are true eye-catchers as they bloom on the bare branches, and sometimes the trunk, in early spring. Soon, heart-shaped green leaves appear, which will turn lemon yellow in the fall, accompanied by tan, bean-like seed pods that last into winter. Even in winter, the auburn bark on the open horizontal branches provides some visual interest.

Eastern redbuds (*Cercis canadensis*), which can reach 30 feet high at a moderate growth rate, are not picky trees. They're happy in acidic or alkaline soil, damp soil, sun, or semi-shade. They need deep watering only about every four weeks during the growing season. This deciduous tree is tolerant of almost any type of garden condition. However, you do have to keep an eye out for insect pests.

■ *The distinctive leaves of Eastern redbud are preceded by pea-like flowers that are magenta in bud and open to pale pink.*

The eastern redbud is extremely popular, but the western redbud (*C. occidentalis*) gives it lots of competition. This is a much smaller tree, usually growing about 18 feet tall. It's often multi-trunked, and also can be grown as a shrub.

More flowering trees:

- Acacia (*Acacia*)
- Catalpa (*Catalpa*)
- Coral tree (*Erythrina*)
- Crabapple (*Malus*)
- Flowering almond (*Prunus triloba*)
- Flowering ash (*Fraxinus ornus*)
- Franklinia (*Franklinia*)
- Fringe tree (*Chionanthus*)
- Golden-rain tree (*Koelreuteria paniculata*)
- Golden chain tree (*Laburnum*)
- Hawthorn (*Crataegus*)
- Jacaranda (*Jacaranda*)
- Japanese lilac (*Syringa reticulata*)
- Japanese snowbell (*Styrax japonicus*)
- Smoke tree (*Cotinus*)
- Tulip tree (*Liriodendron*)

Instant arbors

IF YOU'RE EAGER *to get your garden trees going quickly, you may want to plant some that are known for their rapid growth. These might be considered "temporary" trees, to be removed when slower growing trees reach the height you want. Trees in the fast lane include the favorites I'm about to describe.*

Ash

People seem to like to name ash (*Fraxinus*) trees after colors: red, claret, green, velvet, and white, among others. These are pretty much wash-and-wear trees: none of the ashes demands a lot of attention. Among the hardiest of the hardy is the popular *F. pennsylvanica*, commonly known as both the green ash and the red ash. I'll call it the green ash here. This tree can survive severe cold (to -30°F!), semi-soggy soil, and drought conditions.

■ **Ash trees** *are popular for their foliage of paired leaves.* Fraxinus angustifolia (shown here) *has slender, dark green leaves that are attractively glossy.*

Like all ash trees, it's big, so even if you want a lot of shade really fast, buy only one. The tree is slim in youth, rounds out in middle age, and reaches at least 50 feet in height. In the fall, the lance-shaped leaves turn a lovely yellow and the bark may develop a red tinge.

More eye-catching ashes

If you're feeling a little more flamboyant, consider the claret ash (*F. angustifolia*), whose dark green leaves turn wine red in autumn. For dry areas, the Arizona ash (*F. velutina*) grows from 30 to 50 feet high, depending on the variety. If you want lots of tree in a little time, the Arizona ash is a favorite among deciduous tree fans. At one time, wood from the Arizona ash was used to make wagons. The bark is dark gray, and in fall the leaves turn bright yellow. Note, however, that with its shallow roots, you probably won't have much luck getting anything to grow under it, nor will you want to try to mow nearby for fear of damaging the roots.

Maple

Some of the maples (*Acer*) are bonsai material and some are towering specimens. There seem to be infinite varieties, most of which are breathtaking in autumn for beauty, including the snakebark maple (*A. capillipes*). The giants are usually the ones that grow super quick, such as the red maple (*A. rubrum*) and sugar maple (*A. saccharum*), both reaching 70 feet. If you have limited space you'll want the smaller ones, but if you are fortunate enough to have enough land, the larger trees provide a brilliant seasonal prize. In general, maples make good shade trees. They do well in most good garden soils, and are seldom harassed by pests or diseases.

■ **The red maple** (Acer rubrum) *grows quickly to give a stunning display of red and bronze leaves, but it needs plenty of space.*

It's difficult to say which maple has the best fall color. The sugar maple, with its silver-gray bark, turns crimson, orange, and yellow, and is considered the most extravagant of the American maples. Leaves of the Norway maple (*A. platanoides*) and big-leaf maple (*A. macrophyllum*) turn a clear, deep yellow. In the shorter varieties, you'll get bright crimson red leaves from the amur (*A. tataricum*), the Japanese burgundy lace (*A. palmatum* Burgundy Lace), and the vine maple (*A. circinatum*). There are even maples with dark purple leaves for yet more variety.

INTERNET

main.tellink.net/~sues/

Learn all about how to turn your sugar maple sap into sweet syrup. This site includes an historical photo album, a cookbook, and a guest sugarer you can send questions to.

My advice is to buy any maple when you can see its fall color, even though the cost will be somewhat higher than when leaves are bare.

Even within the same variety there are variations in color and leaf shape. If you can, make a fall foray to a well-labeled **arboretum** before you buy. It's a simple matter to jot down the name of the tree you like, and then buy it in the following spring.

DEFINITION

An **arboretum** *is a tree garden cultivated by horticulturists. Often open to the public, arboretums are a great way to learn about trees you may wish to plant in your own garden. They're also nice for a casual stroll.*

Russian olive

The Russian olive tree (*Elaeagnus angustifolia*) is a fast-grower that's very useful for erosion control on slopes. Even the tallest Russian olive is not too imposing, reaching a maximum of 25 feet high. However, it also expands to 25 feet wide. This is a good background tree, with willow-like, olive green leaves. It is easily pruned to make a hedge.

This is a sturdy garden addition with fragrant, greenish-yellow flowers, even if it's not an eye-catcher like the maples. Site it in sun or light shade. It patiently tolerates dust, smoke, wind, and seashore exposure, and very cold or very hot, dry weather. The Russian olive's only true nemesis is poorly drained soil, but it will withstand soil that's damp. Pests seem to avoid it, and transplanting is easy. Birds love its ample, yellow, olive-like berries in winter.

RUSSIAN OLIVE (*Elaeagnus angustifolia*)

Like anything else, the Russian olive does have a drawback: messy berries and leaves. But its semi-thorny branches make it a good barrier plant, and on a slope, a bit of organic debris is only a minor distraction. There are other *Elaeagnus*, equally super hardy, that grow in shrub form. Keep an eye out for the attractive silverberry (*E. commutata*).

Weeping willow

Weeping-style trees with flexible, drooping branches provide a focal point for the garden, and for many people they seem to bring on waves of nostalgia. The weeping willow's (*Salix babylonica*) branches will cascade toward the ground, even from a height of 30 foot or more. If you simply must have one, a deciduous willow will come into your garden despite known drawbacks. Yes, they drop leaves. Yes, they seem to send party invitations to bugs. Yes, the wood is brittle. And no, you can't garden around the roots – don't even try. So why bother?

Because they are beautiful, grow rapidly, tolerate almost any soil, and if you give them lots of water, weeping willows will thrive in any drainage conditions. If you have a stream on your property, this is definitely a tree to consider. Our early American pioneers, moving westward over dry territory, were jubilant when they saw willows because it meant water was nearby.

Trivia...

In the first century AD, *a Greek physician discovered that a concoction made from willow bark, despite causing an upset stomach, decreased both pain and fever. Native Americans brewed willow leaves into a bitter tea to cure headaches. Much later, researchers discovered that both the bark and leaves contained a chemical closely resembling aspirin.*

The willow family tree

A relative, the golden willow (*Salix alba* var. *vitellina*), which tolerates both beach conditions and floods, is equally fast growing. Quite pretty, it has yellowish-brown bark, bright yellow stems, and leaves that are yellow-green underneath and bright green above. Of the hundreds of willow species, there are also shrub-like ones and small trees. Consider planting a decorative pussy willow (*S. discolor*), whose soft, silky, gray catkins are a popular feature in dried flower arrangements.

More instant arbors:

- Acacia (*Acacia*)
- Birch (*Betula*)
- Catalpa (*Catalpa*)
- Empress tree (*Paulownia tomentosa*)
- Eucalyptus (*Eucalyptus*)
- Honey locust (*Gleditsia*)
- Linden (*Tilia*)
- Pin oak (*Quercus palustris*)
- Poplar (*Populus*)
- Silk oak (*Grevillea robusta*)
- Silk tree (*Albizia*)

Fall color

CHOOSING A TREE *for its fall color can be a real challenge. Some provide brilliant displays of color, but can be a little dull at other times of the year. Here I have listed those trees that really earn themselves a place in your garden.*

American sweetgum

Often used in endless rows to line public streets, the sweetgum (*Liquidambar styraciflua*) provides fall colors that make you feel as if you're in Vermont (which you might be, but most of us aren't). I really like this tree, although by the time mine hit 30 feet high, it was too big for my suburban yard. It would have grown to 80 feet if I'd let it. But looking out my window was really something! Even when the tree was young, it had great fall colors: crimson, oranges, purples, and yellows.

■ **The American sweetgum** (Liquidambar styraciflua) *is a conical spreading tree with glossy, dark green leaves that turn brilliant orange, red, and purple in fall.*

Each tree seems to have its own color personality, so this is another example of a good purchase to make in the fall. Although the sweetgum doesn't have any flowers to speak of, the prickly, golf-ball-size fruits that follow hang on bare branches throughout most of the winter. Full sun and moderate water are all the care you need to nurture a sweetgum. Other sweetgum species are quite attractive, but the American sweetgum provides the best overall fall color.

Birch

If you're into fall yellows, try three birches planted in a triangle. Picturesque peeling bark, often white or gray, delicate branches and 1-inch cone-like fruits that follow the fall shed make the trio even more attractive.

Don't be afraid to try one of the more obscure species, but because there are different birches (*Betula*) for different climate zones, your best bet is to choose your tree in a neighborhood nursery. Most commonly marketed are the 70-foot monarch birch (*B. maximowicziana*) and the 50-foot European white birch (*B. pendula*). The latter has weeping varieties, so if you like the drapery, shop around a bit. If one nursery doesn't have it, another will. Birches do demand lots of water in addition to sunlight. Some are susceptible to insect pests, including aphids – those tiny insects that drip sticky, sugary waste matter all over your new car.

My birches, which have never gotten over 20 feet tall in 30 years, are a focal point of my backyard, and I've never had insect problems. And the bush tits adore the little brown fruits that hang on throughout the winter.

■ **A graceful tree** *with a narrow crown,* the Laciniata is *a form of the European white birch* (Betula pendula) *that bears yellow-green catkins in spring.*

Smoke tree

If you have rocky or otherwise decrepit soil, this may be just the tree for you. It's simple to grow, multi-stemmed, and fairly small, growing only about 15 feet high and almost as wide. Leaves may be blue-green or purple throughout the spring and summer, changing to orange-red in the fall. The name "smoke" comes from its greenish blooms, which, as they fade, send out stalks covered with fuzzy, grayish-purple hairs. This makes the tree seem as if it is in a smoky, almost surreal cloud. The appearance lasts through until late summer.

The smoke tree (*Cotinus coggygria*) grows in full sun or light shade, and although somewhat drought-tolerant, it prefers low to average water with good drainage. It can be grown as a shrub, or, if you don't mind a tad of pruning, as a small, single-trunked tree.

SMOKE TREE (*Cotinus coggygria*)

Washington hawthorn

Of all the hawthorns (*Crataegus phaenopyrum*), this is truly the best one for fall color. The 25-foot-high deciduous tree dons a fall ballgown of absolutely the most vivid orange-red. If you have the space for more than one, two make a real showstopper. In spring, pure white grouped flowers appear. They are followed by clusters of scarlet berries that seem to cling to the branches forever, and are great for attracting birds. Hawthorn also grows well along highways, at salt-sprayed seashores, and in the city, including inner city parks. Hawthorns come with and without thorns, the benefit of those with sharp spines being that they make a nice barrier.

What do they need in the way of care? Not much other than sun and an average amount of water. Other hawthorns include the cockspur (*C. crus-galli*), English (*C. laevigata*), and the toba (*C. x mordenensis* Toba) – a Canadian hybrid that performs exceptionally well in cold winter climates.

INTERNET

ag.ohio-state.edu/
~ohioline/hyg-fact/
1000/index.html

Ohio State University Extension has a large library of horticulture fact sheets, incuding many on growing trees.

More trees for fall color:

- Black tupelo (*Nyssa sylvatica*)
- Chinese pistachio tree (*Pistacia chinensis*)
- Chinese tallow tree (*Sapium sebiferum*)
- Crape myrtle (*Lagerstroemia indica*)
- Franklinia (*Franklinia*)
- Katsura tree (*Cercidiphyllum japonicum*)
- Larch (*Larix*)
- Maidenhair (*Ginkgo*)
- Mountain ash (*Sorbus*)
- Ohio buckeye (*Aesculus glabra*)
- Persimmon (*Diospyros*)
- Poplar (*Populus*)
- Sassafras (*Sassafras*)
- Scarlet oak (*Quercus coccinea*)
- Serviceberry (*Amelanchier*)
- Sourwood (*Oxydendrum*)
- Tulip tree (*Liriodendron*)

A simple summary

✔ Evergreen trees keep their leaves right throughout the year. Deciduous trees shed their leaves in the fall and grow new ones in the spring.

✔ Before you buy any tree, learn how big it will grow and determine if this will realistically fit in your garden space. You don't want to have to move it later on when it is large.

✔ Buy younger, smaller trees, rather than those that are larger, to ease transplant shock, which could kill your tree. The smaller ones soon catch up in size.

✔ Install deciduous trees during their dormant, or resting, season. Make the planting hole as big as you can – about 50 percent larger than the extended root ball. Soak roots before, and water immediately after planting.

✔ You can buy trees to fill just about any niche in your garden: flowers, leaf shape, color, seasonal beauty, size, protective barrier, camouflage.

✔ Part of the fun of gardening is doing some research. Study the trees you might want before you buy them.

Chapter 9

Successful Shrubs

SHRUBS SERVE MANY GARDEN FUNCTIONS. They are hedges, screens, boundaries, noise reducers, windbreaks, background plantings, garden dividers, prowler deterrents, and focal points. In addition to front-, back-, and side-yard shrubs that go directly into the ground, you can buy shrubs to plant in big containers on your porch or patio. There seems to be a size and style for just about every need.

In this chapter...

✓ **What is a shrub?**

✓ **Too many choices**

✓ **Proper pruning**

✓ **Shrubs for hedges**

✓ **Scented shrubs**

✓ **Shrubs for visual fruit**

GRACEFUL, ARCHING *NEILLIA THIBETICA*

What is a shrub?

WHAT'S THE DIFFERENCE *between a shrub and a tree? That's a good question, and one that nobody has truly succeeded in answering. You can say a tree has one trunk and a shrub has several, but there are some trees with multiple trunks. You can say that trees are bigger than shrubs, but horticulturists have brought us trees that are quite tidy in size – unlike some shrubs, which grow wild and woolly.*

In general, though, trees usually (but not always) have a single woody trunk and are fairly to very tall, beginning perhaps at 20 feet high and ending at, well, towering. Shrubs usually (but not always) have several woody stems and may be from 12 inches to 15 feet high. There are also tree-like shrubs, tall shrubs pruned to look like small trees, and shrub-like trees. Whew! We definitely need to keep it simple. Even if you can't really define a shrub, will you know it when you see it? Probably.

The secret language of shrubs

When selecting a shrub, especially from a catalog, you may see words that describe its shape. These words aren't always as clear as they should be, so let's go over them briefly:

- A **low-branching** shrub is one where the lowest branches come very close to, or touch, the ground.

- A **prostrate shrub** is lower than a low-branching shrub. Its branches grow sideways, and may even rest on the ground. A prostrate shrub is often used as a ground cover.

- If a shrub is described as **pyramidal**, it has a pointy top and a wider base, like an Egyptian pyramid.

- A **columnar shrub** resembles a column, or a round pole.

- Like the columnar and the pyramidal shapes, the **compact shrub** has dense foliage, or leaves. It is, however, shorter, and almost square or rectangular in appearance.

- If you want a more airy touch, an **open shrub** is one where all the branches are spaced a bit apart.

- A **specimen**, or **focal point shrub**, is an open-style shrub.

- In the **weeping style shrub**, the branches grow upward and arch toward the ground.

Too many choices

THERE ARE SHRUBS *that flower in early spring, some that flower a little later in the season, and summer and fall bloomers. Some shrubs have fragrant flowers, many have berries. Although most have green leaves, others have leaves with yellow-green, blue-green, green-white, or purplish markings. Some are deciduous, others evergreen. The leaves of deciduous shrubs may change colors in autumn, becoming red, orange, or yellow before they drop. On some deciduous shrubs, the bark has its own fascination.*

■ **The American holly** (Ilex opaca) *looks like a shrub before it becomes a tree.*

You may be tempted to select a little bit of everything. Try to resist. To create a successful garden picture, plant at least three shrubs of the same variety, so they form a little group. The exception is when you want a specimen, or focal point shrub. A plain old shrub is not a focal point, so choose your specimen plant carefully. You want a focal point to offer something special, such as colorful leaves, fantastic flowers, or delightful shape.

Planning first

Once again, just a little planning and a little bit of research before you shop will go far in helping you make the right choices.

The best advice I can give you is to look at a mature size specimen if possible, and visualize it in your selected spot. Then buy a smaller version of your chosen plant. Regardless of how small it looks when you plant it, it will grow.

To be extra-confident in your choice, do some background research on the plant's favorite habitat and any special needs, so you'll be sure it will do well in your garden.

Do not count on adapting the site to your shrub by changing the soil around it. Choose a shrub that is already suitable by its very nature.

How and when to buy your shrub

There are two best times to buy a shrub. One is in early spring, before new leaves appear on the branches. The other is in late fall, approximately 6 weeks before the first hard freeze. This allows for some root growth.

Most often, shrubs are sold in containers, usually in 1- to 5-gallon sizes. Deciduous shrubs are sometimes sold early in the season with their roots bare, and this is the least expensive way to buy them. As the season moves on, the bare-rooted plants are placed in containers and the price goes up. Evergreens are sold in containers or balled and burlapped (B&B, you remember from Chapter 8, right?).

Picking a healthy shrub

Before you buy your shrub, make sure the soil is damp. If the root ball of an evergreen dries out, you are likely to be getting a half-dead plant. Chances are slim that you'll be able to help it recover. Whether it is deciduous or evergreen, always check to see if the roots are ramming their way through the container bottom or circling the trunk. If they are, the plant is root-bound. Shrubs grown in cramped surroundings like this are quite often water stressed. When you place them in the garden, the roots have limited capacity to reach out for moisture. A root-bound plant of any kind seldom adapts well when transplanted. Should you inadvertently buy one, loosen the roots and spread them out as best you can before planting.

PERFECT PLANTING

If you buy a container plant and haven't had the sides cut at the nursery, loosen the root ball by dipping the entire container in a bucket of water and letting it soak for a few minutes. This will make getting it out of a tight container fairly easy. Regardless of the way your plant is packaged when you buy it, you must loosen the soil clinging to the roots so you can spread them out when you get ready to place the shrub in its planting hole. Roots tangled into each other will continue to grow that way. Spread-out roots anchor the plant and have more space for survival.

1 **Dig a big hole**

Dig a hole about 50 percent larger than the size of the spread-out roots, and add some good organic soil. If planting in spring, mix in a cup of general-purpose fertilizer (5-10-5).

Help it along

To protect the newly planted shrub from wind and sun while it adjusts to its new environment, place a cover (made from paper or a similar material) over the plant for a week or so. Don't forget to water.

If your new shrub is less than 4 feet high, you don't need to stake it. But if it's taller, put a solid stake in the hole before you place the shrub. Fix the trunk to the stake with garden tape. Don't use wire, because as the shrub grows the wire will cut into the trunk.

There is continuing (and heated!) discussion among experts about whether you should prune a new shrub. Some say not to prune the shrub in any way. Others say not to prune evergreens, but do prune deciduous shrubs. I say don't prune at first. The plant is traumatized enough by the moving, so keep it simple.

Heeling in your shrub

Plant your shrub within a few hours after you buy it, and certainly within 24 hours of bringing it home. If this is not possible, you can heel the plant in to preserve its health, and your investment. This is really simple. In a shady spot, dig a trench about 18 inches deep. Place your shrub, tipped sidewise about 45°, into the trench. Cover the roots with soil. In autumn, you can leave it this way for a week. In spring, leave it for a few days only, as the shrub will start to grow and will be traumatized if you move it.

2 **Remove the pot**

Gently remove the shrub from its container. If necessary, water the pot first to make removal easier. Try not to disturb any of the soil around the roots while moving the plant.

3 **Plant your shrub**

Position the plant in the middle of the hole. Gradually fill around the plant with a mixture of local soil and organic soil. Give the plant a bit of a jiggle to fill any air pockets around the roots.

4 **Water it well**

Tap the soil down gently with your foot after each few shovels of soil. Once it is stable in the hole, give your new purchase a hearty drink of water to help its roots get established.

Proper pruning

SOME FOLK LIKE SHRUBS *with a natural look. Others want to clip them to look like porcupines or candelabra. You'll find the majority of people hacking away on the weekend. Whether inherited from a prior owner, or planted in great enthusiasm a decade ago, the pretty little shrub is now 15 feet tall and equally wide. It is perhaps blocking the view of their picture window, making midnight noises under their roof, or prolifically dropping leaves into their roof gutter. Eventually they'll probably chop it down or try to dig it out. In between, they'll just keep pruning it.*

Before you begin chopping away, do a little research about when your shrub should be pruned. Some shrubs should be pruned before they flower. Other shrubs should be pruned after they flower. If you don't do it at the proper time, you won't get many flowers or nice little berries for the birds.

When it's time to prune, give the about-to-be-trimmed plant a thorough watering. Now begin, using the proper equipment, such as pruning shears or lopping shears. Make sure that you trim carefully and slowly.

Never cut a branch flush to the trunk. This is an invitation to decay.

Careful cutting

Remove dead wood and branches that don't have a healthy appearance, and any that are trying for the odd-growth Olympics. If you want to make a shrub more compact, cut where there is a bud pointing downward. If you want to make a shrub taller, cut where there is a bud pointing upward. After you have done just a bit of trimming, stand back and rest. Refocus. While indiscriminate cutting may work off human angst, you don't want to strip the plant, just shape it.

■ **Proper pruning** *needs proper tools. Always use sharp pruners to cut back dead, diseased, or dying wood. When you have done this you can then prune for shape.*

General care

Deciduous shrubs need fertilizer applied about once a year. This is of greatest benefit if you do it in early spring or late fall, after the plants have lost their leaves. Do not fertilize shrubs in late summer or early fall. This will encourage new growth that is very susceptible to frost. Resist the temptation to just toss the fertilizer against the shrub trunk. Instead, see how far the roots fan out by looking at and poking into the soil. Water well afterward.

■ **Spread fertilizer** *evenly around the plant so that none of your shrub's roots miss out on essential nutrients.*

INTERNET

ag.usask.ca/cofa/depart
ments/hort/hortinfo/
yards/landsca.html

The University of Saskatchewan College of Agriculture has an extensive list of gardening articles. Check it out for help in choosing plants for home landscaping, including practical information on selecting shrubs and trees for a home garden.

New plantings need more regular watering than sedate, older plantings. After the first year, depending on the shrub, you can let it go almost dry between waterings. If you live in a cold area, lay some mulch around the shrub to keep the roots warm.

RESCUE FOR SAD SHRUBS

(1) Is your shrub in a frost pocket? Tender shrubs dislike the cold. Try moving it.

(2) Is your evergreen shrub in a windy spot? Wind increases water evaporation. Either create a way to break the wind, perhaps with a tree in the wind's path, or increase your watering.

(3) Is your shrub under or near a tree with wide-spreading shallow roots? These roots absorb the water and nutrients in the soil around them, depriving your shrub. You must either move the shrub or remove the tree.

(4) Is mulch piled high around the shrub trunk? A high blanket of mulch holds moisture that attracts rot fungi and causes other problems. Check it out and lower the mulch.

(5) And the usual suspects: Is there enough sun for a sun-loving shrub? Have you put a shade-lover in the sun? The solution to these problems is obvious.

Shrubs for hedges

A HEDGE SERVES AS A PRETTY (and if it's thick enough, a prowler-deterring) boundary. Easy-to-grow shrubs favored by hedge-lovers include the ones I'm about to describe.

Common privet

I have no great love for privets (*Ligustrum vulgare*), mostly because they tend to be seasonally messy. However, I have grown them for decades simply because they thrive in just about any soil, any place, sun or shade, never seem to contract disease, tolerate forgetfulness – you get the picture. You also will get dozens of little deciduous baby privets to keep or pull out, as the falling seeds seem to have a high birth rate. Should you want to make a really large hedge, plant these youngsters about 18 inches apart. Each heartily growing youth will reach about 5 feet high, although some have grown as tall as 15 feet.

Privet is easily pruned, and some people do so to avoid the prolific, small, white flowers that have a sort of unpleasant aroma. The flowers appear only for a short time in early summer, and pollinators do like them. When pruning young shrubs, make the shrub top slightly narrower than the broader base. This lets sun reach the base, promoting a preferred, bushy growth pattern.

There are several privets to choose from, including evergreens, and those are easily pruned and kept in small tree form. Simply put, if you want a shrub that ranks among the hardiest (and ranks highly with birds too), privets are for you.

Hedge cotoneaster

There are more than 50 species of cotoneaster, all with abundant small fruits that last well into the winter. The red, scarlet, yellow, or black ornamental fruits also attract birds if you like a little wildlife. Some cotoneasters are groundcovers, others are upright, ranging in size from dwarf to 15 feet tall. The taller varieties are easily pruned to a desired shape.

Trivia...
Cotoneaster is so hardy, there are even cotoneasters that thrive at the seacoast, such as rockspray (Cotoneaster horizontalis).

Hedge cotoneaster (*Cotoneaster lucida*) grows as a rounded evergreen shrub eventually reaching 6 to 8 feet high and equally as wide. When the plant's pinkish-white flowers subside, round black berries will appear. Cotoneaster is hardy and has no special soil requirements. It grows well in clay and even in deprived, stony soil. Although semi-shade tolerant, planting in full sun will yield the best results in attaining flowers and fruits.

The only caution with cotoneaster is to plant it where it is to grow. Cotoneaster does not transplant cheerfully.

Deciduous varieties, such as cranberry cotoneaster (*C. apiculatus*), offer a nice alternative to the evergreens. Cranberry cotoneaster has dark green, glossy leaves turning reddish-purple at the season's end. Its flowers are small and white, but profuse in mid-summer. It grows to only 3 feet high, but will spread to 8 feet wide.

Japanese holly

Japanese hollies (*Ilex crenata*) make attractive informal or trimmed hedges. Densely packed leaves are dark green on a neat, rounded plant that grows slowly. Usually about 4 feet high, this plant can reach 10 feet or be as short as 12 inches.

There are a fair number of varieties among the Japanese hollies, and the Convexa variety is one of the best of the group for hedge use. Its berries are black and inconspicuous. This holly adapts to sun or semi-shade, and to almost all climates. It will even put up with some pollution. Although it will adjust to most soils, there is a definite preference for organic, moist, well-drained soil. If you want to prune Japanese holly into a formal hedge, do so after the new growth has matured in the spring.

JAPANESE HOLLY (*Ilex crenata*)

Laurustinus

There's quite a choice of viburnums, including some with phenomenally fragrant white flower clusters. Some viburnums are evergreen, some are deciduous, and many are listed for general use. The evergreen laurustinus (*Viburnum tinus*) is specific for screens and hedges, reaching 6 to 12 feet high and almost as wide. Laurustinus leaves are dark green and the foliage adapts well to formal pruning. Its 3-inch-wide clusters of flowers are initially pink, later becoming white. It doesn't have the pleasant aroma of some of the other viburnums, but it does bear an attractive, bright blue fruit. For informal hedges, pruning in alternate years is sufficient.

This shrub will tolerate a shady site, but if you want more flowers, do give it some sun. It's not soil fussy – acidic or alkaline is fine – and a location near a swimming pool is acceptable. Planted near the ocean, however, laurustinus' leaves may develop mildew.

Where it is marginally hardy, don't water laurustinus in late summer as this encourages lush growth that may not survive the winter.

Rosemary

If you'd like a short to medium-size hardy shrub, and fragrant flowers would be a plus, think rosemary (*Rosmarinus officinalis*). It grows most happily in fairly dry or gravelly soil, as long as it has good drainage. Full sun is fine, even against a white reflecting wall. Happy to 15° F as well as warm winter areas, rosemary tolerates oceanfront sites reasonably well. And once the plant gets started, watering can be kept to a minimum. Moreover, rosemary rarely has pest or disease problems. It's hard to find something objectionable about rosemary. I've seen it grow healthily in yards that, for one reason or another, are completely unattended.

Choose carefully for the height you want, as some varieties are groundcovers and others, such as Tuscan Blue, grow to 6 feet tall. This variety has clear blue flowers, but other, smaller varieties have lavender-blue or violet flowers. You might want some of each.

■ **Rosemary not only** *looks pretty when in flower, it also smells wonderful, and, being a culinary herb, it's a useful shrub to have in your back yard.*

Trivia...

Rosemary symbolizes affection and remembrance. At one time, it played an emblematic role at weddings. Bridesmaids would present the groom with a ribbon-bound rosemary bouquet. The bride would bring a wreath of rosemary to her new abode, in remembrance of her former home and loving hearts that had cared for her so well. A bridesmaid would also plant a sprig of rosemary in the bride's new garden. When this rosemary grew, it would be used for the bride's daughters when they married. In a prelude to marriage, a young woman wishing to dream of her future husband would place a sixpence, our equivalent of a few pennies, and a rosemary sprig under her pillow.

More shrubs for hedges:

- American arborvitae (*Thuja occidentalis*)
- Box honeysuckle (*Lonicera nitida*)
- Boxwood (*Buxus*)
- Burning bush (*Euonymus alatus*)
- Cherry laurel (*Prunus laurocerasus*)
- False cypress (*Chamaecyparis*)
- Glossy abelia (*Abelia x grandiflora*)
- Juniper (*Juniperus*)
- Myrtle (*Myrtus*)
- Osmanthus (*Osmanthus*)

- Photinia (*Photinia*)
- Pittosporum (*Pittosporum*)
- Rosebay rhododendron (*Rhododendron maximum*)
- Rose of Sharon (*Hibiscus syriacus*)
- Scarlet firethorn (*Pyracantha coccinea*)
- Silverberry (*Elaeagnus commutata*)
- Warty barberry (*Berberis verruculosa*)
- Yew (*Taxus*)

Scented shrubs

THERE'S AN ABUNDANCE of sweet-smelling shrubs to choose from. Whether you are planting a whole border or just want one dramatic specimen plant to set off the rest of your plantings, there are shrubs ideally suited to your needs. Of course, they all have different care requirements, but you're bound to find one you to suit you from the list of my favorites that follow.

CLOVE CURRANT (*Ribes odoratum*)

Clove currant

Maybe you just want something different. Great! If you like the scent of cloves, try this shrub. A deciduous shrub, clove currant (*Ribes odoratum*) likes quite dry soil and a somewhat shady spot – an alternative to many other shrubs that demand sunlight. It's multi-purpose, because besides the fruit and the spicy clove scent, there are cascades of tubular, sunny yellow flowers in spring, and leaves that transform into scintillating scarlet in autumn. You will have to allow this Great Plains native ample garden space, as it enlarges by means of underground *suckers*. The better the soil, the faster this plant spreads.

> ### DEFINITION
>
> *Yes, sucker is a gardening term. Suckers are shoots springing from below the ground, typically from a plant's roots, instead of from its stem. They eventually push their way to the surface to make new plants.*

Clove currant, like other Ribes species, can carry the fungus that transmits white pine blister rust. If you live near an area where white pines grow, this plant is a no-no.

To see if it is possible to grow a clove currant in your area, visit your local nursery. If they sell it, it's probably safe to bring it home. Birds just love its small, black, sweet-tart fruits. Another bird attractor is golden currant (*R. alpinum* 'Aureum'). This hardy species likes full sun, does well in all soil types, and doesn't mind air pollution. It is often planted in groups and makes a good hedging shrub.

Daphne

In the language of flowers, daphne means "sweets to the sweet." Sweetness notwithstanding, daphnes (*Daphne*) are inclined to be prima donnas. If you simply must have that delicious fragrance next to your patio door or living room window, you'll just have to do the extra coddling to make these shrubs comfortable. Daphnes require very well drained, neutral soil and full sun, although they tolerate partial shade. Always place some mulch around the shrub after planting and, once planted, do not move. Daphnes resent transplanting. Never over-water these shrubs, as their dislike for soggy soil is almost immediately apparent.

The winter daphne (*D. odora*) has a particularly beautiful scent. It grows from 3 to 5 feet high and almost as wide. As a note, all parts of this pretty shrub are poisonous if ingested, especially the berries.

WINTER DAPHNE (*Daphne odora*)

Gardenia

The gardenia's (*Gardenia augusta*) fragrance is legendary, and while you can buy it in a perfume bottle, you can also grow it in your garden. One large, waxy, white cut flower can perfume a small room, and a mature shrub is covered in midsummer with flowers. The plant's leaves are a shiny dark green. Native to China and Japan, this attractive evergreen is now available in many *cultivars* ranging in size from 2 feet to 8 feet. So you can keep a gardenia as a container shrub or as a full-size background shrub.

■ **The waxy beauty** *and sweet scent of gardenia (Gardenia augusta) once made it a popular buttonhole flower for men.*

> **DEFINITION**
>
> Cultivar *is a contraction of "cultivated variety." It's the progeny of a deliberate breeding effort which is known only in cultivation and produces plants with predictable, uniform characteristics.*

Gardenias demand very well drained, acidic soil that's high in organic matter. They prefer full sun, but light shade may suffice. Avoid planting gardenias in windy areas. Water regularly, and don't let the soil dry out completely. A 2-inch mulch of pine needles or peat moss can help keep gardenias in good health.

This shrub must be regularly fertilized. Look for fertilizer that says "azaleas" on the label (it's also good for gardenias), and read the instructions carefully before applying. *Fish emulsion* is another fine fertilizer for gardenias.

Promoting new blooms on your gardenias is a piece of cake. Just take a moment to cut the faded flowers.

Lavender

If I could have only one type of plant in my garden, it would have to be lavender (*Lavandula*). I like this small evergreen shrub so much that I collect books about lavender, make lavender wands, put lavender in my cut flower displays, attempt to make lavender sachets, and order odd varieties from catalogs. Although some lavenders can be a bit sensitive, they make me happy nonetheless, and their fragrance is fabulous.

Trivia...

For centuries, lavender has been used to scent soaps, bath water, and linen. According to some, the name derives from the Latin lavare, "to wash." Way back when, in Europe, people thought washing was unhealthy, and sanitary conditions were pretty awful. Because of this, people tended to have quite distinctive body aromas, some of which weren't very pleasant at all. To hide the unpleasant smell they used to drench themselves in lots of homemade perfume, lavender included.

In general, the common lavenders, such as the French (*L. stoechas*) and Spanish (*L. stoechas pedunculata*), are quite hardy if you provide dryish, rather limy soil and bright sunshine. Frankly, lavenders like my clay soil, which is why we get along so well. Soil must be well drained, so if you have any problems whatsoever, including lengthy winter rains on clay soil, plant lavender on a mound. Depending on the variety, lavender will grow from 18 inches to 3 feet high. The narrow leaves and flowers are carried on slim, slender stalks and the plant will bush out nicely if it can grow in the right soil.

■ **Spanish lavender** *doesn't need much attention in the right soil – and butterflies and hummingbirds love its fragrant purple flowers.*

The flowers are usually light to medium purple, but there are white, pink, and even green flowering lavenders. But these are not, in my experience, as hardy as the purple ones. If you live in a mild climate, lavender may bloom almost all year; otherwise you'll have spring and summer flowers. Experiment a bit to see what grows well in your climate. Given all the choices, you might try a more "exotic" lavender, which you can find from a catalog. I just read in an English magazine about a type of lavender that has reddish flowers.

Mock orange

Some folk consider the orange blossom fragrance overly sweet, but most find mock orange (*Philadelphus coronarius*) a joy. In spring, white flower clusters transform this otherwise plain, deciduous shrub into a star. Unlike the more fussy gardenia or daphne, mock orange grows in just about any garden soil, seldom gets any serious pests or diseases, and tolerates occasional drought. Give it full sun or light shade. The *P. coronarius* species is among the hardiest of the mock oranges, and in a sheltered spot may survive fairly cold winters. To avoid disappointment, select shrubs when they're in bloom, as some mock orange varieties don't have that famous fragrance.

> **INTERNET**
>
> ### botanical.com
>
> *Botanical.com has details on a wide variety of medicinal herbs, including nine pages of historical and growing information on lavender, plus how to make some lavender concoctions.*

VARIEGATED MOCK ORANGE (*Philadelphus coronarius*)

Mock orange is a great plant if you like butterfly visitors. In the language of flowers, it signifies "Remember me."

More scented shrubs:

- Bouvardia (*Bouvardia*)
- Buddleja (*Buddleja*)
- Carolina allspice (*Calycanthus floridus*)
- Deutzia (*Deutzia*)
- Fothergilla (*Fothergilla*)
- Frangipani (*Plumeria*)
- Glossy abelia (*Abelia x grandiflora*)
- Holly olive (*Osmanthus heterophyllus*)
- Jasmine (*Jasminum*)
- Lilac (*Syringa*)
- New Jersey tea (*Ceanothus americanus*)
- Russian olive (*Elaeagnus angustifolia*)
- Star magnolia (*Magnolia stellata*)
- Summersweet (*Clethra*)
- Sweet box (*Sarcococca*)
- Virginia sweetspire (*Itea virginica*)
- Wintersweet (*Chimonanthus*)

Shrubs for visual fruit

VIVID FRUITS ARE THE SELLING POINT of some shrubs. As you probably know, the fruit of these plants is for visual (not internal) consumption. In fact, some can be poisonous so make sure young children don't get their hands on them. Here are just a few of my favorites.

Barberry

The barberry (*Berberis*) is a low or medium-size shrub. It provides winter-persistent blue, black, or red super-showy berries, adored by birds. The berries follow yellow flowers that attract honeybees. The flowers do well in indoor arrangements, and appear during May and June amidst glossy, green leaves. The barberry's branches have thorns, so watch your fingers! All of the numerous barberry species are extremely easy to grow in average garden soil and several tolerate climate extremes. However, each has its own climate preference, so it's best to buy them from a local nursery.

The most popular purchase is the wintergreen barberry (*B. julianae*), an evergreen from 4 to 6 feet high, but be aware that its blue-black berries don't last as long as those of some others. Of all the barberries, this is the thorniest, and hence is often used as a barrier shrub. Berries do last on the deciduous Japanese barberry (*B. thunbergii*). They're profuse and bright red, so they really stand out against winter snow. The leaves turn brilliant scarlet, orange, and yellow before they drop in the fall from this 4- to 6-foot-high shrub. Barberrys do well in full sun or light shade. They don't need very much water in order to thrive, and are generally a healthy, pest-free shrub.

Firethorn

I have 10-foot-high firethorn (*Pyracantha*) all along my back fence. Its bright red berries arrive in the fall by what seems to be the thousands. Birds, especially robins, love the berries. Even the elusive cedar waxwing sneaks in when the berries are especially ripe and tasty. Firethorn also has sharp thorns, so anybody who wants to crawl over my fence has to run a formidable gauntlet. In summer pretty, small white flowers with an odd but mostly mild aroma attract foraging bees. I am always trying to get pollinators in my garden, so this is a great thing, and I just move my lounge chair away from the shrubs for a while.

There are many different types of firethorn, ranging from 3 feet to 18 feet tall. Berries might be yellow, orange, or red, and would last well into winter if the birds didn't eat them all. Purchase firethorn in the spring and place in a site that gets full sun. Water regularly but don't overwater or give a lot of fertilizer. Place this evergreen where it is to grow, as firethorn resents moving around.

Usually very hardy, the only hazard that I've encountered is an occasional plant disease called fireblight. Literally overnight, the entire plant turns black with a scorched appearance.

Fireblight is caused by a bacterium that becomes particularly destructive when daily temperatures average above 60° F and rains come during the blooming season. It may spread to nearby susceptible plants, such as apple trees, pear trees, hawthorn, and mountain ashes.

Sometimes the blackened plant is dead, other times it only looks dead. I leave mine alone for a year, because the affected plant sometimes grows back, although never quite as hardy. Resistant varieties of firethorn are available. Look for those named Mohave and Teton.

■ **Orange Glow** firethorn *bears lots of orange-red berries. Enjoy the sight while you can, before birds devour the lot!*

Oregon grape

Also called grape holly, Oregon grapeholly, and Oregon grape mahonia, this good-natured shrub (*Mahonia aquifolium*) thrives in just about any garden soil, including clay and sandy. Plant several shrubs in a row and you have a nice, 3-foot-high hedge. The shiny evergreen leaves are holly-like, and are often used in bouquets and holiday wreaths. In the winter, the leaves turn a reddish color. From March through May, small golden-yellow flowers appear in dense clusters. When the flowers subside, purple-blue berries in grape-like clusters appear. The berries are quite attractive to birds.

If you have a shady area, Oregon grape might just serve as a good fill-in. You do have to give it a moist, well-drained site, shelter from hot, dry winds, and an acidic soil. Although Oregon grape can be a tad fussy as to site, it isn't always easy to find a hardy shade-happy shrub, especially a disease-resistant one that has both pretty flowers and berries for the birds.

OREGON GRAPE
(*Mahonia aquifolium*)

Purple beautyberry

Plant beautyberry (*Callicarpa dichotoma*) in masses to get the full October effect of its lilac berries appearing in enormous clusters, somewhat like small grapes. Each shrub grows about 4 feet high (even taller if it's in the shade), and develops a 4-foot spread. In the spring, pinkish-lavender flower clusters are carried on stalks above medium-green leaves. Purple beautyberry does well in full sun or light shade, needs only average garden soil, and requires below moderate water. In cold winter areas, this deciduous shrub will sometimes freeze to the ground. It will return in the spring, so don't worry. This one is an easy-keeper.

More shrubs for visual fruit:

- Baneberry (*Actaea*)
- Bearberry (*Arctostaphylos*)
- Beautybush (*Kolkwitzia*)
- California lilac (*Ceanothus*)
- Cestrum (*Cestrum*)
- Cotoneaster (*Cotoneaster*)
- Dogwood (*Cornus*)
- Elaeagnus (*Elaeagnus*)

- Heavenly bamboo (*Nandina domestica*)
- Holly (*Ilex*)
- Photinia (*Photinia*)
- Snowberry (*Symphoricarpos*)
- Spice bush (*Lindera benzoin*)
- Spindle tree (*Euonymus*)
- Sweet box (*Sarcococca*)
- Viburnum (*Viburnum*)

A simple summary

✓ Shrubs have many garden uses. They serve as hedges, windbreaks, focal points, yard dividers, noise buffers, and, of course, as decoration.

✓ Always consider the the eventual size of the mature form of the shrub before planting.

✓ Unless you are using the shrub as a focal point, buying in groups of three is preferable from a design point of view.

✓ Shrubs are usually sold in containers, but you may obtain them with bare roots, or balled & burlapped (B&B).

✓ After purchase, always try to plant your shrub as soon as possible – in a hole that's at least 50 percent larger than the spread-out roots.

✓ Select shrubs for their form, leaf color, flowers, autumn hues, or pretty fruit.

Chapter 10

Rosier Roses

PEOPLE OFTEN THINK that roses are difficult to grow, but nothing could be farther from the truth. There are few sites and soils that won't entertain roses. Even when the temperature drops to well below freezing, some roses, particularly old-timers, will make it through the winter.

In this chapter...

✓ Buying roses

✓ Sites made simple

✓ Planting for perfection

✓ Rose maintenance

✓ Rose diseases

✓ A rose by any other name

✓ Recommended roses

✓ Everything's coming up roses

Buying roses

ELIZABETH HARKNESS ROSE

THE EARLY SPRING or fall months are the best time to plant roses, and so these months are also the prime time to buy them. Should you choose to start in autumn, plant in early fall if the weather has started to cool down, mid-fall if it hasn't. If you're on a budget, be aware that most garden centers have a rose sale in the fall.

Choose your rose

When buying, start by doing your homework about what type of rose will best suit your garden site. Bare-root roses, the kind in the pretty plastic packages with a photo and brief description on the front, are usually the most popular. With bare-root roses, you generally don't get the widest selection, but they can be $3 to $10 less than container roses. Read the descriptions on the package. If this is not the rose that you came into the store to buy, go home empty-handed and do some more research. Of course, I know you'll never follow this advice and you'll just bring home the rose you like. It's still a good idea to know something about the plant, so get some information about the rose's requirements before you pop it into your garden.

Rescuing roses

You do not want a rose prone to blackspot, rust, or mildew unless you are willing to give it extra care. You want roses that are hardy, vigorous, and disease free.

Look for roses with three to five canes coming off the enlarged main stem, plus a good fan of strong-looking roots. Do not buy leftover bare-root roses, the kind put in a pile at half-price.

Rose roots in those little plastic containers tend to dry out after a while, and roots really do need something to sink their teeth into for nutrition. So roses on sale for half-price could be substantially deprived and maybe not growing, or they might just need a longer while to adjust. Just so you know, if you're plant "rescuer" like I tend to be.

INTERNET

ars.org

Visit this site to learn about the American Rose Society (ARS). Founded in 1892, the non-profit ARS focuses on the enjoyment, propagation, and promotion of roses. It has 24,000 members. This site provides an opportunity to have rose-related questions answered by experts, and lists events, local societies, and membership information. It also offers a list of the best roses of the month, with details on each, which is invaluable when planning a large or small rose garden.

Sites made simple

BECAUSE ROSES DON'T LIKE TO BE DISTURBED, *you should choose your site carefully. Every time I have to move an established rose (usually because I have placed it incorrectly), there's a 50 percent chance I'll lose the plant. Besides, you're bound to be pricked – a lot – when you try to move a big, thorny rose bush.*

Air circulation

When selecting a site, in addition to ample sunlight, most roses, like most people, do best in an area with good air circulation. Close quarters abet various debilitating fungus diseases such as powdery mildew, rust, and blackspot. Good air circulation means just that; it does not mean placing the plant in a windy area. Heavy winds dry roses out and ruin the pretty flowers.

Water

Roses like to be watered regularly. If you plant them near trees or large shrubs, robber roots will steal water meant for your roses. So either don't plant them where there's competition underground, or plan on watering more often.

Soil

What do roses prefer in terms of soil? Well, there's preference, there's adaptability, and there's tolerance. Ideally, you want to provide your roses with healthy organic soil. If you can, dig it deeply the week before planting, turning it all over so fresh air eliminates any hiding bugs. Then, place your roses where they have ample sun but shelter from harsh winds.

Now that you know the preferred environment, let's talk about adaptability. Many roses will grow in any soil that has fairly decent drainage. As for tolerance, unless you are trying to grow on a bog site or a Sahara desert simulation, you can probably get roses to grow even in your rather inhospitable yard. Of course, if you do happen to have sandy or clay soil extremes, be kind. Before you plant, dig in a couple of buckets of organic matter: garden compost, bagged steer manure, or whatever is inexpensive and healthy.

INTERNET

rose.org

The home page of the All-America Rose Selections, an association of rose growers dedicated to promoting garden roses. You'll find information on buying and growing roses, new hybrids, and rose history and symbolism.

Planting for perfection

THE RULES FOR PLANTING *roses are simple.*
Just follow these instructions and you will get your rose
plants off to a super start.

Homecoming

When you bring a bare-root rose home, unpack it
immediately and dunk the roots in a big pail of
cool water for an hour or more. I have left mine
in a pail overnight with no harm and they seem to
adjust somewhat better than if they had not been
thoroughly soaked. If you've purchased container
plants, give them a huge dose of water when they
arrive home. Excess water will run out of the container
holes. Water again if the container must stand about a bit.
Before planting, place the rose in a wind-free, semi-shady
site so you don't traumatize the plant.

Placement

Dig a planting hole that's big enough to hold all the roots
comfortably. Don't skimp. You should fan out the roots
of cramped bare-root roses. Container rose roots may
remain as is, unless they're root-bound. This may occur
when the rose has been left in the container too long. The
roots continue to grow but begin to curl around each other for lack of an alternative. In
this scenario, you must squiggle them out before you place the rose in the ground. If the
roots are all squished together, they may continue to grow that way, vying with each
other in a limited space instead of reaching outward for nutrition and water.

Set the plant in the hole so that the soil reaches the same level that it did in the
container. Find this spot by looking for a slight color change at the base of the
stem. Backfill the hole with a mixture of 50 percent good organic soil and 50
percent of whatever soil you already have. Tamp it down gently as you fill, or
when you finish, to remove air pockets. Then water well.

Do not let the soil go dry on a newly planted rose. This is a major
reason for new rose failure.

■ **A container rose** *should have*
a healthy root system. If it has
been confined in its pot for too
long, the roots can get tangled
and may need to be cut back.

Rose maintenance

MAINTAINING ROSES *is really no more demanding than keeping any other type of plant. You'll want your plants to be healthy and to look spectacular, so it's important to develop good maintenance habits. Keep reading for the essentials of good rose care.*

Fertilizer

Although the hardier roses will do fine without regular fertilization, all roses benefit from a healthy snack in the spring. The easiest way to feed is to buy fertilizers designed specifically for roses, which usually cost about $3 to $5 a box. One box covers a lot of roses. Just follow the instructions, applying the fertilizer evenly around the plant base and then watering it in well.

PRUNING ROSES

Even if you don't do it the first year or two, after a while you'll begin to wonder about rose pruning. In areas where the winters get very cold, pruning is best done from late winter to early spring. In areas with mild winters, you can prune from fall to early spring, before the leaves emerge. Prune just above a bud with the cut sloping downward. Why not higher? The extra piece is likely to die and turn black, with the *dieback* perhaps progressing down the plant stem.

DEFINITION

Dieback *is exactly what it sounds like. It occurs when a shoot begins to die at the tip, from either disease or damage.*

a **Prune unwanted wood**

Prune out any diseased, damaged, or dead wood from the plant. Also, prune to thin out any crowded or crossed-over stems.

b **Prune for strong growth**

Prune just above a bud with the cut sloping downward. This encourages the plant's energy to go into producing strong stems.

Support

General maintenance also includes checking to make sure trellises and other supports are well fixed, and any rose climber is well attached to it. I remember having an 8 by 10 foot climbing Blaze fall forward off the fence, trellis and all. The wind displaced a lot of things that year, even re-siting a Monterey cypress onto my roof. In order to save the Blaze climber, I had to cut it back to little stubs just to get it out of the pathway. The climber has since recovered, but it's never been quite the same.

Cold weather

It is generally agreed that some protection should be provided if the temperature goes below 15° F. However, there is ample debate on what that protection should be. Some roses are more winter-hardy than others. If you live where the snow piles up, look for cold tolerance in the plant description. Generally, shrub and species roses withstand low temperatures better than other kinds.

Why does cold cause problems? When the temperature drops below freezing, ice crystals form within the plant. The colder it is, the more ice crystals there are. These crystals begin to push at plant tissue and may tear it. When temperatures fluctuate, causing repeated thaw and frost, the damage is increased and can kill the plant.

One popular protection method is to mound soil around the plant's base right after the first killing frost. The mound should be at least 8 inches high. The purpose of this protective mound is to keep the plant as warm as possible, like a blanket, and also to prevent alternate freezing and thawing. This protects only the lower plant part. However, even if the parts above are killed by frost, enough wood may survive to let the rose grow back. Remove the mounded soil in early spring unless a true cold spell is expected.

■ **A mound of soil** *around the base of your rose plant acts like a blanket to protect the lower stems in freezing weather.*

INTERNET

tpoint.net/neighbor

The Gardening Launch Pad covers just about everything you want to search out on gardens, or at least leads you to the information. In the section on roses, local rose societies are listed, as is information on different rose types, rose recommendations, rose hip recipes, and even a virtual tour of an English rose garden.

Suckering

You may see suckers coming from the plant base. Remove them immediately, or they will keep growing and use up energy-giving nutrients, at the expense of your roses. It's easy to spot a sucker as they look different from regular rose stems. They are a lighter green in color, and rather than having thorns, they have a prickly feel. Always remove suckers completely, and keep an eye out for any new ones that appear. Some roses sucker more than others.

■ **Remove suckers** *regularly to prevent them from sapping strength from your roses. Grab the sucker firmly and tug it up from the root.*

A little history of hips

A rose hip is the cup-like receptacle that encloses rose seeds, or the rose fruit. Picture a small pomegranate and you'll have a mental image of a large rose hip. While many are light to vivid orange, ripe rose hips may be yellow, red, brown, scarlet, or black. Rose hips contain an enormous amount of vitamin C – about 400 percent more than an orange. During World War II, when citrus fruits were scarce in Great Britain, the garden roses still had rose hips. These were collected and used to make syrup.

Although all roses make hips of some kind, letting the hips grow takes energy away from the flowers. Most people who want rose hips for a culinary objective grow roses specifically for this purpose. Rose hips, often collected from old-time rugosa roses, have been used for many culinary purposes, including teas, marmalade, sauces, and tarts. Some hips are larger (up to 1½ inches) than others, with better taste.

If you want to find a recipe incorporating rose hips, you may have to search in a cookbook from your grandmother's or great-grandmother's day, or for reproductions of old-fashioned recipes. If you're thinking about collecting rose hips from anyplace, make very certain they have not been treated with systemic or other chemicals. A systemic is a chemical applied to the plant that travels throughout the plant for a specific purpose. A systemic may be a weed killer, a fungicide, an insecticide, or an insect killer. All systemics are poisonous, and unless you have grown the rose yourself, you truly have no idea what it may have been treated with.

Rose diseases

DISEASE IN PLANTS will be discussed thoroughly in Chapter 21. But to select and keep healthy plants, you need to look out for signs of diseases that are somewhat common in roses. The following diseases, simplified and in order of importance, are the most bothersome.

Blackspot

Blackspot is a fungal disease, characterized by circular black spots on the leaves. Leaf tissue around the spots may turn yellow, and later the leaf may drop off. Blackspot weakens the plant and may cause leaves to fall prematurely. Don't bring home a rose plant that shows signs of blackspot, and look for plants stated as resistant to this disease. Do not water roses late in the evening, as water remaining on leaves encourages the spread of this disease.

BLACKSPOT

Mildew

Mildewed leaves are coated with a grayish-white powdery growth. The leaves become distorted. Mildew is most often found on plants growing in high humidity, which encourages the spread of the fungus. Purchase plants described as resistant to mildew.

Canker

Canker appears as brown patches on rose stems, and it is most visible during early spring and late winter. The patches may be several inches long, and may completely surround the stem. Depending on the canker type, the patches may appear sunken. All wood above the canker will eventually die.

RUST

Rust

Red-brown spots on the undersides of leaves are signs of rust. The leaf becomes deformed, and may develop cuplike depressions. Affected leaves may wilt, yellow, and drop off. Prolonged rain, or watering on overcast days or late evenings, encourages this fungal disease.

A rose by any other name

ROSES FALL WITHIN THE GENUS ROSA. *As a rule, roses are known by their trademark names, and that is how I'll refer to them here.*

You'll hear roses described as albas, bourbons, centifolias, Chinas, climbers, damasks, eglantine hybrids, floribundas, Gallicas, grandifloras, hybrid perpetuals, hybrid rugosas, hybrid teas, moss roses, noisettes, polyanthas, portlands, ramblers, and teas. Each of these is a group of roses. For the newcomer, it isn't important to memorize all the groups of roses. The desire for detail will come later, as roses begin holding you in their thrall.

What you will need to know, for starters, is type: miniature, bush, shrub, climber, or tree. Type, basically, represents height and width. And you'll want the fundamentals on the plant – how often it blooms, its fragrance, hardiness, and disease resistance.

I now grow about 60 roses of various kinds. Once upon a time, I didn't think type was important. I have changed my mind. When you put a tall plant next to a short one, the short plant is obliterated. It is also wise to know that a climber is a climber, so you don't have to risk moving a beautiful, healthy growing rose because it's begun to resemble Jack's beanstalk.

■ **Different types of roses** *can be grown together to create a stunning mixed rose garden. Here the roses* Stanwell Perpetual, De Rescht, *and* Marbree *take pride of place.*

Recommended roses

WITH THE MANY GROUPS OF ROSES *and the almost countless number of species, I will narrow the focus to those that are popular with new gardeners. The hybrid teas and the climbers, two of the groups I just mentioned, provide an ample and easy-to-grow assortment.*

■ **Double Delight** *is a multicolor white, cream, and red hybrid tea rose.*

Hybrid tea roses

If you've ever received a gift of a single rose, or a bouquet of roses, chances are the beauties were hybrid teas. Almost all the roses sold by florists are hybrid teas, and about 75 percent of roses sold in garden centers are hybrid teas. They can be grown without formal protection anyplace where winter temperatures are above 10° F. If it gets colder than that, your plants will probably need shelter of some kind.

Hybrid teas are shrub roses. They generally have long and pointed buds carried singly on a stem. Flowers may be single, with one row of petals, but are usually double. Hybrid tea plants range from 2 to 6 feet tall, although most are in the 4- to 5-feet tall group.

The plants bloom on and off from mid-spring to late fall, depending on your climate and general nurturing. Many hybrid teas are fragrant, and fragrance can be mild or intense. I have found that the printed description of a rose fragrance to be of marked variance with what my nose knows.

If the fragrance of a rose is important to you, it's worth spending a bit more to buy the plant when in bloom, rather than as a bare-root bush.

Hybrid tea history

Hybrid teas were developed long ago by crossing tender tea roses and the tough hybrid perpetuals, which themselves were a cross between oriental and European roses. The first officially recognized hybrid tea rose was La France, a pale pink flower, appearing in 1867. After that, the hybrid tea population exploded with new varieties, and fresh ones continue to appear all the time.

The chart on the opposite page is far from complete due to space limitations. All the hybrid tea roses listed here are considered hardy, and the word "durable" denotes vigor and partial or full disease resistance. "Short" indicates a plant that grows from 2 to 3 feet high, "medium" indicates a plant that grows to about 4 feet, and "tall" indicates a plant that grows to the upper ranges, about 5 or 6 feet.

	Fragrant	Height	Repeat bloom	Durable	Comments
White					
Elina		short	■		
Elizabeth Harkness		short	■	■	
Honor		tall			
Mrs. Herbert Stevens		medium			
Pascali		medium	■	■	
Polar Star		medium			
Pristine		medium	■	■	
Pink					
Bewitched	■	tall		■	
Century Two		medium			
Charlotte Armstrong		tall			*very dark pink*
Color Magic		tall			
Confidence		medium		■	
Congratulations		medium	■	■	
Coral Bay		tall			
Duet		medium		■	
Eden Rose	■	medium		■	
Friendship		tall			
Perfume Delight	■ ■	medium			
Radiance		tall		■	
Sheer Elegance		medium		■	
Signature		medium	■		
South Seas		tall			
Tiffany	■	tall		■	
Lavender					
Heirloom		medium			*see lavenders in bloom*
Paradise		medium			
Yellow					
Allspice		tall			
Apollo	■	tall			
Goldstar		short	■	■	
King's Ransom	■	medium		■	
Lowell Thomas		medium			
Oregold		medium			
Peace	■	tall		■	
Rio Samba		tall		■	

Continued . . .

	Fragrant	Height	Repeat bloom	Durable	Comments
Orange					
Fascination		medium		■	
Folklore	■	tall			
Futura		medium			
Mojave		medium			
Montezuma		medium			
Mrs. Oakley Fisher	■	short		■	
Mrs. Sam McGredy		short	■	■	
Red					
Americana	■	medium			
American Pride		medium			
Flaming Peace		medium			
Fragrant Cloud	■	medium		■	
Gypsy		tall			
Ingrid Bergman		medium		■	
Kentucky Derby		tall		■	
Legend	■	tall		■	
Mirandy	■	medium		■	
Mr. Lincoln	■	tall			extra easy
New Yorker	■	medium			
Olympiad	■	medium			
Precious Platinum		tall			
Proud Land	■	medium			
Royal William		short	■	■	
Wendy Cussons		medium			
Multicolored					
American Heritage		tall			
Barbara Bush		medium			
Brigadoon		medium			
Cary Grant	■	medium		■	
Chicago Peace		medium		■	
Double Delight	■	medium		■	
Shot Silk	■	short	■	■	some winter hardiness
Yankee Doodle		medium		■	

The peace rose

The Peace rose, originally known as #3-35-40, was first hybridized in 1937 in France by 23-year-old Francis Meilland. When Germany invaded France during World War II, *budwood* shipments of the plants were smuggled out. There was only one shipment sent to America, and it was in the last diplomatic pouch out of Paris. For 5 years, Meilland did not know what happened to his beautiful rose. In 1944, he found out that it had survived and was thriving in various places under a host of different names. The following year, the world-famous rosarian, Robert Pyle, gave #3-35-40 its official name, Peace. To symbolize the war's end, one Peace rose was given to each member of the United Nations. This rose, which the Duke of Windsor called "the most beautiful rose in the world," was also honored as the World's Favorite Rose. There are color variants of the original yellow Peace rose, and a climbing version. Every garden should have at least one Peace rose.

■ **Peace** is the perfect rose, and a must for every rose grower.

DEFINITION

Budwood *refers to strong young stems that have buds suitable for use in budding. When a professional decides to multiply a desired rose plant, growth eyes, or "buds," are sliced from the budwood of selected roses. These buds are inserted into cuts made in the bark of already-rooted cuttings, or understocks. Understocks are from roses known for their hardy root systems. Almost all bare-root rose bushes are budded plants.*

Climbers

Climbers can be found in medium, tall, and apparently never-ending sizes. The roses can be of any type, including floribunda, grandiflora, hybrid musk, hybrid tea, and polyantha.

Climbing roses can be used to cover old tree stumps, screen out neighboring views, cover arbors, disguise garages, and hide fences. You will need to give all climbers firm support because wind and rain can pull them (and the support) to the ground. And remember, the plants get even heavier when laden with flowers. If you put them against a trellis, make certain the trellis itself is well anchored. To be sure, I always put some nails into the fence, and affix the trellis tightly with wire.

When planting roses, you don't need to be reminded that they have thorns. As you are pulling the thorns out of your hands, make a mental image of how big this climber is going to get. Put climbers out of strolling reach, and away from children's play areas.

■ **Golden Showers** *is a fragrant, upright climbing rose.*

This chart includes just a few of the hardier climbing varieties. The word "durable" means vigorous and partially or fully disease resistant. Winter hardy refers only to 0° F.

	Fragrant	Height	Repeat bloom	Durable	Winter hardy	Comments
Red/Scarlet						
Altissimo		7-13 ft.	■	■		
Blaze		to 15 ft.	■	■		extra easy
Climbing Crimson Glory	■	to 10 ft.		■		
Climbing Etoile de Holland	■	to 20 ft.				
Dortmund		to 10 ft.		■	■	
Paul's Scarlet Climber		to 15 ft.		■		profuse blooms
Pink						
Aloha	■	to 10 ft.	■	■	■	
America		to 10 ft.	■	■	■	
Climbing Cecile Brunner	■	to 25 ft.				good for arbors
Climbing Queen Elizabeth		10-12 ft.		■		
Mme. Gregoire Staechelin	■	to 20 ft.				
Morning Jewel		to 15 ft.		■		
New Dawn		12-20 ft.			■	
Viking Queen	■	8-15 ft.	■			
White						
Handel		to 14 ft.				
Mrs. Herbert Stevens Climber	■	to 12 ft.	■			
Sombreuil Climber	■	to 15 ft.	■			
White Dawn	■	to 12 ft.	■	■	■	
Yellow						
Climbing Peace		to 20 ft.		■		
Elegance	■	to 15 ft.		■	■	thorny
Golden Showers	■	8-12 ft.	■		■	few thorns
Orange/Gold						
Climbing Autumn Sunset	■	to 12 ft.		■	■	
Climbing Lady Forteviot	■	10-15 ft.		■	■	
Royal Sunset	■	12-15 ft.		■		long blooming period
Multicolored						
Climbing Talisman		9-12 ft.		■		
Fourth of July		10-14 ft.			■	
Pinata		to 8 ft.				

Everything's coming up roses

IT IS IMPOSSIBLE TO COVER ALL *the current and old-time roses available, even in a book entirely devoted to roses. Although I've chosen to feature hybrid teas and climbers, you should have a working familiarity with some of the other rose groups. Here I've given some very, very basic descriptions and definitions.*

■ **Alba Maxima** *is a large alba rose that blooms once a year.*

■ **Alba** – these are shrub roses, known to be fragrant and hardy. They grow from 6 to 9 feet tall. They have abundant green foliage but bloom only once.

■ **Bourbon** – these plants are vigorous, but sensitive and fragrant. They will grow up to 6 feet high and may re-bloom. They can be trained to climb.

■ **Centifolia** – also called Provence roses, these shrub roses will bloom only once but will provide huge flowers. The fragrant flowers are often seen in clusters. These plants range from 3 to 7 feet in height.

■ **China** – these roses range from low to tall, have clusters or single flowers, and will bloom repeatedly. They are not particularly hardy, so always try to provide adequate shelter. China roses are one of the ancestors of repeat bloomers.

■ **Damask** – rangy shrubs, these roses grow from 3 to 7 feet high. They are hardy, and will bloom once or twice. They bear fantastically fragrant clusters of flowers.

■ **Eglantine hybrids** – Eglantines produce fragrant, single or clustered flowers on arching shrubs growing up to 12 feet. Look out for bright red hips in the fall.

■ **Floribunda** – these plants are low growing, bushy, and hardy. They may or may not have fragrant flowers, which can either grow singly or in clusters. These roses provide nearly continuous blooms.

■ **Gallica** – Gallicas are compact, hardy shrub roses reaching about 3 to 4 feet high. Their large, fragrant flowers will bloom once per season. Special care for Gallicas includes watching for suckers.

Trivia...

Cleopatra, who knew many ways to enchant Mark Antony, would carpet a room with red rose petals so their scent would rise toward her lover as he strode eagerly in her direction.

■ **Fantin-Latour** *is a vigorous centifolia rose with fragrant cupped or flat flowers in a delicate shade of pink.*

- **Grandiflora** – producing single or clustered large, vigorous flowers, Grandifloras grow from 3 to 6 feet high. The blossoms have limited fragrance.
- **Hybrid musk** – these do well in poor growing conditions.
- **Hybrid perpetual** – hardy, vigorous, and sometimes rampant, hybrid perpetual shrubs have fragrant, large flowers. It's possible that they'll bloom repeatedly.
- **Hybrid rugosa** – select hybrid rugosas if you want a really tough plant. They're drought tolerant, seashore tolerant, winter hardy, and have an extraordinary resistance to disease. They produce pretty red hips, and are happy to bloom repeatedly.
- **Miniatures** – although not all miniatures are small plants (some grow to 6 feet or more!), their flowers are all small.

■ **Boule de Neige** *is a white Bourbon rose, often tinged pink.*

- **Modern roses** – this designation is given to any roses that have been developed after 1867. The floribundas, hybrid teas, and miniatures are among the sub-groups of modern roses.
- **Moss** – when rubbed, the flower stalks and hips of moss rose shrubs will give off a piney scent.
- **Noisette** – these are climbers, and have fragrant, repeat-blooming flowers. They're not winter hardy.
- **Old roses** – these include the sub-groups alba, gallica, and tea roses, among others. These are plants developed before 1867.
- **Polyantha** – shrub roses in this group are low growing and very hardy. They'll have many small flower clusters in almost continuous bloom.
- **Portland** – the portlands are fragrant shrub roses. They resemble the bourbons but have smaller flowers.
- **Ramblers** – ramblers are characterized by their very long, slender, pliable canes. They produce large clusters of small flowers once a season.
- **Species** – these are wild roses, and can be either climbers or shrubs. They are often fragrant and very hardy, and most bloom once a season.

■ **Henri-Martin** *is a strong, upright moss rose. Its rosette-shaped, purple-crimson flowers have a light scent.*

Trivia...

The Roman emperor Nero had rosewater-drenched pigeons fly over his banquets to sprinkle guests with perfume.

- **Tea** – available in both climbing and shrub form, tea roses prefer a mild climate. They have fragrant, large, repeat-blooming flowers.
- **Tree roses** – these are also known as standard roses. Floribundas, grandifloras, and hybrid teas can all be pruned and trained into tree form.

■ **Veilchenblau** *is a rampant rambler rose. It produces clusters of violet flowers streaked with white.*

Trivia...
...and may there be a road before you and it bordered with roses...
(an Irish blessing).

A simple summary

✓ Do a little homework before you purchase roses. Know the type of rose you want, and why, prior to going shopping.

✓ To simplify the selection process, make a list of the characteristics you desire in order of importance before you buy.

✓ Although a few will tolerate some shade, most roses need ample sun.

✓ Don't forget to water your roses. They need adequate water to look their best.

✓ Plant roses where they'll get good air circulation, but do not place them in windy areas.

✓ Take the time to dig a roomy planting hole, and backfill with good soil.

✓ Consider the plant's needs for water, air, and the right soil when you plant it.

✓ Fertilize roses in the spring.

✓ Give climbing roses good support as they can easily blow over in strong winds.

Chapter 11

Vivacious Vines

THERE ARE LOTS OF GREAT REASONS to include some climbers in your garden planning. One is to beautify a barrier, such as a fence or wall, that doesn't add much to the visual appeal of your garden. Another is to hide an eyesore, such as the dustbins, by growing climbers over a free-standing support. A climber-laden arch makes a lovely entrance from one part of your garden to another. Best of all, by planting vines you can erect a barrier to create more privacy in your garden.

In this chapter...

✓ Keep it up

✓ Get a grip

✓ Annual vines

✓ Flowering fence covers

✓ Vines for fragrance

✓ Clingers for concrete

BOSTON IVY SCALING A WALL

Keep it up

MOST VINES HAVE no way to defy gravity and need some type of support system. For some of the lighter annuals, such as black-eyed Susan vines (Thunbergia alata) or morning glories (Ipomoea), a length of string fastened here and there to the nearest support will suffice. For others with a thicker stem, you'll need a heartier support, such as crisscrossed wires, a fence, latticework, trellis, arbor, or pergola.

Support systems

Gardeners who happen to be handy can construct all types of support systems. If you're only marginally handy, you can buy arches and pergolas in kit form that you simply put together. Or you can just have the supports you like delivered and set up for you.

I've tried to be creative in using different types of supports for different plants. I've placed chicken wire along my fences to hold up tendril-climbing vines, used bamboo and metal uprights to guide smaller twining vines in the proper path, and put up Y-shaped trellises to display others.

■ **A pergola** *makes an ideal focal point. There are many different styles to suit every yard, from simple to elaborate, rustic to ornamental.*

It's my goal eventually to have an archway between one section of the garden and another, either to display a fragrant climbing vine or to try again – hopefully with more success – for sweet seedless grapes.

I used to worry about how to support a U-shaped arch without having to dig a trench and set posts inside concrete. Then I saw a garden where the innovative person used two large, deep, steel buckets just set on top of the ground, one for each side of the archway. She set the bottoms of the archway into the buckets, and then filled each almost to the top with sand. They appeared to make a quite solid base for a large clematis. You could paint the buckets to make them more attractive.

Get a grip

HAVE YOU EVER WONDERED how vines cling and climb? Well, there's more than one technique that they use to scramble over just about anything they come across. A simple overview of the various climbing mechanisms follows.

Tendril grabbers

Tendril grabbers, such as grape vines (*Vitis*) and passionflowers (*Passiflora*), reach out to hold onto vertical or horizontal support items, including tree branches, adjacent plants, and latticework. These spiral tendrils are flexible, so when the wind blows, the vine just shifts with the action. The tendrils may also be quite difficult to dislodge. I find it easier to cut them with pruners than to try to pull them off.

TENDRIL GRABBERS

Disk attachments

Sort of like the disks on an octopus' tentacles, these small, circular plant disks are at the end of a tendril reaching out for support. The disks attach themselves to the support with a quite sticky substance. To remove, I've always had to yank the vine off; the little disks stay there as reminders to be careful of what I plant.

There are also vines that don't have a holding mechanism, and need your help. I put screw-in cup hooks into my grape stake fence and attach those vines with green yarn or wire, depending on the vine heft. There are masonry hooks for brick walls, and special ties available at garden centers.

DISK ATTACHMENTS

Holdfast rootlets

Also called clinging aerial rootlets, holdfast rootlets are minuscule roots along either side of a plant's stem. These grab onto any type of roughened surface, including concrete. The rootlets don't feed on the holding material – it is almost like they staple themselves into it. They can pull siding off a house, so use only on brick, concrete, or stone walls, if you must. English ivy (*Hedera helix*), trumpet vines (*Campis*), and wintercreeper (*Euonymus fortunei*) are examples of plants that adhere and climb using holdfast rootlets.

HOLDFAST ROOTLETS

Twiners

Morning glories (*Ipomoea*), clematis (*Clematis*), and wisteria (*Wisteria*) are among the twiners. Twiners wrap themselves around a support, which can be anything that can be wrapped around, including the plant's own stem.

TWINERS

ESPALIERS – FUN FOR VINE LOVERS

INTERNET

ext.msstate.edu/pubs/
pub456.htm

The Mississippi State University Extension Service offers advice on espaliers, including suggested plants for espalier use, planting tips, espalier patterns, how to support espaliers, and training methodology.

You may, from time to time, hear the fancy word "espalier." This is a French word that derives from the Italian *spalliera*, which means something to rest your shoulder on, or from *spalla*, which means against. At one time, it meant a framework for the plant to lean against. Today it refers to plants that have been trained to stand flat against a wall or other vertical site, generally affixed to a trellis.

Espaliers are often trimmed into lovely designs, from informal, such as a fountain shape, to intricate, such as a diamond pattern. Fruit trees were among the earliest to be espaliered for the purpose of catching reflected sun off a wall. Newcomers often begin by working with pyracantha.

If you're interested in this avocation, there's a lot of advice available in books and on the Internet. As with all other plant projects, make certain you know the growth habit and ultimate size of the plant you are planning to espalier.

Annual vines

ANNUAL VINES ARE A FINE WAY to find out whether you want a vine in a particular spot, and if so, what type of vine you want. They are also useful if you are in a rental property and don't want to put too much energy into a perennial vine, but still want fence cover or patio ornamentation. You may see some vines here that are perennials where you live, but in most climates they're treated as an annual.

Do be aware that most annual vines do not transplant well, so put them where they are to grow. Put in their support system, be it trellis, arbor, or strings along a fence, at the same time that you plant them.

Black-eyed Susan vine

Plant seeds for this vine in early spring, once the chance of frost has passed. This fast-growing vine is also called clockvine, and black-eyed clockvine. It does well in full sun or semi-shade, but needs moist, well-drained soil. If given a satisfactory site, it will reach 5 to 8 feet, hanging onto a trellis or other support by twining stems. Its funnel-shaped flowers are bright yellow or orange with dark centers. Easy to grow, black-eyed Susan vines (*Thunbergia alata*) do well in hanging baskets. If you have a sunny windowsill indoors, try it in hanging baskets there, too.

BLACK-EYED SUSAN VINE
(*Thunbergia alata*)

Morning glory

Morning glory (*Ipomoea tricolor*) seeds are available at any garden center and most seed racks in supermarkets. Soak the large, round seeds for a few hours in warm water to speed germination. The flowers are up to 3 inches across, and colors are plentiful, including shades of pink, blue, red, and white, as well as striped varieties. In the spring, plant morning glories in average soil. Over-rich soil will give you lots of heart-shaped green leaves but limited flowers. Give these plants full sun.

Vines reach 10 to 20 feet, wrapping around a support mechanism as they grow. Give them a trellis or multi-branched tree to hold onto. Morning glories, true to their name, have showy flowers during the day that close in the afternoon. For variety, try the night-blooming morning glory called the moonflower (*Ipomoea alba*), which has a white flower. Moonflowers have a pleasant, light perfume that attracts night-flying moths.

■ **The scarlet runner bean** (*Phaseolus coccineus*) *climbs quickly to smother a tripod.*

Scarlet runner bean

If you have a small, open area with good air circulation and full sun, but not much wind, this is a great temporary cover. Quite hardy if you water it regularly, scarlet runner bean (*Phaseolus coccineus*) climbs quickly to 12 feet via tendrils equipped with tiny suction disks. It is perennial in some areas, but it has always died back at summer's close for me. Medium red, pea-shaped flowers are profuse in small drooping clusters. In addition to full sun, this vine needs rich, moist, well-drained soil.

After the flowers have come and gone, long, dark green pods will appear, and some people eat the beans within. The bean-sized seeds are fun for children to plant, as something usually grows even in less-than-ideal conditions. Pink- and white-flowered varieties might be available, but they are harder to find. Be aware that some people call this vine fire bean, and it may be labeled this way where you shop.

Sweet pea

A native of Italy, this annual vine climbs by tendrils to reach about 6 feet in height. Sweet peas (*Lathyrus odoratus*) look great as a long temporary hedge. Put up a lengthy but short wire trellis and let them meander along it. Sweet pea vines do need some fussing. Start out with very rich, organic soil in a well-drained site. For best results, sow them indoors in peat pots and then move them outside. Their preferred growing area has a good deal of sun, but if you live in a warm climate zone, they will need shade in the afternoon. The soil for sweet peas must be kept moist at all times. There are now bush varieties of sweet peas as well as vines. The bushes grow to up to 2 feet high. Butterfly-shaped flowers, some with fragrance, appear in spring or summer, depending on the variety.

Some people have phenomenal luck with sweet peas, which seem to thrive if their owners just smile at them. Then there are others who, despite servitude, can't get them to survive at all. But it's worth a try because the flowers are so sweet smelling.

More annual vines:

- Balloon vines (*Cardiospermum halicacabum*)
- Cup-and-saucer vines (*Cobaea scandens*)
- Nasturtium (*Tropaeolum majus*)

Trivia...

The original sweet pea was a Sicilian wildflower, which was discovered by a Franciscan monk. Father Cupani sent seeds to England in the early 1700s. At the time, sweet peas, while fragrant, were quite plain. But gardeners began making improvements, particularly the gardener to Earl Spencer of Althorp Park, who developed a wavy-flowered variety. It was named Countess Spencer. If the name seems familiar, think of Princess Diana, a relative.

Flowering fence covers

ALMOST ALL VINES will cover a fence. Some are fairly delicate covers, others cover the fence and all the neighboring property. Before installing a fence-cover vine, read on to discover some exceptional choices.

Bougainvillea

For a tropical look and brilliant color, evergreen bougainvillea (*Bougainvillea*) is a standard in gardens, whether as a fence cover, wall curtain, porch cover, or arbor decoration. Vines grow from 25 to 40 feet, and they have hearty thorns, so keep that in mind. Colors include scarlet, various reds, salmon, gold, purples, and off-white. The flowers, which are truthfully rather plain, are provided courtesy of bracts. And if you don't have a fence to cover, there are shrubby bougainvilleas available, too.

Bougainvilleas are really touchy about being removed from their container. Do so very carefully, with as much of the root ball preserved as possible.

You'll have to give this weighty vine some strong support. I've anchored mine to the fence, and at times to a securely sited, tall trellis. Bougainvillea needs a rich, organic soil for maximum growth, but it will do well in any well-drained soil. It is not a heavy water user after it matures. Full sun is best in most climates, but if you live in a really hot, dry area, you should site it with some afternoon shade. To save you the trauma I experienced, realize that anything longer than a few days of frost is going to eliminate many bougainvilleas, even big ones that have been in the family next to forever.

BOUGAINVILLEA
(*Bougainvillea glabra*)

Clematis

Much gentler-growing than the bougainvillea, most varieties of clematis (*Clematis*) reach only 8 to 12 feet tall. The roots should be well spread out in rich, moist soil with super drainage. It's a good idea to place mulch over the entire root area. Fertilize clematis monthly during the growing season. There is a great deal of diversity among clematis. Some varieties want more sun than others, so it is always sensible to research the needs of the type you choose. If you haven't, the general rule is tops in the sun, roots in the shade.

Another issue is the general climate favored by particular clematis plants. For example, sweet autumn clematis (*C. terniflora*), which has white, star-shaped flowers and a lovely fragrance, does well at the seashore.

Clematis flowers, which can be up to 10 inches wide, are quite lovely. Colors include purple, white, lilac, pink, blue, and some multicolored varieties. While most appear in mid-summer, some will re-bloom in early fall. Because the varied types bloom at different times, if you want continuing flowers from late spring until late fall, select accordingly.

Clematis does not have a strong self-support system. When you first plant it, include a tall bamboo stake or similar support, tying it with gardener's string. These vines cling to objects by twining around them, so you must provide a trellis, or even netting along a wall or fence. Lean the stake towards the trellis to encourage the direction of growth. The plant's ultimate size will depend on which variety you purchase. *C. jackmanii*, one of the easiest to grow, can reach 10 feet in one spring-to-summer season, and often grows to 15 feet. Others grow as high as 25 feet.

■ **A vigorous climber,** *this clematis* (Clematis viticella 'Etoile Violette') *will clamber up to 12 feet high and cover an area 5 feet wide with masses of violet-purple flowers.*

While most varieties of clematis are deciduous, which means you won't have that privacy screen or fence cover throughout the year, a few are evergreen. If evergreen interests you, look for *C. armandii*, a fast-growing vine with white fragrant flowers.

As a rule, clematis does extremely well in containers if you meet the soil, water, and light requirements.

Honeysuckle

There are several honeysuckles (*Lonicera*) available, some more controllable than others. The most aggressive is the semi-evergreen Hall's honeysuckle, a variety of *L. japonica*. You'll have to work at keeping this rapidly growing vine on the fence or trellis and off the ground, where it may root at its leisure, creating an extemporaneous ground cover. If you want a honeysuckle that quickly covers a wide expanse, this could be just what you are seeking. Hall's honeysuckle has light yellow, very fragrant flowers in June and intermittently until frost.

Trivia...
An old-time European and American custom was honeysuckle sipping. If the base of the flower is removed, there is a teensy drop of nectar within.

TRUMPET HONEYSUCKLE
(Lonicera sempervirens)

For less haste, trumpet honeysuckle (*L. sempervirens*) will reach 50 feet, climbing by twining stems. Its tubular flowers have yellow interiors and scarlet exteriors. They are very pretty indeed. The flowers are followed by short-lived orange berries. A shorter honeysuckle, just to 15 feet, is Henry honeysuckle (*L. henryi*). This vine works nicely on a small trellis or on a fence section. An evergreen in mild climates, Henry honeysuckle is deciduous where winters are very cold. This vine has pretty, but not striking, purple-red flowers and long-lasting clusters of blue-black berries that are adored by birds.

Honeysuckle will grow in fairly good soil, shade or sun. If you want prolific flowers, however, you should plant honeysuckle in a sunny area. Regular watering is needed, at least to get it started, but soggy conditions will not be tolerated.

Wisteria

Most often with violet-blue flowers, this prolifically flowering, deciduous vine draws tourists to older homes where it covers the walls and sometimes the roof. On average, wisteria (*Wisteria*) will grow to 30 feet tall. The flower clusters are quite conspicuously displayed because they may appear before new leaves develop in spring. Japanese wisteria (*W. floribunda*), with drooping flower clusters up to 12 inches long, has a spicy scent. It is tolerant of both seaside and city conditions. Chinese wisteria (*W. sinensis*) has blue-violet, white, or pink drooping flower clusters, often reaching 13 inches in length. Following the flowers are long, green, bean-like seedpods that last through the winter. Pests seldom bother this hardy vine.

JAPANESE WISTERIA (*Wisteria floribunda*)

Although slow to get started, wisterias eventually demand a large growing space. If you don't provide it, you will be forever pruning. Fortunately, pruning, even rather dramatically, doesn't seem to bother wisteria. Wisterias also need solid support. This is a heavy vine. Give your wisteria well-drained, average soil.

Vines for fragrance

IF YOU TRAIN a fragrant vine over an arbor or pergola, your reward will be a fabulous scented tunnel to walk through or sit under. A long pergola smothered in wisteria can be a heady experience, and it looks stunning, too. Another idea is to train a fragrant vine around your front door; this provides a wonderfully welcoming entrance to your home.

Chilean jasmine

In early summer, white or rich pink trumpet-shaped flowers bloom profusely on this deciduous, woody, twining vine. There may be a second flower display in early fall. The fragrance of these flowers has been compared to that of gardenias. Many gardeners like to place Chilean jasmine (*Mandevilla laxa*) in hanging baskets. Another option is trying it indoors, although flowering will be much lighter.

Chilean jasmine is often purchased in containers, but you can try growing this vine from seed, or even from stem cuttings rooted in a sterile medium, such as vermiculite. Eventually it will grow to about 15 feet.

Easter lily vine

Also called Herald's trumpet, the fragrant 3-to-5-inch-long trumpet-shaped white flowers do resemble Easter lilies. Flowers appear from spring through summer on this enthusiastically growing evergreen vine. This plant may twine up to 30 feet high and equally wide. Among other places, it will do well around swimming pools, providing an authentic tropical appearance. Give this plant good soil, ample water and fertilizer, full sun, and a strong support system. Prune Easter lily vines (*Beaumontia grandiflora*) back after flowering has ended. Should it be apparently frost killed, don't despair. It just may return from the roots.

EASTER LILY VINE (*Beaumontia grandiflora*)

Poet's jasmine

Also called common jasmine, poet's jasmine (*Jasminum officinale*) will surround you with scent from its small white flowers. These very fragrant flowers will bloom from early summer until fall. As a deciduous vine, poet's jasmine will reach 30 feet, but you can also grow it as a mounding shrub, placing it near a window or patio door. Another option, should you not have room for the lengthier version, is to look for Spanish jasmine (*J. grandiflorum*), which only reaches about 10 to 20 feet, or African jasmine (*J. multipartitum*), which is a 3-foot-high shrub. All jasmines need full sun to partial shade and good, well-drained soil.

POET'S JASMINE (*Jasminum officinale*)

Star jasmine

Also called confederate jasmine, the white, clustered flowers of star jasmine (*Trachelospermum jasminoides*) have a fragrance that envelops gardens throughout the world (in addition to its star status in the perfume industry). Eventually, this pleasantly growing vine will reach 10 to 25 feet, starting slowly at first and then picking up the pace. Purple flower buds precede the flowers in early summer. You can also use star jasmine as a ground cover. Put it near a sitting porch, since the fragrance is appreciated best on warm quiet evenings. Give regular water, good soil, and mostly full sun.

STAR JASMINE
(*Trachelospermum jasminoides*)

Vanilla trumpet vine

The vanilla trumpet vine (*Distictis laxiflora*) has 3-inch-long, vanilla-scented, trumpet-like flowers that appear in warm weather, sometimes almost throughout the year. This tendril-climbing vine isn't found in many garden centers, but due to its evergreen status and long blooming period, it is worth looking for. It grows in partial shade or full sun, and requires regular watering. There are "trumpet vines" found in other genera, such as *Campsis radicans*, so you really have to check for the Latin name on the label to get the one you want.

More fragrant vines:

- Carolina jessamine
  (*Gelsemium sempervirens*)
- Climbing hydrangea
  (*Hydrangea petiolaris*)
- Evergreen clematis (*Clematis*)
- Fiveleaf akebia (*Akebia quinata*)
- Honeysuckle (*Lonicera*)

- Madagascar jasmine
  (*Stephanotis floribunda*)
- Moonflower (*Ipomoea alba*)
- Sweet autumn clematis
  (*Clematis terniflora*)
- Wisteria (*Wisteria*)

Clingers for concrete

IF YOU WANT TO COVER CONCRETE and keep it hidden forever, you can install one of the following vines. They attach by adhesive disks or holdfast rootlets to upright surfaces, including concrete, stone, wood, brick, and the like. However, there are potential problems with these plants to be aware of before you start. These vines can envelop a multi-story building. Attractive over a small front wall or tool shed, they are a pain if they lodge into your roof. It's one thing to prune a low vine and another to climb on a ladder and prune a second story.

There's always the temptation to purchase something that grows quickly, but keep in mind that this attribute can be a liability as well as an asset.

Creeping fig

Creeping fig (*Ficus pumila*) is a clever little houseplant if you want to drape a window with tiny heart-shaped leaves that just grow and grow and grow. Plant it outdoors and those tiny leaves eventually grow to 4 inches in length. This vine does well in sun or shade, and needs watering only until it gets started.

Creeping fig will attach to just about anything, including metal. There appears to be no limit to how big this vine will get, both in terms of width and length. You must keep cutting it back, or it will cover a four-story building, windows included.

Be careful, because creeping fig roots are invasive. I don't recommend it for ordinary garden use.

Climbing hydrangea

Of all the climbers, climbing hydrangea (*Hydrangea petiolaris*) is one of the prettiest. It attaches to vertical surfaces by holdfast rootlets, reaching an eventual 50 feet by 50 feet. Clusters of small white flowers appear in summer. As with most hydrangeas, this deciduous vine needs rich soil, ample water, and some afternoon sun protection.

Cross vine

Climbing rapidly to 30 feet using adhesive disks and tendrils, cross vine (*Bignonia capreolata*) is planted by some people to cover unsightly poles. In a comfortable site, it can also reach 60 feet, covering trees and fences. Unlike some of the other clingers, it doesn't become overly thick. Cross vine's glossy dark green leaves turn purplish in winter. Although an evergreen in most area, the leaves will drop off in very cold climates. In summer, clustered, small, trumpet-shaped, reddish-brown or apricot flowers appear, followed by pod-like fruit.

■ **The climbing hydrangea** (H. petiolaris) *is one of the most attractive plants for covering a fence or wall. Once established, it grows quite quickly.*

Ivy

There are many kinds of ivy (*Hedera*). Some are used as pretty and tidy container plants, others as topiary, and still others as thick, ever-spreading, 18-inch-high ground cover useful for soil erosion control. On walls and other upright surfaces, some ivies, such as Boston ivy (*Parthenocissus tricuspidata*), will climb using adhesive disks. Others, such as English ivy (*Hedera helix*), will climb by means of holdfast rootlets. The Boston ivy, which prefers a semi-shady or shady spot, has striking fall colors that make it a popular choice; once the leaves have fallen, however, your wall or fence is no longer covered.

Climbing English ivy will reach heights up to 90 feet. A variety, climbing Baltic ivy, will attain 50 feet, and climbing Algerian ivy (*H. canariensis*) will grow to 75 feet.

Once in place, vigorous ivies such as English ivy can be difficult to eradicate, both for you and any affected neighbors.

I admit to a bias, having spent years trying to eradicate English ivy from an adjacent lot that kept crawling through my fence and trying to take root in my garden. Thick ivy is also a snail haven and a rodent hideaway. It will smother small plants and take over trees. However, those that are not thick – and that is most varieties – can be quite satisfactory. There are advocates whose entire gardens are created around yellow, white, green, or variegated ivy. Just study up on the eventual impact of your choice.

ENGLISH IVY (*Hedera helix*)

Most ivies are easy to grow in average garden soil. They do well in full sun if the weather doesn't get overly hot. Otherwise they should be kept in partial shade. Regular watering is necessary, at least until the vine gets a head start. Trim ivy as necessary to shape. For ground covers, light mowing may be possible if done with great care, or use hedge shears. Each variety has its own tolerance of cold, so once again, it's important to look into the needs of the type you like.

WINTERCREEPER (*Euonymus fortunei*)

Wintercreeper

An evergreen vine, wintercreeper (*Euonymus fortunei*) will creep or crawl up a wall by holdfast rootlets. Depending on the variety, wintercreeper may climb as high as 40 feet, or may grow only to 3 feet. To establish on a wall, spray the wall with a garden hose from time to time, especially during warm weather. By dampening the wall, you help the rootlets cling. Plan on pruning. Wintercreeper does best in shade or a semi-shady spot.

Wintercreeper has dark glossy leaves, and there is a variegated form with a creamy white leaf margin. Inconspicuous greenish-white flowers appear in summer. Pinkish berry-like fruits may follow, which later open to reveal orange seeds that are well liked by birds. Wintercreeper can also be grown as a shrub, but keep an eye out for trailing branches that just may root hither and yon. It is useful for erosion control, so you might try wintercreeper as a ground cover.

A simple summary

✔ Vines serve to enhance the beauty of vertical surfaces and to cover those that are less attractive. A vine-covered arbor is a pretty addition to almost any garden.

✔ Vines' climbing mechanisms include twiners, tendril grabbers, holdfast rootlets, and disk attachments. Most vines need some type of strong external support on which to grow.

✔ There are annual vines, which must be re-planted each year. Many self-seed, and others have large seeds that are fun for children to plant and grow.

✔ Some vines are perennial, but aren't too hardy in many regions, so they are grown as annuals.

✔ Fragrant vines add a touch of scented luxury to a pergola or transform an arch.

✔ Vine growth varies widely. While some vines are gentle, others are rampant and will cover the side of a garage or even an entire house in no time at all.

PART FOUR

SWEET BASIL, READY FOR PICKING

EXPLORING EDIBLES

THERE'S ABSOLUTELY NOTHING in the garden gourmet world more delightful than eating a fruit or a vegetable you have nurtured yourself. If you can pick it off the tree and crunch into it while basking in the summer warmth, you may feel as if the whole world is yours at that moment.

Visions of vegetables, fruit trees, and berries may make you think of the farm. But there's no need for acres of land. Smaller versions of just about everything have been created by hybridizers. Tomatoes indoors and on patios, 5-foot-high dwarf fruit trees, tiny carrots, and berries that grow on 2-foot-high bushes are just a small part of your decorative yet edible garden. Tuck in a few home-grown herbs here and there, and you send out an invitation to pollinators, butterflies, and birds. Best of all, you can also season the delicacies you *create* with your home-grown produce.

Chapter 12

Volumes of Veggies

YOU REALLY DON'T NEED a green thumb to have a successful vegetable garden. What you do need is a simple understanding of how to arrange your vegetable plants and the fundamentals of planting and maintaining your little crops.

In this chapter...

✓ Shopping for veggies

✓ Arranging the vegetable garden

✓ Terrific tomatoes

✓ Carrots for crunching

✓ Please pass the peas

✓ Perfect peppers

✓ Great pumpkins

Shopping for veggies

GOOD ADVICE ON *where and how to shop for your garden vegetables essentially applies to all of your plants. I've chosen to elaborate on catalog shopping in this chapter because so many people use catalogs, and rely on catalog descriptions, to purchase their garden edibles.*

If you do decide to shop at a garden center or nursery, be sure to buy bare-root plants and bulbs early in the season – that is, when they first appear at the retailer.

■ **Home-grown vegetables** *are rewarding to grow and they always seem to taste so much better than their store-bought counterparts.*

Do not buy vegetable plants with veggies already on them, as they don't transplant well.

Winter reading

In winter, the catalog companies get busy. There is nothing more cheering during a miserable, cold, wet winter than looking through catalogs just bursting with plants that will make your garden resemble Eden. Most catalogs offer seeds, but there are some that offer plants already growing in small or medium-size containers.

I do not wish to think about all the plants I have ordered that are totally unsuitable for my little suburban mild-winter space. But I love catalogs, have a jillion of them, and still order regularly. On occasion I even try to be sensible. But this is a challenge, as I do love greenery, especially greenery that claims to flower fragrantly, or attract birds, butterflies, and beneficial insects, or give me a fruit or a vegetable I can eat.

Decoding descriptions

I am also particularly attracted to the word "easy," which seems to have various meanings, depending on the author of the catalog text. Some of the descriptive phrases you'll find in lovely catalogs include:

a **Does well in most areas, or adaptable:** *This means the plant will grow in most climates, but not in areas where winter temperatures are sub-zero and not always in areas where the summers get hot and humid. If the plant tolerates warm and sticky conditions, the catalog will say so directly, as this is a prime selling point.*

b **Requires winter protection in cold, frost, etc. areas:** *In cold climates you must either bring it under shelter or cover it with something that conserves heat.*

c **Disease tolerant/disease resistant:** *The word "tolerant" means the plant may get the disease but the disease doesn't bother it very much. The word "resistant" means the plant usually doesn't get the disease. Diseases you may see mentioned are anthracnose, aster yellows, blight (many types), downy mildew, fireblight, fusarium wilt, leaf spot (many types), mosaic virus, peach leaf curl, powdery mildew, red stele, root rot, rust, scab, tobacco mosaic virus, and verticillium wilt. In Chapter 21 you'll get more information on some of the more common plant diseases. There are books and Internet sites that deal entirely with plant diseases. I seldom worry about these plant problems, but do try to purchase disease-resistant plants, especially vegetables and fruit trees.*

d **Hybrid:** *A mixture of two usually well-known proven plants of the same type that have been combined to obtain their best qualities, such as one with large fruit and one that is vigorous. Hybridization is an art form done by specialists, but you can try it in your garden too.*

e **Cool-season plants:** *Plants that thrive in cool weather, such as asparagus, beets, broad beans, broccoli, cabbage, carrots, cauliflower, celery, chive, leek, lettuce, onions, peas, radishes, roquette, and spinach. Plant cool-season crops as early in the spring as the soil will allow. Most cool-season crops have matured by May.*

f **Warm-season plants:** *Plants that do well in warm weather, such as lima and green beans, corn, cucumbers, eggplant, melons, peanuts, peppers, pumpkin, squash, and tomatoes. Warm is not the same as desert heat, for which you must seek a specific description. Warm-season crops should be planted after the last sensible frost threat has passed. Nowadays, with all the wonderful hybridization going on, you will find crops designed to cross these seasonal barriers. For example, there are now numerous tomatoes that will grow in cool weather, and broccoli that thrives in warmer weather.*

g **Short-season vegetables:** *These plants will germinate, grow, and produce quickly. Beans, beets, carrots, lettuces, and radishes are short-season plants.*

h **Long-season plants:** *Plants that take a while to grow, flower, and produce a crop. Long-season plants include corn, cucumber, eggplant, melons, pepper, and squash.*

i **Prize-winning or award-winning:** *Usually a superior variety judged against others of its kind for good growth, production, vigor, and other nice facets. Look for those designated as part of the All American Selection (AAS). They're the cream of the crop.*

Catalogs vary greatly in their descriptions of plants and it's fun to read a whole batch of catalogs before you decide on anything. You will see many of the same plants offered again and again, each with a different nuance. Names of catalog companies are provided in the Appendices (see pp. 420–1).

Arranging the vegetable garden

ONCE AGAIN, *the essential advice here is to plan ahead. For the best results, you'll need to have a good idea of what you want to plant, when you should plant it, and where you should plant it. It's really very simple!*

Design

Beginning gardeners tend to plant too much too close together. Well, it's a live-and-learn world. Just as using graph paper is helpful in designing a flower garden, it is useful in figuring out your vegetable garden. Outline the area you have available, and remember it must have plenty of sunshine. After you have decided what you are going to plant first, begin marking rows on the graph paper.

Try using the little self-paste multi-colored dots sold at stationery stores to represent veggies on your graph paper. The dots come in various sizes, which allows for great flexibility. Place the dots, color-coded, at the approximate spacing recommended for your vegetable.

Mark all your trees and large shrubs on your graph. Keep your vegetable garden as far away from them as possible, as they block sun and wide-ranging root systems are bossy about who owns soil nutrients and moisture.

Spend one day making note of how the sun travels across your garden. When you make your graph design, you want rows of vegetables that run north and south, so they get the best sun exposure. The taller vegetables should be at the rear of the garden. These include pole beans and peas, high-vined tomatoes, and corn. The shorter veggies, such as bush varieties, can be in the middle, and the little ones, such as spinach and salad greens, should be placed down front where they won't be shaded.

■ **In a cottage-style garden** *every inch of space is used in a seemingly random way. Tepees and screens support beans and peas.*

Out in the garden, don't forget to identify each row of vegetables with indelible pen on plastic labels or Popsicle sticks. Paper labels won't withstand precipitation, and are a popular snack for snails, slugs, and bugs.

Sequential crops

To make the most of your space, grow vegetables in sequence. Check the maturity date of the vegetable you want to grow on the seed packet. If it says, for example, 52 days, you've selected a short-season crop. In that case, you may want to plant a second crop of something else. Leaf lettuce and radishes may be followed by carrots, spinach followed by beets, beets followed by leaf lettuce, and the like. For long-season crops, you have to decide how much ground you want to devote to them for the duration.

As you can see, much of your planning will depend on the size of your planting area. However, since the best practice is to *rotate crops* whenever possible, you may have ample opportunity to grow a bit of everything eventually.

Double cropping

Double cropping is the practice of planting quicker growing crops among slower growers, giving a larger harvest. For example, you might plant radishes amid slower-growing carrots, rapid-growing beets among pokey broccoli, or scallion onions among cabbage.

■ **Vegetables planted** *in neat, well-organized rows make the maximum use of space and allow you easy access to each crop when it's ready to harvest.*

Placing your perennials

Perennial vegetables, such as asparagus and artichoke, can simply have a sunny corner of their own. Or, if you like, mingle them with your medium-size flowering plants that get sun and enough water. Just remember where they are, so you don't dig them up in the plants' sleeping, or dormant, season.

Companion planting

Companion planting usually refers to placing specific herbs among specific plants to deter insect pests and diseases. Examples are using garlic to ward off Japanese beetles, using mint to deter aphids, and using pot marigold to slow down the onslaught of asparagus beetles.

Companion planting may also describe plants that grow better when grown next to each other. Examples include onion and carrots, radishes and cucumbers, and basil and tomatoes. Companion planting has both its advocates and those who scoff. It certainly won't hurt to try.

Raised beds

When it comes to veggies, planting on raised beds (an elevated mound of soil) means you can plant earlier and grow later.

Do not use any type of preservative-treated wood for vegetable gardens.

■ **Nasturtiums** *can be used near a vegetable garden both for color and edible capers.*

Terrific tomatoes

PLUM TOMATO

TECHNICALLY, YES, TOMATOES (Lycopersicon *lycopersicum*) *are a fruit. But let's face it, you slice up tomatoes for the top of a salad. You don't slice them up to combine with grapes and chunks of watermelon. Everybody thinks of tomatoes as vegetables. So without further ado, let's make some sauce!*

Endless variety

You see quite a few different types of tomatoes in the supermarket, but did you know that there are at least 2,600 tomato varieties? Various types include heirloom, early-season, mid-season, late-season, beefsteak, small fruited, paste, and winter storage. Tomato shapes include accordion, egg, heart, oblong, pear, ribbed, round, and even square-round. If that isn't enough, tomatoes come in yellow, white, red, green, green with yellow stripes, gold, pink, brown-red, purple-brown, bicolor yellow/orange, bicolor red/yellow, and orange.

If you truly get into tomatoes, you can have an entire garden of native American tomatoes, Italian tomatoes, American heirloom tomatoes, or hybrid tomatoes. Ninety-five percent of home vegetable gardeners grow tomatoes. It is actually easy. It's even easier if you buy them in a little container at the nursery, but more fun if you grow them from seed. I won't say anybody can grow tomatoes, because they do take some care, but for a vegetable they are extremely cooperative.

■ **Bush tomatoes** *don't need any form of support – they simply sprawl along the ground.*

Trivia...

The original tomotl, *or tomato, is believed to have come from Peru's Andes Mountains. In the early 1600s Spanish explorers brought seeds home to Europe. In Italy, they were called* poma amoris, *or the apple of love, in France it was* pomme d'amour. *Most people, however, didn't eat them, using them as ornamental plants. The Pilgrims brought tomato seeds to North America and the tomato later found its way into most colonial gardens. Still, there was a belief that the tomato was poisonous. It wasn't until the French military, stationed in New Orleans, began using tomatoes in their daily meals that the tomato gained culinary acceptance.*

Starting tomato seeds

Begin with a few pots containing a sterile potting mix, which you can buy in little plastic containers at the garden center or supermarket. It is best not to use garden soil because the soil may carry some insect or disease that will destroy the susceptible seeds. You can place your tomato seeds in individual Styrofoam cups if you like; just make a little hole in the bottom for drainage and put the whole batch of cups in a waterproof tray. Poke a few seeds in a cup, just half an inch deep. They will germinate, or sprout, in about 1 week if they are in a reasonably warm (about 75° F) site. A sunny kitchen windowsill often is a great spot for sprouting. If the area is only about 60° F, the sprouting can take up to 2 weeks. Don't despair if you have no sunny windowsill or if yours is already filled with plants, as mine is. Try starting them under a lamp that you leave on most of the time.

Once you see the seedlings, add water so the soil stays slightly damp. You don't want the soil to be wet, as the teeny roots drown quickly. When seedlings are about 3 inches high and have a few sturdy leaves, you must give them more room to grow. You can transplant them to other Styrofoam cups or cottage cheese containers, or to something more charming, such as a 4-inch pot. Your new tomato plants need a good amount of sun at this point, so you may just have to rearrange your windowsills after all.

Into the garden

As the weather warms up, move your outdoor tomato plants into the garden. The tomato is strictly a warm-weather fruit. If you plant it outside too early and the temperature takes a sudden dip below 55° F, the emerging flower buds will fall off. Each pretty yellow bud = one tomato.

I love plucking ripe, exquisitely crunchy, teeny tomatoes growing indoors, for breakfast. Try it.

You can also continue to grow tomatoes, such as the tiny cherry tomatoes, indoors. Each plant requires a nice-size pot with a drainage hole if you tend to over-water at times. A sunny site is mandatory. Provide an occasional (but skimpy) liquid fertilization when you do your other houseplants. A tomato fertilizer is best, of course, but I find these plants are not overly selective in this respect.

Transplanting tomatoes

With plants that are to go outside, place the plant, whether home-started or nursery-raised, into a soil hole that is about 6 inches wider and deeper than the container. Soil should be composed of 50 percent good organic soil and 50 percent whatever you have naturally. Some people with only one or two raised beds use them strictly for tomatoes. These are nice people to know if you want tomato gifts.

Gently remove the transplant from its container. Tomatoes from the nursery may be somewhat root-bound, especially if you've bought them late in the season. If you can be extraordinarily gentle, separate the roots a bit so they move outward instead of curling inward. Otherwise, leave well enough alone. Place the transplant with the lowest set of leaves at soil level. Backfill the hole with good soil, and gently firm the soil down. Give your plants a nice drink of water. Start fertilizing your tomatoes when they are about 2 feet tall. Fertilize every 2 to 4 weeks with a commercial fertilizer that has a big picture of a tomato on the label and says "for tomatoes."

Of course, you can seed your tomatoes right in the garden. Poke little planting holes half an inch deep with a stick or an old screwdriver. Install two seeds per hole, and cover with very fine organic soil. Keep slightly moist until seedlings appear.

Support systems

There are those who like their tomatoes sprawling all over the ground and those who like their tomatoes growing neatly on some type of support. I am a lazy gardener, but I now support my vining tomatoes. I usually do it on plastic shoe racks, but there are a multitude of choices, from tomato cages to 3- to 5-foot stakes of anything you have around or want to buy inexpensively. Put stakes in the ground before you install your tomatoes. If you decide to do it later, you'll have to hammer the stakes through the root system. As the vines grow, tie them to your support system with strips of soft cloth – a good use for clean rags.

The goal of the support system is to keep the tomatoes off the ground, because the part that's in contact with the soil may get discolored or a bit rotten, especially as the tomato matures. In general, tomato plants should be placed about 3 feet apart, but of course, each type has its own preference.

■ **Staking tomatoes** *need to be trained, or tied to support stakes or wires as they grow, to ensure that all the fruits receive enough sunlight.*

Patio pots

Tomatoes have a long, wide root system, and if you want to grow tomatoes on your patio make sure the pot is big enough. Even the roots of cherry tomatoes can develop heartily.

The most critical care you can give all tomatoes, and patio tomatoes in particular, is to water them regularly, preferably at soil level.

Without adequate water, patio tomatoes develop leaf wilt quickly. If you notice early signs of leaf wilt, give some water and the plant will probably resuscitate without major harm. A few days of untreated leaf wilt and you'll have to go back to the nursery or supermarket. Regular under-watering causes blossoms to drop, and you'll end up with misshapen and/or undersized fruits.

Note that although tomato plants are self-fertile, each flower does need to be pollinated. If you live in a wind-free area, your patio is well enclosed, or you're growing the plants indoors, not enough pollen will naturally meander from one part of the flower to the next. Play matchmaker and brush the blossoms gently with your hand a few times.

Tomatoes of all types

It's so much fun looking through garden catalogs trying to decide which tomato to grow, from itsy-bitsy grape tomatoes to 5-pound monsters. To help you choose among the many types, the following list sets out the qualities of some delicious tomatoes.

For the small tomatoes only, I've included the number of days from seed to tomato if you start from a transplant – add 2 months if you plant from seed. The phrase "determinate" indicates a sort of stalky plant that stops bearing fruit when it reaches a determined size. The fruit of these plants tends to ripen all at the same time, which is a benefit if you do canning or preserving. All of the large tomatoes are "indeterminate," which means they continue to grow and bear fruit until frost kills the plant. Large tomato plants may need support. For our purposes, "large" means 1 pound or over.

Finally, because the high summer humidity of the south is a problem for some types of tomato, "good for south" indicates that this plant can often overcome sticky conditions.

■ **Here, tumbling bush** *tomatoes share a hanging basket with French marigolds, grown as a companion plant.*

Cherry tomatoes

These are tiny and short tomatoes, under 2 inches.

CHERRY TOMATO

- **Golden Nugget** – 50 days, determinate, dark gold, early in season.
- **Micro-Tom** – 25 days, red, 8 inches tall, can be grown in a 4-inch pot.
- **Pixie** – 50 days, dark red, grows to 18 inches.
- **Sub-Arctic Plenty** – 40 to 60 days, early in season, very cold tolerant.
- **Tiny Tim** – 60 days, good for south, red, grows to 18 inches, can be grown in a 6-inch pot.
- **Tumbler** – 50 days, red, sweet fruit, early in season.

Small vining tomatoes

- **Green Grape** – 70 days, good for south, yellow-green and sweet.
- **Juliet hybrid** – 60 days, plum-like red fruit, crack resistant, late-season, blight and leaf spot tolerant.
- **Mini-Orange** – 66 days, good for south, 1½-inch orange, tangy fruit.
- **Pink Ping Pong** – 75 days, 1½-inch pink, sweet fruit, prolific, tall.
- **Riesentraume** – 70 days, good for south, 1½-inch pear-shaped red fruit, huge flowers.
- **Sugar Snack** – 65 days, ½-inch red fruit.
- **Sun Gold** – 60 days, 1-inch dark gold fruit, early-season.
- **Sweet 100 Hybrid** – 65 days, 1-inch red fruit, vigorous.
- **Sweet Quartz** – 65 days, dark pink, vigorous, disease resistant, long fruiting.
- **Yellow Pear** – 75 days, good for south, 2-inch yellow fruit, productive.

VINE TOMATOES

Large tomatoes

- **Big Rainbow** – good for south, 2-pound golden fruit with pink and red highlights, disease resistant.
- **Brandywine** – good for south, 1-pound red fruit, tall, Amish heirloom.
- **Brimmer** – good for south, 2-pound pink/purple fruit, Virginia heirloom.
- **Bull's Heart** – 2 pounds or over, vigorous, Russian variety.
  - **Delicious** – good for south, 1- to 3-pound beefsteak variety.
    - **Giant Belgium** – 2- to 5-pound, dark pink, sweet fruit, Ohio origins.
    - **Giant Oxheart** – 2-pound, dark pink, heart-shaped fruit, vigorous, humidity tolerant.
    - **Goliath** – 3-pound red fruit, vigorous, 1880s heirloom.
    - **Lillian's Yellow Heirloom** – 1-pound, lemon yellow, citrus-like flavor, vigorous.
  - **Mortgage Lifter** – good for south, 2- to 4-pound, pinkish red fruit, disease resistant.
  - **Wins All** – 1-pound, slightly flat pink fruit, originated in 1924.

BEEFSTEAK TOMATO

Harvesting hints

Once you have eaten a home-grown tomato, supermarket tomatoes tend to taste like cardboard. Why? Because they are usually picked while green and ripened artificially. You just can't wait to pick your first tomatoes, but leave them on the plant as long as possible. Try not to tear the fruit when you pick it off. Store extra fruit at room temperature, out of direct sunlight.

■ **Yellow tomatoes** *turn a golden-yellow color when ripe.*

To maintain the fresh taste of your tomatoes, don't store them in the refrigerator.

Carrots for crunching

CARROTS *(Daucus carrota) actually grow in a variety of colors, including purple, red, yellow, white, and, of course, orange. The orange carrot originated in the 1700s, but the wild carrot, which was branched rather than conical, was around long before that and was often used as food for cattle. Now young carrots are a gourmet item in the grocery store.*

Planting carrots

Sow carrot seeds where they are to grow every 2 weeks from February through August. Those planted from July to mid-August will provide the winter harvest. The seeds may take up to 3 weeks to germinate. It is better to sow them thickly and then thin out the extras. Because the seeds are so small, mix them with some sand before sowing.

■ **Thin seedlings** *to about 1 inch apart for early carrots and at least 1½ to 2 inches apart for late carrots to give them room to develop.*

Gardeners often mix 20 percent radish to 80 percent carrot seed when sowing. The radishes mark the site of the slower-germinating carrots, and are ready long before carrots need their full space. Early carrots will be ready for picking about 3 months after they're sown; late carrots will take about 4 months.

If you want long carrots, your soil should be fine, sandy loam. If you have clay or other heavy soil, plant short carrots. The longer ones will be tough and misshapen from trying to drill their way downward. Raised beds work well for growing carrots. They may also be grown in a container, using commercial potting soil.

Here are some favorite types of carrots – they're all orange unless otherwise noted.

Short rooted carrots

Short roots are about 3 to 5 inches long. These carrots are the earliest to appear and the easiest to grow. They include:

- **Baby Spike** – grows to 3 inches, stores well.
- **Kinko** – grows to 4 inches, very early.
- **Little Finger** – dark orange, grows to 3 inches, very early.
- **Minicor** – grows to 3 inches.
- **Oxheart** – grows to 6 inches, triangular.
- **Parmex** – nearly 1 inch and round, does well in rocky or shallow soil.
- **Short 'n Sweet**
- **Sweet Treat hybrid**
- **Thumbelina** – round to oblong, 2 inches, good for heavy soil.

THUMBELINA

Midsize carrots

Medium carrots are 7 to 8 inches long. Some popular midsize carrots are:

- **Autumn King** – large roots, good for winter storage and freezing.
- **Danvers** – grows well in heavier soil.
- **Danver's Half Long** – good in heavy soils, stores well, originated in 1871.
- **Gold Pak**
- **Nantes Mexican strain** – good for hot, dry climates.
- **Red Cored Chantenay** – 2 inches wide, good for heavy soils, stores well, originated in 1829.
- **Scarlet Nantes** – orange red.
- **Sweet Sunshine** – yellow.

DANVER'S HALF LONG

Long carrots

The long carrots will grow to 10 to 12 inches. If you don't mind spending a few minutes chopping each one, look for:

- **Burpee** A#1 hybrid
- **Healthmaster**
- **Imperator**

- **Long carrots** *are best grown in light, fertile soil that is reasonably deep and free of stones.*

Maintaining your carrot crop

Carrots prefer very slightly damp ground, so remember to water them evenly. Root cracking is too often caused by soil that swings between wet and dry. Be sure to remove weeds as they emerge, making a point to differentiate between weeds and carrot leaves that look somewhat like weeds. A hint to help you along: Carrot leaves are vertical, or upright, while weed leaves tend to flop to the side. Continue to thin the plants so that the carrots intended for mature size are about 2 inches apart.

Your best defense against disease in your carrots is a good offense. In this case, be sure to buy the strongest type of plants. Look for the disease-resistance of your choice, which is noted on the package. The only insect of consequence to a carrot crop is the carrot rust fly. The young of this insect, appearing as maggots, chomp away on the carrots. There's not much to be done about this pest – just make sure you plant enough carrots and cut away any damaged parts.

Harvesting

Carrots get sweeter the closer they get to maturity, and in this case the simple taste test is best. After you remove the carrot from the ground, cut off all but about 1 inch of the greenery, as the root continues to try to supply it with nutrients. This eventually dries out the root.

Some gardeners simply leave their carrots in the ground as a means of storage. But make a point of removing them by February before they get tough, and definitely before the ground freezes. A frozen carrot will rot. Note: If you like the look of carrot flowers, leave a few. They attract pollinators.

Please pass the peas

UNTIL THE 1800s, PEAS (Pisum savitum) *were eaten dried – unless they were boiled to make pease pudding. Later, peas were cooked in the pod, and when served at the table, diners licked the peas out of the pods. Move along a bit and people began eating peas with a knife. I'm not sure how they did that, since when I tried the peas rolled off the knife. I eat mine with a fork if they are cooked, and crunch them out of the pod when fresh. It's considered lucky to find a pod with a single pea in it.*

■ **Best eaten soon after picking,** *peas are a good source of protein and fiber.*

Today, 40 percent of home gardeners grow peas. There are pea types that appear early in the season, types that appear mid-season, and others that come late. If you have enough space, try a few of each, planted at the same time for a long harvest season.

Planting peas

Where winters are cold, plant peas as early in the spring as possible. They don't mind light frosts and tolerate cold nights as chilly as 20° F. Sow a second crop from mid-July to August. If you live in an area with mild winters, plant in early spring to get a spring crop and then again in early autumn for a winter crop. If you live in the south, sow in the fall for a winter harvest. Peas are generally not heat lovers. If you plant peas in late spring or summer, and the temperature tops 80° F, they tend to grow poorly. These pea plants are likely to have wilted leaves, fallen blossoms, and tiny pods, and to develop powdery mildew problems.

Peas require full sun in a wind-free site and rich, well-drained, organic soil. Because of the good drainage they supply, raised beds are ideal for pea plants. Dig a long trench about 2 inches deep where you want to place your peas. Dwarf varieties should be 3 feet apart and don't need trellising or support systems. Tall varieties should be placed about 4 feet apart. When placing the tall pea varieties, it helps to provide some support for the tendril-climbing vine. Some type of approximately 2- to 4-inch mesh will work well.

Because peas germinate slowly, many gardeners soak the seeds overnight before planting.

SUPPORTING PEAS

Peas range from 18 inches to over 6 feet tall and all will benefit from the support of twiggy branches known as peasticks as they are growing.

1 **Push sticks into the ground**

When seedlings have developed tendrils, push peasticks into the ground, as upright as possible, along the outside of the block or row.

2 **Watch your peas climb**

As the peas grow, the tendrils are able to wrap themselves around the peasticks and clamber upward on the supports.

Varieties of peas

There are basically two kinds of pea plants. There are bush, or dwarf, pea plants and pole, or vining, peas. With bush peas, you'll need many plants to obtain a large quantity of peas. All of the pods tend to be ready at about the same time in a 2-week period. Vining peas produce from 2 to 5 times more peas than bush plants, but they do take up more room. Vining peas develop blossoms and pods over an extended period. Good types of peas for the beginning gardener follow.

Bush peas

- **Early Frosty** – grows to 28 inches with 2-inch pods.
- **Lacy Lady** – grows to 20 inches with 2-inch pods, semi-leafless, compact, good in cool and warm weather, good for small gardens.
- **Little Marvel Wrinkled Pea** – grows to 15 inches with 3-inch pods, tastes good fresh.
- **Novella** – grows to 28 inches with 3-inch pods.
- **Pioneer Shell Pea** – grows to 24 inches with 3-inch pods.
- **Sugar Ann Snap Pea** – reaches 24 inches with 2-inch pods, sweet and crisp.
- **Sugar Pod 2 Snow Pea** – grows to 30 inches with 3-inch pods.

Vine peas

- **Dwarf Grey Sugar Pod Pea** – grows to 30 inches, red or purple flowers, 3-inch pods are good for steaming, climate adaptable.
- **Extra Early Alaska** – grows to 30 inches with 2-inch pods, good plant for northern areas, smooth-skin pea.
- **Golden Sweet Edible Pod Pea** – grows to 6 feet, produces two-tone purple flowers and bright lemon-yellow pods, best eaten when small, excellent for stir fry.
- **Knight** – grows to 24 inches with 4-inch pods, disease resistant, peas are good fresh or cooked.
- **Mammoth Melting Pod Pea** – attains 6 feet with 6-inch pods.
- **Oregon Giant Snow Pea** – grows to 36 inches with 4-inch pods, white flowering, vigorous, disease resistant.
- **Sugar Snap** – grows to 6 feet with very tasty 3-inch pods, good vine for southern climates.
- **Tall Telephone Wrinkled Pea** – grows to 6 feet with 5-inch pods.
- **Thomas Laxton Wrinkled Pea** – attains 30 inches with 3-inch pods, widely adaptable, disease resistant.
- **Wando Wrinkled Pea** – grows to 30 inches with 3-inch pods, more heat tolerant than most peas and does well in southern areas, also tolerates cold and coastal weather well.

Easy pea plant care

Water your peas regularly so the ground doesn't quite dry out, but do not over-water. Peas seldom need any type of fertilizer, but adding mulch to the base of the plant will help conserve moisture. Because pea vines are quite delicate and can be broken easily, weed around them very carefully by hand.

Diseases commonly seen in pea plants include wilt, root rot, and downy mildew. Aphids, bean maggots, cucumber beetles, pea weevils, snails, and slugs are all pea pests, so keep an eye out for insects while your plants are growing.

Picking peas

Depending on when they are planted and what type they are, peas will bear pods from 2 to 4 months. The first pods will appear at the plant base. Pick these quickly to encourage the plant to form more pods. Harvest about every 2 days. Pick the pods when they are somewhat slim and about 2 to 3 inches long. As they plump up, the peas become hard and lose flavor.

Eat your harvest as quickly as possible after picking. If you must refrigerate, put the pods, in their entirety, in a plastic bag. They will last up to 1 week. Sugar and snow peas have tender, sweet pods that can be eaten pod and all when still small. Smooth peas are best for drying; wrinkled peas are best for eating fresh.

Perfect peppers

PEPPERS (Capsicum annuum, C. frutescens) *are another of America's favorite home-grown vegetables. There are so many varieties, from sweet to phenomenally hot, that you could plant an entire garden in peppers and it would look just as pretty as a flower-filled one. Peppers grow well in containers, too.*

MIXED SWEET PEPPERS

Planting peppers

Plant peppers in spring about 1 week after the last frost. The preferred temperature for sweet peppers is 70 to 75° F, for hot peppers between 70 and 85° F. Night temperatures below 60° F may cause blossoms to fall off. Each blossom represents one pepper. Because their roots don't care to be disturbed, peppers grow and fruit better if you plant them from seed. However, pepper plants are available from nurseries if you don't want to start from scratch. Just handle young plants gently and water them after placing.

Do not purchase pepper plants if they have flowers or fruit. Once the plants are at this level of maturity, they will not adjust well to transplanting. To select, look for strong stems and dark green leaves.

Peppers need full sun, reasonably good soil, and good drainage. Avoid placing them in windy areas. Indoors, start peppers in peat pots so you can place the entire plant and pot in the ground. Put about three seeds in each pot, each half an inch deep and 1 inch apart, keeping the soil slightly damp. After the seeds sprout, put the containers in a sunny window. Thin to one plant per container when the seedlings are 3 inches high. Move the plants outdoors when each is about 6 inches high and when night temperatures don't fall below 45° F. Space the plants about 2 feet apart.

Pepper particulars

There's a lot of diversity among peppers. There are even ornamental varieties, such as Varingata with its variegated leaves, purple and white blossoms, and small green and purple fruits that turn red when they mature. But assuming you plan to eat your harvest, check out the following. (Note that the sizes listed are for the pepper, not the plant.)

Sweet peppers

- **Bananarama** – 8 inches long, yellow fruit becomes orange-red.
- **Big Bertha hybrid** – 7 by 4 inches, dark green to red, great for stuffing and roasting.
- **California Wonder** – 4 by 4 inches, green to red, stuffing pepper.
- **Chocolate Beauty** – 4 inches long, chocolate color, sweet and crispy.
- **Corno di Toro** – 8 by 2 inches, curved bright red fruit, good for frying, also known as horn of the bull pepper.
- **Giant Aconcagua** – 11 inches long, light green, very sweet, good for stuffing and roasting.
- **Gold Standard** – 5 inches long, gold, good for stuffing.
- **Purple Beauty** – 4 by 3 inches, purple, spicy sweet.
- **Red Heart Pimiento** – 3 inches long, red, heart shaped, very sweet.
- **Sweet Pickle** – 2-inch ovals, yellow, orange, red, and purple fruits on the same plant, good for pickling.
- **The Godfather** – 7 inches long, green fruit becomes red, a frying pepper.

■ **Yellow peppers** *tend to have the sweetest flavor of all sweet peppers.*

Hot peppers

Note that hot peppers get even hotter as they mature.

- **Anaheim chili** – 6 inches long, green to dark red, mildly hot, good fresh, pickled, dried, or in stew.
- **Ancho** – 6 inch fruit on a bushy plant, green to red, mildly hot, good fresh or dried to make chili powder.
- **Big Chili** – 8 to 10 inches long, green to red, mildly hot.
- **Bulgarian Carrot** – looks like a carrot, very hot, good in chutneys, marinades, and salsas.
- **Caribbean Red** – 2 inches long, red, extremely hot.
- **Habañero** – 2 inches square, silvery green, short, wrinkled fruit turns orange, extremely hot.
- **Huasteco** – 2 inches long, green, moderately hot, good disease resistance.
- **Hybrid Thai Dragon** – 7 inches long, red, extremely hot, good for drying.
- **Jalapeño** – 3 inches long, dark green to dark red, hot.
- **Pimento Select** – 2-inch plump fruit, scarlet, mild and juicy.
- **Rellano Chile** – 10 by 3 inches, green, mild, good for stuffing and for chile rellano.
- **Salsa Delight** – 7 inches long, green to red, mostly mild, good disease resistance.
- **Thai Hot** – tiny, cone-shaped fruit on a very small plant, extremely hot, good as ornamental house plant if you keep it away from children and pets.

JALAPEÑO

Pepper plant care

Water your peppers regularly. Water stress causes blossoms and growing fruit to drop off, so don't let the soil totally dry out. Fertilize the plants about every 3 weeks with a vegetable fertilizer. Fertilizing is most important just as blossoms are becoming fruit.

If you plant sweet peppers too close to hot peppers, cross-pollination can occur and you may bite into a hot sweet pepper.

Diseases often found in pepper plants include tobacco mosaic virus, mildew, and bacterial leaf spot. Aphids and caterpillars are common insect pests. Peppers need good drainage, and too much rain can stunt plants. Unfortunately, there's absolutely nothing you can do about bad weather.

Picking peppers

Cut peppers off the vine with scissors or pruning shears. Most peppers will begin ripening in July and in some areas will continue until early winter. Many of the sweet and hot peppers become sweeter or hotter as they ripen. But if you leave too many on the vine, new peppers won't develop.

If your hands are sensitive, wear gloves when harvesting hot peppers.

Harvest all peppers before any frost is predicted. They cannot tolerate even a light freeze and are damaged by cold rain. Hot pepper plants can be hung upside down so that the fruit dries slowly. Fresh peppers will keep in the refrigerator for about 2 weeks.

■ **Harvest hot peppers** *once the fruits have swollen. Wash hands after harvesting. Contact with peppers can cause a burning sensation. Avoid rubbing the eyes.*

Great pumpkins

PUMPKIN (Cucurbita moschata) seeds are big and easy for children to handle. If you have a sunny spot in your yard, try one for fun. Of course, there are little pumpkins for decoration, but the best fun comes from growing the Jack o'lantern size.

Pumpkin planting

Plant pumpkin seeds outdoors in late spring. If you put them in the ground any later, the pumpkins won't be ready for Halloween. Besides, they don't do well once the weather cools off in fall, so you must plant in spring even if you just want them for pies. Absolutely any danger of frost must be past before you set seeds out, so to get a head start, you can start seeds indoors. The container must be bottomless and biodegradable, because you don't want to disturb a pumpkin plant once it gets going. Plant seeds ½ inch to 1 inch deep. They will sprout in 1 to 2 weeks.

Pumpkin soil should be as richly organic as possible. If you have a spare, sunny, raised bed, use it for your seedling or seeds. You don't need a fancy raised bed, though; you can just create a large mound and start your pumpkins there. Be sure to select a sunny site where there is some growing room. You'll need 3 feet around each plant for the smaller bush pumpkins, and up to 10 feet for the big vines. A big pumpkin vine can grow 6 inches in 1 day!

■ **Pumpkins come in** *a variety of colors and in many different sizes — tiny, medium, large, and hugely enormous!*

Pumpkin varieties

Pumpkins are available in three major categories: small, large, and huge. The more exotic pumpkin seeds are only available through catalogs. After you have tried a year or so of the standard seeds, you might try catalog shopping. Read on for a simple summary of the different pumpkins you can grow.

Small pumpkins (under 10 pounds)

- **Baby Bear** – 2 pounds, good for pies, stores well.
- **Baby Boo** – about 8 ounces, white skin, white flesh.
- **Heirloom** – up to 6 pounds, orange, 1800s American heirloom.
- **Jack Be Little** – about 8 ounces, orange.
- **Munchkin Mini** – under 1 pound, dark orange, grows on a vine.
- **Small Sugar** – about 7 pounds, orange.
- **Snack r jack** – grows to 2 pounds, orange, seeds are hulless and can be eaten fresh.
- **Spooktacular** – grows up to 4 pounds, dark orange.
- **Tan cheese** – 6 to 12 pounds, tan skin, orange flesh, hardy, productive, one of the oldest pumpkins in cultivation.
- **Wee-b-little** – up to 1 pound, orange, grows on compact vines.

Large pumpkins (10 to 25 pounds)

- **Connecticut field** – grows up to 25 pounds, bright orange, native American origin.
- **Lumina** – grows from 10 to 20 pounds, white skin with orange flesh.
- **Rouge Vif d'Etampes** – up to 25 pounds, shiny red-orange, flattened top, an old French variety reputed to be the model for Cinderella's pumpkin coach, first offered for sale in America in 1883.
- **Seminole** – about 10 pounds, deep orange, bell-shaped, good for hot, humid, disease-prone areas, grown by Seminoles in Florida in the 1500s.
- **Southern field** – up to 25 pounds, yellow-orange, flattened globe shape, cold tolerant.
- **Styrian Hulless** – up to 20 pounds, green, for food use.
- **White Hopi Jack o'lantern** – up to 10 pounds, white skin, yellow flesh.

Huge pumpkins

- **Amish Pie** – up to 80 pounds, light orange, Amish heirloom.
- **Big Max** – up to 100 pounds, orange with orange flesh.
- **Big Moon** – up to 200 pounds, orange.
- **Dill's Atlantic Giant** – up to 400 pounds (prize winners have come in at over 800 pounds!), yellow to orange fruit, good cold-weather tolerance.
- **The Great Pumpkin** – up to 100 pounds, pinkish-orange.

Maintaining your pumpkin patch

To grow really huge pumpkins, thin to one or two plants per mound and only allow one fruit to mature per vine. Remove the others when they reach grapefruit size. Always water regularly, keeping the soil very slightly moist, and do not allow the soil around your pumpkins to dry out. Use one cup of a complete vegetable fertilizer right after planting, and water it in well. Fertilize each plant again with another cup when it develops about 6 leaves.

As the pumpkins get big, you may want to put a board underneath each one to keep them off damp ground. You may also want to rotate the pumpkin so the bottom part doesn't become flat. These chores should be done gently, as traumatized pumpkins can develop rot problems.

■ **Some pumpkin varieties** *are trailing plants that can be grown very successfully on tripods. Their huge leaves and flowers make quite an impact in a vegetable garden.*

Leaf spot, mildew, wilts, and viral diseases can all produce problems in your pumpkins. You should also be on the lookout for cucumber beetles, squash bugs, and squash vine borers.

Pumpkin sex

Each pumpkin has both male and female flowers. Male flowers show up first and are more plentiful. The female flowers arrive a week later. They attach closer to the vine and have a rounded area underneath the flower. Female flowers must be fertilized for you to get a pumpkin out of the rounded area beneath the flower.

INTERNET

sadako.com/
pumpkin/growing.html

Go to this site for pumpkin-related activities, pumpkin links, pumpkin varieties, and for information on how to plant, care for, harvest, and store pumpkins.

Each flower is open for only one-half day, usually in the mornings. Then they fold shut and do not open again. Female flowers that drop off instead of beginning to form fruit were probably not pollinated.

Encourage pollinators to the area by planting insect-attracting plants near your pumpkins. Or, while wearing gloves to avoid pumpkin vine prickles, you can take a soft brush (an old make-up brush will do) and brush the male flower first, thus obtaining pollen, and then brush the center of the female flower. Doing this always gives me the giggles.

Harvesting the pumpkin crop

Harvest your pumpkins after their skins have turned their full color, which in most cases will be orange. Do not leave pumpkins in the field when the temperature drops below 50° F for a week or more. This type of chilling causes pumpkins to rot in storage. When cutting for storage, use a sharp knife and leave about 4 inches of stem attached.

■ **When pumpkins are ripe,** *cut them off the plant with as long a stalk as possible. Leave the pumpkins out in the sun for about 10 days so that the skin can dry out and harden.*

A simple summary

✔ Determine the boundaries of your vegetable growing area before you buy plants or seeds.

✔ When catalog shopping for vegetable seeds, read the descriptions carefully. If you have the time, read through several catalogs, and see how they compare before deciding to buy.

✔ Plan the layout of your vegetable garden carefully so that you maximize your harvest.

✔ Because vegetables tend to need good drainage, consider planting in raised beds.

✔ Make certain you have enough sunlight for the types of vegetables you want to grow.

Tomatoes and peppers, in particular, need plenty of warm sunshine in order to ripen.

✔ Remember to fertilize and water plants as often as necessary – given the right care and attention your vegetables should reward you with a bumper crop.

✔ You can help to protect your vegetables by placing companion plants among them, or those plants, such as herbs, that are known to deter pests and diseases.

✔ Make sure you visit your vegetables on a frequent basis. You'll want to pick them at exactly the right time to enjoy them at their best .

Chapter 13

It's the Berries

THERE ARE ONLY TWO WAYS to get really fresh berries: Either grow them yourself or buy them from a farm where they're raised. I used to fool myself into thinking those pricey berries in the little plastic containers at the supermarket were the "real thing" (despite the fact that the ones on the container's bottom were either soggy or growing mold). Then I was a lunch guest of Dr. and Mrs. Kent Brown, Sr., of Honesdale, Pennsylvania, who grew blueberries. I went down the rows picking and eating, and it was a revelation.

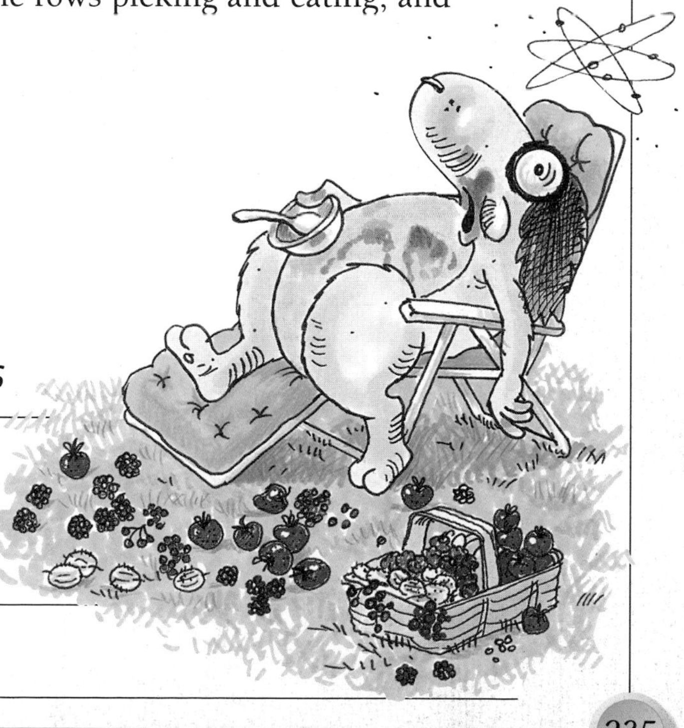

In this chapter...

✓ A bounty of blueberries

✓ Grapes galore

✓ Rolling in raspberries

✓ Succulent strawberries

A bounty of blueberries

BLUEBERRIES are native to North America. In addition to producing tasty fruit, they make wonderful decorative shrubs. Blueberries (Vaccinium) bloom in the spring. Later in the season you'll be picking the berries like mad to get them before the birds do. Some blueberry bushes even develop bright red autumn leaves.

■ **Highbush blueberries**
produce a pretty show of white flowers in the spring.

Buying blueberries

There are three major blueberry species: highbush (*Vaccinium corymbosum*), rabbiteye (*V. ashei*), and lowbush (*V. angustifolium*). Buy plants that are about 3 years old, and from 12 to 36 inches high.

Your local nursery probably stocks the type best suited for your growing site, but you'll want to verify the appropriate climate zones for your selection if ordering by catalog. Although most blueberries can be grown anyplace where the temperature does not drop below 20° F, and some can be grown where temperatures drop to -35° F, a variety's tolerance to cold will depend on other factors too, such as humidity. If you already grow azaleas or rhododendrons, both blueberry relatives, you should be able to grow one or more of the blueberry varieties.

Sites and soil

There are early-season, mid-season, and late-season blueberries. Plant some of each if you have the space, as bigger berries will result from cross-pollination. Place plants about 4 to 6 feet apart, giving even more room to varieties that grow particularly large. A sunny site is preferable, but blueberries do well in light shade too. Blueberries require ample moisture and thrive in high rainfall areas. This is because they have only fine, fibrous roots that grow in a shallow mat, and these roots are not capable of foraging for water. But soil for blueberries should still be well drained. If you have water that puddles, or soggy soil, you absolutely must plant in raised beds.

Acidic soil, with a pH of 3.5 to 4.5, is vital to enable the blueberry plant to make use of the iron and nitrogen it needs to grow. So to improve drainage and add the right amount of acid to the soil, buy a sack of peat moss, preferably sphagnum peat moss, and mix it in a nice big planting hole as follows: ¾ peat moss, ¼ the soil you have. That big planting hole is important. Blueberries don't like squashed roots. After placing your plant, tamp the soil down firmly with your foot.

Early-season blueberries

- **Blue Ray** – early- to mid-season, huge berries with sweet flavor, resists cracking, grows upright to 4 to 6 feet, spreading, cold tolerant.
- **Bluetta** – vigorous, upright, good yield, fair fruit quality.
- **Climax** – spreading to 9 feet wide, large fruit, heat and drought tolerant.
- **Collins** – medium yield, hardy, vigorous, upright, good fruit quality.
- **Duke** – mild, very cold hardy.
- **Earliblue** – hardy, upright, vigorous, fruit keeps well.
- **Misty blue** – large berries, 6 to 8 feet high, heat and drought tolerant.
- **Northland** – very hardy in cold climate zones, low and spreading.
- **Premier** – early- to mid-season, upright to 9 feet, large sweet berries, heat and drought tolerant.
- **Sharpblue** – upright to 6 feet, heat and drought tolerant.

BLUETTA BLUEBERRIES

Mid-season blueberries

- **Berkeley** – hardy, vigorous, productive, upright, sweet large berries, a good choice for northern California.
- **Bluecrop** – tart, good for cooking, hardy, vigorous, productive, upright, drought resistant, high frost resistance.
- **Bluehaven** – moderately hardy, tall.
- **Bluejay** – medium yield, large fruit of good quality, resistant to mummy berry (disease that causes berries to harden and shrivel).
- **Collins** – hardy, vigorous, upright, large sweet fruit.
- **Jersey** – mid-season to late, large spreading bush, scarlet autumn leaves.
- **North blue** – bushy, grows to 2 feet tall, large tart fruit, bright red fall color, cold hardy to -35° F.
- **North country** – bushy, grows to 2 feet high, wild berry flavor, cold hardy to -35° F.
- **Stanley** – hardy, vigorous, upright.

Late-season blueberries

- **Coville** – moderately hardy, 4 to 6 feet tall, slightly tart flavor.
- **Elliott** – hardy, vigorous, 5 to 6 feet tall, some mummy berry resistance.
- **Friendship** – grows to about 2 feet tall, flavorful fruit, cold hardy to -35° F.
- **Herbert** – compact, hardy, vigorous, productive, excellent fruit quality.
- **Jersey** – vigorous, spreading, large fruit, especially good for West Coast.

INTERNET

ohioline.ag.
ohio-state.edu

For information on growing blueberries in the home garden, see the Ohio State University Extension Fact Sheet on blueberries. It includes local selections.

Maintaining your blueberry crop

Do not dig around blueberry roots, because they are shallow and easily damaged. During the first year, don't fertilize your blueberries. After that, you can add any commercial fertilizer recommended for azaleas or camellias. A mulch helps protect your plants, as well as conserve moisture. Layer about 6 inches of peat moss over the root area and replenish the mulch as necessary.

Because manure is alkaline in nature, never use it as fertilizer, backfill, or mulch for blueberry plants.

You'll want to give your blueberry plants plenty of freedom. Avoid pruning them during the first three years. After that, using pruning shears, you can cut back weak twigs and old canes. Keep in mind that flower buds develop near the branch tips, so if you remove these you are essentially removing the berries. If you don't prune, the world won't end. The berries will just be smaller.

Harvesting your blueberries

You must cover your blueberry bushes with netting, or you won't have any berries to harvest. Protective netting is available at most garden centers and nurseries. Without it, bird and people tasters will pick them all.

Pick your berries when they've attained a good size and color. Many people prefer to taste before picking to determine sweetness, and this method is recommended – as long as you don't eat all of them in the process. Save some of your berries for pies and muffins and to put on ice cream. Although blueberries can be kept in the refrigerator for two days, it is best to eat them right away or freeze them in a container. A cupful of blueberries has only 87 calories.

> ### Trivia...
> There are also blueberries that can be grown in containers and small places, such as Top Hat and the Northblue blueberries that reach only 2 by 2 feet. They have white flowers in spring and full-size fruit. Look for Northblue plants in catalogs.

WINTER PRUNING

You can stimulate an older blueberry bush to produce more fruit by getting rid of some of the oldest wood each year. Cut mature, non-fruiting branches to ground level to encourage the plant to grow new shoots, and cut weak shoots back so that strong new ones can take over.

Grapes galore

GRAPES *were probably one of the first fruits cultivated by humans. It's believed that grapes (Vitis) were initially grown as food, and that growing them to make wine came later. Most students of the grape believe that winemaking resulted from the unintentional fermentation of some edible grapes. It was a popular discovery. Art on ancient Egyptian tomb walls depicts wine being made in a process not unlike the method used today. So things have not really changed much.*

■ **Grapes need** *plenty of sunshine to help the fruits develop.*

Wild grapes are native to the United States. When the Norsemen visited the northeastern shores of what later became known as North America, they called the new land Vinland because of the multitude of wild grapes. Grape cuttings traveled with Columbus and early Spanish explorers, supplementing those that were already established.

Choose your grapes

If you have a sunny spot in your garden, regardless of where you live, you can probably grow grapes. It is important to know what you are planting, especially if you have a small garden and you only have room for one or two vines. I nurtured a grape vine for 2 years — about the time it took for it to produce grapes — only to find out they were wine grapes and I wanted eating grapes.

In this book I'll only discuss what's known as table grapes, the kind you eat as fruit or use to make jelly or juice.

Getting started

It is best to buy the grape type sold at your local nursery, unless you are very familiar with your climate and microclimate. Start by planting 1-year-old vines. Some experts advocate trimming the vine's roots to 6 inches long before you plant. If your winters are relatively mild, it's best to plant grapes in the winter. If your winters tend to be cold, early spring is the time to plant.

Site your vines in an area with ample sun and good air circulation. Without good air circulation, vines are prone to develop mildew. You will also need well-drained, good-quality soil. Grapes like somewhat acidic soil, with a pH of about 5.5 to 6.5. Many major vineyards are built on sloping or hilly areas. If you have a slope to plant on, this can work out well, as the slope to the land will help keep it well drained. Grape vines will develop deep root systems, so dig a big planting hole. Install the vine with the roots fully spread out and at the same soil level as they were when you bought them. After planting, put on a mulch to 3 feet all around the trunk to keep the roots cool and soil moist.

Grape varieties

There are at least 8,000 varieties of grapes, certainly enough to choose from. To help narrow the choices for the new gardener, I'll focus on three major types: American grapes (*Vitis labrusca*), Muscadine grapes (*V. rotundifolia*), and European grapes (*V. vinifera*).

American grapes

You can usually find an American grape suitable for humid and/or cold-winter areas, with a choice between early-, mid-season, and late-ripening types. Grape season is from late summer to late autumn. For beginners, the Concord is one of the easiest to grow if there is enough summer warmth. Space vines for American grapes about 8 to 10 feet apart. Some popular varieties include:

- **Catawba** – late, medium-size reddish grapes, sweet musky flavor.
- **Concord** – mid-season to late, large blue-black, sweet fruit, vigorous, more soil tolerant than most, some resistance to downy mildew but not to powdery mildew.
- **Delaware** – mid-season, small red fruit, hardy, vigorous, productive, somewhat susceptible to downy mildew.
- **Edelweiss** – pale gold, sweet grapes, cold-hardy to subzero temperatures, vigorous.
- **Golden muscat** – very late, gold, somewhat susceptible to mildew.
- **Niagara** – large white, mid-season to late, hardy, vigorous, moderately susceptible to mildew, good for arbors.
- **Reliance** – mid-season, seedless, red, excellent flavor, moderate vigor, very winter-hardy to below zero.
- **Stover** – early, white, resists Pierce's disease.

■ **Edelweiss** *is hardy in colder climes.*

Muscadine grapes

Muscadine grapes are best for the Southeast, where temperatures stay above 10° F. You will usually need to buy at least two vines: one male to act as a pollinator, and one female. Even if you buy ten female vines, you still only need one male. Muscadine vines' productivity improves with age. Individual clusters, however, are small. Space these larger-growing vines about 12 to 15 feet apart. Some favorites include:

- **Cowart** – late-season, purple-black, very sweet grapes, vigorous.
- **Fry** – mid-season, gold fruit, vigorous.
- **Higgins**—mid-season, bronze grapes, vigorous.
- **Hunt** – early, large, very sweet, black fruit.
- **Jumbo** – mid-season to late, large purple-black fruit, vigorous, productive.
- **Magnolia** – mid-season, bronze, vigorous.
- **Nesbitt** – black fruit.
- **Scuppernong** – early, large bronze, vigorous, productive.
- **Southland** – mid-season, black, vigorous.
- **Summit** – mid-season, bronze, very sweet grapes.
- **Welder** – mid-season, green, vigorous.

■ **Nesbitt** *is a muscadine grape with plump black fruit.*

European grapes

Grapes that we know as European are originally from eastern Europe and western Asia. Sometimes called California grapes, these are the commercial grapes that grow quite successfully in mild winter areas.

They have usually been *grafted* to American rootstocks to make them resistant to the attacks of phylloxera, an aphid-like insect that destroys the roots of European grapes. Space these vines about 8 to 10 feet apart. Popular European grapes include:

- **Cardinal** – early, dark red, extremely vigorous, for large sites only.
- **Emperor** – late-season, large, firm red grapes, likes lots of heat.
- **Flame seedless** – small red fruit, quite vigorous and productive.
- **Orlando seedless** – late-season, pale green, mild flavor.
- **Perlette** – early, seedless, small pale green, vigorous, productive, resistant to sunscald.
- **Red Malaga** – mid-season, berries are not flavorful.

■ **Orlando seedless** *is a late-ripener that needs lots of warmth.*

> **DEFINITION**
>
> Grafting *is the deliberate combination of two plants. To graft plants, a shoot of one plant is inserted into a slit in another plant. The latter plant is called the stock. If the shoot later becomes part of the stock, receiving nutrition from and growing along with it, the two parts are now considered one plant.*

Good grape-keeping

Water your vines regularly, as it is important to prevent drought stress. Drooping leaves are signs of thirst, so take action. After the first growth appears in the spring, put half a cup of 10-10-10 fertilizer around the base of each vine, spreading it about 15 inches outward from the trunk. Increase the amount of fertilizer each year by half a cup, and increase the distance of distribution as well. Do not feed late in the season, as this encourages growth when energy should be placed into the fruit. Never over-fertilize.

Some kind of strong support is a must for grape vines. Shape the growth of your vines by providing a support system that you feel is pleasing to look at.

Pruning the vines

> **DEFINITION**
>
> A cane is a long, slender branch that usually originates directly from a plant's roots.

Resist the urge to prune grape vines during the first growing season. After that, prune them in late winter. Pruning is important to eliminate weak *canes* and to encourage good air circulation. It also helps ensure that you get nice big grapes instead of teeny ones, and to improve fruit quality. But don't get too carried away. You need some of last year's stems to provide the current year's grapes. How can you tell the old from the new? Last year's stems (which will become this year's canes) will be about pencil size with buds a few inches apart.

There are several ways to prune grape vines. The most common method used for American grapes is called the four-arm Kniffin system, which sounds complex but isn't too difficult once you get the gist of it.

To prune using the Kniffin method, start by selecting four fairly well separated healthy canes. These will remain, so flag them with something that you can see easily. A piece of yarn will do. Near the base of these canes, find three other healthy canes. Cut these back to stubs with a few plump buds remaining on each. Now prune the canes you didn't mark with yarn about an inch from the trunk. Firmly affix the yarn-marked canes, called fruiting canes, to your trellis, arbor, or fence.

Grape pests

Pests to watch out for include aphids, grape berry moth (which causes wormy fruit), and leafhoppers.

Grape vines also have their share of diseases, such as mildew, black rot (which shrivels half-grown grapes), anthracnose (which causes sunken brown dots on the grapes), and Pierce's disease (a bacterial disease spread by feeding leafhoppers, which causes leaves to turn yellow, and then red and brown around the edges).

Harvesting grapes

Examine your grapes for a slight translucence. This is a sign that they're mature. Fully ripe grapes have the best flavor, and you should taste before you pick to ensure sweetness.

The tip of the grape has the truest ripe flavor, so just take a nibble at that part to test your harvest.

Cut your grapes off the vine with pruning shears. Muscadine grapes will fall on their own, so you can just shake them into an old sheet. Don't worry if you don't have zillions of grapes the first year. If the site and care are correct, every year will get better. It may take 5 years to get a full harvest.

Suppose you have done everything correctly and you get batches of sour grapes. Leave them for the birds, or plant a variety that's better suited to your climate zone. You can always try moving the recalcitrant vine to a warmer spot in the garden and seeing what happens.

Trivia...

Grapes got their English name from the Old French word grappe, *meaning a cluster of grapes. This word was derived from the Old High German* chrapo, *the small hook used in harvesting grapes. In the language of flowers, the grape signifies cheer, fellowship, pleasure, fruitfulness, lust, and youth.*

■ **Harvest grapes** *by cutting off a ripe bunch with 2 inches of woody stem on either side to act as a handle. This is to avoid touching the fruit and spoiling its bloom.*

Rolling in raspberries

EARLY RASPBERRIES, *mixed with honey, were used more often in Greek and Roman times to cure bloodshot eyes and skin disorders than they were as a dessert. The European raspberry, often called a brambleberry, had been brought to America by the 18th century and was soon hybridized with local species. They were not too tasty at the time, and were most often used for pies, puddings, jams, and raspberry brandy, as well as for red dye and to remove tartar from teeth. Today, garden raspberries (Rubus idaeus) are most often eaten fresh, and the hybridizers continue to achieve marvels with bigger, tastier, and firmer berries. Of all the cane berries, raspberries continue to be the hardiest.*

■ **Red raspberries** *are popular for their sweet, rich flavor.*

Most raspberries found in stores are red, and they have the richest flavor. But you can grow them in yellow, purple, and black, each with its own distinctive taste. Of the four, the black and purple varieties are the liveliest, with arching canes and side branches. As cane tips touch the ground, they have a tendency to take root. Depending on your outlook, you then either have free plants or something to yank out. Yellow and red raspberries cause less of a dilemma. The plants are upright and non-branching, with either prickly or smooth canes. These enlarge by spreading roots that develop buds. These buds grow into new canes.

Planting raspberries

Raspberries should be planted as early as possible in the spring.

If you live in a cold climate zone, select the yellow or red raspberry over the purple or black. The darker raspberries are much more suited for mild winters, so won't do well if it's chilly. If you're looking for diversity, you can order plants from catalogs, but for novices it's probably best to start off with what your local nursery is selling for your climate zone. Each raspberry plant is self-fertile, so you don't need two of each to get berries.

Water well after planting and make sure the roots don't dry out. Do not allow raspberry plant roots to come into contact with fertilizer.

PLANTING RASPBERRIES

Raspberries do best in full sun, but often will tolerate light shade. They like a rich, organic, slightly acidic soil with good drainage, but still plenty of moisture. With the hardier plants, you can probably try them in anything that doesn't get soggy. Reds tend to prefer a sandy loam, while the darker colors like heavier soil, but these tendencies are not fixed in stone.

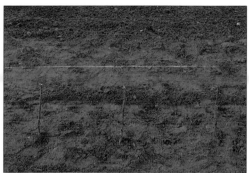

 1 Put the plants in position

Dig a trench and plant the raspberry canes about 3 feet apart. Set them about 1 inch deeper than they were in the nursery, spread out the roots carefully, and fill in the trench with soil.

 2 Trim the canes

Cut back all the newly planted canes to about 5 inches above the ground, except black raspberries, which you may cut almost to the ground. Finally, pat down the soil.

Berries are formed on second-year canes. After these canes fruit, they die back. But you don't have to worry about berry supply. New canes are forming while the older canes are fruiting. Most ever-bearers will give you two crops per year the first year you plant them, usually once in early to mid-summer and again in late summer and fall, but some produce on a continuum from spring until fall. The summer bearers usually produce bountiful crops in July.

 *Do not plant any type of home garden raspberry near wild raspberries, blackberries, eggplant, peppers, potatoes, or tomatoes, as these plants can transmit diseases, such as verticillium wilt. Long-time growers also suggest not planting red and black raspberries in the same garden due to possible disease transmission from the more tolerant red to the more susceptible black.*

SUPPORT YOUR RASPBERRIES

Your raspberry plants will generally do better if you give them something to hang onto while they are growing. One way to do it is to make a wire trellis. Place two heavy-duty, 5-foot high poles in the ground and string three sets of wires at intervals between them. If you don't like to trellis, or have a limited area, you may consider raspberries that grow upright, such as the red Heritage raspberry.

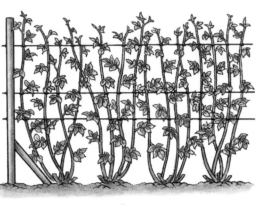

Raspberries are often categorized by their color, and so that's how I've listed my favorite types.

Black raspberries

- **Allen** – fairly disease resistant, good in northeastern and north-central states.
- **Black Hawk** – disease resistant, berries in July, does well in dry hot weather, drought tolerant, good for canning.
- **Bristol** – upright, large sweet berries, good for freezing and canning.
- **Cumberland** – a favorite since 1898, large July crop, adapts well to a variety of climates.
- **Jewell** – large berries ripening almost simultaneously.
- **John Robertson** – very hardy, cold tolerant.
- **Munger** – somewhat disease resistant, good in northwest.
- **Starking black giant** – productive, drought tolerant.

Purple raspberries

- **Clyde** – large flavorful tart berries, mid-July crop.
- **Royalty** – large tangy berries, cold hardy, productive, freeze well.
- **Sodus** – big berries, large crop, hardy, drought resistant.

INTERNET

extension.umn.edu/
distribution/horticulture/
DG108.html

Go to this site for information on raspberries for the home garden from the University of Minnesota. You'll find recommendations on local varieties, care, pruning, and diseases.

Trivia...
Some people think that black raspberries are blackberries. These people are wrong.

Red raspberries

- **Autumn Bliss** – ever-bearing, high yield, berries from early summer until fall.
- **Bababerry** – ever-bearing, very vigorous and sprawling, berries tangy, for areas with mild winters and hot summers.
- **Boyne** – cold hardy, productive, upright, dark red and fairly sweet berries.
- **Canby** – almost thornless, viral disease resistant, cold hardy, heavy yield, vigorous sprawling plants, best in northwest.
- **Fairview** – very large berries, moderately hardy, good for western Washington.
- **Fall Red** – ever-bearing, with a crop in June and one in September, heavy yield, tolerates cold to -25° F.
- **Heritage** – ever-bearing, ripening in July and September, hardy, vigorous, upright canes requiring little staking, adaptable to various areas including cold winters.
- **Latham** – very large berries in mid-July, very cold hardy, widely adapted, good East Coast variety, vigorous, disease resistant, productive.
- **Mammoth red** – thornless, huge berries ripening in late June.
- **Newburgh** – compact, good viral disease resistance, ripens in early summer, cold hardy, good in north and west.
- **New Washington** – good in coastal areas around California.
- **Nova** – upright, high yield in July, hardy, good disease resistance.
- **September red** – ever-bearing with crops in June and August, generally does well in the south.

AUTUMN BLISS

Yellow raspberries

- **Fall Gold** – ever-bearing, with a crop from July until frost, large sweet berries, upright, productive, adaptable to various areas but especially good in the northern part of country.
- **Goldie** – ever-bearing, heavy crop from July to frost.

Raising raspberries right

It's not necessary to fertilize raspberry plants, but it does help to mulch them, especially in warmer areas. Mulch keeps the soil cool and prevents root disturbance. Raspberry roots are shallow, so be careful when cultivating nearby.

Black raspberries are the most disease prone. Commonly seen are rust spots on leaf undersides, partial and full cane dieback, and spots on canes. Remove canes with leaf spot, and cut canes with partial dieback about 6 inches below the dark damaged spot. Immediately remove the entire plant if bright orange rust starts taking over or if entire canes are dead. If you want to replant, do it in a new location. Most raspberry bushes last about 7 to 10 years. You can tell they are aging by the ever smaller berries produced.

PRUNING AFTER FRUITING

Prune your raspberries each year, either when they finish fruiting or in late winter. With the yellows and reds, cut all canes that gave fruit off at their base. Thin out the new canes, leaving only the heartiest. Then cut all remaining canes to about the 6-foot level. Why do you do this? If you don't, you will have an unruly mass of raspberry bushes which may become prone to disease.

1 **Cut back**

When you have finished picking all your berries, cut back to ground level all those canes that have produced fruit.

2 **Tie in canes**

Thin out the current season's canes, keeping the healthiest, then tie these to the support wires about 4 inches apart.

3 **Loop tall canes**

At the end of the growing season, loop any tall canes over the top wire and tie them in securely.

Ever-bearing care

Ever-bearing berries need slightly different treatment. One choice is to follow the advice I just gave you, but instead of cutting the remaining strong canes at the 6-foot mark, cut them below their fruiting height. Another option is to cut the entire bush to the ground in the fall. This will prevent cold weather from killing the entire plant, and decreases disease and deer predation. By doing so, you will also eliminate the next year's summer berries, which would have developed on second year canes. Nonetheless, you still get berries the following fall as the plant re-grows. For purple and black berries, *pinch* the growing tips of new canes in summer when they are about 3 feet high.

DEFINITION

Many plants, including berries, grow fuller if you cut off the rapidly growing tips. This is known as pinching. To authentically pinch, pick off the end bud of a twig or stem with your fingers. But if you prefer to avoid getting pricked, you can use pruning shears.

Succulent strawberries

EVEN INTO HER 90S, *my mother-in-law often spoke of the wild strawberries she gathered as a child in Europe, saying their flavor was beyond delicious. Today, you can grow a cultivated "wild" strawberry, the fraises des bois, or woodland strawberry (Fragaria virginiana) in your home garden. These summer-bearing plants are petite, so you need a dozen to make a true gourmet feast for the family, but they take up so little room that it's worth the effort.*

■ **Strawberries** *can be grown in pots on a sunny patio if space in the garden is limited.*

Trivia...

In Latin, the strawberry is fragra, *meaning fragrant. From this word was derived the French, Italian, and Spanish word* fraise, *or fragrant berry, and the species name* Fragaria. *Nobody is quite sure how the word "strawberry" came into being, which it did in about 100 AD. One of the more common theories is that straw was used to mulch the plants during the winter. In England, children would pick the berries, string them on straw, and then sell them in the open markets as "straws of berries." Another common theory is that adults would string dried berries on straw and use them as decorations.*

Identifying healthy strawberry plants

Always buy strawberries from a reputable nursery or from a catalog rather than getting plants from friends. Unfortunately, strawberry plants attained through informal channels can carry disease.

Healthy dark green leaves

Even growth

Plant not yet in flower

Moist weed-free soil mix

HEALTHY STRAWBERRY PLANT

Strawberry diseases caused by a fungus include verticillium wilt, powdery mildew, leaf spot, and red stele. Verticillium wilt causes one side of the plant to wilt upward or outward from the plant's base. The leaves turn yellow, and the plant may die. Powdery mildew causes whitish powdery patches on leaves that gradually spread to the entire leaf. The leaves become distorted and may drop. Leaf spot displays as tiny spots of varying colors on the leaves. The spots gradually enlarge to form blotches, and the leaves turn yellow, die, and drop off. Red stele, a root rot, is generally considered the most damaging disease of strawberry plants. Plants with red stele will be stunted with markedly discolored leaves: blue-green, yellow, or red. The afflicted plant's leaves wilt, it produces only a few berries, and the plant eventually dies.

Viral diseases, transmitted to strawberry plants by aphids, cause distorted, yellow leaves and stunted plants. Few runners emerge and fruit, if present, is minimal.

When buying strawberry plants, look for healthy ones without any signs of disease. Also look for a plant's level of resistance, usually shown on labels as initials:

LS = resistance to leaf spot

PM = resistance to powdery mildew

RS = resistance to some types of red stele

V = resistance to virus

VW = resistance to verticillium wilt

You'll also see these initials, where appropriate, in this book's list of types of strawberries.

POWDERY MILDEW

Planting strawberries

Strawberries are usually planted in early spring, about 3 weeks before the last expected frost. If you live in an area where the winters are mild you can plant strawberries in early summer, early autumn, and during the winter, if you can find them in the stores.

Prepare the ground well before you plant strawberries, digging in lots of organic matter. Strawberries need plenty of sunlight, rich, slightly acidic soil, and lots of water.

Good drainage is absolutely critical for success with strawberries. The plants will die if the soil is too soggy.

To improve drainage, plant in raised beds about 6 inches high and 2 feet wide. Remove weeds as soon as they appear. Choose a site that is separate from any area where you have grown such plants as eggplant, pepper, potato, raspberry, or tomato. You don't want any pests or diseases from these plants to move onto your new strawberry plants. For the same reason, avoid planting strawberries in areas that were recently part of a lawn. In addition to the threat of underground lawn pests, lawn weeds will compete aggressively with shallow strawberry roots for nutrition.

When putting plants into the ground, place the crown base (the semi-pointed area where the roots converge together) at soil level. Fan out the roots, completely cover them, and afterward firm the soil down. Some strawberry plants have *runners*, and some don't.

Strawberry selection

Constantly hybridized for quality and performance, today's garden strawberries are big and sweet. There are three common types of garden strawberries: June-bearing, which give a single crop per season in spring; ever-bearing, which give two crops per season, in spring and autumn; and day-neutral, which can flower and fruit from spring until fall. Day-neutral strawberries are not affected by day length, which controls the fruiting of other strawberries.

The easiest way to choose strawberries for your climate zone is to buy those sold in your neighborhood nursery. Strawberries can be selective about where they thrive, and even a "preferred" area will vary from year to year depending on that year's climate. For the best selection, grow one or more of each kind: June-bearing, ever-bearing, and day-neutral.

But if you want to experiment or just can't find what you want locally, here are just a few of the varieties available. As a note, day-neutral plants are often listed right alongside ever-bearing types in catalogs, so read carefully.

DEFINITION

Runners are the new baby plants that come off the parent plant via trailing stems. The stems will eventually root. Running strawberries are a fine way to multiply your strawberry bed, but they do need room. Place each prospective parent plant about 18 to 36 inches apart. To get larger berries from running strawberries, limit the trailing stems to four per plant, spacing them well.

June-bearing strawberries

- **Dunlap** – drought resistant, good in all areas when mulched.
- **Earliglow** – early, resistance to RS, VW, LS, partially susceptible to PM.
- **Guardian** – vigorous, ample runners, best for East Coast, resistance to RS, VW, susceptible to PM and LS.
- **Honeoye** – excellent flavor, hardy, vigorous, heavy yield, best in midwest and north, resistance to LS.
- **Kent** – hardy, and very cold tolerant, susceptible to LS, RS, VW.
- **Midway** – freezes well, very productive, mulch for winter, best in northeast and northwest, resistance to RS, susceptible to LS.
- **Redchief** – good for freezing, grows best in midwest, resistance to PM, RS, susceptible to LS.
- **Robinson** – good choice for midwest and northeast.
- **Sparkle** – good for freezing, vigorous, productive, many runners, hardy, resistance to RS.
- **Sequoia** – very large berry, does best in California and northwest, some virus tolerance but susceptible to RS, VW.
- **Sunrise** – drought resistant, good in east, south, and central states, resistance to VW, RS, susceptible to LS.

HONEOYE

Ever-bearing strawberries

- **Fort Laramie** – vigorous, cold hardy, adaptable to most areas.
- **Ogallala** – early, many runners, vigorous, hardy, adaptable to dry conditions and low temperatures, resistance to LS.
- **Ozark Beauty** – good for preserves as well as eating fruit, vigorous, high yield, winter hardy.
- **Quinault** – resistance to LS, RS, susceptible to virus.
- **Shortcake** – large berries.
- **Sweet Charlie** – does well in high temperatures and high humidity, good for south.

■ **Ever-bearing strawberries** *give two crops of fruit a year.*

Day-neutral strawberries

- **Selva** – large berries.
- **Tribute** – hardy, vigorous, resistance to RS, VW, PM, and some resistance to LS.
- **Tristar** – productive, vigorous runners, good for hanging baskets and strawberry barrels, tolerant of temperatures up to 95° F, resistance to LS, RS, PM, and VW.

■ **Day-neutral strawberries** *flower and fruit from spring through fall.*

Maintaining your strawberry patch

Probably the most important aspect of good strawberry plant care is to mulch. Mulching keeps the plant's shallow roots cool and moist, and it keeps the strawberries off the ground. If the weather gets really cold, cover the strawberry bed with a 3-inch-deep light mulch, such as straw. Remove the mulch in the spring when the plant centers are a yellowish-green. If an unexpected frost comes along just as your strawberry plants have started to flower, put the mulch back on or just cover the bed with a light blanket.

Don't put slug bait around ripening or ripe fruit. It could be harmful to birds, pets, and tasting children.

INTERNET

**ohioline.ag.
ohio-state.edu**

Work your way to the Ohio State University Extension Fact Sheet on strawberries. It includes info on how to grow them and the various types and their attributes.

Birds like strawberries as much as you do, so you either will have to plant enough to share, or cover your beds with netting. The netting is sold at garden centers, and must be held somewhat above the berries so the birds don't peck through it. If your ripe strawberries have round or elongated holes, there's a chance that slugs are enjoying your efforts. I find that picking strawberries once they become ripe helps to keep slugs away, as they seem to prefer overripe berries.

Strawberry beds don't last forever. The parent plants gradually give smaller and smaller berries. Three years is considered a long life for a strawberry plant. When a bed's berry production decreases, remove the oldest plants and thin out the younger ones. Add mulch and water well afterward.

A simple summary

✓ Familiarize yourself with the different types of berries and grapes available. Choose a type that does well in your climate and that serves your purposes in planting.

✓ Be prepared to put in a little maintenance work with berries and grapes, which need regular pruning, thinning, and mulching.

✓ Well-drained soil is a must for berries and grapes. Planting on raised beds will help plants thrive.

✓ To prevent birds eating the fruit, cover with garden netting.

Chapter 14

Fun With Fruit Trees

IT ISN'T ABSOLUTELY NECESSARY to know how a plant works. You can grow plants for years without understanding their anatomical or functional details. But when it comes to fruit trees, if you understand a bit about how they grow, you will be rewarded with home-grown delights. So I've chosen to begin this chapter with a little lesson.

In this chapter...

✓ Super simple plant anatomy

✓ Fruit tree fundamentals

✓ The apples of autumn

✓ Fabulous figs

✓ Plentiful peaches

✓ Three cheers for cherries

✓ Oranges for all

ROSY GLOUCESTER CROSS APPLES

Super simple plant anatomy

PLANTS, WHETHER TINY HERBS OR GIANT TREES, are basically made up of three parts: roots, stems, and leaves. Roots are the parts growing downward into the ground. They take in part of the plant's nourishment, including water, from the soil, and they anchor the plant into the soil. Roots usually branch out many times as they grow. The smaller branches are called rootlets.

Growing upward from a root is a stem. At certain places along the stem, according to plant type, there are leaves. Leaves, as a group, make up the plant's foliage. The stem acts as a conduit, carrying nourishment from the roots to the leaves. Leaves also take in food from the air. These nutrients, along with the nutrients transferred to the leaves from the root system, begin to change within the leaves. When exposed to sunlight, the nutrients change into a form that the plant can actually use for its health and growth. This process is called photosynthesis.

A healthy growing plant extends its roots and rootlets further and further out into the soil. Reaching out lets it have access to more soil nutrients and more water. Meanwhile, in a healthy plant, the stem becomes longer. It develops more leaves, or sends out more branches, which in turn develop more leaves. The many leaves obtain more light and air, aiding plant nutrition. Your job as a gardener is to help each of your plants meet its growth needs.

Reproduction

In addition to roots, stems, and leaves, plants also produce flowers. From flowers come fruits. From fruits come seeds. Flowers, fruits, and seeds don't have any part in nourishing, or feeding, the plant. Their purpose is to produce individual new plants, as well as making certain, if at all possible, that the species doesn't die out and disappear from this earth. The flowers, fruits, and seeds are a plant's reproductive organs.

Flower parts

Each flower generally has four parts: calyx, corolla, stamens, and pistils. In spite of their fancy names, the jobs done by each part are quite simple. The calyx, or flower cup, usually green, partly covers the outside of the flower. It looks almost like a little cap or cup. Each piece of the calyx is called a sepal, and each sepal resembles a little leaf.

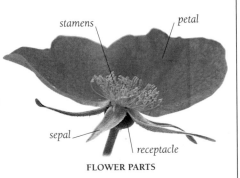

stamens

petal

sepal

receptacle

FLOWER PARTS

The corolla is what we think of when we imagine a flower; each separate piece is called a petal. The petals, besides being part of the pretty flower, have a practical purpose. They provide a protective covering for the flower's reproductive interior and attract pollinators.

Pollination parts

Within each flower are the stamens. Each stamen is usually made up of two parts: a filament, or stalk, and an anther, or little sac, on top of the stalk. Within this little sac is a powdery substance called pollen.

Also within each flower are one or more pistils. The pistils are in the flower center. Each pistil has three parts: an ovary, a style, and a stigma. Don't leave yet, we're just coming to the good part. The rounded ovary, at the bottom of the pistil, will be the seed holder. The style, a slim supporting mechanism, supports the stigma. The stigma has a sticky or furry surface.

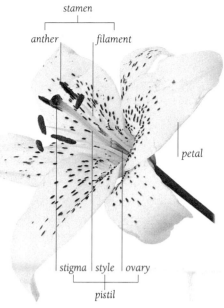

■ **Each male stamen** consists of an anther and a filament, while the female pistil has three parts – a stigma, style, and ovary. When pollen lands on the stigma, pollination occurs.

When pollen is carried by the wind, or transported by bees or other pollinators, some of it may land on a similar flower's stigmas. If this happens, pollination occurs.

When the flower fades and falls, all that is usually left is the ovary of the pistil. This, if it has been properly fertilized, becomes larger and larger. Eventually it becomes a fruit, or a seedpod, or a nut, or whatever. Within the fruit are one or more seeds. If the ovary hasn't been fertilized properly, it doesn't develop. It remains a small ball that dries up and falls off. This is why you may think your cherry tree or apple tree will have lots of fruit because it has lots of flowers. But they develop into little balls, and nothing more. For some reason, fertilization has not occurred.

Fertilization

Plants can be self-fertile or require a pollinator plant. Cross-fertilization occurs with plants that rely on a pollinator plant.

When planning a fruit tree purchase, it is important to know whether the plant is self-fertile or whether it requires a pollinator. If a plant is self-fertile you only need one tree of that kind to produce fruit. If a plant requires a pollinator, you will need two trees to get any fruit.

257

There are fruit trees that are only able to cross-fertilize with specific types of similar fruit trees, so sometimes the tree's "brand name" is very important.

Plants are pollinated in a number of ways, but insects do most of the legwork. And probably the hardest worker is the honeybee. Watching a honeybee load up her pollen baskets is fun. Her body is covered with feathery hairs. Both hind legs have a hollowed-out section that acts as a basket. As the honeybee goes from flower to flower, pollen literally sticks to her. She brushes this off with leg combs into her pollen baskets. Sometimes the baskets get so heavy that the honeybee can barely carry her load around. Eventually, heavily laden, she flies home. But in the meantime, pollen from one flower has brushed against the stigma of another flower, and perhaps a cherry, or peach, has begun. Other bee types, such as the bumblebee, act as good pollinators too.

■ **A bumblebee** *is an effective pollinator, carrying pollen from one flower to another. Yellow flowers are particularly attractive to insects.*

In addition to insects, you'll want to encourage other pollinators to visit your garden, such as hummingbirds. Bats are good pollinators of some plants too. I'll discuss how you can attract pollinators to your yard in Chapter 20.

Fruit tree fundamentals

IT PROBABLY SEEMS AS THOUGH the world of plants is simply a bunch of categories, each with big sub-categories and each sub-category with more sub-categories. And yes, in some ways this is true. A quick overview of the basic types of fruit trees will help you understand how the trees work, and so will help you succeed as a gardener. I've chosen to categorize them as follows.

APPLE SEEDS

Fruit with seeds

There are many types of seeded fruits, including apple, fig, pear, persimmon, and pomegranate. The most common in home gardens throughout North America are the apple and the fig, and I'll focus on growing these trees.

Stone fruits

Better known as fruit with pits, stone fruits include apricots, avocados, cherries, nectarines, peaches, and plums. Of these, peaches and cherries are the most popular for the garden.

Citrus fruits

Citrons, grapefruits, kumquats, lemons, limes, oranges, and pummelos are all citrus fruits. To grow even the hardiest citrus tree outdoors, you should live in a climate zone where the temperature doesn't fall below 17° F. However, even though the citrus plant may survive at that temperature, the flower buds may be killed, thus eliminating the season's crop.

Sour oranges, kumquats, satsuma mandarins, and calamondins are among the hardiest low-temperature citrus fruits. And if you can offer frost protection, Meyer lemons may do well. But don't let ultra-low winter temperatures deter you from growing citrus trees. Plant the smaller types in large, well-drained containers full of good organic soil. Put the containers on rollers, because they will go outdoors during the warmer seasons and inside during the winter.

Trivia...

When you get involved with planting fruit trees, you'll eventually hear the terms rootstock and scion bandied about. Rootstock, sometimes called understock, are the roots of a tree selected for its predictable vigor, size, disease resistance, and the like. A scion is a fruiting variety that is budded or grafted onto the rootstock. The fruit from this scion is predictable for characteristics such as size, color, taste, and cold hardiness. The aim is to combine the best of both for the purchaser.

■ **Fruit trees** *are really rewarding to grow, because they allow you to harvest an array of healthy, delicious produce all through the year.*

259

The apples of autumn

PROBABLY THE EASIEST TO GROW *of all the fruit trees, apples (Malus domestica) are very popular. There are well over 1,000 varieties, ranging from the antique apple to newer disease-resistant types. A few years after planting you will have apples to eat, and apples to spare. You can even train apple trees, particularly dwarf varieties, on espaliers.*

APPLE
(Malus domestica)

Planting apple trees

Put bare-root trees into the ground in the fall when they are dormant, or without leaves. Container-grown trees may be planted at any time when the ground is not frozen or very wet. With apple trees, you have a wide choice of sizes and a wide choice of fruiting time. Mini-dwarf trees grow from 4 to 8 feet tall and do very well in containers. Dwarf trees are from 8 to 14 feet tall, semi-dwarf trees from 12 to 20 feet tall, and standards will grow up to 40 feet. Expect semi-dwarf trees to start bearing fruit in their second or third year, and standards in the fourth or fifth year.

Choosing trees

All apple trees are deciduous. It is important that you select an apple variety that will grow happily in your climate zone, especially when buying from catalogs, as the descriptions tend to be quite general. If you cannot buy a tree locally, read up as much as possible on the apple varieties you like.

If you can buy your trees at a local nursery, chances are good that you'll get a type that does well in your area. Ask the staff members for their recommendations and about a particular type of tree's *chilling requirement*, especially if you live in an area with mild winters.

Apple trees require full sun, regular watering, and well-drained, average soil. They don't like hard and persistent wind. Because apple trees bloom in early spring, select a site that isn't subject to late spring frosts. If you are putting in more than one tree, place smaller trees about 15 feet apart, and larger ones up to 35 feet apart.

DEFINITION

You will hear the term chilling requirement, *or see it on tags at the nursery. These are the hours in which the plant must be cold during the winter. For example, an apple or peach tree's chilling requirement may be 400 to 900 chilling hours. That's how much time it needs to be chilled and dormant during the winter. A chill is basically between 52 and 68° F. There are lots of fruit trees with reasonable chilling hours, but it's best to find out what the previous year's hours were, or the general track record is, for your neighborhood.*

Picky pollinators

You should know whether your prospective purchase is self-fertile, or whether you need a pollinator apple tree. Some apple trees are generic pollinators, helping just about every apple tree in sight, and other apple trees are picky pollinators. So if you are buying for pollinator purposes, do a bit of homework. Of course, if your neighbors have an apple tree or two, that pollen will meander in your direction, which often helps things along.

An abundance of apples

If you've ever been to a farmer's market, you'll know that it's impossible to mention here all the possible apple types for your garden. Still, I've gone ahead and listed some to give you an idea of what is available in the nurseries and catalogs, as well as some of the characteristics you might be looking for.

Unless otherwise noted, all apples require 600 to 900 chill hours below 45° F and have a cold-weather tolerance of -30° F. It is extremely important to select an apple variety that will survive and thrive where you live.

INTERNET

ag.arizona.edu/pubs/
garden/mg/fruit/care

This helpful site calls itself Fruit Trees: Planting and Varieties. You'll get general information on all kinds of fruit trees, including apple, apricot, cherry, fig, nectarine, olive, peach, pear, plum, pomegranate, and quince. Fertilization, thinning, pollination, irrigation, and pruning are also discussed, with tips on named varieties.

Disease-resistant apples

- **Carefree Liberty** – red, tart, crunchy fruit, August to September ripening, stores up to 4 months, fireblight, rust, and scab resistance.
- **Chehalis** – yellow skin, crisp juicy fruit, August to September ripening, does not store well, scab resistance, mini-dwarf trees available.
- **Freedom** – red crisp fruit, September ripening, fireblight, mildew, rust, and scab resistance.
- **Haralson** – red, crisp, tart apples, vigorous, good cold tolerance, September to October ripening, fireblight and rust resistance.
- **Hudson's Golden Gem** – tan-russet skin, crisp fruit with sweet nutty flavor, October ripening, holds onto tree through January, scab and mildew resistance, mini-dwarf trees available.
- **Liberty** – red skin, crisp, juicy fruit, productive, needs thinning, fall ripening, holds onto tree through January, fireblight, rust, and scab resistance, mini-dwarf trees available.
- **Spartan** – purple-red skin, crisp fruit, productive, needs thinning, September ripening, hardy to -45° F, fireblight, rust, mildew, and scab resistance, mini-dwarf trees available.

■ **Newer varieties** *of apples have been specially bred to be more robust and less prone to disease.*

Popular apples

- **Braeburn** – green skin with red blush, large crisp tangy fruit, productive, October ripening, keeps well, doesn't like high heat, susceptible to mildew and scab.
- **Fuji** – red blushed, sweet crunchy fruit, November ripening, fruit keeps through April if refrigerated, only 100 to 400 chill hours needed, fireblight susceptible, scab resistant, mini-dwarf trees available.
- **Gala** – reddish-orange blush, crisp fruit, good keeper, September ripening, needs excellent drainage, 500 to 600 chill hours needed.
- **Granny Smith** – green, late October ripening, keeps up to 6 months in cold storage.
- **Jonagold** – yellow with red blush, crunchy sweet-tart fruit, vigorous, productive, ripens September and October and keeps until January, mini-dwarf trees available.
- **McIntosh** – red, mild tart flavor, soft, good for cooking, September ripening, likes coastal areas, fairly cold hardy, rust resistance.
- **Yellow delicious** – self-fruitful, yellow skin, crisp sweet-tangy fruit, good pollinator, September to October ripening, fireblight, mildew, and scab susceptible, mini-dwarf trees available.

Old-timer apples

- **Black Gilliflower** – black-red, mild soft very aromatic fruit, good winter dessert apple.
- **Doctor Matthews** – faded red, crisp juicy apples, short storage period.
- **Golden Russet** – dates to 1800s, yellow, crisp sweet fruit.
- **Lady** – very small, flat pretty apple that stores well, usually used for decorations, especially holiday wreaths.
- **Paragon** – dark red, spicy apples, good keeper, from 1800s Tennessee.
- **Swaar** – russet, not pretty but sweet and fragrant, grown by Dutch settlers on the Hudson River in the early 1800s.
- **Tolman sweet** – yellow, sweet fruit, very popular in early 1800s Massachusetts.

Pruning your orchard

To give your apple trees the extra nutrients they need, fertilize in the spring with a fertilizer marked "for apple trees." You might want to put off pruning while your apple tree is young. Overly enthusiastic pruning encourages growth in lieu of fruiting. However, once a tree reaches full size, an annual pruning is beneficial to keep the branch structure open. But don't cut off the old branches, as this is where fruit appears. When baby apples grace the scene, you may have to thin the branches out so that the apples are about 5 inches apart.

■ **Golden Russet** *apples, renowned for their sweet, wholesome flavor, are often used to make cider.*

It always bothers me to thin a fruit tree. However, when I initially didn't thin my apple tree, I ended up with lots of itty-bitty fruit instead of big crunchy apples.

Apple pests and diseases

Of course you want your trees and your fruit to be healthy. There are several diseases you should keep an eye out for, and some of them were mentioned in the listing of apples. Fireblight, caused by a bacterium, turns the leaves black, as if they have been scorched by fire. The fungal disease cedar-apple rust shows up as orange spots on leaves and fruits. Powdery mildew, also caused by a fungus, is displayed as a white powder that coats leaves. Another fungal disease, scab, is the worst of the apple diseases. It is particularly prevalent where spring weather is mild and wet. Brown corky spots, gradually enlarging, appear on fruit and leaves.

The best way to avoid disease in your apple trees is to make sure you plant resistant varieties.

> ### Trivia...
> The legendary Johnny Appleseed was born John Chapman in Massachusetts in 1774. At 23 he set out westward, planting apple trees as a way of staking a claim on land he someday hoped to own. John wanted to sell trees to other travelers, too, but realized there was no room for them on the wagons. So he collected apple seeds from local cider mills and, traveling ahead of the wagon trains, he planted thousands of them. When the wagons arrived, he sold the young trees to the settlers. John died at age 70, responsible for nearly all the apple orchards at the time in the new American settlements.

I have had my green apple tree for 20 years and never had a major problem of any kind, and I do not use chemical controls at all.

In addition to diseases, apples have their share of pests, including aphids, the codling moth (that white worm that you can find in your apple), the plum curculio (it eats crescent-shaped scars in the fruit), and the apple maggot (another white worm, which makes the surrounding fruit become brown and pulpy).

Reaping the apple harvest

Some apples stay comfortably on the tree longer than others. If you don't have ample storage space, consider planting trees that hold apples up to 4 months. If the fruit separates easily from the branch, that's a good sign of readiness, but the taste test is the best.

The color of the apples often shows only how much light the tree has received. Looks can be deceiving when you think it's time to harvest.

Fabulous figs

FIGS ARE AMONG THE OLDEST *of cultivated fruits. Records show that people have been planting figs (Ficus carica) since at least 2500 BC, but their history certainly pre-dates that time. While Adam was strolling around the Garden of Eden, he ate the apple Eve had given him and then had to cover his nakedness with a nearby fig leaf.*

FIG BRANCH WITH
YOUNG FRUIT

Planting figs

Figs do best in areas with a long, hot growing season. However, people do grow them successfully in regions where the winter temperature drops to zero or below. Even if cold winters kill the tree to the ground, new growth may appear in spring. You can also enhance your success with fig trees by planting in a warm, wind-protected, corner where heat bounces off concrete or the house, or place them in a large container on wheels that can be moved to a protected site as necessary. Deciduous fig trees, without leaves, do not need light, but must be moved outdoors as soon as possible in spring.

In the spring, buy fig trees as container plants. I was lucky and was given a rooted sucker from a fig tree. I now have a lovely old-timer. Figs are self-fertile, so you don't need more than one unless you want different types of figs. Their chilling requirement is less than 300 hours.

Fig trees need full sun, and do best with rich, slightly alkaline, very well-drained soil. Although some fig trees are smaller than others, all need plenty of space unless you intend to prune regularly. The average fig tree grows to between 15 and 30 feet, with a wide branch spread.

Figs for the fickle

There are hundreds of fig varieties, although you may find only a few for commercial sale. Others you must get from the suckers of friends' fig trees. The following are just a few of the more common fig trees, but be aware that most have several names. For example the kadota is also called white kadota, dottato, and Florentine. In garden catalogs, the few figs offered are often not named at all, but are described with great zeal. Unless you really like to experiment, make a point of finding out exactly what you are buying.

Favorite figs

- **Adriatic** – greenish-yellow skin and reddish pulp, large tree, two crops per season (one on old branches, one on new branches), vigorous, somewhat drought tolerant, does well in cool coastal areas but subject to frost damage.
- **Brown Turkey** – brownish-purple skin and pinkish pulp, small, hardy, vigorous, adaptable, good in the southeast.
- **Celeste** – light brown, sweet, small fruit, good fruit for drying, fairly cold hardy, grows well in the southeast and west.
- **Kadota** – large all-purpose figs, yellow skin and amber pulp, vigorous, likes hot dry areas.
- **King** – dark green skin and pink pulp, very sweet, fruits on old branches only, good for cool coastal areas.
- **Magnolia** – reddish-brown skin with pinkish pulp, fruit is best eaten fresh and does not dry well, vigorous, hardy.
- **Mission** – large fruit, black skin and reddish pulp, vigorous, large tree, two crops per season, good for southeast and hot dry climates.
- **Verte** – small greenish-yellow fruit with dark pink pulp, good fresh or dry, small tree, does well in areas where summer is short.

■ **Brown Turkey figs** (Ficus carica) *have particularly attractive pinkish flesh and brownish-purple skins.*

A fig fitness program

Caring for your fig trees couldn't be simpler. When the weather gets hot and dry, remember to give them plenty of water.

As with many plants, mature trees require much less water than young trees. Potted figs need regular watering at all times. A mulch will help to preserve moisture, because fig roots grow close to the surface. Because of the shallow root system, don't plan on digging or cultivating around your fig trees.

Figs need little pruning, and most pruning should be done for size and shapeliness when the tree is young. If you are into pruning, be aware that some fig trees fruit mostly on new shoots, and others fruit on both old and new branches.

I've never had to wrap my fig trees, but some people advocate wrapping them for the winter in colder climates. A simple way is to tie the branches together to make a cylinder. Use a wire cage to enclose the branches and fill the empty spaces with dried leaves. Cover the cage with a waterproof fabric. Few insects or diseases annoy fig trees, but in the southeast the dried fruit beetle is a serious pest. Gardeners in this area can only successfully grow certain types of figs that the beetle can't sneak into.

Harvesting figs

Figs will ripen from June through October, depending on the variety of tree and its location. Figs will not ripen after they are picked. Pick them when they're slightly to moderately soft. Eat them the same day you pick them if at all possible. Figs will keep in the refrigerator for a maximum of about 4 days. If you let them hang on the tree, the figs get softer and softer and birds and ants have a picnic. You probably will have lots of figs ripening at one time.

I have found that people appreciate gifts of just-ripe fresh figs more than just about any other fruit, because these are almost impossible to find at the market in really good condition.

Plentiful peaches

YOU CAN BUY *only a few types of peaches (Prunus persica) in the market – the kind that ship well and store well. Some of the best, the sweetest, the juiciest, the most aromatic just don't make it onto supermarket shelves. They're the kind you just want to eat off the tree – that is, if you have a tree.*

■ **Choose the site** *for your peach tree carefully and you will be rewarded with plenty of ripe, succulent fruit.*

There are dwarf peach trees reaching only 4 to 6 feet in height, semi-dwarf trees growing from 7 to 9 feet tall, and standards, reaching 18 feet tall and almost as wide. All have beautiful pink blossoms and shiny green leaves. You can even grow peach trees from seed, and will often get good results and early fruit.

Delightful dwarfs

Dwarf trees are very popular in this age of small yards. They are also well adapted to growing in pots. Dwarf trees produce fruit of the same size and color as standard trees. Although standards produce more peaches than the dwarf trees, it takes them longer to do so. Care is the same for dwarf and standard trees, except with dwarf trees you don't need a ladder when pruning!

Planting peaches

The best time to buy a peach tree is about 30 days before the buds open. This should be between January and March, depending on where you live. Choose a peach tree variety that is disease resistant, especially if you live on the East Coast.

Don't let your peach tree roots dry out before you plant them. This will markedly hinder its growth.

It is best not to buy trees in containers full of dry soil. If you do so, soaking the roots for about 12 hours may revitalize the tree. Always water a container well when you get it home.

When planting, you should choose your peach tree site carefully. All fruit trees need full sunlight and exquisitely drained soil. The planting hole should be slightly wider and deeper than the spread-out root system. Place the tree in the hole so the upper roots are about an inch or 2 below the soil surface. Partially fill the planting hole with a mixture of good organic soil and local soil, then water. Do this again until the soil is at the same level as it was in the container. Tamp down the soil and water well.

It's just peachy

In freestone peaches, the pit just falls out. In semi-freestone peaches, you have to wiggle the pit a bit to remove it. The pit stays in place in cling peaches.

CLING PEACH

The cling variety is the standard in the grocery store, but these are not nearly as tasty as the others. Unless you are into canning, most home gardeners plant freestone or semi-freestone peaches.

In most instances peach trees are self-fertile so you won't need two. It does help to encourage pollinating insects in your yard, however, so the pollen is moved from one blossom to the other on the same tree.

All types of peaches are available in early-, mid-season, and late-season varieties. The fruiting season may vary according to where you live, so this is just a general guideline. For the novice, it is best to ask your local cooperative extension agent or master gardener before you buy peach trees at a local nursery. Peach trees can be really picky about where they'll grow. There's no point in being disappointed when you could have selected another peach tree for the same price.

Early-season peaches

EARLIGRADE PEACHES

- **Babcock** – freestone, white flesh, juicy sweet fruit.
- **Earligrade** – large yellow fruit, excellent flavor.
- **Flordaprince** – large red blush fruit, semi-clingstone, must be thinned.
- **Red Haven** – firm gold and red fruit with yellow flesh, prolific, vigorous, requires thinning, very resistant to cold, bacterial leaf spot resistance.
- **Sunhaven** – freestone, yellow skin with red blush and yellow flesh, does well in cold winter areas, bacterial leaf spot resistance.
- **Suwanee** – freestone, large yellow fruit with red blush skin, excellent for deep south.
- **Tropic Snow** – freestone, white flesh and white skin with red blush.
- **Tropic Sweet** – freestone, large yellow fruit.

Mid-season peaches

- **Belle of Georgia** – soft juicy fruit with white flesh, vigorous, good producer, blossoms are somewhat frost resistant, bacterial leaf spot resistance.
- **Cresthaven** – freestone, firm yellow juicy fruit, hardy, productive.
- **Fay Elberta** – freestone, large, good flavor, good producer, requires thinning.
- **Frost** – freestone, medium-size fruit, resistant to peach leaf curl.
- **Midpride** – freestone, yellow fruit.
- **Ranger** – freestone, large yellow peaches, bacterial leaf spot resistance.
- **Red Globe** – freestone, yellow skin with red markings, large firm yellow fruit.
- **Rio Oso Gem** – freestone, large red fruit with firm yellow flesh, susceptible to bacterial leaf spot.

Late-season peaches

- **Madison** – freestone, yellow flesh, medium vigor, productive, tolerant of late frost, bacterial leaf spot resistance.
- **Reliance** – freestone, winter hardy to -25° F, yellow-gold skin, soft yellow flesh.

Simple care for your peach crop

Water your trees regularly. In general, fertilize with a fruit tree fertilizer in the spring and after you harvest. Sprinkle the fertilizer evenly and keep it away from the tree trunk.

A peach tree begins forming next year's flowers at the same time as it is growing this year's fruit. This is tough work for the tree and so good watering is a must.

PRUNING AND THINNING PEACH TREES

You should prune every year, preferably while the tree is in bloom. This helps to decrease the fruit production – too much fruit will leave you with very small peaches. You also want to stimulate the growth of new wood, because new wood is where peaches form the following year. Even with pruning, you will probably have too many fruits, in which case you will need to thin them out.

 Thin once

As they form, thin the peaches to one fruit per cluster, removing any fruits growing away from the sunlight or toward the wall or fence.

2 **Thin again later**

Thin the fruits again to leave one fruit every 6 to 9 inches. The only time you might not want to thin is if frost has ruined young fruit.

Peach pests

A very common disease in peach trees is peach leaf curl. Its hallmark sign is the puckering of the tree's leaves, which become quite distorted and discolored. Brown rot disease is displayed as a gray fuzzy fungus, eventually causing peaches to darken and shrivel, although they don't always fall. Bacterial leaf spot shows up as brown or black spots on leaves. The leaf tips may die, and the leaves may turn yellow and drop. The fruit of a tree may be pitted with brown and black spots. How you deal with these problems is up to you: some people use chemical deterrents and some go organic and put up with the problems.

Watch out for pests. Plum curculios chew on developing fruits, leaving a sickle-shaped scar that damages the fruit and makes it susceptible to disease. The Oriental fruit moth caterpillar eats a large hole in fruit and bores into the stems, making the tips wilt.

Picking peaches

How do you know when the time is right? Start by feeling your peaches very gently as they mature. As they begin to soften slightly, pick a peach and taste. Is it tasty? Not yet? Wait a bit. Try again a few days later. When peaches are sweet, they are ready to be picked.

Be aware that peaches getting the most sun will ripen first, so your tasting trials should begin on the upper and outer branches. When harvesting, do so carefully, as ripe peaches bruise easily and those brown bruises start the spoilage process.

The best way to remove peaches from the tree is with a little twist combined with a slight upward pull. If you do pick some that are not quite ripe, let them ripen at room temperature. They'll taste much better than peaches ripened in the refrigerator.

Three cheers for cherries

I CANNOT TELL A LIE. You are going to love growing your own cherry (Prunus) trees. And once you get started, you'll know why chopping one down is such a bad idea, be it a sweet cherry (P. avium) or a tart one (P. cerasus).

Planting cherry trees

Cherry trees should be planted in early spring while they're still completely dormant. The trees should not be leafing out – if they are, plant them immediately. Why? Trees that are developing leaves and trying to set down a strong root system seldom accomplish both activities well. Plant cherry trees in rich soil. They like a very well drained area with full sunlight. There is a direct relationship between lots of sunshine and good-quality, tasty fruit.

Plant your sweet cherry trees in a site that doesn't get late frosts, because sweet cherries blossom quite early in the spring and a frost will kill the blossoms.

If you live in a mild winter area, you can also plant cherry trees, completely dormant, in the fall. By doing so, you will give the tree's roots a chance to get comfortable for the following year.

To help prevent the roots from developing crown rot fungus damage, don't plant too deeply. Place the trees in the ground at the same soil level they were in when you brought them home from the nursery. To provide good air circulation, dwarf trees require at least 8 feet of growing space, and standard trees should have about 25 feet in which to stretch out.

> **Trivia...**
> Many cherries are not dark red when ripe. Some are yellow, some are bright red, and some are almost black.

Choosing cherries

Most sweet cherry trees require another sweet cherry tree as a pollinator. The pollinator tree doesn't have to be in your yard, but it sure helps to have one nearby. Tart cherry trees, producing the kind of fruit used in canning and pies, are self-fertile. The varieties I've chosen to feature are all trees producing sweet eating cherries. Some can be found as dwarf trees, such as Compact Lambert, Compact Stella, and Garden Bing. Dwarf cherry trees are self-fertile.

Good cherries for beginners

- **Black Tartarian** – juicy sweet purplish-black fruit, productive.
- **Compact Lambert** – sweet dark red fruit, vigorous.
- **Compact Stella** – sweet dark red fruit, hardy, vigorous, self-fertile, a good pollinator for all sweet cherries.
- **Emperor Francis** – yellow fruit, productive, cold hardy.
- **Garden Bing** – large juicy reddish-purple fruit, productive, vigorous.
- **Hedelfingen** – large black fruit, hardy, very productive.
- **Kristin** – large sweet purplish-black fruit, cold hardy to -25° F.
- **Lapins** – large sweet dark purple fruit, self-fertile, a good pollinator for other sweet cherries.
- **Rainier** – very large yellow fruit with yellowish-white flesh, hardy, vigorous.
- **Royal Ann** – juicy yellow fruit, productive, vigorous.
- **Sodus** – large red fruit with white flesh.
- **Sweet Ann** – sweet yellow fruit, excellent flavor, cold hardy.
- **Van** – dark red fruit, productive, hardy.

■ **Compact Stella** is a late, self-pollinating cherry that has an excellent sweet flavor and beautifully lush flesh.

Pruning cherries

Keeping your cherry trees in good shape is really simple. In summer, be sure to water regularly and deeply. Don't do any pruning until the tree has completed a season of bearing fruit. Any pruning should be very light, since cherry trees bear fruit on both new and old branches. It's best to just remove any damaged or diseased branches.

However, if you have a standard tree, as I do, it may get too tall for you to reach the cherries without a long stepladder. Birds are delighted to get the tastiest cherries at the top of the tree, but you may want them for yourself. If you dislike ladder climbing as much as I do, you can shorten the top of the tree.

The goal of pruning is to create an open center. Rather than have one main trunk growing upward, you want four to five significant branches growing outward at about a 45° angle. The branches should be separate from one another. An open center gives each of the different areas more sun, and makes fruit easier to reach.

■ **Morello cherries** *have an excellent flavor which makes them among the best for cooking. They make particularly tasty cherry pies and jams.*

Cherry pests

Cherry trees are susceptible to some pests. In particular, look for plum curculios. When these insects feed on the cherries, crescent-shaped scars will appear and the fruit may drop off the tree. Cherry fruit fly larvae can be identified as white worms within the cherries. Deformed leaves will result from an infestation of aphids. As for diseases, you should be most concerned with cherry leaf spot, which shows up as purple spots on upper leaf surfaces; powdery mildew, a powdery white coating on the leaves that eventually distorts them; and bacterial canker, which will be seen as oozing patches of sap.

Is it fruit yet?

Knowing when to pick your cherries could not be simpler. Let your taste buds be your guide. Pick a cherry by pulling carefully on the stem with a slight upward twist. Ripe fruit will separately easily from the stem. Be gentle when picking to avoid bruising your fruit. Eat or cook cherries right away. Don't let them pile up – one rotten cherry can cause rot in the whole batch.

Oranges for all

THE BIG ORANGE (Citrus sinensis) *groves that are but a memory in some areas had trees that reached 30 feet and were just as wide. For the home garden, consider the dwarf trees. A dwarf navel orange tree reaches 8 feet by 8 feet at maturity, a mandarin orange about 6 feet. All citrus trees are usually self-fertile, so you don't have to worry about buying two of a kind.*

■ **Bitter or sweet**, *oranges take a lot of beating. Their vibrant color and zesty fragrance enhance any yard. Rich in vitamin C, they can be squeezed for their delicious juice or used in preserves.*

273

Planting your orange orchard

In most areas you'll get the best results by planting orange trees from mid-spring through early summer. However, if summer temperatures where you live are consistently high, plant in the fall to late winter. This allows the tree to establish itself before the hot, dry weather comes. Container citrus trees are really simple – they can be planted at any time of the year.

Orange trees need a lot of sunlight, regular watering, fertilization with a citrus plant food, and protection from the wind.

If you select a citrus that needs warmth and you don't live in a consistently warm area, augment the heat your house gets by planting on the south and southeast sides of the house. Here the tree will be protected from some cold winds, and will also get some heat from the building itself. If there is an unexpected or heavy freeze, you can try draping the tree with blankets or other coverings.

DEFINITION

On a tree, the **bud union** is the place where the trunk joins the roots.

When planting, keep the *bud union* at the same level as it was in the container the tree came in.

Never bury the lower trunk of an orange tree and never water the trunk directly. A damp trunk is an open invitation to fungal diseases.

Since mulching orange trees can also lead to fungal problems such as crown and root rot, it should be avoided. Orange trees prefer loose, well-drained soil, which is a mixture of loam, peat, and sand. They like soil with a pH of 6 to 8. These trees do not tolerate salty soil, so if this is a problem, plant in a container with purchased soil. If the drainage in your yard isn't excellent, create a raised area for the trees.

An array of oranges

Sweet oranges include navel oranges, the type with a thick skin that peels easily. Juice oranges are just that – juicy. They tend to have a thin, hard-to-peel skin. They demand extended seasonal warmth. Mandarin oranges (*C. reticulata*) are small fruits with loose, easy-to-peel skins. Their trees are generally tough, but their heat requirements vary. Some can tolerate a bit of light frost. They are slow growing, eventually reaching 10 to 20 feet high and 5 to 10 feet wide. The dwarf trees grow from 4 to 6 feet, and are ideal for the small garden or patio.

SWEET ORANGE

Sweet oranges

- **Robertson** – productive, November to December ripening.
- **Summer navel** – spring ripening.
- **Trovita** – spring to summer ripening, cool weather tolerant.
- **Washington** – October through February ripening, large seedless fruit, easy to peel, segments separate well, does not do well in prolonged, high heat.

Juice oranges

- **Dillar** – August to September ripening, very juicy, vigorous, good for desert areas.
- **Hamlin** – fall to winter ripening, very juicy fruit with few seeds, good for desert and other hot summer areas.
- **Valencia** – spring through fall ripening, round medium-size juicy fruit, vigorous, also available in a seedless variety.

Mandarin oranges

- **Clementine** – winter to spring ripening, large sweet fruit with few seeds, moderate vigor, prefers high heat but is fine in some coastal areas, does better if a pollinator is present.
- **Dancy** – November to December ripening, seedy, bright green leaves, needs high heat, good for desert areas.
- **Encore** – summer to fall ripening, semi-dwarf tree, does well in cooler summer areas.
- **Kara** – spring to summer ripening, large sweet-tart fruit, likes warmth but not prolonged high heat.
- **Kinnow** – winter through spring ripening, needs mild climate, has columnar growth.
- **Mediterranean** – May to July ripening, juicy, needs high heat to ripen.
- **Owari satsuma** – fall to winter ripening, seedless, very hardy, small but spreading growth pattern.

CLEMENTINES

Caring for the orange crop

Citrus trees tend to be fussy about having their root system and lower trunk remaining dry. Although watering regularly is an absolute necessity, soggy soil will kill the plant. I recently lost a 20-year-old lemon tree that had survived all sorts of calamities because my daughter let the hose run unattended for several hours, creating a lemon swimming hole. The plant never recovered.

For young trees, you should fertilize with citrus food every month through October. Sprinkle the fertilizer on the ground about a foot from the tree trunk and immediately water it in well. For mature trees, you should fertilize in February, May, and September.

Thinning orange trees isn't necessary unless a branch looks as if it's about to break. The only pruning will involve clipping off any dead or diseased twigs. If you have planted dwarf citrus, you may see suckers emerging from the rootstock. Cut these off as far down as possible. If parts of your citrus have been frost damaged, wait until late spring to see what has survived before pruning.

INTERNET

plantanswers.tamu.edu/fruit/fruit.html

Click here to learn how to grow all kinds of fruits. Information is provided by the Agricultural Extension of Texas A&M University. Although the information is targeted toward Texas, most of it is applicable nationwide.

The right amount of water is very important for your orange trees. Too much or too little water, as well as too little sunlight, can result in bud, flower, or small fruit drop. Similarly, too much water and/or poor drainage can cause the leaves to turn yellow. You might also see this happen if there is too little sunlight or if pests attack. If you see a black coating on the leaves, along with sooty mold, you are likely to have an aphid infestation.

Collecting your oranges

Good things come to those who wait. Orange trees usually start full fruiting in their third year, so you just have to exercise some patience. After the flowers bloom, you may see a lot of them fall off the tree. This is natural. Typically, you'll also see a second drop a few weeks later of pea-size fruit, and another slightly later of golf-ball size fruit. Expect this 80 percent drop and don't get upset.

If at all possible, allow citrus to ripen on the tree for best flavor. So, not only do you have to wait a while for your oranges to appear, you also need to let them hang around on the tree. Something else in your garden could probably use a little attention. Go busy yourself there!

A little bit on lemons

Lemon trees (*C. limon*) require less heat than orange trees to thrive, so a lemon tree might be just right for your yard. The standard lemon tree reaches 35 feet, and dwarf lemon trees grow from 5 to 10 feet high. Lemons ripen throughout the year, with the largest crop in spring and fall. My favorite lemon trees include:

LEMON (*C. limon*)

- **Eureka** – egg-shaped fruit with very few seeds, tree has few thorns, at its peak in summer, the type you buy in stores.
- **Lisbon** – thorny, heavy fruiting with most fruit in winter, will grow in desert areas.
- **Meyer** – not a true lemon, but enough like one to be accepted as such, sweetish peel and less tangy fruit, quite cold hardy.
- **Ponderosa** – mild flavored, very large fruit, bears quickly.

A simple summary

✓ The roots anchor a plant and the stems support it. The roots and leaves work together to provide the plant with nutrition. Everything you do to help each part of a plant complete its job will make for a healthier garden.

✓ Fruit trees can be self-fertile or require a pollinator.

✓ The most popular fruit trees with seeds for the home garden are the apple and the fig. There are types of each that can be grown in most climate zones.

✓ There are many peaches and cherries that are never found in the marketplace since they do not ship or store well. These delicious varieties can be grown in a home garden.

✓ Citrus trees, such as lemon and orange trees, do not always tolerate very low temperatures outdoors. The right amount of water is important for success.

Chapter 15

Herbal Harvest

I CAN THINK OF LOTS of reasons to grow herbs. It's easy. It's fun. Herbs don't take up a lot of space and so are a great choice for people with small yards. In fact, you don't need a yard at all to raise many herbs. You can do it in your kitchen; which will be convenient, because that's ultimately where you'll want them.

In this chapter...

✓ Herbal history

✓ Herb gardens

✓ Favorite garden herbs

✓ Easy-to-grow herbs for cooking

✓ Easy-to-grow fragrant herbs

✓ Preserving your harvest

DILL IN FLOWER

Herbal history

LONG BEFORE *recorded history, people enjoyed herbs. How do we know? Well, pollen grains from a long-ago relative of wild marjoram have been found in cave dwellings dating back 60,000 years. No doubt, there are all sorts of stories of herbal use that we'll never know! Fortunately, there are many ancient writings about herbs.*

■ **Herbs have been** *harvested over the centuries because of their health-giving properties.*

Legendary herbs

The Mt. Olympian gods of early Greek mythology ate only *herbs* and drank only herb tea. In this way, the gods remained ever youthful and healthy. These same deities washed their hair with herbal brews and washed their faces with herbal juices. They took herbal baths and consumed herbal brain tonics. All this made for beauty as well as long life.

> **DEFINITION**
>
> *The term* **herb** *generally refers to the seeds, leaves, flowers, bark, roots, or other parts of any plant that is used for cosmetics, dyes, flavoring, fragrance, or health purposes.*

The Greek gods, so it is told, wanted to hide these prized herbs away from the common folk. So they made certain herbs grow in forests, where the ordinary mortal would not think to look for them. Diana, goddess of the hunt, was put in charge of guarding herb-growing sites. But, being a kindly sort, she felt sorry when women came begging for medicinal help, so she shared her information.

The angered gods took control of their herb garden again, later putting it in charge of Hebe, the goddess of youthfulness, warning her to keep their secret. However, Hebe felt sorry for warriors who were injured in war without any medicine to help cure them. Since her capabilities included restoring youth and vigor to gods and men, she snuck medicinal herbs into the warriors' food. Which, so the story goes, is how herbs came to be used in cooking.

The warriors, upon returning home, went seeking the source of this culinary delight. They got ample assistance from young maidens, who had had brief trysts with various gods. These gods were indiscreet in their conversation. And gradually the sources of ambrosia – the food of the gods – were discovered by ordinary folk.

■ **Cookbooks have many** *delightful recipes using herbs.*

Get it in writing

Only a few educated persons could write in ancient Greece, so information on how to grow and use herbs was passed down orally from one generation to another. Herbs were rumored to do many things that they were far from capable of accomplishing. But at the time, medicines such as we know them didn't exist and people needed help with all sorts of problems.

A scholar named Theophrastus (c. 372–287 BC), began to compile information about herbs and put it in writing. Quite a few years later, around 65 AD, the botanist and physician Dioscorides detailed information on 579 medicinal herbs. His book, *De Materia Medica*, which included formulas on each herb's use, became a standard medical reference until the 1600s.

Herbal medicine

Eventually herbs took a firm place in a physician's cure-all for assorted ailments. In addition, herbs were used to season and preserve food, bring good luck to a household, discourage evil spirits, eliminate nightmares, act as love potions, and improve beauty. They were also carried to ward off the implacable stench of an unwashed world. Many people grew their own herbs, and to get the best results they listened to the advice of assorted astrologers. Herbs were planted and harvested for a particular disease or disorder according to the positions of the planets.

The Romans, bent on conquest, and therefore carrying their own body-mending kits, brought herbs to Britain. Initially, monks working in monastery gardens were the chief cultivators. But before too long, every estate and small farm had an herb garden.

■ **Some herbs** *grown in modern-day windowboxes would once have been essential to a physician's medical kit for treating a wide range of illnesses.*

Herbs in the Americas

Herbs came to the New World with the first colonists. In a very early American garden catalog, the listings include anise, coriander, dill, chervil, fennel, parsley, sage, and thyme. Westward ho went the wagons, and herbs and instructions for use went along too. The settlers were quick to add to their home pharmacy those herbs long used by Native Americans.

The Shakers started the first medicinal herb garden in North America in 1800. They soon expanded their operations for business purposes, and eventually sold dried native and European herbs that were used in herbal extracts throughout the commercial world. In urban areas, peddlers sold herbs from baskets as they called out their wares along busy streets. In rural areas, vendors in horse-drawn wagons traveled door to door, selling everything an isolated housewife might need, including helpful herbs.

Herbs in print

Over the years, thousands of books and pamphlets in all languages have been written on herbal use. Some very early texts are still available today. If you go to a large bookstore or do a book search online, you'll find *Gerard's Herbal*, a book first printed in 1596. It has since been expanded several times. Author John Gerard grew more than 1,000 herbs in his garden. Also found on modern bookstore shelves is Culpeper's *Complete Herbal*, a reprint of a text originated by Nicholas Culpeper (1616–1654), a London physician, pharmacist, and astrologer.

Recently there has been a true resurrection of herbs for health, and grocery store shelves are filled with expensive containers of St. John's wort, kava kava, echinacea, valerian root, and the like. Herbal teas have become a standard on household shelves, and if you order tea in a restaurant, chances are chamomile and peppermint teas are among the selections offered.

There are books on how to cook with herbs, how to dry herbs, how to stuff pillows with herbs for a good night's sleep, and how to use herbs to enhance your beauty. There are also innumerable Web sites devoted to herbal information. Just type in "herbs" and see where it gets you.

■ **The striking** *flowers of echinacea* (E. purpurea).

Herb gardens

BECAUSE HERBS HAVE A SPIRITUAL NATURE to many, and perhaps to you, sit in the garden space for a while before designing your herb garden. Visualize how you would like your special herbal space to appear, and think about the plants you would like to grow. You might want to visit the herb gardens at various arboretums. Do you have adequate sun for what you want? With a few exceptions, herbs like at least 6 hours of sunlight per day and reasonably good drainage.

You can often create a sunny spot for a herb garden by trimming back trees and bushes, and drainage can be improved with the use of raised beds. Raised beds in an herb garden lend a very lovely rhythm to the visual scene. An alternative is to mingle herbs – here and there, in pots and in the ground – among other sun-loving plants. Some gardeners prefer to interplant herbs among their vegetables, acting on beliefs that some herbs have protective powers against pests. You can also grow a multitude of herbs on your sunny windowsills.

It is never recommended that you gather herbs from the wild. Some healthful herbs are look-a-likes of extremely poisonous varieties.

The knot garden

Initiated in the 1600s, a formal English herb garden is a fun challenge to re-create. The herbs are planted in intricate geometric designs, with a specimen plant in the center of each knot. A knot garden is often placed in full view of a patio or terrace.

■ **An Elizabethan-style** *knot garden is characterized by geometric shapes of rectangles, triangles, and circles. A popular feature of the original knot gardens was to enclose a wide variety of herbs and medicinal plants between the rows of clipped boxwood hedges.*

You can create a traditional design for an herb garden, or design your own. A drawn-to-scale plan is a very important first step.

Then, using garden sand, mark the lines on a prepared, leveled site. Don't forget to leave pathways for strolling and care. The pathways can be left bare, or covered with a mulch such as decorative wood chips or rock. In the traditional versions, colored earth and pebbles are used to fill open spaces.

Herbs selected for the design of a knot garden should be compact, and it's best to go for texture variations. This type of garden is labor intensive. In order to maintain its appearance, you must clip the plants about every 2 weeks from spring through fall to keep a uniform plant height. To lighten the work load, start by selecting plants that don't grow too wildly.

The Japanese herb garden

Often favored by gardeners living in rocky areas, the Japanese herb garden design incorporates rocks. A true Japanese herb garden is a highly structured affair, so you must be prepared to do a lot of preparatory manual labor to correctly set one up. Of course, you can hire someone to do this for you, if you're so inclined.

A traditional garden will have formal pathways between the rocks made of stepping stone, crushed rock, or steps. Then you encircle the open space between each rock group and close it off with large pebbles or small rocks. Good organic soil will fill the open area, and this is where you will place your carefully researched purchases. Select plants that will create some tracery as they grow, but will not overwhelm their rock-rimmed site.

The theme garden

Are you fond of butterflies? American history? Shakespeare? Are you raising herbs just for teas? For cooking? Would you prefer a garden that includes only those herbs grown in Biblical times, such as anise, cumin, garlic, mint, and wormwood? Or would you like a garden with a color theme, such as all gray leaves?

There are almost endless possibilities for theme gardens, and obviously this choice is up to you. Regardless of the theme you choose, make sure you leave a place for a bench or a comfortable garden chair within your herb garden. You deserve a front-row seat in your own special place.

INTERNET

gardenweb.com/ directory/hsa/

Go to this address to find the Herb Society of America reference site. You'll find the society's history and purpose, membership information, a discussion of the herb of the month, a speaker's list, news of the many local societies, a calendar of events, meetings and conventions, seed exchange information, and publications, projects, and programs of interest.

Favorite garden herbs

WHEN IT COMES TO HERBS *for the outdoor garden, or for the kitchen, container gardeners have a lot of options. Among the many herbs you can grow are:*

- Anise *(Pimpinella anisum)*
- Basil *(Ocimum)*
- Bay *(Laurus nobilis)*
- Caraway *(Carum)*
- Catnip *(Nepeta cataria)*
- Caper bush *(Capparis spinosa)*
- Chamomile *(Chamaemelum nobile)*
- Chervil *(Anthriscus cerefolium)*
- Chives *(Allium schoenoprasum)*
- Coriander *(Coriandrum sativum)*
- Cumin *(Cuminum cyminum)*
- Dill *(Anethum graveolens)*
- Fennel *(Foeniculum vulgare)*
- Garlic *(Allium sativum)*
- Ginger *(Zingiber officinale)*
- Lavender *(Lavandula officinalis)*
- Leek *(Allium ampeloprasum)*
- Lemon balm *(Melissa officinalis)*
- Lemon verbena *(Aloysia triphylla)*
- Marjoram *(Origanum majorana)*
- Mint *(Mentha)*
- Nasturtium *(Tropaeolum majus)*
- Oregano *(Origanum vulgare)*
- Parsley *(Petroselinum crispum)*
- Rocket *(Eruca versicaria)*
- Rosemary *(Rosmarinus officinalis)*
- Sage *(Salvia divinorum)*
- Savory *(Satureja hortensis)*
- Scented geraniums *(Pelargonium)*
- Sweet woodruff *(Galium odoratum)*
- Tarragon *(Artemisia dracunculus)*
- Thyme *(Thymus vulgaris)*
- Watercress *(Nasturtium officinale)*

■ **Potted garden herbs** *provide an aromatic focal point. Combine interesting foliage shapes and textures with the odd flowering plant for a great effect.*

Some of the easier-to-grow varieties are reviewed in this chapter. Others, such as chamomile and thyme, are discussed in greater detail in Chapter 16 on groundcovers. You'll find more on nasturtium in Chapter 18.

Easy-to-grow herbs for cooking

IF YOU'RE LOOKING FOR HERBS *that will grace your table (without a lot of effort on your part), try the simple plants that follow.*

No-jive chives

Indoors or out, chives are easy to grow. If outside, give them a spot with full sun. If you want to grow chives indoors, place them in a pot of standard commercial potting soil. Use a fairly large pot to accommodate their extensive root system, and be sure to place them under good lamplight. Gently scatter the seeds, and then lightly cover them with soil. Sprinkle with water until the soil is just damp.

In about 2 weeks, your first grass-like seedlings will appear. These are edible, although you should rinse them off first and remove the tiny roots. Thin the seedlings (you do it by simply eating them). Mature chives are from 8 to 12 inches tall. When you cut leaves for garnishes or to add to salads, cut from the outside.

Don't remove all the leaves unless you intend to terminate the plant. Chives are a perennial plant, and once they get healthily started you can divide their expanding clumps to create more plants.

CHIVES

Gourmet garlic

Garlic may not be as attractive as other members of the lily (*Allium*) family, but if cooks were given a choice of which to grow, the smelly version would win hands down. Garlic has been grown since practically forever. It was nurtured in Egypt while the first of the Great Pyramids was built, about 6,000 years ago. Laborers working on the pyramids under the hot desert sun were fed garlic to stave off heat stroke. It has had, and continues to have, numerous health-related uses, and today you can buy it packaged with and without odor.

To grow your own, you can start from seed, or, more conveniently, you can buy bulbs at any garden center or at the supermarket. There are early- and late-season types of garlic, so try some of each. Planting time outdoors in the midwest and northern states is right after the ground thaws. In the south and on the west coast, where the ground does not freeze, plant around August.

GARLIC

PLANTING GARLIC CLOVES IN CELL PACKS

Garlic bulbs are made up of numerous small bulblets, called cloves. Separate the cloves and place them in the soil with the pointy side up. Use good organic soil, preferably with a little sand mixed in. Plant the cloves about 1 inch deep. Keep the soil slightly on the dry side. Do not over-water, or the bulbs will rot. I have also grown garlic indoors on a very sunny windowsill in good potting soil.

Garlic tolerates a wide range of climates, but needs a period of 1 to 2 months at about 32 to 50° F in winter. Some variants are extremely hardy; use those recommended for your area. Garlic grows best in an open, sunny position on light soil that does not have to be very fertile. Plant one clove 1-inch deep in each section of a module. Cover the cloves with more compost. Place the modules in a sheltered position.

After about 3 months, the leaves will turn brown. It is now harvest time. Remove any loose dirt and rootlets from the bulbs, and begin cooking. Dry those that you don't want to cook right away. Dried garlic will generally be stronger than fresh.

■ **Braid the leaves** *of several garlic bulbs together, tie the end with a piece of string, and hang them up to store.*

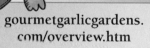

INTERNET

**gourmetgarlicgardens.
com/overview.htm**

Click here for a garlic overview: Garlic, the sweet breath of life! If you like garlic, this is the site to visit to find out more. There are good descriptions of the garden varieties available, history, folklore, harvesting information, cooking tips, growing tips, health benefits, garlic chemistry, reference books, on-line purchase catalogs, and how to braid. Lots of fun information!

Elephant garlic (Allium ampeloprasum) is not a true garlic; it is a leek and has a relatively placid taste. Try growing some of this too.

Marvelous mint

Mint can be found in many varieties, including apple, orange, peppermint, pineapple, and spearmint. All mints are perennial, and grow rapidly if they're given plenty of water.

Mints are great for places where you can keep them confined. Given good care, they may grow so rapidly by underground root runners going this way and that, that you'll wish you never saw a mint.

Culinary advocates grow a garden of mints in colorful pots. In fact, they are among the very few herbs that do nicely in pots that don't have good drainage. For mint grown in pots, it is best to pinch the tops to keep them at about 10 inches high.

PLANTING INVASIVE HERBS

When planting invasive herbs, such as tansy or woodruff, in open ground, you can restrict their spread by growing them in a sunken container. Old buckets, large pots or even heavy-duty plastic bags are suitable, although it is usually necessary to make drainage holes. For best results, lift and divide the plants each spring and replant young, vigorous pieces in the containers using fresh compost.

1 **Position your pot**

Dig a hole large enough to accommodate a large pot or old bucket. Make drainage holes in the pot, then place it in the hole and fill with a soil and compost mixture.

2 **Plant the herb**

Plant the herb in the pot, firming it in well. Add enough compost to conceal the pot's rim, and water thoroughly. Each spring, replant and replace the soil mix in the pot.

CORSICAN MINT (*Mentha requienii*)

Mints need about 3 hours of sun each day. (An exception is Corsican mint, a dense groundcover that does very well in semi-shade.) Each plant grows from 1 to 4 feet high, and most have small white, pink, or lavender flowers in mid-summer. To start new plants, just take a cutting from an older one and stick it in a glass of water until roots form, then plant.

Mints are high in vitamin A, vitamin C, and calcium, and also contain some niacin and potassium. They are used in teas, liqueurs, jellies, salads, soaps, to flavor chewing gum, scent perfumes, scent candy, and in sauces. Long ago, before toothbrushes were invented, Roman women chewed a paste made of mint and honey to sweeten their breath.

Parsley particulars

Parsley roots have long been prized for their medicinal value. Dried leaves were used to make tea, and the fresh leaves, chewed, help make breath fresher. There are several parsley varieties, some with curly leaves and some with flat. Parsley is primarily a potted plant, kept either indoors or on a sheltered patio or porch. However, you can get good results outdoors if you plant in good soil and in a sheltered spot. There are reports of gardeners successfully growing parsley (well mulched) under the snow in Maine.

Parsley grown indoors prefers partial sun, and will do fairly well under bright lamplight. Grow it in a commercial potting mix. Drainage must be good, so don't forget that the pot needs a drainage hole. Feed once a month with a weak-strength liquid plant food.

Growing parsley is easiest if you buy young plants in the herb section of your local nursery. However, if you want to plant from seeds, be aware that it does take about 6 weeks for the seeds to sprout. Begin the process from March until early May. To speed it up, soak seeds overnight before planting. Eventually plants will become 6 to 12 inches high. Parsley is a biennial plant, and small yellow flowers appear the second year. After this, the leaves become tough and bitter, so you will need to install new plants. Prolong your plants' productivity by cutting off flower stalks as they first form.

Trivia...

Many people think of parsley as something chefs use to garnish a steak. But aside from its decorative purpose, parsley contains vitamins A and C, calcium, magnesium, potassium, and riboflavin. So be sure to encourage everyone at the table to eat their parsley.

Trivia...

In Greek mythology, the god Pluto was king of Hades, or the underworld. Pluto was married to Persephone, but he fell in love with a beautiful young Grecian nymph named Minthe. In her jealous rage, Persephone decided to get rid of Minthe, changing her into a lowly herb easily stepped on and crushed. The legend goes that this herb is mint, which still sends out runners along the ground to seek her lover. Pluto couldn't do anything about the transformation, but gave the mint a lovely fragrance and the power to make people love her.

Easy-to-grow fragrant herbs

MANY HERBS ARE KNOWN *for their wonderful aroma. Those that I've selected to discuss in detail are also known to be ideal plants for beginning gardeners who may be a bit nervous about choosing and growing herbs.*

CATNIP (*Nepeta faassenii*)

Cavorting with catnip

Certainly cats like catnip, which is precisely why some people plant it. The bruised leaves give off the attractive oil. At one time, catnip was used in foods, flavoring soups, stews, and teas. It does have good amounts of vitamins A and C.

Catnip, called catmint by some, is a hardy perennial. The most common type is a 4-foot bush with gray leaves and spikes of small white flowers that have lavender spots. However, there is also the compact *N. faassenii*, which has gray-green leaves and lavender-blue flower spikes, and another type, called dawn to dusk (*N. grandiflora*), which has rose flower spikes. There is also a Syrian catnip (*N. curvifolia*), available only in specialty catalogs, that has blue-purple flowers.

Catnip attracts honeybees as well as cats. Its flowers will appear in summer and may remain into the early fall. They're excellent for cutting. You can obtain catnip from a friend who will share the roots, or grow it from seed sown directly in the garden in spring or fall. Thin the seedlings to about 24 inches apart. Once the plants have become established they will self-sow.

Catnip isn't picky about where it lives, so it's a good plant for dry, shaded, or sunny areas with subsistence soil. However, a sunny site and somewhat sandy soil will produce catnip with the best fragrance. To keep plants trim, cut them back each year. The only thing that seems to disturb this hardy perennial is over-watering.

Lovely lemon verbena

The leaves of this deciduous South American native give off a distinct lemony scent at the slightest touch. Used by the Incas for stomach ailments, among other purposes, lemon verbena was brought to North America in the 1700s. Dried lemon verbena leaves can retain their scent for years. For use in pot pourris and sachets, the best scent is obtained by picking the leaves during the flowering period.

LEMON VERBENA (*Aloysia triphylla*)

This pale green shrub gets tall and can eventually reach 6 to 10 feet high in the home garden. It can be grown in a container or in a sunny garden corner where it won't overwhelm the smaller herbs. Inconspicuous white to pale lavender flowers appear from July to September.

The planting soil for lemon verbena should be organic, with a tendency toward sandy. Keep the soil moist but provide it with good drainage, and fertilize this plant regularly. Since lemon verbena won't make it through a really cold winter, you can either dig it up or take cuttings in mid-summer. If you decide to dig it up, first cut the plant to the ground. Find a dark place to store the roots in moist sand. Replant your roots in spring for quick growth. If you prefer to take cuttings, the cuttings should have at least two joints: the lower joint, without leaves, will be below the soil line; the other, with just a few leaves, will be above the soil line.

Majoring in marjoram

Marjoram could be considered a true all-purpose herb. Marjoram's aroma comes from its small round bracts that are covered with shiny oil glands. (As a refresher, the bracts are the modified leaves growing just below a flower or flower cluster.) The ancient Greeks and Romans used fragrant marjoram in perfumes, food, and medicine. They crowned young lovers and bridal couples with marjoram wreaths and planted marjoram on the graves of loved ones as a token of good feelings and remembrance. Long before we had carpets, or vacuum cleaners, homeowners would sprinkle marjoram along the ground to sweeten one's step. And of course, today we use marjoram to flavor food. If you plan to use your marjoram in cooking, you'll want to have about a half-dozen plants, as the leaves shrink quite a bit when dried.

Marjoram is a quite tender perennial that is usually grown as an annual. It will not survive a cold winter. However, it is easily grown from seeds sown in spring, or from cuttings taken in summer. If you want, you can start the seeds indoors in March, then transplant outdoors in May. The seed is slow to germinate, or sprout. When it does, thin the seedlings so that they are about 6 inches apart. The plant grows to about 12 to 24 inches, and has gray-green leaves. Like most plants from the Mediterranean, marjoram prefers a warm, sunny location in slightly alkaline soil. Flowers, appearing in late summer, are tiny, white, pink, or pale lilac.

MARJORAM
(*Origanum majorana*)

291

Marjoram does quite well in pots for patio use, and makes a delightful hanging basket plant. It will even grow indoors if given enough light. To grow inside, use potting soil that is equal parts sand, soil and peat moss. Don't forget to water so the soil stays slightly moist. As mentioned above, you can plant it from seed, or you can purchase marjoram in the herb section of most garden centers.

Simple scented geraniums

Scented geraniums were a choice plant during the Victorian era, rivaling ferns in popularity. There seems to be a geranium available in every scent: almond, apple, apricot, coconut, lemon, lime, mint-rose, rose, nutmeg, peach, peppermint, and strawberry, to name a few. The fragrance of geraniums is fine on a sunny day, and at all times when you gently rub the leaves between your fingers and daintily sniff. There are people who grow nothing but scented geraniums. In addition to their lovely fragrance, they also have white to rose-colored flowers. There are also trailing scented geraniums, which are particularly nice in pots, hanging baskets, and even as groundcovers.

Trivia...

In Greek mythology, Amaracus, a young and delicate servant of the cruel King of Cyprus, accidentally dropped a precious vial of perfume containing the juice of the world's only red pearl. In his terror of the ensuing punishment, Amaracus fainted. The local gods, feeling kind, instantly changed the perfume-soaked Amaracus into a fragrant herb, amarakos. The Latin word somehow transformed into the word "marjoram," which means "joy of the mountain." The oil is still used in some perfumes.

Most geraniums will start easily, if quite slowly, from seed, but I find it much simpler to grow them from cuttings. Just take a stem that's a few inches long, let it dry off for an hour, then set it about one inch deep in a mixture of sand and peat moss. Or you can just stick the stem in a glass of water until the roots appear. If that isn't simple, nothing is.

Outdoors, these geraniums aren't too fussy about soil, but a good organic, well-drained soil always helps things along. These plants prefer a slightly dry environment, but not too dry or their lower leaves will drop off. Most geraniums eventually reach from 2 to 4 feet in height and will grow equally wide. Pinch the top growing tips to inspire fullness rather than ranginess. Leaves for the different scented geraniums vary greatly, from fernlike to large and round. You'll also see a wide array of shades of green in the leaves and some have variegated foliage.

■ **Rober's Lemon Rose**
is a scented geranium with a heady rose and lemon aroma.

Indoors, or in patio pots, plant scented geraniums in equal portions of sand, soil, and peat moss, and plan on fertilizing about once a month with a liquid plant food. You'll probably find a limited selection in the herb section of a garden center, and it's likely you'll want to browse through some garden catalogs for variety.

Preserving your harvest

IF YOU'RE SUCCESSFUL with your herbal efforts, which of course you will be, the chances are pretty good that you just won't be able to use all the herbs you have grown when they're fresh. Moreover, having your own herbs on hand through the winter makes the drearier months of the year pass by just a little more quickly. So here we'll explore some ways you can enjoy the fruits of your labors year round.

Harvesting herbs

Culinary herbs harvested for their leaves should always be cut just as flower buds appear. By cutting at this time, dried herbs will have the strongest flavor. Do this first thing in the morning, right after the dew dries off the leaves, but before the sun's heat has evaporated or changed the plant's basic oils, decreasing its quality. It's best to do most of your harvesting when the weather is dry rather than damp or rainy. You can get several harvests off most of the leafy herbs, as long as you don't remove too much of the plant at one time.

Herbs grown primarily for their flowers, such as chamomile, should also be harvested right as the plant begins flowering. For both types of herbs, you will need a sharp knife or good pruning shears to harvest properly. Use a sharp spade to dig up garlic and other root crops.

■ **Dry seed heads** *by covering them with muslin or a paper bag, secured in place with string or a rubber band. Hang them upside down in a warm place until dry.*

■ **Dried seeds of aromatic** *dill (Anethum) are often used for culinary purposes.*

If you are into seed gathering, do this as the seed heads form by cutting the flower with a few inches of stem attached. Immediately place each herb group upside down into labeled brown paper bags. The seeds will fall into the bag as the plant dries. Always handle carefully when harvesting to prevent most of your seeds from dropping onto the ground. Why not let them dry on the plant? It's too chancy that the seedpods will open and disperse the seed before you collect it.

HERBS IN ICE CUBES

Several different herbs can be used to flavor and enhance the appearance of ice cubes when added to drinks. Suitable herbs include borage, pineapple mint, and parsley, as shown here. Put chopped herbs, or herb flowers like borage, in ice-cube trays, adding about 1 tablespoon of water to each tablespoon of herb. This method is a good way of protecting delicate flowers like borage, which could get crushed during storage.

Freezing your herbs

Herbs with soft leaves, such as basil, chives, dill, marjoram, mint, and parsley, freeze best. If you intend to freeze your harvest, go out when the dew is still on the plants. After you bring them indoors, rinse the plants well and gently shake them dry. To freeze, put sprigs of each herb type into individual bags, and then store them in your freezer. Store frozen herbs in small quantities and don't refreeze once thawed.

Another way to freeze herbs in small amounts is to chop them into very fine pieces, and freeze them with water in ice cube trays. Pop out the frozen cubes and place in freezer storage bags. When cooking, it is not necessary to defrost frozen herbs.

Drying herbs

Proper herb drying is essential to retain as much of the original color, flavor, and fragrance as possible. Good drying techniques remove moisture, thereby preventing chemical changes, mold, and enzyme activity that can destroy your best growing efforts. There are various methods for drying herbs. For limited amounts, use string or rubber bands to fasten the collected herbs loosely in small bunches. The fastener should be tight, because the herbs will shrink as they dry. But the bunches themselves should not be too thick, or the inner parts may rot. Hang the bunches upside down in a warm, not hot, dry, shady place that has good air circulation.

Do not allow sunlight to reach the drying herbs, as it will cause the leaves to darken considerably, even turning them black.

Drying times for each herb will vary, but on average, 1 to 2 weeks will be required. All herb bunches should be left until they are crisp to the touch, but not powdery. If you let them hang too long, some herbs begin reabsorbing moisture, making them useless for storing purposes.

Once the bunches are dry, remove the leaves, or flowers, from the stems. Store the dried leaves in dark, airtight, glass jars. Do not store in paper or plastic containers, as they will allow the herbal oils to evaporate. Canning jars, on the other hand, are excellent for storing dried herbs. Put a dark jacket around each one, and be sure to label and date the contents. Keep the jars in a cool place out of direct light. Dried culinary herbs will keep their flavor for about 6 months.

■ **Air-dry herbs by** *spreading them on a mesh-covered rack. Leave them in a warm place until dry.*

An alternate drying method, if you have a lot of herbs, is to spread them loosely on wire mesh racks or on racks covered with paper towels, newspaper, or muslin fabric. Again, shade, warmth, and good air circulation are musts. The herbs should be stirred gently every day to encourage even drying. When the plants feel dry to the touch, they are ready. Do not wait until they crumble when you touch them.

A simple summary

✔ Herbal gardens range from the rather formal to the very expressive. They provide a great opportunity to plan your own special place.

✔ When selecting herbs, consider how many of each you'll need for a gratifying harvest. A few herbs are rampant growers, and you should know this before planting.

✔ Most herbs need full sun for good growth.

✔ Determine how much land you have to dedicate to herb use exclusively, or what sites intermingled with other plants are suitable.

✔ Decide whether you want herbs for cooking, for fragrance, for craft, or if you want a mixture of each.

✔ The majority of herbs grow well in containers, so you can have your herbal garden on your patio, or even in your kitchen.

PART FIVE

SUCCULENT HOUSELEEK

TYING IT ALL TOGETHER

EVERY GARDEN NEEDS *unifying elements* – some common thread, like a leitmotif in music, that joins your home and garden together. And bringing *harmony* to all aspects of your outdoor space means providing a nice smooth segue from one area to the next.

How do you do this? You *keep it simple*, of course. In this part I'll take a look at some of the ways you can create a complete, beautiful environment.

Chapter 16

Glorious Groundcovers

GROUNDCOVERS ARE LOW-GROWING PLANTS that spread (gradually or rapidly) to form a moderate or dense cover over the soil. They are used for many purposes, such as to control erosion, to cover slopes, to unify a garden scene, to provide plantings beneath shrubs, to deter weeds, and to serve as an alternative to grass, concrete, or mulch. Some groundcovers can be walked on, others serve more decorative purposes.

In this chapter...

✓ Low-profile groundcovers

✓ High-speed groundcovers

✓ Dry climate groundcovers

✓ Beach covers

✓ Cool in the shade

GROUNDCOVER HERBS CREEPING THROUGH PAVING

Low-profile groundcovers

SOME LIKE IT SUBTLE. If you do, consider a very low-growing groundcover. Some of these recommendations are most often used between stepping stones or in other somewhat limited areas; others spread quite quickly, so they need a wider expanse. My choices include these, and some that I'll describe in detail:

Baby's tears

This moss-like, creeping, light green groundcover doesn't get higher than 3 inches, and usually stays lower than that. It will root easily from any piece of stem, so you can either buy it at the nursery or find some at a friend's garden. Place plants about 6 inches apart for quick cover and to deter weeds.

BABY'S TEARS (*Soleirolia soleirolii*)

Baby's tears (*Soleirolia soleirolii*), so named because of the tiny round leaves, will need regular watering and good soil, but this evergreen doesn't require a lot of sunlight. You can even try growing it in almost full shade. It is hardy to 25° F, and in perfect surroundings can be somewhat aggressive. Try it between stepping stones around the perimeter of the house. Baby's tears' little flowers are white and are not easy to see.

Chamomile

Small, yellow, button-like flowers cover the bright, medium green leaves of this perennial evergreen herb. It will grow from 3 to 6 inches high in ordinary garden soil. Buy seedlings in the multipack, and place 12 inches apart. Buy several packs if you need a lot at once, because chamomile (*Chamaemelum nobile*) will meander along gradually and take its time filling up space. This groundcover forms a thick enough cover that weeds don't get much of a foothold. Chamomile prefers sun. It's a good choice for areas that don't get much rainfall, as it's somewhat drought tolerant after it gets started, and likes to be kept slightly on the dry side.

Trivia...

In addition to being pretty, chamomile has a number of uses. It has long been believed to have a soothing effect. The soft aromatic leaves, placed in a muslin bag, can be floated in the bathtub and are supposed to encourage relaxation. Of course, chamomile tea recipes abound. If you're a blond, and you want to have more fun, use this sweet-smelling herb to make a hair rinse. Put the chamomile flowers in a saucepan, and pour very hot water over them. Let sit until cool, then strain.

Creeping thyme

Creeping thyme (*Thymus praecox arcticus*) makes an almost flat, dark green ground cover. It is super hardy after it gets well started. Buy them in six-packs or by the *flat*, and place plants 6 inches apart in full sun or light shade and average soil. Small flowers, which attract bees (good for pollination!), are usually purple, but you may find some with pink, lilac, red, or white flowers. Thyme blooms from summer to fall. Although this evergreen perennial withstands both neglect and drought, it does much better with occasional watering. There are several types of creeping thyme, but this is the hardiest (it will tolerate below-zero temperatures) and spreads the most quickly. It is also occasionally used as a seasoning, but common thyme (*T. vulgaris*) is more often the culinary choice.

DEFINITION

A flat is a container, usually made of wood, about 18 by 18 inches wide and 2 inches high. It's used to hold a whole batch of groundcover plants.

Mazus

This groundcover will grow from 1 to 2 inches high. An evergreen in mild-winter areas, mazus (*Mazus reptans*) disappears in cold climates, reappearing quickly in spring if it's protected by mulch. It likes regular water and good soil that never quite dries out. In hotter areas it will do well in part shade; otherwise you should give it full sun. The tiny flowers are purple-blue, appearing in clusters in late spring. Mazus will eventually form a dense groundcover. It roots at the joints and is easily increased by division.

MAZUS (*Mazus reptans*)

INTERNET

muextension.missouri.
edu/xplor/agguides/
hort/g06835.htm

Visit this site for recommended groundcovers, where to place them, selection, and culture. Although this is from the University of Missouri horticultural department, the information is applicable throughout North America.

More low-profile groundcovers:

- Australian violet (*Viola hederacea*)
- Cinquefoil (*Potentilla*)
- Creeping Jenny (*Lysimachia nummularia*)
- Creeping speedwell (*Veronica repens*)
- Creeping wire vine (*Muehlenbeckia axillaris*)
- Green carpet (*Herniaria glabra*)
- Mint (*Mentha*)
- Parrot's beak (*Lotus berthelotii*)
- Purple rock cress (*Aubrieta deltoidea*)
- Sea pink (*Armeria maritima*)
- Stonecrop (*Sedum*)
- Wall rockcress (*Arabis caucasica*)
- Woolly yarrow (*Achillea tomentosa*)

High-speed groundcovers

WITH EXCELLENT TREATMENT and rich soil, rapidly growing groundcovers can become rampant. However if you, like me, have tough-toil soil, "rapidly growing" can be actually moderate – but it does grow, which is nice.

Greater periwinkle

With plenty of water and light shade, this 18-inch groundcover has been used to control highway erosion. Introduced to North America in 1769, it tolerates below-zero temperatures, and once established it deters just about all weeds. Also called big periwinkle or blue buttons, greater periwinkle (*Vinca major*) is a favorite for large, sloping areas where fussing is inconvenient. Place the plants 18 inches apart. It does well in sun where the summers are not very hot and long, and is also happy in quite a bit of shade. It spreads by rooting stems, with pretty blue flowers appearing among dark green leaves in both spring and fall. A relative, lesser periwinkle (*V. minor*) grows to only 6 inches high. Usually seen with lilac-blue flowers, there are varieties with white, blue, pink, reddish, or purple flowers, and also some with variegated leaves. Also called dwarf periwinkle, it is somewhat less aggressive than greater periwinkle, but is still quite energetic if watered regularly.

GREATER PERIWINKLE
(*Vinca major*)

Indian mock strawberry

This plant gets its name from its pretty, half-inch berries that resemble strawberries. But these berries are inedible, so just enjoy them for their good looks. They're followed by petite, bright yellow flowers that bloom all spring and into the early summer. I use Indian mock strawberry (*Duchesnea indica*) in semi-shade to blanket a hard-to-reach side yard. Growing only 4 inches high, the only problem is convincing it to stay on its site, rather than wander by trailing and rooting stems into adjacent areas of the garden. Other than occasional watering, this plant needs virtually no care. It tolerates below-zero temperatures and so is good for colder climates. I've read that birds like the berries.

Serbian bellflower

There are so many campanulas that entire books have been devoted to them. Most are exquisitely pretty plants, but for cranky soil, Serbian bellflower (*Campanula poscharskyana*) is one of the best. Its dainty blue bells can appear from spring to early fall. It likes full sun in cooler climates, but is happy in partial shade elsewhere.

Although this evergreen perennial tolerates occasional drought, it needs regular watering to thrive and form low, up to 4-inch-high, undulating growth. It is occasionally mislabeled as Dalmatian bellflower (*C. portenschlagiana*), its cousin. The latter has purple flowers and it is not as aggressive. Both are hardy in below-zero temperatures.

SERBIAN BELLFLOWER
(*Campanula poscharskyana*)

Snow-in-summer

Quite happy in dry, poor soil, this 3-inch-high gray groundcover makes an interesting contrast to taller plants. In a suitable situation, very few weeds dare to emerge. This is one of the few groundcovers that does well in reflected heat from concrete. Just water it enough to get started and, once underway, water occasionally. In early summer white flowers blanket the leaves, looking almost as if they are covered with snow. Easily multiplied from segments and tolerant of below-zero temperatures, snow-in-summer (*Cerastium tomentosum*) may even straggle along in sand.

■ **Rampant groundcover** *is furnished by snow-in-summer* (Cerastium tomentosum). *This is a very tolerant plant, happy in just about any sunny situation, provided you give it a little water when thirsty.*

More high-speed groundcovers:

- Cape weed (*Arctotheca calendula*)
- Creeping gold wallflower (*Erysimum kotchyanum*)
- Creeping Jenny (*Lysimachia nummularia*)
- Creeping speedwell (*Veronica repens*)
- Fleabane (*Erigeron*)
- Fountain grass (*Pennisetum alopecuroides*)
- Green carpet (*Herniaria glabra*)
- Ground ivy (*Glechoma hederacea*)
- Ground morning glory (*Convolvulus sabatius*)
- Ivy (*Hedera*)
- Ivy geranium (*Pelargonium*)
- Kenilworth ivy (*Cymbalaria muralis*)
- Mint (*Mentha*)
- Rose carpet knotweed (*Polygonum bistorta*)
- Rosea ice plant (*Drosanthemum*)
- Sage-leaf rockrose (*Cistus salvifolius*)
- St. John's wort (*Hypericum calcyinum*)
- Spreading myoporum (*Myoporum parvifolium*)
- Stonecrop (*Sedum*)
- Sweet woodruff (*Galium odoratum*)
- Trailing African daisy (*Osteospermum fruticosum*)
- Trailing gazania (*Gazania rigens*)
- Trailing ice plant (*Lampranthus*)

Dry climate groundcovers

THE ABILITY TO TOLERATE DRYNESS, *or drought, is a variable. Dry to one plant means never watering; dry to another is watered seldom. It is best to be aware of this if you are thinking of placing a groundcover in an area that can't be reached by a hose or sprinkler.*

When most of us think of plants for dry areas we think of cacti. All cacti are *succulents*, but there are many more types of succulents, including stonecrop. Stonecrops are low-growing succulents with creeping stems. Their leaves are green and come in a variety of sizes, shapes, and colors. You'll see stonecrop included in the following list of good groundcovers for arid areas:

Blue fescue

Often used in dry landscaping, the serene blue-gray leaves of blue fescue (*Festuca ovina glauca*) accent taller, brighter perennials. Only 7 to 10 inches high, blue fescue develops into a tufted, mounding groundcover that usually displays moderate growth, expanding from individual plants that may each get to 12 or more inches wide. During the summer months brownish, rather bland flowers appear on little spikes. Blue fescue markedly prefers sun, but it will also tolerate light shade. To keep it looking its best, just water it occasionally.

BLUE FESCUE (*Festuca ovina glauca*)

Silver brocade artemisia

My 6-inch-high groundcover artemisia (*Artemisia stelleriana*) started when a dinner guest gave me a home-grown flower bouquet set up with stems of gray. Out of curiosity, when the flowers faded I tucked the stems in a glass of water on a sunny bathroom windowsill and forgot about it. Three weeks later, the stems developed roots. The plant went into the sunny, dry spot where just about everything had refused to grow because of concrete-reflected heat. The artemisia thrived. I clipped a few stems, rooted them in water, and placed them into more tough, small areas, such as the inside of an ancient truck tire that has been transformed into a raised bed. To get groundcover, you must place each plant about 10 inches apart. Expect artemisia to reach about 15 inches wide. This evergreen perennial has silvery-gray leaves about 2 to 4 inches long.

Trailing gazania

A true sun lover, the daisy-like flowers of gazania (*Gazania rigens*) close up on shady days and at night. Tolerant of pretty much any soil, they need regular watering until they settle in. With hybridization, flower colors are seemingly limitless, including pink, cream, yellow, orange, rose, and scarlet.

Although most of the groundcover flowers are about 1½ inches wide, there are varieties with 3-inch flowers. (These larger versions are better for individual placement rather than groundcover – place them 12 inches apart, and you have a good-natured plush carpet.) Gazania tolerates temperatures to 30° F, but markedly prefers warm and dry surroundings. If you want to play with it a bit, you could always try raising gazania from seed.

GAZANIA
(*Gazania* Chansonette series)

Trailing ice plant

Soil- and drought-tolerant varieties of trailing ice plant (*Lampranthus*) are most often used in planting strips that get limited water. Trailing ice plant has tiny, succulent-type, fleshy leaves, and belongs where temperatures don't drop below 25° F. Because its growth can be rather rapid, an area surrounded by concrete suits it quite well, although it is easy enough to pull up if it becomes annoying. In spring, bright purple, orange, yellow, or florescent pink flowers make a vivid display. Trailing ice plant grows to 6 inches high and is useful for erosion control, seaside gardens, and on slopes. Some people even put it in hanging baskets that aren't easy to water.

More dry climate groundcovers:

- Cape weed (*Arctotheca calendula*)
- Chamomile (*Chamaemelum nobile*)
- Common winter creeper (*Euonymus*)
- Creeping coprosma (*Coprosma*)
- Creeping thyme (*Thymus praecox arcticus*)
- Fountain grass (*Pennisetum alopecuroides*)
- Garden lippia (*Phyla nodiflora*)
- Ground morning glory (*Convolvulus sabatius*)
- Hottentot fig (*Carpobrotus edulis*)
- Lavender cotton (*Santolina chamaecyparissus*)
- Pink Australian fuchsia (*Correa pulchella*)
- Purple rock cress (*Aubrieta deltoida*)
- Red valerian (*Centranthus ruber*)
- Rockrose (*Cistus*)
- Rockspray cotoneaster (*Cotoneaster horizontalis*)
- Snow-in-summer (*Cerastium tomentosum*)
- Spreading myoporum (*Myoporum parvifolium*)
- Stonecrop (*Sedum*)
- Sunrose (*Helianthemum*)
- Trailing African daisy (*Osteospermum fructicosum*)
- Trailing verbena (*Verbena*)
- Woolly lamb's ears (*Stachys byzantina*)
- Woolly yarrow (*Achillea tomentosa*)

Beach covers

FORTUNATELY FOR THOSE AT THE SEASHORE, *a good number of groundcovers work nicely in this environment. Try some of the following plants if your yard gets beach winds and salt sprays:*

CAPE WEED (*Arctotheca calendula*)

Cape weed

I use cape weed (*Arctotheca calendula*) in a really hot, dry, side yard where nothing else wants to tolerate the living conditions. The only problem is it keeps trying to escape into an area with soil less like hardened adobe. It's aggressive enough to require vigilance, but then, that's exactly what you may need. Cape weed can grow to about 8 inches tall, but will hug the ground in dry situations. It can tolerate temperatures down to 25° F and is quite useful on neglected slopes and for erosion control. If you plant it in any form of shade, it will grow with great determination toward sunlight. Cape weed's flowers are daisy-like and yellow, opening during bright days.

Hottentot fig

Hottentot figs (*Carpobrotus edulis*) have thick leaves, and each stem can reach 6 feet long. In some hot, dry areas it is called "freeway ice plant." It helps stabilize beach sand, and tolerates coastal soil spray and some soil salt. The large flowers are yellow and pink. Hottentot figs tolerate temperatures to 25° F.

Hottentot fig does have its advantages, but I don't recommend it for ordinary garden use because it has a bulky appearance and spreads rapidly. Initially lying flat, it may mound gradually as long stems pile on top of one another.

HOTTENTOT FIG
(*Carpobrotus edulis*)

Sage-leaf rockrose

There are many types of rockrose, all originating on dry, stony soil in warm climates. They are grown in parks as well as gardens, and if watered occasionally and given full sun, they'll reward you with lovely springtime flowers in white, light pink, or rose pink.

Although some types of rockrose reach 5 feet high, sage-leaf rockrose grows to only 2 feet in height but has a fast-paced spread up to 6 feet wide. It has white flowers with yellow centers, and is not particular as to soil, other than the necessity for good drainage. Sage-leaf rockrose (*Cistus salvifolius*) tolerates wind, salt spray, and desert conditions, and can withstand temperatures down to 15° F.

St. John's wort

Full of vigor, this 12- to 18-inch-high groundcover, also called Aaron's beard, is quite aggressive, spreading by underground stems. It's better for large areas, and has been used for erosion control and on slopes. Usually evergreen, dark green leaves show off bright yellow, 3-inch flowers from spring through summer. Bees like this plant. Not at all particular about its soil, and often able to compete with tree roots, St. John's wort (*Hypericum calycinum*) tolerates drought well once it gets started. Plant it in full sun to light shade. It looks best if cut back every other year, after all frost danger has disappeared.

ST. JOHN'S WORT (*Hypericum calycinum*)

There are several types of St. John's wort. If you want to take St. John's wort as an herbal supplement, do not try to grow your own. Some varieties contain phototoxins and should not be ingested. Herbal St. John's wort is best purchased at the pharmacy.

More beach covers:

- Basket-of-gold (*Aurinia saxatalis*)
- Bergenia (*Bergenia*)
- Blue fescue (*Festuca ovina glauca*)
- Cotoneaster (*Cotoneaster*)
- Creeping coprosma (*Coprosma*)
- Dwarf rosemary (*Rosmarinus officinalis*)
- Garden lippia (*Phyla nodiflora*)
- Lavender cotton (*Santolina chamaecyparissus*)
- Lilyturf (*Liriope*)
- Mondo grass (*Ophiopogon japonicus*)
- Scotch heather (*Calluna vulgaris*)
- Shrub verbena (*Lantana*)
- Snow-in-summer (*Cerastium tomentosum*)
- Stonecrop (*Sedum*)
- Sunrose (*Helianthemum*)
- Trailing African daisy (*Osteospermum fructicosum*)

Cool in the shade

YOU MIGHT BE LOOKING to soften a shady area. If so, there are a number of lovely groundcovers that aren't unhappy to get a little relief from the sun. I suggest:

CARPET BUGLEWEED (*Ajuga reptans*)

Carpet bugleweed

There are several new varieties of this long-time semi-shade favorite. The older varieties have dark green leaves and grow about 4 inches high. In spring and early summer, the area becomes a carpet of blue as each leaf rosette has a 5-inch-high flower spike. Among the new hybrids are those with larger, variegated pink, green, and white leaves, bronze leaves, and pink flowers. Moderately spreading by creeping stems that root, carpet bugleweed (*Ajuga reptans*) will form a thick enough groundcover to eliminate all but the most persistent weeds. Fertilize it in early spring and water regularly. It will be fine if temperatures don't drop below 5° F.

Creeping Jenny

Also known as creeping Charlie and moneywort, this is truly a hardy, takeover groundcover. Flat and fast, it is sometimes called a weed. But if you have tough soil to cover, where shade and almost soggy soil forbid most else, this is a delightfully pretty perennial plant with bright green, rounded leaves and inconspicuous, bright yellow flowers in summer. I quite like it, and sunlight often helps keep this shade-lover in place. Creeping Jenny (*Lysimachia nummularia*) tolerates below-zero temperatures. There is a gold-leafed variety sometimes offered, but be aware that it needs coddling.

Sweet woodruff

Give this delicate-looking, medium green, aromatic groundcover shade, average soil, and ample moisture, and it will thrive, spreading by rhizomes, or horizontal underground stems. It is easy to divide; space new plants about 12 inches apart. It tolerates temperatures below zero. While there is no fragrance when fresh, dried sweet woodruff (*Galium odoratum*) smells like new-mown hay or, some say, vanilla. In days gone by, sweet woodruff was used to make sachets for linen closets.

In spring, tiny, white flower clusters appear on sweet woodruff. If you want to harvest this herb, do so just before it flowers.

Wild ginger

Usually found in a friend's garden, wild ginger (*Asarum caudatum*) makes a thorough, dark green 4-inch-high groundcover if properly sited. Easy to get started, it tends to persist, so plant it where you want it. Aside from shade and regular watering, it is not demanding at all. Inconspicuously held under the leaves, wild ginger has minute reddish-brown flowers. For eastern gardens, the deciduous Canadian wild ginger (*A. canadense*) is hardier.

More groundcovers for shade:

- Baby's tears (*Soleirolia soleirolii*)
- Bellflower (*Campanula*)
- Bergenia (*Bergenia*)
- Bluets (*Hedyotis*)
- Bridal-wreath (*Francoa*)
- Dichondra (*Dichondra*)
- Dwarf African blue lily (*Agapanthus*)
- Ground ivy (*Glechoma hederacea*)
- Greek yarrow (*Achillea ageratifolia*)
- Indian mock strawberry (*Duchesnea indica*)
- Japanese spurge (*Pachysandra terminalis*)
- Lilyturf (*Liriope*)
- Mint (*Mentha*)
- Mondo grass (*Ophiopogon japonicus*)
- Periwinkle (*Vinca*)
- Plantain lily (*Hosta*)
- Strawberry begonia (*Saxifraga stolonifera*)
- Sweet box (*Sarcococca*)
- Trailing fuchsia (*Fuchsia procumbens*)
- Wandering Jew (*Tradescantia zebrina*)
- Wintergreen (*Gaultheria procumbens*)

A simple summary

✓ Groundcovers are low-growing plants that form a moderate to dense soil cover.

✓ Regardless of the soil conditions that exist where you live, there's a groundcover to suit your situation.

✓ Several groundcovers grow extremely fast once they get started. Make sure you know the speed at which the groundcover you select grows, and plan accordingly.

✓ Groundcovers are very valuable in coordinating a landscape plan, moving the eye easily from one site to another.

✓ Some groundcovers grow slowly, so that weeds emerge, but they eventually will form a mat. Some do not ever grow thickly enough to shut out weeds.

Chapter 17

Luscious Lawns

A NICE GREEN LAWN is what a yard is all about. It's a resting place, a status symbol, sometimes even an obsession. You should know something about your planting area, and your willingness to spend time maintaining it, before you rush out to buy sacks of grass seed.

In this chapter...

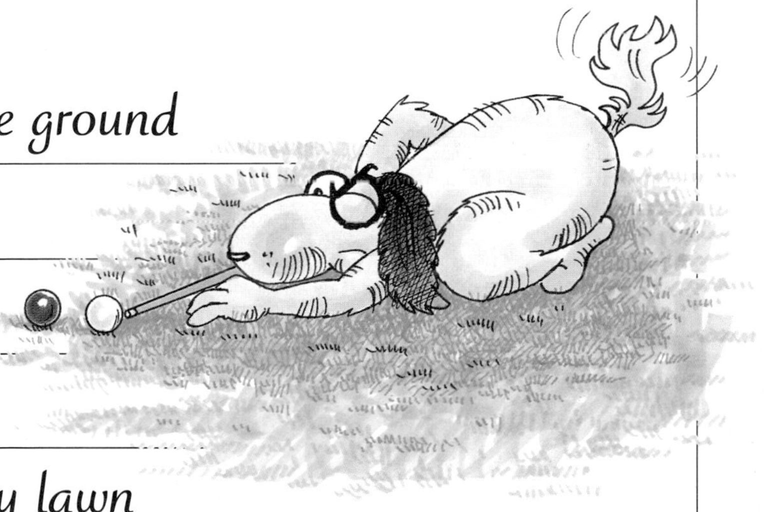

✓ Getting grass off the ground

✓ Northern grasses

✓ Southern grasses

✓ Starting from seed

✓ Maintaining a lovely lawn

✓ Common lawn problems

Getting grass off the ground

ASK YOURSELF THE FOLLOWING QUESTIONS:

1. Will you, the family, the neighbors, or assorted tradespeople be walking across this area? Some grasses like a lot of foot traffic, some just tolerate it, and others are squashed beyond redemption.

2. Being completely honest and looking at your track record for this type of thing, how much time and energy are you truly going to devote to the perfect lawn? (There's a home in my neighborhood that has been sold several times. Each time, the new home-owner rips out the old scraggly lawn and spends a lot of money getting it reseeded, replugged, or laying sod strips down. A year later, suffering from advanced neglect, the new lawn looks like the old lawn. This isn't to say you shouldn't put in a lawn, if you like lawns. But some types of lawn grass are more good-natured than others.)

INTERNET

lawninstitute.com/ guide.html

Take a look at the Lawn Institute Homeowner's Resource Guide to a Beautiful Lawn, with explanations of grass types, seed selection, and how to plant and maintain a lawn.

3. How much water is available? Some areas have occasional droughts when water use is strictly limited. Does this happen in your neighborhood? What about your usual water bill? Do you wince? Lawns can be heavy-duty water users.

4. Is your site in full sun? Partial shade? Some grasses are particular. You will soon realize this if you plant the wrong one.

5. Do you live in the south? If so, you will need what is called a "warm-season" grass. If you live in the north, defined as an area that gets at least some winter snow, you will need a "cool-season" grass. Keep reading to learn the differences between the two.

■ **Choose your grass** *with care. High-quality fine grass (top) needs good growing conditions, regular maintenance, and little use. Coarse grass (bottom) is less fussy and much more hardwearing.*

Cool mixes

Cool-season grass seed mixes contain a variety of seeds designed to grow where the weather turns chilly in the winter. You may not have much choice about what's in the prepackaged mixes. Generally, a mix will contain some Kentucky bluegrass, some narrow-leaf perennial ryegrasses, and some fine fescue. If you are really into a fine lawn, take note of the ingredients and the percentage of each type of grass seed included in different mixes. Armed with this knowledge, evaluate which type of grass you want to predominate, and purchase accordingly.

Some grass seed mixes are more expensive than others. If you're wondering whether it is worth it to buy a more expensive mix, the answer is usually yes.

The more expensive grass seed mixtures should be specific as to what type of grass is in the package, and broadly speaking, "brand name" grasses will be of better quality than "generic" grasses. For example, look for names such as bonnieblue Kentucky bluegrass, rather than Kentucky bluegrass; fortress fine fescue, rather than fescue; and Manhattan perennial ryegrass, rather than ryegrass.

Resistance is not futile

You may be tempted, after looking at the fine, green lawns in picture books, to get only one type of grass, such as the legendary Kentucky bluegrass.

It's not a good idea to buy only one type of grass — lawns do tend to get lawn diseases, and some of these target one type of grass more than others. If you only have one variety and a fungus comes upon the scene, there goes all your hard work.

All the northern, cool-season grasses come in mixtures. If one doesn't work out, the others may be fine. Just so you know.

When shopping for grass seed, you may see the word "endophytes" in descriptions of the grass cultivar. This means the cultivars have been inoculated, or implanted, with organisms that make them resistant to certain insects and diseases, as well as more tolerant of heat and drought. I recommend these cultivars.

Northern grasses

SNOW AND COLD WEATHER *translate into cool-season grasses. They will not do well in areas where summers are long and hot. Plant cool-season grasses in the spring or fall. To get the inside scoop on some common cool-season grasses, keep reading.*

Bentgrass

Ample sunshine enables bentgrass (*Agrostis*), also called bents, to create a thick, lush lawn in cool, moist areas, such as coastal regions. But it does require nurturing, so if you don't want the fuss of precise fertilization, watering, and mowing, avoid too much bentgrass in a seed mix. Bentgrass grows rapidly where it's happy, requiring you to mow more than once a week to a preferred ½-inch height. Tolerant of only light foot traffic, this is a "show" and putting green lawn. Look for the type named colonial bent – it's more versatile than creeping bent, which requires a special mower.

Fine fescue

Quite a few types of fine fescue (*Festuca*) are available, including red fescue (*F. rubra*), chewing fescue (*F. rubra* Commutata) and hard fescue (*F. ovina durisuscula*). Fine fescues' leaves resemble tiny soft needles. They're ideal for heavy traffic areas, and tolerate partial shade. Although fine fescues are neither soil fussy nor water demanding, they do better with good growing conditions. They should be kept about 2 inches high. Hard fescue has the best heat and drought tolerance of the bunch.

Kentucky bluegrass

Overwhelmingly popular, the dark green, fine Kentucky bluegrass (*Poa pratensis*) forms a lush carpet. It is usually mixed with fine fescues or perennial ryegrasses for cover purposes, as it takes a while to establish itself, and it requires regular water and fertilizer. Most members of the *Poa* genus prefer sunlit glades. Rough bluegrass (*P. trivialis*) cultivars will grow in shade and damp soil, but are not as hardy as the *P. pratensis* cultivars. I recommend the more disease-resistant adelphi, bonnieblue, and touchdown.

Ryegrass

Ryegrass (*Lolium*) is used as a part of grass mixes, seldom on its own. Although ryegrass is available in annual and perennial varieties, it is best used for lawns in the perennial (*L. perenne*) form. A sun lover, it may adapt to very light shade. Perennial ryegrass makes a good quick, temporary cover until another grass in the mix takes over. To look its best, it needs to be mowed with a very sharp, clean mower. Give it regular watering and fertilization.

Southern grasses

THE SUMMER HEAT AND HUMIDITY in the south creates special needs for lawn enthusiasts. Warm-season grasses, also called hot-season and sub-tropical grasses, are generally more resistant to heat, drought, and weeds than cool-season varieties. Warm-season grasses should be planted in late spring or early summer.

Bermuda grass

There are many cultivars, or named varieties, of this medium to dark green grass. It is medium-textured, and is probably among the best for southern states. Easy to grow and amenable to foot traffic, including sports fields, Bermuda grass (*Cynodon dactylon*) enjoys hot weather, prefers slightly acid soil, and demands full sun. In exchange for all this good behavior, you must feed it regularly with lawn fertilizer. However, Bermuda grass doesn't thrive in temperatures below 55° F. Once it gets slightly chilly, the grass turns drab brown. If you like short grass, it can be mowed down to ½ an inch high.

Bermuda grass can be somewhat aggressive. If it invades your flower area, it can be extremely difficult to get rid of.

Bahiagrass

This fairly coarse grass is heat loving, drought-tolerant, and doesn't mind poor-quality, sandy soils – the bane of some gardeners' grass-growing existence. It will also tolerate a fair amount of neglect. It is available as seed, as well as pre-seeded soil. Because bahiagrass (*Paspalum notatum*) grows quickly, it does need frequent mowing. The grass should be cut when it reaches 2 or 3 inches.

Zoysiagrass

This slow-growing, dark green grass is thick and attractive, at least during spring and summer. In winter it turns brown and stays that way for several months. The planting site should be sunny, as it grows even more slowly in semi-shade. It will take about 2 years to get full coverage of this grass in a sunny site. To get a thicker lawn quickly, combine it with one of the faster-growing fescues. Zoysiagrass (*Zoysia*) does not like soggy or poorly drained soil. It also demands a bit more care than other grasses, because **thatch** must be removed regularly. However, it is especially resistant to weeds, insects, and diseases and is quite drought-resistant.

DEFINITION

Thatch is a layer of dead roots and stems that builds up between growing grass and the soil.

Starting from seed

THIS WILL REQUIRE *some heavy tilling, and you may end up sharing some seeds with the birds. Just make sure you get enough to go around.*

Tilling the soil

If you are planting from seed, you begin by either tilling the area with a rotary tiller (you can rent them) or digging out the area where you'll be planting to a 6-inch depth. Remove all rocks, roots, and miscellaneous items.

PREPARING THE SOIL

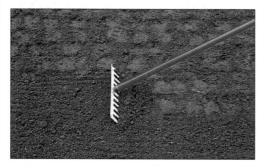

1 **Rake the soil**

After firming the tilled soil by treading evenly over the whole area, rake it very finely, removing any debris or weeds.

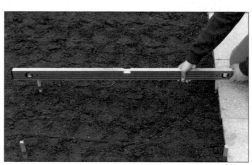

2 **Check the level**

To ensure you get a lovely flat lawn, check that the area is level after firming down the soil. Measure at regular intervals with a level.

After making sure your soil level is even throughout, relaxation then ends, because now weed seeds, deprived of competition and given more sunshine, will begin sprouting. Let them have their way for about 3 weeks, and then *rototill* or chop them out. Now you have to level the ground again. Buy a truckful of good topsoil, and rake this about 1 inch deep into the entire area. Let the topsoil fill in any low-lying areas. Smooth everything out again. You may want to rent a plastic or metal lawn roller for this purpose.

DEFINITION

When you rototill, *you dig. Also called rotary tillers or power cultivators, they have sharp rotating tines. They are also used to aerate, de-thatch, or make planting rows.*

Fertilize obediently

Now, using a hand-held or other spreader, distribute a lawn fertilizer over the area. Ask your local nursery staff what type of fertilizer is best for the soil in your area. Obey all instructions on the fertilizer container. Then, once again, add a topsoil layer, up to 6 inches deep, and level this out.

SOW YOUR SEEDS

 Make a grid

For large areas, it's better to mark out a grid system before sowing, so you can be sure you spread the seeds evenly. Use stakes to divide up the site into many equal squares. Weigh out each portion of seed, scattering half of it up and down and the other half side to side.

 Rake over the soil

Once you have finished sowing, lightly rake over the surface of the soil. Work across the whole area carefully to cover the seeds. In the following days and weeks, water the site regularly. Be sure not to walk on the area for at least 2 months.

Aftercare

You'll need to water at least twice a day using the fine mist nozzle on your garden hose. Use a sprinkler only after the seeds have germinated. Germination takes from 1 to 3 weeks, depending on the grass species. Do not let the young grass dry out. You will not be able to resuscitate it. Do not walk on it for about 2 months. Mow only after the grass is about 3 inches high. Fertilize again in the fall with a lawn fertilizer.

Warm plugs

Warm-season grasses, for the south where summers get hot and humid, are usually not sold in seed form. You buy a specific variety as *sod*, *plugs*, or *sprigs*. You can buy pre-seeded soil segments in the north too.

Planting plugs

As with seeding and sodding, you must prepare the area by removing any existing plants and, of course, rocks and larger detritus. When your new lawn area is ready, dig holes about 12 inches apart. Your plugs, kept moist and covered until planting time, will be placed individually in the pre-dug holes. Each plug is from 2 to 4 square inches, so the pre-dug holes must be large enough to accommodate them easily. Water your new lawn regularly, not letting the soil dry out. Keep weeds at bay by weeding between the plugs. Install sprigs using the same procedure as plugs.

■ **Space the plugs** *evenly over the area, planting them 6 to 12 inches apart. When they are all planted, apply a top-dressing of soil over the whole area and make sure they are kept well watered.*

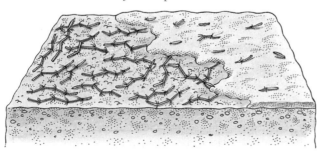

■ **Distribute the sprigs** *over the surface of the soil and then cover them with top-dressing of fine soil. Water well.*

DEFINITION

Sod *gives you an instant lawn. It is mature grass with roots set in good soil.* **Plugs** *are smaller, cut-out sections of good growing lawn inserted into prepared ground.* **Sprigs** *are individual grass plants.*

Trivia...

In Middle English, the word laund *was used for a woodland glade, or a place without trees. Eventually, the word "lawn" was derived from it.*

■ **When buying sod,** *make sure all pieces look healthy and of good quality, and that none is showing any bare or brown patches.*

SIMPLE SODDING

 Make a start

Begin by laying the first row of sod against a straight edge, such as a path or board, so that you can use it as a guide. Each piece should lie flat and be positioned so that it's flush against the next one.

 Kneel on a board

Once you've finished the first row, place a board on top of it and kneel on the board. Lay the second row of sod, staggering the joins against those of the previous row. Keep going until you have covered the entire area.

 Firm the sod down

With the back of a rake, firm down the turf to get rid of any air pockets and to create good contact between the grass roots and the soil. Or, you could use a light roller to do the job.

 Water thoroughly

Give the newly planted sod a good drink of water and keep watering it daily for at least 2 weeks. The roots in the sod will eventually take hold in the soil below.

Maintaining a lovely lawn

THERE'S NOTHING DIFFICULT *about keeping your lawn looking beautiful. It does take some time and some dedication, but it doesn't take an advanced degree in horticulture. Just follow these simple steps.*

Mowing made meaningful

If mowing the lawn were a complex task, you wouldn't hire a neighborhood kid to do it. But there is a bit to know about mowing. For example, if your mower blades aren't sharp enough they'll tear the grass instead of cutting it. So get them sharpened if you haven't done so in a while.

Begin mowing in the spring as soon as the grass starts growing. Don't let grass grow too tall because it may then be traumatized by the cutting and slow down future growth. Some gardeners remove the grass clippings mechanically or with a rake after each mowing job. Others prefer to leave a light layer of grass clippings to act as a moisture-protective barrier. This might be a good idea if you live in a particularly dry area. Continue mowing until the fall or when growth ceases. Over-long grass continuing into winter is an open invitation to lawn disease.

Do not let thatch pile up. If it gets to be a thick layer, rake it off and place in the compost pile or the garbage can. If this layer gets more than ½ an inch thick, it can keep water and fertilizer from penetrating into the lawn. If you go over the lawn with a heavy-duty garden rake every few weeks, you can deter thatch buildup. Otherwise you should remove it with a special de-thatching rake sold at most nurseries, or rent a power de-thatcher. De-thatching is best accomplished in early spring on cool-season or northern lawns, and in late spring on warm-season lawns. After de-thatching, always fertilize appropriately.

DE-THATCHING RAKE

■ **Pull the rake** *vigorously when de-thatching, pushing the tines well down into the surface to aerate the lawn and get rid of any buildup.*

Fertilizing facts

Lawns are big nitrogen users and must be fed regularly. Use a lawn fertilizer that has a nitrogen content of about 20 percent. Fertilize during the season when lawns are most capable of absorbing the nutrients.

In the north, that means feed in the spring, early summer, and autumn. In the south, start fertilizing in the spring and continue until cold weather approaches.

An energizing meal in March and April is extremely important, because a rapidly growing lawn quickly uses up soil nutrients. Snow thaws and spring rain will dissolve the fertilizer and help transport it downward through the soil. Apply fertilizer evenly, preferably on a calm day. Otherwise there will be dark green sections you have fertilized, and yellowing areas that have been deprived. A broadcast spreader is most helpful in getting even coverage.

Be water-wise

If possible, water the lawn early in the morning on days when there is no wind. Water only when the lawn is dry. Do not over-water. If you are seeing runoff, the ground may be soaked. One of the more common over-watering problems is caused by not adjusting a sprinkler system for cooler weather or rain. We have all seen sprinklers going full spurt ahead when it's been raining all day. Drowned roots do not produce healthy lawns. It is also possible that the water pressure or amount is excessive, with more water being applied than the soil can absorb at one time, so it runs off. Underneath the top layer, the soil may be dry.

Before you decide that you're over-watering, check out whether the water is actually sinking in. If it's not, you'll need to try a more moderate approach to watering.

Under-watering can be a problem too. Grass roots will only survive with some moisture. If there isn't enough, the grass may be unable to withstand drought or temperature spikes. Check your sprinkler system as the seasons change. The heat of summer is simply going to require more water for your lawn. Check how deeply the water has been absorbed with a shovel, digging to about 6 inches. The soil should be damp. Check several spots, as absorption on slopes or in hollows will differ. If you don't like digging, buy a lawn-water measuring gadget.

■ **Grass roots** *will soon show the signs of a lack of water. If roots remain too close to the surface (top) it means they're just not getting enough moisture down in the soil where they need it. To ensure healthy roots (bottom) make sure that water is getting down to a depth of at least 4 to 6 inches.*

Weeding wisely

Patience is most definitely a virtue when it comes to picking out weeds from pretty green lawns. Among the many perennial and annual weeds you may encounter are bindweed, black medic, clover, crabgrass, dandelion, and plantain. The most effective weed deterrent is a healthy, dense lawn that is well fertilized, watered, and has plenty of air circulation and the sunshine it needs. Always mow to the recommended height. If you mow too short, low-growing weeds have more space to spread and thrive. Pull weeds out consistently so as not to let them get a foothold and just use herbicides on the areas where pulling just won't do the job. There are some organic weed sprays on the market, but you may have to look in specialty catalogs. Chapter 21 covers the use of herbicides in detail.

BINDWEED   CLOVER   PLANTAIN

Common lawn problems

THERE ARE A THOUSAND REASONS *your lawn could drive you crazy – or to the poorhouse. I'll address the most common ones here.*

Too much fertilizer

Fertilizer or other chemical overdoses cause irregular yellowing areas with a dark green border. Water well, and if your grass doesn't recover, remove it and replant with new grass in the afflicted spot.

Wandering Weimaraners

It's a fact of life that passerby dogs peeing on your grass won't do much to improve its appearance. When canines wander onto your lawn, you'll probably notice characteristic browning areas. Female dogs squat when they urinate, so they are the likely suspects if you see canine-caused round lawn circles. Male dogs lift a leg, so shrubs at favorite corners can turn brown or yellow. Grass by these areas will also be affected.

What's in animal urine that's so disturbing? Urine contains nitrogen, and the fertilizer you buy also contains nitrogen. An overdose of either will cause lawn damage or death.

What to do? Water well. Try to keep dogs off your lawn (which may be impossible). You can try fencing off your lawn, or planting a border of something less beckoning (if you can figure out what plant life is unattractive to your neighbor's dog). Some grass types, such as fescue and perennial ryegrass, are more resistant to urine burns than others. Kentucky bluegrass is quite sensitive to it.

Diseases and pests

For more information on how to cope with disease and insect pests, see Chapter 21. But if you want a quick overview, common lawn diseases include anthracnose, brown patch, dollar spot, fusarium patch, fusarium blight, leaf smut, powdery mildew, pythium blight, red thread, rust, septoria leaf spot, slime mold, spring dead spot, and take-all patch. Pests of note are ants, bermuda grass mite, billbugs, cutworms, leafhoppers, mole crickets, white grubs, and sod webworms.

A simple summary

✔ Be honest with yourself about how much time you actually have to spend on lawn care, and how willing you are to use that time for lawn work.

✔ Be aware of any water limitations in your area, current or pending.

✔ You will need a warm-season grass in the south, and a cool-season grass in the north.

✔ You can plant grass with seeds, sod, sprigs, or plugs.

✔ Different grasses have different needs. Check out the strengths and weaknesses of the grasses you like so that you select the correct variety for your site.

✔ Do not over-water, and check to make certain water is soaking down into the soil rather than running off.

✔ Fertilize your lawn regularly and in the recommended seasons. Lawns need lots of nutrients to be healthy.

Chapter 18

A Bounty of Balcony and Patio Plants

Setting up your plants in a large container on a balcony, porch, or patio can be as challenging as moving the furniture, yet again, in your living room. You may like everything orderly, so your pots are in a precise arrangement and all your plants are almost equal height. Then again, you may like the natural look where everything is helter-skelter.

In this chapter...

✓ Container choices

✓ Re-potting like a pro

✓ Potting particulars

✓ Picking plants for the patio

✓ Cacti and other succulents

✓ Seasonal sensations

✓ Basking in baskets

Container choices

YOU HAVE A MOST marvelous choice of containers for balcony and patio plants. You can be strictly economical by using pretty cups with broken handles for small plants, old pots for medium-size greenery, and plastic garbage cans for the larger tree-like versions. Just remember that most objects that did not start out as plant pots don't have drainage holes, so you must not over-water.

■ **Containers in groups** *provide maximum impact. Mix flower colors as well as leaf textures for a truly eye-catching display.*

Another great way to collect containers is to do your shopping at garage sales. You'll find the most expensive planter pots for as little as 50 cents when people move away and just can't take the pots with them. Sometimes you even get plants in the pots for free. Reviving them might be a challenge, but a fun one.

Then, of course, there's the vast array at your nearby garden center, and an even more grandiose selection at the nursery. What do you have to know about containers to get the best results?

■ **You'll find containers** *in just about every size, shape, and color. It's important that your container is the right size for the chosen plant and has good drainage.*

glazed earthenware

unglazed ceramic

wooden Versailles planter

painted Versailles planter

terracotta urn containing New Zealand flax (Phormium tenax)

molded concrete urn

period-style reconstituted stone urn

terracotta trough

Clay pots

Clay pots are everywhere. I think that they have a nice natural look, but you should know that they allow rapid water evaporation in hot weather. Cacti are quite happy in clay pots provided they have drainage holes.

Wood containers

Made of redwood, oak, or cedar (all long-lasting woods), wood containers seem to become part of the plant because they are so well suited to each other. They may be square or round, small or huge. If you are going to plant a dwarf tree on your patio, consider using a wooden half-barrel as the container. At one time these were inexpensive . . . now they have become trendy and so the prices have risen. But they have a charming rustic appearance, and if properly constructed, will last a long time.

Like any large container, they are heavy when filled. A cubic foot of soil can weigh up to 90 pounds. So unless you are quite certain you'll remain where you are currently living for a long time, and during that time you will never have to move that 300 pound-plus container, consider placing it on a low wheeled platform.

There are many other types of wood containers, including the ubiquitous redwood boxes. Make certain they don't leak water as fast as you pour it in. Test them first, and if there seems to be a problem, install a heavy-duty plastic liner.

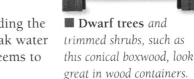

■ **Dwarf trees** *and trimmed shrubs, such as this conical boxwood, look great in wood containers.*

Plastic containers

Lightweight and not overly charming, plastic containers have the advantage of being inexpensive and usually transportable without much stress. You can get small to large pots in identical fuchsia, blue, or black color schemes, which is nice. These pots almost always have drainage holes, and are accompanied by a little saucer that has a tendency to fall off. I usually put a larger saucer underneath to be on the safe side.

Thrift stores often have a section of used plastic kitchenware, where everything often goes for about 25 cents. These can be good places to find old saucers to put under plants.

Ceramic pots

Purchased for their design, ceramic pots are usually quite functional as well as attractive. Most have a drainage hole, and if they don't come with a sensible water-holding saucer, that's easy enough to remedy. The only disadvantage to ceramic pots is that they break. If you have a cat or a dog, or a rambunctious youngster who might push over the pot or its stand, you may have a re-potting emergency.

Hanging pots

Both lightweight ceramic and plastic are preferable for hanging pots, because lightweight containers are less likely to fall, and if they do, they're less likely to hurt someone.

Any hanging plant container should be very firmly affixed into the overhead support, and should never be low enough to be a head bumper.

On the same safety-first note, no container filled with soil should be placed on any windowsill without being very strongly attached. Patio plants are better on a solid stand away from the rail. If you insist on putting them on a wide rail, they must be anchored very, very securely. A pot filled with soil can fall if given an accidental push, or if there's earthquake activity, or even heavy winds. It can kill or seriously injure a passerby.

■ **Hanging pots** *provide greenery for even the smallest patio or yard.*

Potting tips

Unless your container is brand new, wash it out well with hot water and a scrub brush before putting in a new plant. You don't want to inherit pests or diseases from the pot's prior occupant. If the pot doesn't have a drainage hole, put in a 1-inch bottom layer of coarse sand mixed with gardening charcoal. Despite your best efforts to avoid over-watering, water may well pool at the bottom of the container. This mixture will do a nice job of preventing the water from developing an unpleasant odor.

If your pot has a drainage hole, put a saucer underneath with a 1-inch lip at the edges. Water-holding saucers shouldn't be too shallow; they are meant to hold excess moisture, not let it flow over the rim.

Re-potting like a pro

MOVING A NEW PLANT *from its garden center plastic container to your pretty pot can be accomplished without traumatizing the plant. Why is this important? Traumatized plants take a longer time to get going, and in a few cases don't get going at all. Be sure the plant's new container is several inches wider than the one you bought it in, so the roots have room to grow.*

Transplanting from six-packs

If your plants come in little black or gray six-packs, water them lightly while they're in their original container. Doing so holds the soil together a bit, rather than it all falling off the little plant as you remove it. After dampening, gently pinch the bottom of each cell to extract the plant. Always support the root ball with one hand and don't dangle the little plant by its delicate leaves.

Don't take all the plants out of the container at once and leave them lying around to bake in the sun as you plant. Remove each plant individually after you have prepared its new space and are ready to gently pop it in.

Transplanting from containers

Today, most nurseries put their plants in plastic containers. Occasionally you may find some in metal containers. If so, have the nursery staff cut the sides of the container for you to make plant removal safer and easier. Once you get the plant home, wet the container soil to help keep the root ball together. After dampening, gently remove the plant. If it doesn't come away easily from the container and seems stuck, it may have overgrown roots. If the roots are overgrown, you must loosen or cut them so you can remove the plant.

The best way to cut roots is to cut those at the side of the plant. Cut from top to bottom, rather than chopping off the bottom roots. Only cut off what you have to, then spread the roots out carefully in your selected container. Of course, you'll try to avoid purchasing *pot-bound* plants, but it does happen. Some plants don't like having their roots disturbed, so give them a little time to adjust to their new container, taking extra care when following their particular watering and feeding needs.

> **DEFINITION**
>
> *Overgrown roots may hold tenaciously onto the pot's drainage hole, or even grow out of it and circle the pot. In gardener's language, this is a pot-bound or root-bound plant.*

329

RE-POTTING A CONTAINER PLANT

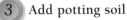

1 **Soak the root ball**

An hour or so before re-potting, and keeping the plant in its original pot, soak it in water. This reduces the impact of the move and helps to establish the roots in the new soil mix.

2 **Loosen the roots**

Encourage the roots to grow into the new soil mix by gently teasing out congested roots with your hands. Trim off damaged or dead roots with a sharp knife.

3 **Add potting soil**

Add some potting soil, firm lightly, and position the plant, leaving room for watering. Fill around it with more soil, firming as you go.

After planting

Water the new resident well. It is better to water directly onto the soil or into the saucer beneath the container. Watering from above can leave unattractive leaf spots caused by the water drying out on the leaves. More importantly, it can invite fungal disease. To help minimize transplant trauma, keep the plant in a shady spot for the first day or two to let it get used to its new container before it has to acclimatize to its outdoor site.

■ **Trim off any dead leaves** *and straggly or damaged stems, as this will help encourage new growth. Give the plant a good start with some fertilizer, and water well.*

Potting particulars

IT IS ALWAYS BEST to buy commercial potting soil for any type of potted plant, including houseplants. Although it is often easier to take shortcuts and use your garden soil, this may contain almost invisible insect eggs, or the remnants of various diseases. Moreover, with clay soils it tends to form an almost impenetrable clump in the pot once it settles in.

Just like fish in an aquarium, plants in pots don't have a place to go if they don't like things where they are. Potting soil may cost somewhat more than the home-dug variety, but it's less expensive than having to buy a new plant, and more cheering than watching your carefully nurtured seedlings disappear to some inherited bug.

Soil components

Good generic potting soil may be a combination of any or all of the following:

- Peat moss
- Sawdust
- Leaf mold
- Ground bark

- Sand
- Vermiculite
- Perlite

You also may want to look for potting soil that contains water retention crystals. These are a relatively recent invention designed to let the user be less compulsive about watering.

Water retention crystals are tiny, sheer, whitish granules that swell up to many times their original size when water is added to them. Mixed with soil on a specific ratio, depending on the product, they very slowly release their moisture, enabling you to avoid watering for up to 2 weeks.

Each product is different, and you must be careful that you don't end up with soggy soil, the bane of so many potted plants. Check the plant's needs first, but I would urge you to test-drive an unplanted pot of soil using these crystals before using it with a favorite new plant.

Picking plants for the patio

WITH SO MANY CHOICES, you may be wondering where to begin. I'll help simplify things by offering some beautiful plants that don't grow too large for containers and will keep your patio looking good throughout the year.

■ **Group pots** *to hide ugly features or to brighten up a boring part of your yard. Try mixing permanent plants with seasonal ones that you can add to keep the display looking fresh.*

Cacti and other succulents

ALL CACTI ARE SUCCULENTS but not all succulents are cacti. Cacti are just part of the large selection offered in this fleshy-stem plant group. The word succulentus means "juicy sap" in Latin, and generally, cacti don't need a lot of water. Other succulents, including the sedums, need occasional water lest they begin to look like deflated balloons.

Can you tell a cactus when you see one? Cacti have little cushions, called areoles, dotting their shapes, and their flowers, new growth, and spines arise from these.

■ **Bold shapes and outlines** *are typical of cacti and succulents. Display them to even greater effect by choosing pots that are just as bold and dramatic as the plants.*

Cacti care

Many people buy cacti and other succulents in the winter, when they just need to buy a plant but are discouraged by cold weather. These plants are happy outdoors in sun, and you can over-winter them indoors – not too close to a very sunny window, but close enough. The greatest thing about succulents is that many grow so slowly that you can have an entire and completely varied collection in a limited area. Lest you think they are dull, wait until they flower. It's like an unexpected gift, and when your cacti are outside, hummingbirds come right up to admire and taste them.

Perhaps the second greatest thing about succulents is the minimal amount of care they require. Place them in potting soil mixed with some sand, or better yet, buy a bag of cactus soil. There's no need to fertilize. With most types of succulents, let the soil dry out briefly before you water again. Those that do like a slightly moist soil are the tropical, so-called "jungle" cacti. Jungle cacti include the Christmas cactus (*Schlumbergera* x *buckleyi*), Thanksgiving cactus (*Schlumbergera truncata*), Easter cactus (*Hatiora rosea*), and Orchid cacti (*Epiphyllum*). But, be they jungle or desert, should you over-water, it's goodbye, so all pots must have a drainage hole.

THANKSGIVING CACTUS
(*Schlumbergera truncata*)

It's highly advised, when touching or handling any form of succulent that has teeny prickles, or what even resembles a spine, to wear heavy-duty gardening gloves. If you forget this once, you will probably not forget it again.

Okay. Now that you know how to handle them, let's look at some pretty, popular succulents.

Delightful donkey's tail

Donkey's tail (*Sedum morganianum*) is an extremely popular hanging plant for placement in partial shade, but it's grown primarily where summers are hot and dry. The multiple long, trailing stems may grow to 3 feet, with light green, plump, small leaves overlapping one another. With age and the proper site, red or pink flowers may appear. If you don't have the climate to put this outdoors, try it indoors near a sunny window. Don't forget to water once in a while.

Easy echinopsis

The spines on an echinopsis (*Echinopsis*) look and are formidable, but that's what a cactus is all about: self-protection. Members of this genus are adaptable to temperatures from 40 to 85° F and actually enjoy some water during the hottest summer months. But let the pot soil dry out completely before you water again and do not water at all in the winter. Expect flowers, often night-blooming, in lemon yellow, peach-pink, white, pink, or dark orange in late spring or early summer.

Many species will produce offsets – new plants growing off the parent. You can leave them on, or remove them and start a new potted cactus. Again, gloves, gloves, gloves.

Elusive living stones

Living stones (*Lithops*) really do look like pebbles. These brown, gray, or pale green, often mottled succulents are charming in their own container, and are even more so when bright yellow flowers emerge from what look like clefts in the pebbles. Some people grow nothing but living stones, since there are more than 40 species to choose from. They like lots of sun, and will put up with temperatures up to 120° F. Like most succulents, they aren't fond of very cold weather, but don't let that deter you. Bring the pot indoors in winter, where a house heated from 40 to 60° F suits them fine. Do keep them away from the kitchen sink or the bathroom, as these plants like the air to be pretty dry.

LIVING STONES (*Lithops*)

OLD MAN CACTUS
(*Cephalocereus senilis*)

Old man cactus

Bearing a resemblance to Rip Van Winkle, this columnar cactus can reach 40 feet high in a 200-year period, as it does in its native Mexico. On your quite sunny front porch it will stay contentedly at 12 inches, maybe picking up an inch a year. It looks best in a vertical pot. Old man cactus (*Cephalocereus senilis*) will produce no flowers, but it's still quite a conversation piece.

INTERNET

graylab.ac.uk/usr/hodg
kiss/bcss.html

Visit this site for a listing of national and international cactus and succulent societies that offer growing advice, as well as cutting exchange information.

Seasonal sensations

ALMOST ANY SMALL TO MEDIUM-SIZE annual plant, and many perennials, can be grown in an appropriate-size container. The four detailed below are among the most colorful and easiest to grow, but others may be even better where you live. Some of my first choices follow:

- Alyssum (*Alyssum*)
- Bachelor's buttons (*Centaurea cyanus*)
- Balsam (*Impatiens*)
- Calendula (*Calendula*)
- China aster (*Callistephus*)
- Cockscomb (*Celosia*)
- Cosmos (*Cosmos*)
- Dusty miller (*Senecio cineraria*)
- Fairy primrose (*Primula malacoides*)

- Floss flower (*Ageratum*)
- Flowering tobacco (*Nicotiana*)
- Lobelia (*Lobelia*)
- Pansy (*Viola*)
- Petunia (*Petunia*)
- Phlox (*Phlox*)
- Snapdragon (*Antirrhinum*)
- Sweet William (*Dianthus barbatus*)
- Zinnia (*Zinnia*)

Countless chrysanthemums

Every autumn, pots replete with festive chrysanthemums (*Chrysanthemum morifolium*) are the color plants of choice. I like the burnt orange and sun yellow ones, but fall mums are available in red, pink, purple, lavender, and white, as well as multicolors. While the *anemone* and *pompom* forms are usually supermarket gift plants and table brighteners for the upcoming holidays, there are *spider* and *spoon* flowers, among others, available at nurseries and garden centers. These are perennial plants, and will return each year.

C. morifolium, also known as florists' chrysanthemum, is but one of the many different *Chrysanthemum* species. Besides my fall-flowering mums, there's ox-eye daisy (*C. leucanthemum*), costmary (*C. balsamita*), painted daisy (*C. coccineum*), shasta daisy (*C. maximum*), and feverfew (*C. parthenium*).

POMPOM CHRYSANTHEMUM

> **DEFINITION**
>
> *The flowers of chrysanthemums can be found in many shapes. The* anemone *form is a semi-double flower with a raised, pillow-like center. The* pompom *form is fully rounded. The* spider *is a double flower with long, tubular, graceful florets. A* spoon *flower's florets expand slightly into a* spoon *shape at the end.*

The feverfew chrysanthemum's not much to look at, but it thrives in the garden corner where my dogs pee, so it is a wonderful plant indeed.

Caring for chrysanthemums is a piece of cake. Just give them a sunny spot, self-respecting soil, fairly regular water, and good drainage. Good drainage means mums like life a tad on the dry side. Fertilize your chrysanthemums occasionally.

Colorful coleus

These partial shade-loving plants are grown for their absolutely brilliant leaves: reds, oranges, greens, yellows, scarlets, sometimes seemingly all together on one tidy, 12-inch plant. Tropical natives, coleus (*Coleus blumei*) require rich, loose soil (sterile potting soil is by far the best choice), plus a warm, protected growing site. Soil should be kept a little damp, and the plants should be fed fertilizer once a month. Clay pots absorb heat and lose water too quickly for coleus, so find a pretty alternative. If you don't treat them courteously and they get too much shade or too much sun, they will become straggly, lose their color, and wither. Plant several together in a large pot for maximum impact from spring through early fall. To get bushier coleus, pinch out the tops so the sides grow wider.

Coleus act as annuals in most areas, so expect to replant them the following year. They are relatively easy to grow from seed started in the late winter or spring. You can also *propagate*, or start new plants, by putting some stem cuttings in water at any time. They will form roots. If you've got a favorite coleus leaf color scheme, keep some to grow indoors in a window where the light filters in.

■ **Coleus come in** *an infinite variety of colors, often with strikingly contrasting margins to the leaves.*

> ### Trivia...
> The name chrysanthemum derives from the Greek words chrysos, meaning "gold," and anthos meaning "flower." Garlands made from mums served as protection against demons. Drinking dew collected from chrysanthemum flowers was supposed to make one live longer.

> ### DEFINITION
> With the exception of starting seeds, all plant propagation is called vegetative propagation, where you use a part of the original plant as the basis for the new one. Propagation techniques include stem cutting, budding, dividing, and grafting.

Miraculous marigolds

From the plethora of marigolds (*Tagetes*) that festoon balconies and patios from early spring until fall, it seems just about everybody has at least one specimen. The most commonly seen are the annual French marigolds (*T. patula*), probably because of their compact size on sturdy, upright stems. Colors range from yellow to almost mahogany red, including the spectrum in between. Flowers are found in single and double varieties. Give marigolds full sun with regular water and they will bloom from the late spring until fall, especially if you pluck off fading flower heads.

Marigolds are reasonably easy to start from seed. Just make certain to use good potting soil and don't let it dry out while the seeds are trying to sprout. As a note, some people don't like the musty close-up aroma of some marigolds, but in organic gardening, French marigolds are considered great company for vegetables.

MARIGOLD
(*Tagetes erecta*)

The marigold's aroma reportedly masks the odor of veggies, so pests just fly by and keep going. Try marigolds around your patio tomatoes, making an even prettier picture while performing a scientific experiment.

Nasturtiums – naturally

Somebody recently told me they couldn't get nasturtiums (*Tropaeolum*) to grow. I was astounded. Nasturtiums are just about the easiest annual to grow, and once happy, will drop their large, brown, wrinkly seeds all about and give you nasturtiums all over the sunny place. Nasturtiums demand full sun. They are not fussy about soil, and like life slightly on the dry side after they get started. Never fertilize, or you'll get lots of nice, medium-green leaves and few flowers. There are low-growing varieties, from 6 to 10 inches, and vining varieties, reaching 6 feet high. Flowers are found in yellow, white, red, rose, orange, and mahogany, and some are bi-colored. If they don't start out that way, the next generations may provide their own color. Because nasturtiums don't transplant well, sow in place – pot, windowbox, or ground – in early spring to get late-spring to autumn color. Sometimes during the season aphids tend to appear, so it's time to remove the plant, saving the seeds if you want. You can just push them an inch down into the container soil and, come the warm weather, they'll probably give you new nasturtiums.

NASTURTIUM (*Tropaeolum speciosum*)

Basking in baskets

THERE'S SOMETHING *wonderfully carefree about hanging plants – they're like a little bit of bohemia right on your own balcony. I've narrowed this list down to my basket bests:*

Awesome asparagus fern

Don't let the words "asparagus" or "fern" throw you: this plant is neither. Very long (3 to 6 feet) waterfall-style, draping stems have green needle-like leaves. In winter, small, bright red berries dot the stems; in summer, very fragrant, tiny, white flowers appear.

Plant asparagus fern (*Asparagus sprengeri*) in good potting soil in a reasonably large container, as it has thick, fleshy roots that will crowd a smaller pot. Asparagus fern does well in partial shade, but can deal with full sun in cool-summer areas. Fertilize in the spring, and water regularly. If you live in a frost-free area, this perennial stays green and fluffy all year long. A really cold spell will decimate the greenery, but it usually returns come warmer weather if you water it.

Fuchsia forever

Hummingbird magnets all, fuchsias (*Fuchsia hybrida*) look great pruned as small trees, grown as shrubs, or placed in a hanging basket to delight the eye with ballerina blossoms. There are so many types available, complete color palettes with a great variety of ruffled petals, that it's pick and choose at your leisure. A bit fussy, especially in hanging baskets, they require rich, organic soil, regular fertilization, and regular watering to keep the soil slightly damp. Although not prima donnas, fuchsias dislike the cold and they dislike hot, humid weather too. They do like partial sun, fog, or other forms of cool air moisture, and a wind-protected site. Give them their wishes, and you will have hummingbirds hovering from early spring until frost.

FUCHSIA (*Fuchsia hybrida*)

Excelling with ivy geranium

All of the geraniums are good patio and balcony plants. Some grow in a mounding form, others are draping. Ivy geranium (*Pelargonium peltatum*), in spite of its name, isn't an ivy mimic. It only grows to 3 feet long, and is very well behaved, producing white, pink, red, lavender, and purple-pink flowers in spring and summer. In warmer climates, you may see flowers intermittently throughout the year.

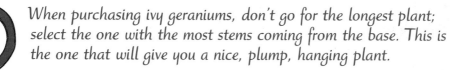

When purchasing ivy geraniums, don't go for the longest plant; select the one with the most stems coming from the base. This is the one that will give you a nice, plump, hanging plant.

It's best to purchase when this hardy plant is in flower – with all the different colors, you'll want to know ahead of time what you'll be getting. Care is the same for almost all geraniums: place in a mostly sunny spot and water regularly. They'll be happy in average soil.

More hanging plants for baskets:

- Balsams (*Impatiens balsamina*, New Guinea Group)
- Cascade petunia (*Petunia x hybrida*)
- Donkey's tail (*Sedum morganianum*)
- Italian bellflower (*Campanula isophylla*)
- Parrot's beak (*Lotus berthelotti*)
- Sapphire trailing lobelia (*Lobelia erinus*)
- Tuberous begonia (*Begonia x tuberhybrida*)

A simple summary

✔ All potted plants should be placed in commercial potting soil if at all possible. Soil from your garden may harbor pests and diseases that potted plants can't tolerate.

✔ Many container types are available. Place your plant in a container that is 1 or 2 inches wider than the container you bought it in.

✔ Containers should have drainage holes. If not, put 1 inch of sand mixed with gardener's charcoal at the base to stop water smelling.

✔ Balcony plants are safer standing back from the railing.

If you do put a plant on a wide railing, firmly anchor it. This also goes for hanging plants. A plant dropping on someone could kill or injure them.

✔ The rims of the saucers around potted plants should be high enough to prevent water spillage.

✔ Potted plants are at your mercy. If you give too much or too little water, the plant has no recourse.

✔ Select the best patio and balcony plants for your growing environment and for your willingness to give proper care.

PART SIX

EASY-TO-GROW SUNFLOWER SEEDS

GARDENING CHALLENGES

ONCE YOU HAVE BEGUN your garden, whether on a small apartment patio or on a piece of acreage, you may decide you want to take a *special direction*, experiment, or learn more techniques. A special direction might include planting a garden for the birds, butterflies, or  beneficial insect *pollinators*. A new technique might include starting plants from seed, either indoors or out, or dividing your daffodils or irises correctly.

Because any garden will get insect and weed pests from time to time, there's information here about which pests may bother you most, and what to do about them, if anything. Before you use chemicals in the garden, read the section on pesticides in Chapter 21 so you *control* them appropriately and safely.

Chapter 19

Making Your Own Plants

IT IS QUITE SIMPLE to make your own plants from seeds or cuttings, or by dividing a favorite plant. Making your own plants is thrifty and fun, and "homemade" greenery makes a wonderful gift for garden-loving friends. A small, or not-so-small, perk is that plant parenting can often be done in late winter, when it looks like spring will never come dancing around the corner.

In this chapter...

✓ Starting seeds indoors

✓ Starting seeds outdoors

✓ Making plants from cuttings

✓ Dividing garden plants

NASTURTIUMS, IDEAL FOR NOVICE GARDENERS

Starting seeds indoors

A PACKET OF 100 OR MORE SEEDS *costs only about $2. That's about two cents a plant. If you wait until a nursery has started the seeds for you, each young plant can cost $2 or more. Nature starts seeds every day, and with a little skill, you can too.*

Smart seed buying

Most seeds are purchased in little paper packets. Do not buy or use commercial seed packets with last year's date printed on them. They were meant for last year's use. Fresh seed germinates well. Old seed, or improperly stored seed, does not.

When you buy a seed packet, place it in a container and store it in a cool, dry place. To help hasten germination, some people like to put flower and vegetable seed packets in the refrigerator (not the freezer) for a week before sowing. You can always try a test packet and see what happens.

If you're concerned about the easiest seed to nurture indoors, look for those packets stating that seeds will germinate within 10 days. Anything longer than that requires extra vigilance.

Start with the right soil

Always use sterile potting mix for your seeds. Ordinary garden soil contains a host of bacteria and fungi that cause damping-off and other miserable seed and seedling disorders. You can buy potting soil in a ready-made bag, or purchase sterile soil components. A satisfactory generic mixture is 25 percent vermiculite, 25 percent perlite, 25 percent horticultural sand, and 25 percent sphagnum moss or peat moss.

Containers

You can start some seeds in something as plain and simple as a Styrofoam or yogurt cup that is ¾ full of sterile potting mix, or in sturdier but more esthetically pleasing containers.

PEAT POT

Containers for seed starting must be at least 2 inches deep, and should have drainage holes at the base. You can buy starting trays, or little *peat pots* (the simplest solution), at garden centers. Peat pots should definitely be used for vining plants, such as tomatoes.

If you're re-using containers that previously contained soil, each must be thoroughly cleaned to prevent the transmission of bacterial and fungal diseases that can communicate via just one small leftover lump of soil. While a good hot water and detergent solution will do if the container is rinsed very well, an even better way is a washing with hot water to which about 2 tablespoons of bleach have been added. Again, rinse well.

You're now ready to plant your seeds (see pp.346-7). To avoid shifting the seeds about when watering them, place a piece of paper towel over each seed container and lightly sprinkle water onto this.

You must never allow seeds to dry out at any time after you have planted them.

Allow the soil to drain, remove the paper toweling and place sheets of plastic wrap over each container. Don't let the plastic touch the soil. Label each container with a waterproof marker, stating both the plant's name and the planting date.

Now place your containers near a window, but out of direct, hot sunlight. If a sunny window is all you have, cover it with a sheer curtain. Seedlings may grow toward any light source, so rotate the containers regularly. Keep the soil moist at all times but don't let the soil become soggy, or the small seeds will drown.

> **DEFINITION**
>
> Peat pots *are little pots made of pressed and dried peat moss. When you use them, you can place pot and plant directly into the garden soil for transplant, without damaging the root system.*

When you see the sprouts

After the seeds germinate, or sprout, remove the plastic covering. Place the container in a sunny indoor site. If the site really gets hot, give the seedlings a little paper covering during the warmest part of the day. If you don't have a sunny indoor site, you can create your own sunshine.

Garden centers and hardware stores usually sell plant growth lights. A 2-tube fluorescent fixture holding 40-watt bulbs is a standard variety. Place the lights about 6 to 8 inches above the seedling containers. To avoid burning the delicate seedlings, raise the light fixture as the seedlings grow. You can leave the lights on full time, or use a timer to provide about 12 hours of light a day.

PLANTING SEEDS

When starting seed, the indoor temperature should be between 65 and 75° F. Fill your chosen containers with sterile soil. It is very important to moisten the soil and let it drain before inserting seeds. When adding the seeds, barely cover with soil seeds that are the size of rice grains, such as zinnia. Large seeds, such as morning glory, nasturtium, sunflower, or sweetpea, should be covered firmly but just enough so that you cannot see them. Seeds the size of pepper grains, such as foxglove, petunia, and snapdragon, should not be covered with soil.

1 Firm the soil

Fill a planting container with soil and then firm it down to about a ½ inch below the rim of the pot. You can do this by hand, or by using a presser.

THINNING SEEDLINGS

When seedlings reach about 1 inch high, thin them out a bit, using your fingers to extract them by the roots. With the point of a pencil, poke holes about 1 inch apart in a new pot and put the removed seedlings in the pre-moistened hole, filling and firming around the roots. When seedlings are about 2 inches high, they are ready to move into the garden if the last spring frost has already occurred. You will need to *harden them off*.

1 Harden the seedlings off

Cover your seedlings with glass or clear plastic and place the pots in a sheltered spot outside a few hours each day for about a week.

DEFINITION

Hardening off *a plant means making it a bit tougher so it can withstand cold, wind, or other outdoor natural weather conditions. You do this by gradually exposing it to the harsher outdoor environment.*

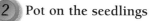

2 **Sprinkle the seeds onto the soil**

Use a folded piece of paper to hold the seeds and help provide an even distribution. Scatter the seeds sparingly over the surface of the soil.

3 **Sieve soil over the pot**

Once you have distributed the seeds, gently sieve a shallow layer of soil over the surface of the pot, taking care not to dislodge the seeds.

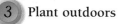

2 **Pot on the seedlings**

When the seedlings are 2 inches high, move them into a bigger container. Lift the seedlings out by the leaves, as the stems are very delicate.

3 **Plant outdoors**

When the seedlings have grown into small plants with good, strong roots, you can either transplant them again or plant them outdoors.

COLD FRAMES — TRANSITIONAL HOUSING FOR YOUNG PLANTS

A cold frame is a transitional place where small young plants can harden off before they are placed directly in garden soil. Cold frames are particularly helpful in areas with late spring frosts. They are used for interim seedling transplants, rooted cuttings of deciduous and evergreen trees and shrubs, softwood cuttings of such plants as chrysanthemums, pelargoniums, and fuchsias, and leaf cuttings of rex begonias and African violets.

Cold frames use the sun's heat. Soil within the box is warmed during the day and gives off its retained warmth at night, keeping the plants comfortable. If you live in a cold winter climate, you can surround your cold frame with straw or another protective material to insulate it from the outside air and increase heat retention.

The basic cold frame is nothing more than a bottomless box with a removable top. The box is usually made of wood pieces (either 3 feet by 4 feet or 3 feet by 6 feet) that are about 1 inch thick. My favorite design has a wooden back about 18 inches high, and a front that is 12 inches high. The sides should be cut diagonally to accommodate this 6-inch slope.

The top is usually made of glass or clear plastic, such as clear plastic sheeting. If you have good drainage, you may place this directly on top of the soil. If not, you must dig down about 6 inches. Fill the dug-up area with coarse sand or gravel. Pack this down firmly and water well. Then, place the cold frame over the dug-out area and fill it with a commercial sterile potting mix. If you use garden soil you risk bringing in all the fungi and bacteria that eliminate seeds and/or seedlings.

■ **Protect your young plants** *from the elements by keeping them in a garden cold frame.*

Your cold frame should not be sited where it gets baking sun, or its interior will become an oven. Where this is unavoidable, put a covering over the glass, and/or ventilate the cold frame by opening the top slightly. You can also buy more elaborate cold frames with glass tops that open and close automatically to keep the air temperature constant.

Starting seeds outdoors

BECAUSE OF SEED PREDATORS, *such as snails, slugs, cutworms, and birds, sowing seeds outdoors can be something of a challenge. However, with vigilance and some pre-planting preparation, you can be quite successful. Fortunately, there are some seeds that tend to provide good results, regardless of the color thumb of the gardener.*

Good choices for beginners

Maximize your chances of success by starting with plants that tend to do well when they're sown outside. The easier annual flower seeds to grow include:

- Common sunflower (*Helianthus annuus*)
- Forget-me-not (*Myositis sylvatica*) (a perennial usually grown as an annual)
- Marigold (*Tagetes*)
- Morning glory (*Ipomoea*)
- Nasturtium (*Tropaeolum*)
- Sweet alyssum (*Lobularia maritima*)
- Zinnia (*Zinnia*)

■ **Pretty blue** *forget-me-nots are ideal plants for novice gardeners to grow.*

349

Among perennial flowers, the easiest seeds to grow include:

- Columbine (*Aquilegia*)
- Coneflower (*Rudbeckia*)
- Delphinium (*Delphinium*)
- Four o'clock (*Mirabilis jalapa*)
- Shasta daisy (*Leucanthemum* x *superbum*)
- Snow-in-summer (*Cerastium tomentosum*)

CONEFLOWER (*Rudbeckia hirta*)

SWEET PEPPERS (*Capsicum annum*)

Finally, the easiest vegetable seeds to grow are:

- Peppers (*Capsicum*)
- Pumpkin (*Cucurbita moschata*)
- Tomato (*Lycopersicon*)
- Zucchini (*Cucurbita pepo*)

Shortcuts with seed tapes

If you're looking for a shortcut, you can buy seed tapes at some garden centers and nurseries. The tapes are about 15 feet long, with seeds integrated into them. You can cut them into smaller segments if you want. Place the seed tapes along the area where you want these particular plants to grow, and you get straight rows and correct, even spacing. Seed tapes are more expensive than seed packets, but they do make sowing easier. On a grander scale, you can also buy lightweight fabric seed carpets about 5 feet square. Often a mix of flower seeds, annuals and perennials, the carpets are placed on pre-prepared soil. The roots grow through the fabric into the soil.

SEED TAPE

Sowing successfully

Preparing the soil properly is as important as obtaining fresh seeds. You cannot just dump seeds on the ground and expect them to survive. If you need a refresher course on how to improve your soil so that it's ready for planting, look again at Chapter 2.

Be sure to read through the instructions on your seed packet. They may recommend planting dates in your region.

Before planting, you must have some idea of when the last frosts have usually occurred. This information is important because a sudden frost will quickly kill almost all emerging seedlings.

Check on the packet to see if the seeds need sun, semi-shade, or shade. This will affect where you place your seeds. A final, and important, instruction is how deep to plant the seeds, so always check on the package. Seeds that are planted too deep do not get enough light and will not germinate. Seeds that are planted too shallow will get too much light and will not germinate.

Seed in the hole

When you're ready to plant, make a series of small indentations in the ground. I use my finger, but a pencil eraser makes a nice, tidy dent too. Sprinkle the area lightly with water. Insert your seed at the proper depth.

Some seeds are exceedingly small. You can finger-pinch the seeds into your planting hole. You may get several seeds in one planting hole, but you can always thin the seedlings out later.

Mix very small seeds with horticultural sand, about ½ a cup per seed packet, right before sowing. This is a little haphazard, but it beats dumping all your itsy-bitsy seeds in one place, as often happens to people such as myself who lack great finger dexterity. The lighter sand displays where you are setting the seeds.

Planting in furrows

An alternative method of sowing is to make shallow, V-shaped furrows about 4 to 6 inches apart along your planting area. Water the furrows and allow the water to soak in. Now make a cone of your seed envelope, and gently shake the seeds out along the furrows. Alternatively, you can use the mix of seeds with sand, put some in a used envelope, and shake out the results from the corner of the envelope.

Cover the seeds with a sterile soil mix and press the soil down firmly with your hands or another solid object. Label your plantings with Popsicle sticks or pre-purchased plastic or metal tags – whatever the garden critters won't eat. They will often munch on paper labels, such as seed packets.

Seedling care

Never let the newly planted area totally dry out. In warm climates, you may want to cover the seeded area with newspaper held in place at the edges with rocks or the like.

Use a fine mist from the hose to keep the area slightly damp. Of course, you don't want to flood the planting site with water, which will drown seeds and seedlings, or use a strong spray from the garden hose, which will wash the seeds hither and thither.

When the emerging seedlings are about 2 inches high, remove any covering and begin thinning. Thinning is best done using your fingers, because you can feel what you are doing. Hopefully, you won't mind getting your hands dirty. If you're worried about your manicure, you can gently use a kitchen fork or the tip of a butter knife to remove seedlings, or you can snip off the excess seedlings with a slim pair of scissors. You can try transplanting rooted seedlings to another prepared area. Remember, they do best when taken out of the ground with some soil around the roots. Protect transplants with a light covering, such as a box, for a day or two if the weather is really hot. Be sure to water these transplants regularly.

■ **Be sure to water seeds well** *after planting. Use a watering can or hose with a nozzle that provides a very light spray so that you don't dislodge the seeds from the soil.*

Trivia...

From time to time you may find flowers and trees starting in your garden, even if you haven't planted them. Seeds travel to a garden in many ways. They arrive on the wind, with the rain, and in bird droppings. Your pet may also deposit seeds that have become attached to its fur after a walk in the park. Seeds stick to slacks, socks, and shoes, and you might bring them home from the woods, or even the nursery.

Making plants from cuttings

THERE ARE FOUR basic types of cuttings: softwood, hardwood, leaf, and root. For the novice gardener, softwood and leaf cuttings are the easiest to work with. The advantage of cuttings of all types is that the offspring are identical to the parent plant. This is not true when plants are started from seed, especially from the seed of hybrid plants.

Softwood cutting choices

Some of the easiest perennial flowering plants to multiply from softwood cuttings are:

- Aster (*Aster*)
- Balsam (*Impatiens*)
- Cane-type begonia (*Begonia*)
- Chrysanthemum (*Chrysanthemum*)
- Coleus (*Solenostemon scutellarioides*)
- Fuchsia (*Fuchsia*)
- Geranium (*Pelargonium*)
- Lavender (*Lavandula*)
- Penstemon (*Penstemon*)
- Rose (*Rosa*)
- Sage (*Salvia*)

GERANIUM (*Pelargonium*)

Get your cuttings going

Softwood cuttings are usually taken in spring when the parent plant has almost fully developed new shoots on it. The cuttings are easy to grow, provided you give them clean, healthy compost, the right amount of light, and water them regularly. Cuttings deprived of water tend to keel over very quickly. Always plant up several cuttings in one go, as this reduces the chances of failure. If you lose them, try again later in the year.

It's important to use a sharp implement to make cuttings, because a dull blade squashes the cutting base, damaging the growing cells.

Containers for cuttings

Once you have made your cutting proceed promptly with setting it. You will need containers that are about 5 inches deep, have a drainage hole, and are filled ¾ of the way with sterile potting mix. Poke holes in the planting mix with a pencil or with a screwdriver. Remove the leaves from the lower third of each cutting.

Trivia...

The ancient Romans dipped their plant cuttings in ox manure to encourage a strong root system.

TAKING SOFTWOOD CUTTINGS

Always select a strong, healthy plant from which to take your cuttings. Make your cuttings early in the morning before the sun becomes too hot and the plant begins to lose water. If the parent plant has nodes, or eyes, which are little growing bumps along the stems, try to obtain about 3 to 5 nodes per selected cutting.

1 **Take a cutting**

Make an angled cut on the stem, taking approximately 3 to 6 inches. Use a sharp knife or sharp-edged pruning shears.

2 **Give it a trim**

Remove the lower leaves from the cutting and trim the stem just below a node. You should be left with a nice, clean stem.

Lightly dip the bottom of the cutting into plant-rooting hormone powder. The powder, although not absolutely necessary, is a great help in stimulating quicker and stronger rooting. It is available at all garden centers. Keep in mind that the cuttings you've taken have no roots, and therefore, for the time being, they don't need nourishment such as fertilizer. Instead, they need to form roots as quickly as possible.

Insert the cuttings gently into the prepared holes so that the lower leaves are just above soil level. Firm the potting soil around each cutting, and water lightly.

Softwood cutting care

Cover the cuttings with plastic bags. Place the cuttings in a well-lit but not overly sunny area, with a temperature of about 70° F. Check your cuttings at the 3-week mark. They should not be wilted. If you tug lightly, the newly formed roots should hold a cutting in place. If your test cutting resists a bit, lift it out of the soil. You should see thread-size white roots.

The plastic bags you get in the supermarket vegetable section or at the checkout counter are great for covering cuttings.

3 **Plant up cuttings**

Place several stems into a pot of soil. Water well and then cover the pot with a plastic bag to encourage the roots to grow.

4 **Divide plants**

After the cuttings have developed strong and healthy roots, separate them by gently pulling each cutting away from the clump.

5 **Repot cuttings**

You can now repot all the cuttings into their own individual pots, as each cutting has become a separate plant. Water well.

SOFTWOOD CUTTINGS IN WATER

① Remove a stem

With your hands, scissors, or pruners, remove a piece of stem about 4 inches long from the growing tip of the plant. Take off all the leaves except the three topmost ones.

② Place in water

Fill a tall glass or jar about ¾ full of tap water. Place up to 3 stems in the glass, depending on their size and width. Ensure the stems are covered with the water.

③ Allow roots to form

Keep the cutting in a semi-shaded spot for about a week, and then move it to a semi-sunny site. You will be able to see how well the roots are forming in just a few weeks.

④ Plant your cutting

Half fill a pot with soil, lower the softwood cutting into the pot and add more soil. Gently firm the soil around the newly developed roots and water well.

Softwood cutting choices for water

Some indoor plants are incredibly easy to multiply in water. These include:

- Angelwing begonia (*Begonia coccinea*)
- Arrowhead vine (*Syngonium podophyllum*)
- Corn plant (*Dracaena fragrans*)
- Dumb cane (*Dieffenbachia seguine*)
- Ivy (*Hedera*)
- Philodendron (*Philodendron*)
- Golden pothos (*Epipremnum aureum*)
- Wandering Jew (*Tradescantia zebrina*)
- Wax flower (*Hoya carnosa*)

You can also take dangling offshoots of spider plant (*Chlorophytum comosum*) or piggyback plant (*Tolmiea menziesii*) and root them in water.

Many of the plants I've just listed will thrive for quite a while in their watery home, but eventually the roots will fill the glass and you will have to plant the cutting.

WAX FLOWER (*Hoya carnosa*)

COMPACT CORN PLANT (*Dracaena fragrans*)

LEAF STALK CUTTINGS

Leaf cuttings are best begun in the spring and summer. Have ready a container ¾ full of horticultural sand. Cut 2 inches of leaf stalk off the original plant using a razor blade or a pair of scissors. Make a slanted cut. Dip in water, and then lightly in plant-rooting hormone powder, shaking off any excess.

1 **Planting a cutting**

Insert the leaf stalk (here an African violet) in moistened sand, right up to the leaf base.

2 **Cover with plastic**

Water the stalks well and cover with a plastic bag. Place in a well-lit but not too sunny, hot site.

■ **Always keep the soil** *slightly moist. When tiny leaves appear, you can either transplant the leaf cutting into a permanent pot, or leave it where it is.*

GETTING YOUR LEAF CUTTINGS GOING

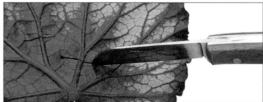

1 **Remove leaf and stalk**

Remove a large leaf from the parent plant (here a rex begonia leaf) and remove the central stalk, using a sharp cutting knife.

2 **Cut through main leaf veins**

Turn the leaf upside down, so the veins are showing. With a sharp knife, make some straight cuts in a few of the main leaf veins.

The best plants for leaf cuttings

Houseplants that you can multiply via leaf cuttings include:

- African violets (*Saintpaulia*)
- Christmas cactus (*Schlumbergera* x *buckleyi*)
- Florist's gloxinia (*Sinningia speciosa*)
- Peperomia (*Peperomia*)
- Piggyback plant (*Tolmiea menziesii*)
- Rex begonia (*Begonia rex* group)
- Sansevieria (*Sansevieria*)
- Wax flower (*Hoya carnosa*)

Sedums do well too, if you let the leaves dry for 24 hours before you put them into soil.

INTERNET

telework.ucdavis.edu/ Propagation/ Propagation12

This is a lengthy and somewhat scientific site, but it has excellent discussion on all types of plant propagation, including the most modern techniques used by commercial nurseries.

AFRICAN VIOLET (*Saintpaulia*)

 Place leaf onto soil

Place the leaf, topside upward, onto the soil in the growing container. You might need to weight the leaf down with a few small pebbles.

4 **Divide the new plants**

New plants will form where the cut leaf veins touch the soil. These new plants can be lifted, divided, and then repotted.

Dividing garden plants

PERENNIALS THAT GROW IN GROUPS *originating from a single plant, such as aster, primrose, and Shasta daisy, often get rather sad looking in the center, start producing smaller flowers, or just grow too large for the site. When this happens, it may be time to divide. There is a continuing discussion on the best time to divide clumps of roots. I recommend dividing in the early spring, just as the plant starts rapid growth. My second choice would be after the plant has flowered. For bulbs, divide after the flowers have come and gone.*

DIVIDING BEARDED IRIS

Every type of iris has a preferred planting time. If you don't know the best time for your iris type, look for when the bulbs or rhizomes appear in your local garden center. At this time, lift and divide overcrowded clumps in your garden. Lift the entire clump with a spade or garden fork and shake off the soil.

1 **Divide the rhizomes**

Cut the rhizomes apart with a sharp knife. Each of the sections should have green leaves, as well as roots. Discard the old and leafless center sections.

2 **Transplant the sections**

Cut the leaves to about 3 inches high, removing any discolored parts. Transplant the sections at least 10 inches apart. Firm into place, with the rhizomes just below the surface of the soil.

Dividing clumps

Divide shallow-rooted plants, such as chrysanthemums or violets, by lifting the entire clump with a spade or a garden shovel that has a pointed end. Gently break off rooted sections. If the roots are entangled you can cut them apart carefully with a sharp knife or pruning shears. If extracting the entire clump from the ground is a chore, just slice it with a spade and lift out a cut-off section. Do not make the divisions too small. Leave or place one section in the original site, and place the sections elsewhere, ensuring each section has roots. Water the new plant well, but do not overwater.

Dividing bulbs

Divide bulbs after flowering has finished, and the leaves die back and turn yellow. Dig carefully, to avoid bruising the bulbs, as this encourages disease. Do not cut off the leaves. You may see little bulblets on the plant, which you can gently pull off and replant in groups (but not as deeply as the parent bulbs). Alternatively, store the bulblets in a dry, cool site for the winter, and replant in early spring. The bulblets will mature and bloom the second or third year.

■ **Separate the bulbs** *by gently breaking the clump apart. If the bulbs have bulblets, pull them off carefully and replant for new plants.*

A simple summary

✔ The easiest seeds to grow usually sprout within 10 days.

✔ Start seeds indoors to get a head start on plant growth and an earlier harvest for vegetables.

✔ Use sterile potting soil for indoor planting. Prepare soil thoroughly.

✔ Don't let seeds or seedlings dry out. They will die rapidly without water.

✔ When transplanting seedlings, water the area first so that a little soil remains on the roots.

✔ Late winter is a good time to start houseplant cuttings. Many can be easily rooted in water.

✔ Early spring is the best time to divide overgrown perennial clumps. Divide bulbs after the flowering and when leaves have turned brown or yellow.

Chapter 20

Wonderful Wildlife

Even if you have a tiny garden in the city or the suburbs, you can still design it to attract birds, butterflies, and beneficial insects. A hummingbird sipping a flower you have placed there just for it is a marvelous sight on any lovely day.

In this chapter...

✓ Attracting birds with berries and seeds

✓ Hailing all hummingbirds

✓ Bird feeders

✓ Bringing in butterflies

✓ Attracting beneficial insects

BIRD- AND BUTTERFLY-ATTRACTING LOVE-IN-A-MIST

Attracting birds with berries and seeds

IT IS AMAZING the variety of birds attracted to your garden if you invite them with a plenitude of food and shelter plants. Food plants are those providing berries or other fruit, nuts, or seeds. Shelter should include some evergreens, especially in cold winter areas. First, we'll take a look at the berries birds love.

The joy of juniper

There are junipers (*Juniperus*) that lie on the ground and never get more than 6 inches high, and junipers that grow into 60-foot trees. In between there are any number of choices, including evergreen shrubs, some with dark green foliage, others blue-green, blue-gray, silvery-blue, bright green, turquoise, and golden needles. Bluish-black, cone-like berries appear in winter.

Junipers attract brown thrashers, cardinals, cedar waxwings, evening grosbeaks, flickers, juncos, mockingbirds, phoebes, robins, scarlet tanagers, thrushes, vireos, woodpeckers, and warblers, among others birds. Junipers are sun-loving plants needing moderate water. Although they're not particularly soil fussy, junipers don't thrive in constantly damp soil.

COMMON JUNIPER

Fabulous photinia

Cedar waxwings, finches, flickers, mockingbirds, quail, robins, and thrashers enjoy the fruit and shelter of both evergreen (*Photinia fraseri, P. glabra, P. serratifolia*) and deciduous (*P. villosa*) photinias. White flowers appear in the early spring, followed in the fall by red or black berries that remain on the shrub until mid-winter, that is if they're not eaten by birds.

When new, the leaves are quite colorful. Most photinias develop reddish leaves, while others have leaves that are an appealing copper color. Ranging in height from 6 to 15 feet, photinias are good screening and background shrubs. Photinias require full sun and moderate water.

Brewer's saltbush for southerners

Doves, finches, quail, sparrows, thrashers, and towhees are among the birds that visit this extremely hardy gray-leafed evergreen shrub. Brewer's saltbush (*Atriplex lentiformis*) thrives in hot, dry climates and is seen throughout the southwestern states. Also called quail bush, it's not at all flamboyant, but if you have alkaline soil and need a 6-foot-high shrubbery screen, it may fit the picture perfectly. The dense branches provide both shelter and nesting sites. Saltbushes are fire retardant and drought tolerant. They'll put up with poor soil, but they do need full sun and shelter from cold wind. Some, such as the four-wing saltbush (*A. canescens*), tolerate salt spray and do well in coastal areas.

Thrush-loving thorny elaeagnus

Brownish-red, olive-like berries provide autumn and winter bird food, and prickly stems keep predators away from this dense evergreen shrub, which ranges in height from 10 to 15 feet. Attracted to it are bluebirds, cardinals, cedar waxwings, evening grosbeaks, jays, mockingbirds, robins, thrushes, towhees, waxwings, and wrens. Thorny elaeagnus (*Elaeagnus pungens*) is frost hardy, and will thrive in just about any garden soil. It does equally well in sun and partial shade, needing only moderate water. Its small, white, bell-shaped flowers have a gardenia-like fragrance. There are also deciduous varieties, such as Autumn olive (*E. umbellata*), with fragrant yellow-white flowers. Its silver-green berries ripen to red in the fall when they'll be surrounded by yellow foliage.

Bringing in birds with berries

To bring birds to your garden, plant any or many of the following shrubs with berries:

- Barberry (*Berberis*)
- Bearberry (*Arctostaphylos*)
- Beautiberry (*Callicarpa*)

- **Birds just love elderberries,** *the tiny clusters of dark berries that appear on elder shrubs after flowering.*

- Carolina laurel cherry (*Prunus caroliniana*)
- Chokeberry (*Aronia*)
- Coffeeberry (*Rhamnus californica*)
- Cornelian cherry (*Cornus mas*)
- Cotoneaster (*Cotoneaster*)
- Elder (*Sambucus*)
- Evergreen huckleberry (*Vaccinium*)
- Firethorn (*Pyracantha*)
- Flowering currant (*Ribes*)
- Holly (*Ilex*)
- Northern bayberry (*Myrica pensylvanica*)
- Oregon grapeholly (*Mahonia aquifolium*)
- Privet (*Ligustrum*)
- Rose (*Rosa*)
- Sargent crabapple (*Malus sargentii*)
- Snowberry (*Symphoricarpos*)
- Spice bush (*Lindera benzoin*)
- Viburnum (*Viburnum*)

In addition to berries, birds are also partial to the delectable seeds that are produced by your flowers.

Lovely love-lies-bleeding

Also called tassel flower, this annual plant is quite aptly named after its tiny, bright red flowers that appear in long, cascading tassel-like clusters surrounded by green or red leaves. The grain-like seeds that follow often produce more plants, if the birds don't nibble them all first. Give this plant full sun, wind protection, and slightly below average amounts of water. Even in relatively poor soil, expect Love-lies-bleeding (*Amaranthus caudatus*) to grow from 3 to 5 feet high, and to provide a long-lasting sea of dangling red strands from summer to fall.

LOVE-LIES-BLEEDING
(*Amaranthus caudatus*)

Pretty purple coneflower

Place this daisy-like perennial plant among your taller sunflowers for an eye-catching flower border. Purple coneflowers (*Echinacea purpurea*) will reach from 3 to 5 feet tall. They'll expand in diameter from 2 to 5 feet, so be sure to leave enough room between plants when planting. Purple coneflowers bloom from July to September, and there are reddish-purple as well as white varieties. The name derives from the conical purple or brown center. This native North American plant is drought and wind tolerant.

SUNFLOWER (*Helianthus*)

Sunflowers for supper

The official state flower of Kansas, the sunflower (*Helianthus*) is the ultimate in seed producers for birds. I buy sunflower seeds by the huge bagfull at the supermarket and pet supply store, both the bigger striped sunflower seeds for the jays and the smaller black seeds for just about every other bird that crowds the feeders. There are huge, old-fashioned sunflowers that reach almost 10 feet high (these gangly plants will require staking), and also smaller sunflowers about 1 foot high. If you have bird-feeding stations near sunflowers, your visitors will leave behind mementoes in the form of a sprinkling of sunflowers growing here and there in sunny sites. Although you may remember the yellow-petaled, brown-centered sunflower from childhood, there now are ivory, orange, brown, rose, and maroon, single and double-flowered varieties. All sunflowers require full sun, and do better in good soil. They must have regular water and well-drained soil, or they will droop and then die.

Zoom in on zinnias

Zinnias (*Zinnia*) are easy-to-grow annuals that can be found in a wide selection of flower shapes and colors. They may have button-size flowers on 12-inch-high plants or dinner-plate-size flowers on 3-foot plants. Because zinnias bloom in late summer when other annuals are getting ready for winter shutdown, they provide a special treat for the gardener. You can plant entire sections in one color – apricot, cream, violet, or red – or you can mix and match as you like.

Zinnias are strictly warm-weather plants and they do best when placed in rich soil. Plenty of water is a must. To keep them happy, water them with a soaker hose or something like it. Don't water them from above, as doing so encourages the growth of mildew.

ZINNIAS (*Zinnia*)

Bringing in birds with seeds

Birds love seeds. Here are a selection of those they like best:

- Aster (*Aster*)
- Bachelor's buttons (*Centaurea cyanus*)
- Black-eyed Susan (*Rudbeckia hirta*)
- California poppy (*Eschscholzia*)
- Columbine (*Aquilegia*)
- Cosmos (*Cosmos*)
- English marigold (*Calendula officinalis*)
- Floss flower (*Ageratum*)
- Forget-me-not (*Myositis*)
- Foxglove (*Digitalis*)
- Globe thistle (*Echinops*)
- Goldenrod (*Solidago*)
- Love-in-a-mist (*Nigella*)
- Marigold (*Tagetes*)
- Mexican sunflower (*Tithonia*)
- Nasturtium (*Tropaeolum majus*)
- Pincushion flower (*Scabiosa*)
- Rose moss (*Portulaca*)
- Sea lavender (*Limonium*)
- Snapdragon (*Antirrhinum*)
- Sweet alyssum (*Lobularia*)
- Tickseed (*Coreopsis*)

Hailing all hummingbirds

THERE ARE AT LEAST 150 FLOWERING PLANTS that *attract hummingbirds. Hummingbirds are attracted to bright pink, bright yellow, orange, and red flowers. The hummingbird has a long, slim bill that fits perfectly into long, tube-shaped flowers while its tongue laps up the nectar stored at the base of the flower's tube. While inserting their long bills into the flower to sip nectar, they also feed on tiny insects and, of course, pollinate the flower.*

INTERNET

hummingbird.org/faq. htm

For questions and answers on hummingbirds in the garden, visit the web site of the Hummingbird Society.

■ **Hummingbirds** *are tiny, beautiful birds with magnificent plumage. Encourage them into your garden by growing a few of the plants listed on these pages.*

Bee balm bonanza

Native to the eastern United States, bee balm (*Monarda didyma*) will generally proceed at a mild pace in the garden, or, if it's in rich soil and shade, will spread to form dense clusters. If you want to keep it in check, plant it in average soil with full sun, give lots of water, and avoid fertilizing it. Colors include white, purple, rose-pink, and scarlet, with the scarlet being most attractive to hummingbirds. Butterflies and bees like the fluffy flowers, too.

The beauty of crimson bottlebrush

This fast-growing evergreen shrub attracts all kinds of birds, and is so easy to grow that all my neighbors seem to have one someplace. It reaches a hearty 15 feet high and about 5 feet wide as a shrub. I prune my bottlebrush (*Callistemon citrinus*) to look like a tree with weeping branches. Every morning the birds have tea and crumpets up there. The term bottlebrush comes from the bright red "brushes" that appear on and off throughout the years. Bottlebrush is easy to keep; it's tolerant of heat, cold to 30° F, and poor soil. Its only demands are full sun and moderate water.

BOTTLEBRUSH (*Callistemon citrinus*)

Penstemon perfection

Penstemons (*Penstemon*) are sometimes called beard tongue. There are at least 250 species to choose from, although only a few are commonly found. Chase down the rest in catalogs, because when you see how easy these plants are to grow, even in clay soil, you will want more. Flower colors include rose, scarlet, lavender, purple, and white. Penstemons will grow in sun or light shade, but they do need good soil, regular water, and good drainage. Most references will tell you that you'll see flowers in June and July, but I have them into November during a mild winter.

PENSTEMON (*Penstemon isophyllus*)

Spectacular scarlet sage

All the sages (*Salvia splendens*) are hummingbird magnets, and you can make quite a varied garden with the numerous varieties that are commonly available. They're all easy to grow. Most sages do best in full sun, but several prefer a slightly shady spot. Regular watering is necessary, at least to start, but a few – generally the shrubby perennial types such as purple sage (*S. officinalis*), autumn sage (*S. greggii*), and Mexican bush sage (*S. leucantha*) – are drought tolerant.

Scarlet sage is a perennial but is usually grown as a summer-blooming annual, particularly in cold winter areas. Red, pink, or purple flowers appear all summer long. I use a lot of pineapple sage (*S. elegans*), a perennial that has bright red, tubular flowers from late summer through early winter.

Plant a sage by a window with a clear view and watch the hummingbirds dance.

More plants for attracting hummingbirds:

- Butterfly bush (*Buddleja davidii*)
- Butterfly weed (*Asclepias tuberosa*)
- California fuchsia (*Zauschneria*)
- Canada columbine (*Aquilegia canadensis*)
- Cape fuchsia (*Phygelius capensis*)
- Cardinal flower (*Lobelia cardinalis*)
- Common foxglove (*Digitalis purpurea*)
- Coral bells (*Heuchera sanguinea*)
- Crimson bottlebrush (*Callistemon citrinus*)
- Delphinium (*Delphinium cardinale*)
- Fuchsia (*Fuchsia* – red varieties)
- Hollyhock (*Alcea rosea*)
- Lion's ear (*Leonotis leonurus*)
- Red-hot poker (*Kniphofia uvaria*)
- Shrimp plant (*Justicia brandegeeana*)
- Snapdragon (*Antirrhinum*)
- Star cluster (*Pentas lanceolata*)
- Star glory (*Ipomoea quamoclit*)
- Tobacco plant (*Nicotiana*)
- Trumpet creeper (*Campsis radicans*)
- Trumpet honeysuckle (*Lonicera sempervirens*)

Bird feeders

MANY PEOPLE THINK *of bird feeders for winter use, when snow is on the ground and plants are dormant. But placing out food throughout the year brings birds that you might not see otherwise. In spring, especially, that extra supply of edibles might encourage birds to make their nests in your yard, perhaps in view of a picture window.*

Perfect placement

Birds have many predators, including household cats. All feeders must be placed within 5 to 10 feet of protective cover so the birds can seek quick shelter if threatened.

You may not think that birds need to be protected from predators, as feeders tend to be placed high in a shrub or tree. Even though the feeders are high, seeds will fall to the ground, where many birds prefer to dine.

To get the largest variety of bird visitors, use different types of feeders scattered throughout the garden. Place the feeders at various levels and distances from the house. Feeders should not be in a windy site, and you might want to screen off wind with a plant barrier or a fencing arrangement. Most birds prefer to eat in a sunny area.

■ **Position a hopper feeder** *where you want to attract birds. These dispensers automatically re-fill.*

Hopper feeders

Hopper feeders keep seed in enclosed bins that have a seed tray at the base. Birds feed from the base, which is automatically replenished from the bin. Hopper feeders may be hung, or attached to trees, poles, or windowsills. Hopper feeders may attract cardinals, jays, grosbeaks, house finches, mourning doves, pine siskins, and purple finches, among other types of birds.

Platform or tray feeders

Platform feeders are trays or shallow pans used for birds that like fruit, suet, and nuts, as well as grains and seeds. They may be mounted on flat sites such as retaining walls, poles, and tree stumps. Platform feeders attract a very wide variety of birds, including brown thrashers, buntings, cardinals, catbirds, chickadees, flickers, goldfinches, jays, juncos, mockingbirds, mourning doves, northern orioles, nuthatches, sapsuckers, thrushes, warblers, and woodpeckers.

Suet feeders

Suet feeders are mesh or wire holders for suet, peanut butter, or various mixtures that are compacted together in a cake. You can place them on tree stumps or on poles. It's best not to place them directly against a tree, as the birds' pecking can result in some nasty damage to the tree. Birds that love suet include chickadees, flickers, jays, mockingbirds, sapsuckers, titmice, and woodpeckers.

SUET BALL

Tube feeders

Tube feeders are usually made of plastic and are suspended from trees. Perches for the birds are attached near the holes. Tube feeders may attract chickadees, finches, linnets, pine siskins, sparrows, tanagers, titmice, and warblers.

Hummingbird feeders

Site your feeder within viewing distance. Hummingbirds will come to feeders with red markings. If the feeder is not well colored, attach a bright red ribbon. Do not use red dye in the feeder, as it is harmful to them. To make a sugar syrup that hummingbirds will enjoy, combine 1 part sugar with 4 parts water in a small saucepan. Boil to dissolve the sugar, let it cool, and pour it into the feeder. You will need to clean the feeder at least once a week to prevent black mold forming on the sugar water.

Birdbaths

Concrete birdbaths are more stable than the plastic or ceramic types. Birds like to stand in the birdbath, so the water shouldn't be too deep. To control water height, add pebbles to the bottom. All birdbaths must have clean water. Do not place them under shedding trees unless you clean and refill the bath daily. Provide some type of high protective cover within 5 to 10 feet of the birdbath, and do not place the birdbath near or over shrubbery where predators can hide.

■ **Attract birds** *by setting up a bird bath in your garden. Not only will they drink from it, but they will also, literally, take a bath.*

Bringing in butterflies

BUTTERFLIES ARE PARTICULAR *about their food and residence. Many will starve rather than feed from just any plant. They are also extremely selective as to where they place their eggs. Butterflies avoid shaded sites and need shelter from the wind. If you live in a windy area, plant windbreaks that are also butterfly food, such as butterfly bush. A mud or sand puddle will provide water.*

■ **To attract** *butterflies to your garden, you need to consider three elements: color, shape, and fragrance.*

Color

Butterflies prefer feeding on purple, violet, orange, and yellow flowers. They are guided to the flower nectar by light patterns that we cannot see.

Shape

Although butterflies fly easily, they do not hover in one place very well. They therefore must have a place to perch. Large bloom clusters, *umbels*, and daisy-like flowers are good landing pads.

> **DEFINITION**
>
> *Flowers sprouting from stalks that spread from a common center, similar to umbrella ribs, are known as umbels.*

Fragrance

Butterflies have a very acute sense of smell. They are most strongly attracted to heavily scented flowers. Sadly, many pretty hybrids, bred for color and size, have had the fragrance bred out of them. When buying plants to attract butterflies into your garden, seek out heirloom varieties that still have their own heady fragrance.

Beckon with butterfly weed

This perennial, also called butterfly milkweed (*Asclepias tuberosa*), gives rise to 3-foot-high stems topped with 2-inch-wide clusters of bright orange, red, or yellow nectar-rich flowers. The flat-topped flower clusters present perfect landing fields for Monarch butterflies arriving in summer and fall. Narrow seedpods follow the flowers, each containing flat brown seeds with long, silky hairs that aid wind distribution.

BUTTERFLY WEED
(*Asclepias tuberosa*)

Butterfly weed is a wildflower native to the eastern United States. It requires full sun, good drainage, and moderate water. Not only does it make a great garden plant, but it also is a long-lasting cut flower, and the dried pods look charming in winter bouquets.

As a warning: parts of the butterfly weed plant may be poisonous if eaten, so keep it away from the kids.

Butterfly bush bonus

This well-known butterfly attractor was named after the Reverend Adam Buddle, a noted amateur English botanist of the 17th century. Clustered flowers can be pink, blue, purple, magenta, or white. Shop for plants that are in bloom to be sure you end up with the flower color you like. Older varieties grow to 12 feet tall, and the newer dwarf varieties will grow to about 4 feet. Every garden should have a butterfly bush (*Buddleja davidii*), and the smaller ones fit fine in a large patio pot. Give this attractive semi-evergreen shrub full sun and regular water. Members of the *Buddleja* genus do well in coastal areas and will tolerate some air pollution. The bush may die down in cold winter climates, but it generally returns in the spring.

BUTTERFLY BUSH (*Buddleja davidii*)

Netting with nightblooming jessamine

I have always called this nightblooming jasmine (*Cestrum nocturnum*), but the textbooks like "jessamine." This 12-foot-high, narrow shrub grew outside my bedroom when I was a youngster, and the powerful fragrance instantly transports me back in time.

The fragrance of nightblooming jessamine is best if the shrub isn't out in the open, but in a warm sheltered area. I have one in the entryway to my house, and another in an alcove.

Nightblooming jessamine will thrive if it is positioned in partial shade and given occasional fertilizer and regular water. It has white flowers and its fruit – pretty, but poisonous if ingested – is white berries.

Summoning shrub verbena

This is a delightful shrub, usually growing from 2 to 6 feet high. Depending on the variety, shrub verbenas may have quite a wide spread, possibly reaching 8 feet. In warm climates, shrub verbena (*Lantana camara*) will serve as an evergreen, but expect it to act like an annual in frosty areas. Numerous ½-inch flowers, usually in two-color pairings such as orange and yellow, or magenta and yellow, form multiple 2-inch-wide bouquets from spring until fall. The tiny black fruits that appear after the flowers are gone are poisonous – do not eat them! Shrub verbenas require a sunny site, good soil, and lots of water in the summer. Seemingly omnipresent in warm winter areas, weeping lantana (*L. montevidensis*) is an attractive relative.

INTERNET

naba.org

For fascinating information on butterflies, how to attract them, and how to join a butterfly society, visit the site of the North American Butterfly Association.

Beckoning butterflies

Butterflies are most drawn to gardens with generous patches of a nectar flower. Butterflies' favorite plants for nectar include:

- Aster (*Aster*)
- Bee balm (*Monarda didyma*)
- Black-eyed Susan (*Rudbeckia hirta*)
- Butterfly weed (*Asclepias tuberosa*)
- Cosmos (*Cosmos bipinnatus*)
- Goldenrod (*Solidago*)

- Lilac (*Syringa*)
- Mexican orange blossom (*Choisya*)
- Purple coneflower (*Echinacea purpurea*)
- Red valerian (*Centranthus ruber*)
- Viburnum (*Viburnum*)
- Yarrow (*Achillea*)

Caterpillars feed on plants to gain strength for their metamorphosis into butterflies, and adult butterflies tend to stay around areas where their caterpillar foods can be found. You must plant enough plants so the caterpillars have a continuing meal. Great host plants to help them along are:

FLOWERING TOBACCO

- Borage (*Borago*)
- Dill (*Anethum*)
- Hollyhock (*Alcea*)

- Parsley (*Petroselinum crispum*)
- Red clover (*Trifolium pratense*)

Moths are generally night-flyers and feeders, and so they like flowers that open in the evening. The best plants for attracting moths include:

- Four o'clocks (*Mirabilis jalapa*)
- Hyssop (*Hyssopus*)

- Lavender (*Lavandula*)
- Tobacco plant (*Nicotiana*)
- Zinnia (*Zinnia elegans*)

Attracting beneficial insects

IF YOU HAVE A GARDEN set up for birds and butterflies, chances are your garden is a haven for beneficial insects too. Beneficial insects include bumblebees, flower flies, ground beetles, honeybees, lacewings, ladybugs, and parasitic wasps. To keep these wonderful garden helpers around, you must provide shelter, water, and flowers. They prefer many of the same flowers as butterflies do.

Of course you should not use pesticides of any kind in your garden if you want beneficial insects, including butterflies, to thrive.

Flower flies

FLOWER FLY

Also called hover flies and syrphid flies, these North American native insects are striped like bees, but much slimmer. Adults have only one pair of wings, never buzz, and hover over flowers seeking nectar and pollen. They are good pollinators as they move from blossom to blossom. The young, resembling tiny, light-brown caterpillars, feed on pest aphids and mealybugs. To encourage flower flies plant:

- Baby blue eyes (*Nemophila menziesii*)
- Black-eyed Susan (*Rudbeckia hirta*)
- Cosmos (*Cosmos bipinnatus*)
- Marigold (*Tagetes*)
- Spearmint (*Mentha spicata*)
- Tickseed (*Coreopsis*)

Ground beetles

I love ground beetles because they eat slugs and snails. Ground beetles are plain, usually shiny black, fast-crawling beetles, up to 1 inch long, with a small head, small antennae, and long legs.

GROUND BEETLES

Ground beetles also feed on cutworms and root maggots, among other nuisances. I encourage ground beetles by giving them some log pieces to hide under. They prefer sheltered sites during the day, emerging after dark, and occasionally will meander indoors.

Shoo ground beetles outside, but do so wearing gloves, because a few species will try to protect themselves by giving off a skin-irritating fluid.

Lacewings

These insects are about 1 inch long, green or brown, and have lacy, long wings. Lacewing larvae, or young, can each devour 60 aphids per hour, and also feed on leafhoppers, mites, thrips, and other small pest insects. The adults feed on flower nectar and pollen. To encourage lacewings to your habitat, plant:

- Archangel (*Angelica archangelica*)
- Butterfly bush (*Buddleja davidii*)
- Campion (*Lychnis*)
- Common tansy (*Tanacetum vulgare*)
- Goldenrod (*Solidago*)
- Red cosmos (*Cosmos*)
- Tickseed (*Coreopsis*)
- Yarrow (*Achillea*)

Ladybugs

Most ladybugs are shiny red, orange, or yellow with black markings, but there are black and gray ladybugs too. Each adult ladybug, or "ladybird beetle," is about ¼ inch long. The wrinkled larvae, or young, are orange and black. Both adults and larvae feed on aphids, mites, whiteflies, and scale. In addition, each ladybug can eat hundreds of aphids per day. To encourage ladybugs, plant:

- Butterfly weed (*Asclepias tuberosa*)
- Marigold (*Tagetes*)
- Spindle tree (*Euonymus*)
- Yarrow (*Achillea*)

LADYBUGS

Trivia...

The Vedalia ladybug beetle (*Rodalia cardinalis*) was the first successful predator to be introduced into a country for the control of a pest insect. In 1885 an outbreak of cottony-cushion scale threatened to destroy the California citrus industry. Once introduced, the beetles began chomping on the cottony-cushion scale.

Archangel ecstasy

This tropical-looking biennial plant, sometimes called angelica, offers bright green, deeply divided leaves and fragrant greenish-white flowers in large clusters. A rapid grower, it does best in rich, damp, soil planted in partial shade. In medieval times, archangel was believed to be sent by angels. It provided a cooked vegetable for the dinner table, candied stalks for desert, kept evil spirits from entering the body, and offered protection from the plague. Archangel (*Angelica archangelica*) can grow to 8 feet high. The seeds may self-sow for next year's garden.

Cosmos companions

Cosmos (*C. bipinnatus*), sometimes called Mexican aster, can be found in perennial and annual varieties. The annuals may be white, pink, lavender, crimson, or bicolor, but it's the white cosmos that is most attractive to beneficial insects. Ranging in height from 2 to 6 feet, cosmos prefer full sun, average soil, and moderate water.

Glorious goldenrod

Once considered our national flower, these plants are popular with beneficial insects. Although the wild species can be invasive, hybridizers have produced several goldenrods (*Solidago*) suitable for the home garden, including the seaside-happy *S. sempervirens*, the groundcover *S. sphacelata* Golden Fleece, and the clumping, 3-foot-high *S. rugosa* Fireworks. True to its name, goldenrod's flowers are bright golden-yellow, and provide lovely color into the fall.

Tempt them with common tansy

All species in the *Tanacetum* genus prefer full sun and well-drained, dryish soil, but will thrive in anything that's not soggy. They are hardy plants, quite frost tolerant, and a good perennial for areas where the growing gets tough. In really comfortable surroundings, some, such as common tansy (*Tanacetum vulgare*) and costmary (*T. balsamita*), may become slightly invasive. Others, such as painted daisy (*T. coccineum*), tend to behave themselves quite well. The common tansy is the one that ladybugs like best.

INTERNET

acorn-online.com

Type "native plant societies" in the search engine and you'll find a state-by-state listing of plant societies in North America.

A simple summary

✓ Even a small urban garden can attract butterflies, birds, and beneficial insects.

✓ If you have room, plant shrubs or trees, including evergreens, for winter bird shelter.

✓ Birds like plants with berries or other fruit, nuts, and seeds.

✓ Bird feeders will attract a nice variety of birds. Place a feeder where you can easily see it, but away from where a cat can hide.

✓ Hummingbirds like plants that provide a rich source of nectar, especially those that have bright pink, bright yellow, orange, and red flowers.

✓ Bring butterflies to your garden with nectar plants, particularly those that have orange, yellow, and purple flowers.

✓ If you want beneficial insects, including butterflies, to thrive in your garden, it is essential that you do not use any pesticides.

Chapter 21

Garden Nasties

THE SIMPLEST WAY to avoid having to read this chapter is to buy and maintain healthy plants. When your plants are in the right site and get the right nourishment, they'll be more resilient to pests. But even the accomplished gardeners have problems with disease, weeds, and the like.

In this chapter...

✓ Hole punchers

✓ Sap suckers

✓ Fruit and veggie varmints

✓ Tree and shrub shredders

✓ Common plant diseases

✓ Weed world

✓ Pest controls

✓ Animal visitors

Hole punchers

SOME PESTS DO NOT SEEM TO BE PARTICULAR *about what part of a plant they eat, but you'll know they've set up shop from the holes you see in leaves, flowers, fruit, whatever. Some of the most common hole punchers are earwigs, flea beetles, snails and slugs, and weevils.*

Earwigs

Earwigs are pincer-tailed insects. They usually eat decaying fruit or other garden litter. Occasionally you may get large earwig populations in the garden, and they'll snack on flowers or ripe fruit, creating small ragged holes. No chemical controls are usually necessary if you clean up garden debris and eliminate (to the extent possible) the bugs' hiding places.

Flea beetles

If you find very tiny black beetles jumping around your plants when disturbed, your plants have flea beetles. Their hopping movement is similar to that of the fleas that bother dogs and cats. They eat dozens of tiny round holes in leaves, preferring vegetable seedlings and young plants. These holes cause the leaves to quickly lose moisture, and the rapid drying may kill seedlings. No chemical controls are usually necessary. If an infestation is truly annoying, spray with an insecticidal soap, following the directions on the product.

Sneaky snails and slimy slugs

Not all garden pests are insects. Snails and slugs, which are mollusks, are frequent garden visitors. Although there are many different types of snails and slugs, they share a common feature: thousands of "teeth" on their tongue. The teeth act somewhat like a saw, chopping food into bits before making it a meal.

Both snails and slugs prefer seedlings, young plants, and damaged plants. Usually working at ground level, they will also crawl up trees to feed on fruit. These creatures feed mostly at night, and

Trivia...

Unlike most other insects, earwigs are good parents. After both the male and the female create an underground nest, the female chases the male out. She then takes good care of the tiny white eggs, licking them clean to make sure no destructive fungus takes hold. When the babies emerge, the female earwig makes certain they stay close to home until they are ready to fend for themselves.

BROWN SNAIL

you'll see silvery slime trails in the morning as one clue to their nocturnal appearance. The other clue will be large, ragged holes in leaves, or possibly a total disappearance of your vegetable seedlings.

Snails and slugs hide in dark places during the day. Natural predators are frogs, snakes, and ground beetles. You probably don't want to lure frogs and snakes to your yard, but you might want to encourage ground beetles as a way to keep these pests in check.

If you can deal with it, you can just pick the snails and slugs up with your hand, place them in sealed containers or bags, and discard. Another option is to buy one of the many compounds available at garden centers that kill snails and slugs. These products have to be reapplied regularly.

INTERNET

colostate.edu/Depts/ IPM/ento/j515.html

For more information on slugs, their history, habits, cultural controls, traps, barriers, and baits, click here.

Be cautious — all slug- and snail-killing compounds can cause serious illness or death if ingested. Keep children and pets away from areas treated with these products, and store products in a secure, locked place.

Weevils

Notches on your plant leaf margins are telltale signs that root weevils have been dining. There are more than 2,000 different types of root weevils in North America, and they attack most plants. Those that feed on fruit and nut plants are usually called curculios. Those that feed on other plants are called weevils. The latter are usually about ¼ inch long. Adult weevils destroy leaves, and the larvae feed on plant roots. Infestations initially cause plant wilting, and if severe on small plants, can kill a plant.

VINE WEEVIL

Keeping the garden free of debris helps decrease weevil populations. Knowing which insecticide to use can be a problem, because different weevils require different treatments. Moreover, different insecticides are necessary for food and nonfood plants.

To address a weevil problem properly, ask a knowledgeable nursery person for advice, or your country agricultural extension service, bringing a weevil sample in a closed jar.

Sap suckers

INSECTS THAT SUCK SAP from leaves can infest annuals, perennials, and many other plants. Sap-sucking insects include aphids, leafhoppers, mealybugs, scales, spider mites, spittlebugs, thrips, and whiteflies.

Sap-sucking insects have mouth parts adapted both for piercing and sucking. Imagine, if you can stomach it, one or two needles surrounded by a few straws. The mouth parts puncture the leaves, and then the insect sucks up leaf sap or juices.

The insect gorges itself, while the plant loses its nutrition. A severely infested plant loses vigor and blossoms or fruits poorly. Some sucking insects may carry a plant virus in their saliva, which they inject into the plant.

Aphids

There are more than 800 aphid species, all of which suck sap from just about every type of plant. Aphids are sometimes called plant lice or green flies, because many aphids are green. But aphids, like the plants they love to trash, come in a variety of other colors, too: white, pink, blue, dark brown, red, black, or yellow. Aphids multiply with extraordinary speed, and if they're heavily infested, buds and flowers are deformed, and leaves are curled, yellow, and distorted.

■ **Black aphids** *infesting an allium plant.*

I ignore the infestation if it's on my roses. If my nasturtiums are infested, it's usually time to pull them up. Systemic insecticides (described in detail in the next chapter) may be used to control massive aphid infestations, but realize that when you use them, you are killing the beneficial insects also.

Leafhoppers

LEAFHOPPER

Leafhoppers feed on grapes, apples, and cantaloupes, plus many other fruit, vegetable, shade, and ornamental plants. There are 2,500 leafhopper species and although most are plain brown or green, leafhoppers can be quite pretty, with red, blue, yellow, or black markings. Most leafhoppers are about ⅓ inch long. When disturbed, leafhoppers run sideways, and may jump or fly. Leafhopper feeding causes small yellowish spots to appear on leaves. Leaf edges may turn dark brown, and leaves may drop early. Some leafhoppers transmit plant viral diseases. For severe infestations, use an insecticide spray.

Read the container label carefully to be absolutely certain your plant can withstand the insecticide. You can do more damage with the wrong insecticide than the leafhoppers do.

Mealybugs

These powdery, whitish insects are the bane of many outdoor garden plants. Mealybugs are usually found in groups, initially clustered within leaf-stem junctions and at fruit-stem junctions. If not controlled, they will take over an entire plant. Each female can deposit as many as 600 eggs, and there may be three generations each year.

A severe infestation may require a systemic spray or an external dust. You must treat the entire plant, including stem and leaf undersides.

Do not treat fruit trees when they are blooming, as you will kill the bees that are pollinating the trees for you.

MEALYBUG

Mites

There seems to be a mite for every plant: bamboo mite, citrus mite, fuchsia mite, tomato russet mite. Each mite puncture results in a little white dot where sap, containing chlorophyll, has been removed. Infested plants gradually become speckled, and then begin to yellow and shrivel. On plants that are heavily infested with spider mites, the leaves may be covered by webbing.

SPIDER MITE

Under-watered plants are more frequently infested with mites, and suffer more damage. Always water plants adequately, with special care in dry, dusty areas.

There are pesticides that will slow down the mite population, but before you try them, see if you can decrease the mite infestation by hosing down the plants with a sturdy water stream from the garden hose.

Whiteflies

If you disturb a plant and a cloud of white flies start flying about, you've got whiteflies. Whiteflies suck sap from many annuals, perennials, fruits, and vegetables, and the plant leaves may become yellow and curled. They excrete a waste substance called honeydew. A sooty fungus grows on the honeydew, turning the area black. Many beneficial insects feed on whiteflies, so try an insecticidal soap before resorting to stronger chemicals.

Fruit and veggie varmints

IF YOU LOVE A JUICY, sweet peach picked right off the tree, you're not alone. Some insects attack fruit crops with the same gusto you apply to a bowl of fruit salad. If you plan on growing fruit, look out for citrus thrips, codling moths, curculios, fruit flies, and fruit tree leafrollers. There are many unwanted vegetable visitors including cabbageworms, cucumber beetles, hornworms, and Mexican bean beetles.

Citrus thrips

There are over 600 species of thrips, including onion thrips, flower thrips, and citrus thrips. Citrus thrips over-winter in egg form, emerging as adult thrips in March. They can reproduce at the rate of 12 generations per year, with each female depositing about 200 eggs within leaf tissue.

On plants infested with thrips the flowers may not open, or if they do, they drop before fruits appear. Affected mature fruits display silvery-scarred areas. The leaves of thrips-infested plants take on a silvery or bronzy color as green chlorophyll-containing sap is removed, and you can often see little black spots all over the leaves.

Thrips can be difficult to control, and prevention is the key. Make sure trees and other plants are adequately watered. Thrips are attracted to drought-stressed trees. If you see an initial infestation, try washing it off with the garden hose, repeating as necessary. If an infestation is severe, insecticides are available for use on food and nonfood items. To prevent citrus and other fruit scarring, spraying must be initiated just as flower petals fall.

Codling moths

The most common cause of wormy apples, these whitish-pink moth larvae also feed on apricots, cherries, peaches, pears, plums, and nut trees. When codling moths have invaded, you'll see small holes in the fruit skin with dark brown, crumbly matter around the holes. As if the larvae damage weren't bad enough, the holes are perfect sites for bacterial and fungal growth.

Severe codling moth infestations can totally destroy a fruit crop. Damage is worse in years that have warm, dry springtime weather, because the moths lay more eggs. The larvae drop to the ground or crawl down tree trunks when they are ready to spin cocoons. They may over-winter under tree bark or in garden litter. To protect your garden, clean up garden fruits as they fall, and place rejects in a covered container for eventual disposal. Remove weeds and other debris to eliminate larvae hiding places.

Curculios

Adult curculios, also known as snout beetles, puncture newly formed fruits and then lay their eggs inside. You will see crescent-shaped scars or small holes if curculios have invaded your trees. The punctures enable rot fungus to enter the fruit. Fruits infested with curculio larvae are deformed. If you look inside the fruit, you may see grayish-white legless grubs with curled bodies. These will feed inside the fruit for a few weeks. The larvae crawl out of the fallen fruit and pupate underground, emerging as adults.

Once curculio grubs are within the fruit, they are protected from all chemical controls. Don't spray the fruit. You will not harm the insect, but might harm anyone who eats the fruit.

If infestations are severe, you can spray tree branches with an appropriate insecticide when the flower petals have just fallen and before the fruit forms. Read and follow all instructions quite carefully.

Fruit flies

There are, among many others present in this country, apple fruit flies, Caribbean fruit flies, cherry fruit flies, Mediterranean fruit flies (medflies), Mexican fruit flies, Oriental fruit flies, and walnut husk flies. Apple fruit fly maggots will destroy apples, blueberries, cherries, and plums. The maggots, resembling short, white worms, tunnel through the fruit as they feed, leaving behind brown, decaying areas.

Prevention is the best start toward keeping your garden free of fruit flies. Remove all dropped fruit daily and put it in a covered container, so flies don't emerge from the maggots within. If infestations are a severe problem, a spray is available, but its use must be timed correctly to have any effect. Once fruit fly maggots are within fruit, it is not possible to eliminate them and still eat the fruit.

Fruit tree leafrollers

It's easy to see how these pests got their name. You'll know they've come to visit by your tree's rolled leaves, which are held together with a web. Inside the leaves are pale green worms with brown heads, each about ½ an inch long. These worms are the larvae of brown moths. They feed on the blossoms, leaves, and developing fruit, and may wrap leaves around ripening fruit.

To limit the number of egg-laying moths that will emerge, remove and destroy the webbed leaves. Insecticide sprays are available to eradicate leafrollers. As with all insecticides, make sure the one you choose is designed for your tree, and follow all label instructions carefully.

Cabbageworms

Your kids may object to eating the cabbages from your garden, but cabbageworms will be happy to tuck in. There are several caterpillars known as cabbageworms. Cabbageworms eat large, ragged holes in the leaves of cole crops, such as broccoli, Brussels sprouts, cabbage, and cauliflower. Infested plants wilt during warm days even if they are watered; they will eventually turn yellow.

To deter infestations of cabbageworms, rotate your crops, planting cole crops in different places each year. If you're not squeamish, you can pick the caterpillars off the plants with your hands. Otherwise, try a Bacillus thuringiensis (BT) spray, an organic method of destruction. Spray as soon as the white butterflies are seen in the spring.

CABBAGEWORM

Cucumber beetles

Striped and spotted cucumber beetles are the most common in a garden. They feed on plants in the cucumber family, such as cantaloupe, cucumber, pumpkin, squash, and watermelon, as well as many other vegetables and some flowers, including roses. These voracious beetles devour your emerging seedlings, often eliminating them within a few days. If the seedlings survive the attack, the beetles make holes in the plant's leaves, shred the flowers, and chew on stems and fruits. Cucumber beetles can also transmit plant viruses in their saliva.

There are ways to prevent these beetles from making your garden their picnic grounds. Select plant varieties with stated resistance to cucumber beetle attack. Remove all plant litter regularly, discarding any unwanted fruit. Keep plants as healthy as possible. If your efforts fail, there are insecticides available to control this pest.

Hornworms

If you grow tomatoes, you have probably seen hornworms. If you haven't actually seen these large, 3-inch-long, plump green larvae, you have seen the damage they cause – disappearing leaves and fruit, with sometimes only a ragged stem remaining by morning. During the day hornworms hide under leaves, pooping away the leftovers as dark green droppings. Hornworms attack pepper, eggplant, and potato leaves, and fruit as well as tomatoes.

If you can deal with it, the easiest way to deal with infestations of hornworms is to pick them off the plant by hand and place them in a sealed jar or bag. You should then place the jar or bag in the trash can to avoid further problems. Praying mantids help control hornworms. Chemical contact sprays and BT sprays are the alternative.

Mexican bean beetles

Sometimes confused with ladybugs, Mexican bean beetles are about the same size and shape, but are copper colored with 16 spots. Adult beetles and their yellow young chew on the leaves, pods, and stems of green beans, lima beans, and soybeans. The leaves of an afflicted plant develop a ragged lace appearance. These beetles over-winter in garden litter, emerging in early spring at about the same time as your bean plants.

The easiest way to deter them is to select bean varieties that are somewhat resistant to attack. Remove garden debris after you harvest to reduce places where adult bean beetles spend the winter. Otherwise, there are a number of sprays and dusts available.

Tree and shrub shredders

APHIDS, BAGWORMS, BARK BEETLES, borers, fall webworms, gypsy moths, inchworms, Japanese beetles, lacebugs, leafminers, leafhoppers, leafrollers, mealybugs, scales, spider mites, thrips, and western tent caterpillars are some of the undesirables that may visit your trees and shrubs. You don't want an up-close and personal encounter in your yard, so let's do it here instead.

Bark beetles

Adult bark beetles lay their eggs in tunnels that they have eaten under tree bark. The emerging ½-inch white larvae, often called borers, continue making the tunnels. These tunnels destroy a vital layer of the tree's inner bark, which is responsible for trunk and limb growth. The resulting damage is seen in the form of dead twigs and branches, or worse, in the form of dead trees or shrubs.

There are hundreds of species of bark beetles, each making its own distinctive tunnel patterns. Bark beetles prefer unkempt trees and those suffering from drought, over-watering, transplant shock, or mechanical injury, such as that caused by lawnmowers.

As with most pests, the best defense is a good offense. Keep your ornamental, evergreen, and fruit trees healthy. Fertilize them regularly, water deeply during dry spells, and plant in appropriate sites. Prune in late fall or early winter, allowing the tree's branches to heal before bark beetles become active. Remove grass from around trees, and replace it with groundcover or pebbles. There are insecticides available to control bark beetles, but it is important to know which type you're trying to eradicate. To identify the species, put a sample in a closed container and consult a county agricultural extension agent for advice.

Gypsy moths

The leaves of a single tree can be fodder for as many as 30,000 gypsy moth caterpillars. With severe infestations, which occur about every 5 to 10 years, entire forests may be defoliated. Although these gray-brown, ½-inch to mature 2-inch-long, hairy caterpillars prefer oak trees, they are wide ranging in their tastes. They'll attack apple, birch, cedar, cherry, crabapple, linden, pine, and willow trees, among hundreds of others.

Gypsy moths usually start their work in June and July. The defoliation will probably not destroy the tree in the first year, but it does weaken it, making it susceptible to various fungal diseases. BT sprays are an initial defense, to be used when the caterpillars are small, and stronger chemical gypsy moth sprays are available. Make sure the container label states that the product is for use against gypsy moths and names your tree type.

Inchworms

Depending on where you live, you may know inchworms as cankerworms or measuring worms. They're all the same critter. Swinging from tree to tree on silken threads, these approximately 1-inch-long caterpillars devour the leaves of shade and fruit trees, as well as those of roses and rhododendron. Bits of leaves and caterpillar waste may drop down from infested trees. If the inchworms are numerous, you can hear the crunch, crunch as they feed. The parents are gray moths, about 1 inch in size, which stay fairly well hidden. There are two types of inchworm, one emerging in spring and the other in the fall. The larvae, or caterpillars, of the spring inchworm can be brown, green, or almost black, with yellow, green, or brown body stripes. The larvae of the fall inchworm are brown on top and green below, with white body stripes.

Although infested trees can be almost completely stripped of foliage, the damage usually occurs early enough in the season for trees to develop new leaves. It is only if infestation occurs year after year that it will cause permanent weakness. BT sprays are usually effective against inchworms, but repeated applications may be needed.

Japanese beetles

Metallic green with copper wings, Japanese beetles are quite pretty. The young emerging, grayish-white, C-shaped grubs feed on the roots of grass and groundcovers, resulting in brown, dead areas. The adults chew up leaves until only leaf skeletons remain, weakening the plant. In addition to fruit trees and shrubs, Japanese beetles feed on rose bushes, annuals and perennials. To eliminate the beetles, you'll need to use insecticidal sprays or *granules*.

> **DEFINITION**
>
> *A variety of gardening aids come in the form of* granules. *Granules may be smaller than a grain of rice, but most resemble white bath crystals. Both fertilizers and pesticides are available as granules. Obviously, you want to be careful not to confuse the two. As a pesticide, some granules are scattered, and others are strategically placed in batches. In keeping with all good pesticide use, always follow the directions on the packaging to the letter. If a chemical is harmful to insects or snails, it is also harmful to other living things.*

Scales

Scales, resembling little white, brown, or gray bumps on plant stems, are found on just about every type of outdoor fruit, shade, and evergreen tree. There are two types of scale insects: soft-shelled scales, and hard-shelled or "armored" scales with a hard, brown or gray shell.

HARD-SHELLED SCALE INSECT

INTERNET

uidaho.edu/so-id/
entomology/scale_insect
_and_mealybugs.htm

*Click here for descriptions,
photographs, and information
about how to cope with scales
and mealybugs.*

The shell, often made up of waxy fibers and cast-off skins, protects the soft-bodied insect underneath from almost all forms of chemical control. Accordingly, scales are difficult to eliminate once they find a home. Chemicals are generally useless in the home garden.

The best scale control is to encourage beneficial insects to inhabit your garden. They will either feed on young scales before the pests can form their protective shell, or will pierce the shell and deposit eggs that feed off the scale beneath.

Common plant diseases

THERE ARE A SEEMINGLY *infinite number of viral, bacterial, and fungal diseases that may affect plants. Some of them you truly can't do anything about. Others are treatable, but you have to be quite knowledgeable about the proper treatment. By using the wrong spray or by using the right spray incorrectly, you can injure the plant without distracting the disease in the least.*

If you want to be a plant doctor, my recommendation is to go to a knowledgeable nursery or agricultural clinic, take in a sample of the damaged plant, and ask for help. Plant diseases are a specialty.

If you choose to treat your plants in any way, follow the instructions on the container to the precise word. Always make sure the label lists your plant as appropriate for treatment.

The following diseases are quite common, and will give you an idea of the variety that can visit your garden. But don't really worry. If you keep healthy plants growing in a suitable site, you will probably have few problems.

MOLD AND MILDEW

You've probably seen mold on household edibles left to linger too long. (Or, if you're like me, the bread you buy seems to develop it on the way home from the store.) Let's look at the most common molds and mildews you'll see on your garden plants.

Gray mold

Unfortunately, the fluffy gray fungus covering your delicious garden strawberries can occur at any growth stage, including when they are just getting tasty ripe. This mold may be preceded by light tan spotting on the berries. Destroy infected fruit as soon as you see it. Do not let berries become overripe. Avoid overhead watering, because fungi thrive in cool humid weather. When planting the following year, leave enough space between plants for good air circulation and rapid drying.

Sooty mold

This is a blackish fungus that grows on honeydew, and on the sugary waste material deposited by aphids, mealybugs, scales, whiteflies, and other sap-sucking insects. The leaves and fruit of a plant with sooty mold appear dirty, but the mold can be wiped off. You may want to control whatever insect is causing the problem.

White mold

This may appear on bean pods, causing a condition called watery soft rot. The pods become mushy, and the entire plant may yellow, wilt, and die. This fungus spreads quickly to other bean plants, particularly in cool, wet weather. If your beans contract white mold, remove and destroy all diseased plants immediately, and do not replant beans in that area for three years. Keep the disease from spreading by watering at ground level rather than wetting leaves, and water the plants early in the day so that they dry quickly.

Powdery mildew

This disease appears as grayish-white, powdery patches on leaves, flower buds, and fruit. The various fungi involved in powdery mildew cause leaves to become distorted, buds to shrivel, and fruit to take on an abnormal shape. If the problem is serious, there are sprays available to combat powdery mildew. When treating fruit trees, be certain the product you use lists the afflicted fruit tree on the label, because some chemical sprays should not be applied to certain types of trees.

Bacterial soft rot

I love bearded irises, and it bothers me when one develops yellowing, dying leaves. If I pull it up, the rhizome is mushy, rotted, and stinky. Bacterial soft rot has infected the plant, entering by iris borer insects or other wounds – some of them possibly incurred during planting. This disease isn't limited to irises; it also affects melons, cacti, flower bulbs, carrots, and other plants. On potatoes, the slimy texture and vile stink are easy-to-recognize symptoms.

There is no cure, so prevention is critical. Make sure your soil is well drained, and avoid over-watering and overhead watering. Buy healthy plants, because just one unhealthy bulb can bring this bacteria into your garden soil. Try not to damage bulbs and rhizomes during planting, and place all bearded irises in a sunny site.

Fireblight

A bacterial disease, fireblight destroyed several of my towering pyracantha, almost overnight. The bushes turned black as if they were completely scorched by fire, and there wasn't a green leaf left. The interesting thing is that fireblight attacks some of the pyracantha, and skips the others. I don't know why, although I've read that *Pyracantha coccinea* "Lalandei" and *P. fortuneana* aren't as badly affected by the bacteria.

In addition to pyracantha, fireblight seriously affects cotoneaster and is fond of ruining apple, pear, flowering almond, plum, cherry, and hawthorn trees, among others. There is no cure for fireblight. Avoid planting fruit trees in heavy, poorly drained soil, and avoid over-feeding, both of which are said to increase a tree's susceptibility. If fireblight strikes, remove the plant and replace it with another that is not prone to this disease.

Peach leaf curl

If you have a peach tree and if your springtime weather is cool and wet, every so often you will probably have to endure peach leaf curl. Caused by a fungus, it is one of the worst diseases infecting peach trees. Peach leaf curl causes new leaves to pucker and curl up. The leaves develop red or yellow areas, over which a white coating may appear. If fruit forms, it is deformed and usually falls before it is ripe. After awhile, the leaves darken and fall. The leaf loss causes nutritional deprivation, and the tree becomes weaker. Although a tree will survive 1 year of severe peach leaf curl, several years in succession will kill it.

There is no cure for peach leaf curl. If you see it developing, remove and destroy infected leaves. There is a preventive spray available for use in the fall after the leaves drop, or in the spring before the buds open. The entire tree must be treated.

PEACH LEAF CURL

Weed world

WEEDS SEEM TO THRIVE with much more ease than our favorite plants. Weeds are basically any plants that grow where they are not wanted. They tend to be on the vigorous side, which is no surprise, inasmuch as they sprout in our gardens with no help from us. Some weeds are found all over the country, but others are fairly climate specific. Details follow on some weeds that seem to grow just about anywhere.

Crabgrass

Found in lawns, flowerbeds, vegetable patches, and sidewalks, crabgrass (*Digitaria* sp.) is one of the most annoying and persistent weeds. The pale, bluish-green, ⅓-inch blades are from 2 to 5 inches long and may be slightly hairy. This weed can spread out by stems that root at the joints. It can also spread by scattered seeds that are encased in the seed heads growing from each plant's center during the summer and fall. The seeds drop to the ground, remain dormant during the winter, and sprout in the fall. Crabgrass is quite capable, especially in hot, dry summer areas, of taking over most of a lawn. It has a sturdy, fibrous root system that makes it difficult to totally remove by digging. There are herbicides available for control.

Dandelion

The dandelion (*Taraxacum officinale*) taproot easily extends 3 feet down in the soil, and may go even further than that. The taproots

■ **Dandelion roots**
must be pried out carefully – or they will grow again.

are quite thick, in larger plants almost resembling a whitish, skinny carrot. If, when removing the taproot, you leave even a trace of root, the entire plant will regrow. This, among other factors, accounts for dandelions' continued existence in lawns and anywhere else the sun shines. Yellow flowers appear in spring and persist until frost. The flowers are followed by the familiar white puffballs. Each feathery strand acts as a parachute for the seed at its base. A strong wind carries seeds for miles. Herbicides are available to control dandelions.

Trivia...

Dandelions have been used as a food source and as a medicine for at least 1,000 years. The name derived from a German surgeon's commentary that each leaf of the plant resembled a lion's tooth, or dens leonis in Latin. The French were soon calling the plant dent-de-lion. European immigrants carried seeds to America, and our name for the plant was soon dandelion. Dandelion greens were used for salad and tea, roots were served as a vegetable course, or were dried and used as a coffee substitute. The flowers were used to concoct dandelion wine, and to make a yellow dye for wool.

Mouse-ear chickweed

Bothersome around vegetable and flower gardens, lawns, trees and shrubs, and unplanted areas, this dense, low-growing weed can crowd out your plants. It thrives in sunny areas where the soil is poor and damp. This plant's stems root wherever their joints touch the soil, starting more chickweed (*Cerastium vulgatum*), and its seeds are present from the spring until fall, also starting more plants. It is difficult to control this weed. If you pull it up by hand, be sure to remove all plant parts including the roots, which will otherwise re-sprout. There are herbicides available for control.

Nutsedge

Nutsedge (*Cyperus* sp.) is also called nutgrass, cocograss, cocosedge, and chufa. It looks like an ornamental, 8-inch-high palm tree. Initially my yard had one, but soon, in a damp area, there were a dozen, and then two dozen. They multiply rapidly via seeds, underground stems, and drought-tolerant tubers. There are various types, from 6 to 30 inches tall. You can dig them up, but it's best to do so when the plants are small. If any part of the tuber remains, it will regrow. Try covering the area with thick cardboard or heavy, weighted-down fabric. A powerful herbicide can control young plants.

NIGHTSHADE
(*Solanum* sp.)

More garden weeds:

- Barnyard grass (*Echinolchloa crus-galli*)
- Bermuda grass (*Cynodon dactylon*)
- Black medic (*Medicago lupulina*)
- Carpetweed (*Mollugo verticillata*)
- Common chickweed (*Stellaria media*)
- Common groundsel (*Senecio vulgaris*)
- Common lambsquarters (*Chenopodium album*)
- Cudweed (*Graphalium uliginosum*)
- Dallisgrass (*Paspalum dilatatum*)
- Downy brome (*Bromeus tectorum*)
- Field bindweed (*Convolvulus arvensis*)
- Goldenrod (*Solidago* sp.)
- Goosegrass (*Eleusine indica*)
- Green foxtail (*Setaria viridis*)
- Henbit (*Laxium amplexicaule*)
- Horseweed (*Conyza canadensis*)
- Kudzu vine (*Pueraria lobata*)
- Mallow (*Malva rotundifolia*)
- Nimblewill (*Muhlenbergia schreberi*)
- Nightshades (*Solanum* sp.)
- Oxalis (*Oxalis* sp.)
- Pigwood (*Euonymus atropurpureus*)
- Plantains (*Plantago* sp.)
- Poison ivy (*Rhus radicans*)
- Poison oak (*Rhus diversiloba*)
- Prickly lettuce (*Lactuca* sp.)
- Prostrate knotweed (*Polygonum aviculare*)
- Purslane (*Portulacca oleracea*)
- Quackgrass (*Elytrigia repens*)
- Ragweed (*Ambrosia artemisiifolia*)
- Red sorrel (*Rumex acetosella*)
- Redstem filaree (*Erodium cicotarium*)
- Sandbur (*Cenchrus tribuloides*)
- Shepherdspurse (*Capsella bursa-pastoris*)
- Sowthistle (*Sonchus oleraceus*)
- Spotted spurge (*Euphorbia maculata*)
- Virginia peppergrass (*Lepidum viginicum*)
- Wild oat (*Avena fatua*)

Pest controls

YOU MAY, FROM TIME TO TIME, *think about using some type of* pesticide *in or around your garden. You will probably go to the garden center nearest you and ask a staff member what to do about the leaves curling on your peach tree, the green bugs on your roses, or some obvious damage to a plant. Of course, the level of knowledge of staff members at a garden center or even a sophisticated nursery will vary. They may point you to a certain product and say this will take care of your problem. It may, or may not.*

DEFINITION

Of course you know that a pesticide is a pest control mechanism. But pesticides are not just toxic sprays coming out of airplanes. "Pest" is defined by the Environmental Protection Agency as a living organism causing damage or economic loss, or that carries or causes diseases. So a pesticide can be for use against animals, insects, or weeds.

Specifically, a pesticide designed for use against insects is called an insecticide. A pesticide designed for use against fungi is called a fungicide. A pesticide designed for use against weeds is called an herbicide.

The use of pesticides is a science, one that has been made much easier for the novice with the constant work of chemists and other researchers working for manufacturers. But it still requires attention on your part. Some plant treatments may be effective at one time of the year, but ineffective at others. Some plant treatments may work on one plant but be harmful to another. Let's look at how pesticides work.

Organic insecticides

Organic insecticides are composed of natural products, but should be used only as necessary. They may kill some beneficial insects as well as harmful ones. Generally, plants should be treated with organic insecticides either early in the morning or late in the afternoon, when bees are not busy pollinating.

BT (*Bacillus thuringiensis*): There are various types of BT sold, each for a specific group of insects or insect larvae. The bacteria that make up BT act to paralyze the insect's digestive tract, thereby starving it to death.

Insecticidal soap: Insecticidal soap is a spray-on mixture sold in almost all nurseries. It has been used since at least the 1700s. Insecticidal soaps act to paralyze insects and must contact the insect's body to be effective. Target pests include grasshoppers, leafhoppers, mealybugs, mites, young scales, squash bugs, thrips, and whiteflies.

Petroleum-based spray insecticides have been used in the garden for over 100 years. Early products had too many impurities to be used safely on leafy plants. So they were only used on dormant plants, hence the term "dormant" oil.

Oil-based insecticides: Dormant oil, horticultural oil, and summer oil are insecticides derived from petroleum. The newer concoctions are useful throughout the year on most plant types. Oil sprays act by suffocating insects. Read the instructions very carefully, as you cannot combine horticultural oils with many other garden products, or use them during hot or cold temperature extremes. Horticultural oils are used to defeat aphids, leafhoppers, mealybugs, mites, scales, thrips, and other pest insects.

Pyrethrins: These are insecticidal ingredients derived from the pyrethrum daisy (*Tanacetum coccineum*). They are sold as the primary active ingredient in some products, and also can be found in combination with other organic products. Pyrethrin sprays or dusts require direct insect contact to be effective. Pyrethrins are used to demolish such pests as bean beetles, cabbage loopers, Colorado potato beetles, cucumber beetles, gypsy moth larvae, mealybugs, spider mites, thrips, tomato hornworms, and whiteflies. Make a point of distinguishing between pyrethrins and pyrethroids. The latter are chemicals synthesized in a laboratory to resemble pyrethrins, but they have more toxicity to the surroundings.

Some popular organic insecticides include:

- Bt
- Dormant oils
- Horticultural oils
- Insecticidal soap
- Milky disease for Japanese beetles
- *Nosema locustae* for grasshopper control
- Pyrethrins
- Pyrethroids
- Rotenone
- Ryania

Synthetic pesticides

When using any chemical in the garden, always read the label. Read the label before you buy the product, before you mix it, every time you use it, before storing it, and again before discarding it. Every label will tell you what ingredients are in the product, how hazardous the product is, any special use precautions, and the directions for use.

Follow the instructions on pesticide labels to the letter.

When applying a pesticide, wear gloves, goggles, and a covering garment. Wash your hands thoroughly after use, and wash clothing separately from other laundry. Discard or store all chemical products with the utmost safety.

■ **Always wear protective** *rubber gloves when applying insecticide sprays.*

INTEGRATED PEST MANAGEMENT

Integrated pest management (IPM) is a phrase you will hear frequently used among professional garden people. IPM uses multiple controls to try to manage garden pests, beginning with those that are the least harmful to the environment. Education is the key to successful use of IPM techniques. The more you understand about pests, the more successful you will be at getting rid of them. Many insects are beneficial for your garden. Although there certainly are harmful insects, some damage is merely unsightly and doesn't truly hurt the plant.

Practitioners of IPM often find they don't have to use chemicals. If they do need to use an insecticide, they probably will first try an organic product. When used correctly, organic insecticides are usually safer for people and pets than those that are made from synthetic chemicals. They also cause less environmental chaos.

The various methods used by IPM advocates include:

■ **Physical controls:** Hand-picking pests from plants and screening off plants to keep pests away.

■ **Cultural controls:** Selecting the right plant for the right spot, planting disease and pest-resistant varieties, pruning at the correct time of year, using proper pruning tools and techniques, and proper watering and fertilization practices.

LADYBUG

■ **Biological controls:** Taking advantage of living organisms that naturally eliminate pests. They are often present in your garden of their own accord, if the use of pesticides, insecticides, and herbicides hasn't killed them off.

Parasitoids are organisms whose young develop in or on a pest insect, usually causing the pest insect's death.

Biological controls include predators and parasitoids. Predators are spiders and beneficial insects such as ladybugs, ground beetles, green lacewings, and syrphid flies. The beneficial wasp *Apanteles congregatus* lays its eggs on the skin of tomato hornworms. When the larvae hatch, they burrow into the hornworm and feed on it. When mature, the wasps make cocoons from which adult wasps will emerge. Other parasitoids include the whitefly parasite (*Encarsia formosa*) and Trichogramma wasps that lay eggs within the eggs of butterfly and moth caterpillars.

It is extremely important when considering the use of any pesticide in a garden that you do not use it on or near food plants unless the label specifically states that it is safe to do so.

The label will state what, if any, food plants may come into contact with the product. The label will state treatment times, and how long you must wait to harvest after treatment. All garden pesticides can be extremely hazardous to health, and some are suspected carcinogens. It is much better to prevent problems by good garden care and proper plant selection.

■ **Store all chemicals** *safely out of reach of children and animals – preferably in a locked cupboard.*

Synthetic insecticides

Some chemical insecticides work on contact, and others have a systemic action. Contact insecticides must come in direct contact with the insect to have any effect. Contact insecticides for garden use are sold as a dust, spray, liquid concentrate, or soluble powder. When using a contact pesticide, you must thoroughly treat all parts of the plant, because some insects live primarily on the undersides of leaves. Systemic pesticides are those that will travel throughout the plant. An insect feeding on any plant part will ingest the systemic chemical that will kill it.

No pesticide is specific only to harmful insects. Both contact and systemic insecticides will kill beneficial insects as well as pest insects. Common chemicals in synthetic insecticides at this time of writing include malathion, diazinon, carbaryl, and acephate. Although effective against pest insects if used properly, all are extremely poisonous to people, animals, birds, and beneficial insects.

Synthetic herbicides

It is quite tedious to pull out weeds over and over again. Many gardeners find it easier to use a herbicide or weed killer to do the job. There are four common types of synthetic herbicides: pre-planting, pre-emergent, post-emergent, and sterilizers.

Pre-planting herbicides are used after you have prepared the soil, before you plant your seeds. They destroy weed seeds in the soil. After you have followed the directions, plant the seeds. Pre-emergent herbicides are used to destroy seeds as they germinate. They do not affect established plants or weeds. Post-emergent herbicides are used after the grass or other plants are established and you want to eliminate growing weeds. These products, usually sprays, may kill any plant on which they land. Sterilizing herbicides kill all plants that they come into contact with. If sprayed on a plant they will kill the leaves and then attack the roots and kill them. Avoid using these on a windy day.

Herbicides have their practical uses, but they can be quite poisonous to people, pets, wildlife, fish, birds, and insects. Read and follow the instructions on the container.

Synthetic fungicides are used as preventives, not as cures. If your plant has a fungal disease, a fungicide will probably not cure it, but it may prevent the spread of the disease. When using a fungicide, always read the label and apply it as directed.

Animal visitors

AS OUR HOMES IMPINGE ON NATURE, *many animals have learned to adapt and even to use the garden as a food depot. Some people find this nice, others find it cute, and some get quite annoyed. Animal visitors you may find include birds, chipmunks, armadillos, deer, gophers, squirrels, mice, moles, opossums, porcupines, rabbits, rats, raccoons, and skunks.*

Bothersome birds

Most birds are welcome in gardens, and are even invited with bird feeders and birdbaths. On the other hand, some birds are generally a nuisance, such as blackbirds, cowbirds, crows, grackles, house sparrows, and starlings. Birds can get to your ripe fruit before you do, making little holes as they peck hungrily away. Corn can be destroyed. If you have just planted seeds, seed-eating birds seem to know and can scratch away at the soil looking for tidbits that were intended to be vegetables. To keep your seeds in the ground, you can put ¼-inch mesh cover over them, but remember to remove it as the plants begin growing.

To protect fruit trees and bushes, you can try covering them with netting. Or you may be able to scare the birds off (for a while, at least) by dangling strips of shiny aluminum foil to the branches and letting them sway in the breeze. The simplest solution is to plant enough so that you and the birds get a share. Regardless of the number of trees you have, it is wise to pick fruit as it ripens. Overripe fruit serves as an invitation, and once the birds become accustomed to your garden as a dining center, it is very difficult to convince them to go elsewhere.

Deterring deer

Complaints about deer seem to be mounting in suburbia. There isn't much you can do to keep deer out of your yard. Any fencing has to be a heavy wire mesh at least 8 feet high, and must completely surround the garden. If deer can't jump over, they may crawl under, so set the fence into the ground. Less dramatic measures include a garden of daffodils that deer seldom eat, placing plants as close to the house as possible where human presence may deter them, and planting lots of edibles so you have enough to share. Deer are protected by law, and the fines for harming deer can be substantial. Consult your State Department of Fish and Game for advice if you have a serious problem.

INTERNET

thegardenhelper.com

Search here for some bright ideas on how to keep deer from the home garden, with a list of some plants that may be tried for varying degrees of deer resistance.

Ground digging gophers

These small brown animals dig tunnels about 6 inches under your garden and lawn. From these tunnels, which can become extensive, they eat plant roots and lots of bulbs. The tunnels caused by gophers are not easily visible. If gophers are in your yard you usually will see a hole, or a series of exit holes, some of which may be temporarily covered with earth. From time to time during the day, most often in the morning, a gopher sticks its head out to survey the scenery. If you come near, the gopher tucks back in again.

People living in gopher territory give up trying to grow bulbs, except pehaps daffodils, which the gophers don't like. There are all sorts of gizmos sold to deter gophers. If you want to try them, do. Most often recommended are wire cages that surround your bulbs and newly planted shrubs and perennials. Getting a dog may also help.

Opossum problems

Otherwise quiet, these foot-long gray animals with long tails are fond of clanking around garbage cans looking for tasty tidbits. They are not too particular about what they eat, and enjoy ripening fruit, vegetables, insects, fish, green plants, birds, and smaller animals, alive or dead. They travel the neighborhood at night, so you'll seldom see one, but you may catch a glimpse of one making a quick getaway.

Opossums spend the day in sheltered locations, such as the crawl spaces underneath buildings and porches, drainage pipes, attics, or outbuildings. You can persuade them to dine elsewhere by removing fallen fruit, picking ripe fruit and vegetables, bringing dog food indoors at night, and buying garbage cans with tight-fitting lids. Putting leftovers in plastic bags will not help, as opossums will tear these open. Fencing seldom works, because opossums are excellent climbers. Close off their living areas (making certain they are not in residence).

Do not attempt to handle opossums. In some areas they may be carriers of diseases such as tularemia and Rocky Mountain spotted fever.

In some locales, opossums are protected under wildlife laws. Check with your local animal control center or State Department of Fish and Game for further information on how to manage an opossum problem.

Raccoon relief

I thought raccoons were cute until a mother raccoon decided to raise her 5 babies in the crawl space under my house. The babies seemed to squabble constantly – high squeaky chatter beginning in the evening and lasting most of the night. In between bouts, they were apparently jumping on my newly repaired flexible heating pipes. Nobody slept; neither the raccoons nor my family. Raccoons can be dangerous if cornered. They have long nails and sharp teeth. We were even told to keep our dogs inside at night, lest they come upon a raccoon making a foray into the garden or a garbage can. A dog, unless it is quite large, is no match for an angry mother raccoon.

Our instructions were to wait until the mother took the youngsters out for a stroll, and close the entrance. Their entryway was a low vent that had been covered with wire before the mother raccoon ripped it off. We played loud music, turned on lights, tried all sorts of annoyances, none of which had any effect. After about a month, the raccoons departed and I sealed their entrance with double-wire mesh which I check regularly.

Raccoons are clever, nosy, and bold. They will figure out a way to open a tightly closed garbage can lid. And if they fail, they'll flip the can over so that the lid pops off. Then they will scatter garbage all over looking for choice tidbits. They will walk up to your back door and eat the dog's food as you watch. If you live in a rural area, which is true raccoon territory, and leave a door open in the evening, they may march right in and help themselves to the food in the kitchen. Considering how brazenly they'll go for your garbage, you can imagine what they'll do to your prize baby vegetables.

There are people who have become quite attached to a local raccoon family. However, like most wild animals, it is best to be careful due to possible health risks. To diminish visits, leave no food outside, including pet food and any fruit that may have dropped from your trees. Access to edibles will keep them coming back. Secure garbage cans well so they can't be turned over, and get lids that are difficult to pry open. Screen or otherwise block openings to attics and crawl spaces. Consult your State Department of Fish and Game for local restrictions on trapping raccoons and releasing them in a more wild area.

Trivia...

The Virginia opossum is the only marsupial that is native to North America. The offspring of marsupials develop and feed within the mother's pouch. An opossum may have 18 or more babies per year, each initially about the size of a kidney bean.

A simple summary

✓ A well-planned, well-tended garden, clean started with healthy plants is the simplest way to prevent disease and to deter unwelcome wildlife.

✓ If you are going to treat plants with any type of pesticide, make sure the product is designed to address the specific problem that your plant has, and that it is safe to use on the afflicted plant.

✓ Always follow the directions on the label of all pesticides.

✓ Organic pesticides are readily available and generally less toxic to the surrounding environment than synthetic pesticides.

✓ To deter unwanted animals and birds, remove dropped fruit and pick fruit when ripe.

✓ Generally, insects are good for gardens. They pollinate flowers and feed birds. Some insects are pests. There are beneficial insects that eat these pests.

✓ Pesticides of any kind, organic or chemical, kill beneficial insects as well as harmful ones.

✓ Use a control method designed for use against the insect. If you're not sure, have a professional help you identify it.

✓ Clean up all garden debris.

✓ Never use a pesticide directly on fruit. If a pest insect is inside, no control will reach it, and someone eating the fruit might get sick.

✓ Never spray fruit trees in bloom, as you will kill pollinating bees.

✓ Always read the directions on any pesticide container before you buy it, before you use it, and afterwards. Re-read the directions the next time you use it.

✓ Water your plants appropriately, use the correct amount of fertilizer, and plant them where they will get the proper amount of sunlight.

Chapter 22

A Time to Every Purpose

THERE IS SOMETHING to do in an outdoor garden throughout the year. It's easy in the spring, when just the thought of blossoms draws you outdoors. Summer is a lazy time, but a warm day with a breeze is ideal for a garden center visit or a day spent playing in the dirt. Fall is garden clean-up time. In winter, you can order catalogs to peruse, admire your indoor plants, and by January, start deciding which roses to choose.

In this chapter...

✓ Projects for spring

✓ Special projects for summer

✓ Autumn activities

✓ Whiling away the winter

Projects for spring

IT'S NEVER TOO EARLY to get busy. In February, plan your vegetable garden and plant bare-root roses. (February may not really be spring; your roses might go in a month later.) In March, begin installing summer-blooming bulbs. After the last frost, plant avocados and citrus trees. Prune rose bushes for shape. In April, fertilize the lawn and plant annuals and vegetables. See where you can use time-saving groundcovers and perhaps purchase plants for a water garden. You might need to check and refurbish supports for your climbers. You can always try some fun projects indoors, such as the ones that follow.

Start a lemon tree

To grow a lemon tree (*Citrus limon*) inside the house, begin with 3 seeds taken from different lemons. Soak the seeds overnight and then let them dry. Fill 3 containers with sterile potting mix. The containers can be Styrofoam cups or something more elaborate, as long as they have a small drainage hole in the base. Place each container on an old dish or pie pan. Set a seed in each container, pushing it ½ inch into the soil, and cover with soil. Water lightly, so that all the soil becomes damp. Shelter the containers loosely using a sandwich bag. Place the containers in a warm, not hot, place. You can place them near, but not under, a table lamp that is on about 3 hours a day. Water the containers whenever the soil feels slightly dry.

In a few weeks, small plants will appear. Uncover the containers and put them in a sunny site. Continue to water lightly. When the trees reach about 4 inches, move them to larger pots and keep them in the sun.

Don't forget to water your lemon tree, but don't over-water.

Fertilize the soil every 6 weeks with a citrus fertilizer. As your trees grow, you will have to move them into larger pots. Eventually you may want to move them directly into the garden. Depending on the conditions, your trees should bloom in 3 to 5 years. You can also try orange, mandarin orange, lime, and grapefruit seeds.

Grow a sweet potato vine

If you have an organic fruit and vegetable stand near you, buy your sweet potatoes (*Ipomoea batatus*) there. If the only choice is the supermarket, buy several sweet potatoes, because many of these have been treated not to sprout. Look for those that have started little white roots, or have little purple root bumps sticking out.

Fill three large glass jars or three clear vases with tap water. Place four toothpicks around each sweet potato. The containers should be large enough to hold the sweet potato dangling in place, without its sides or bottom touching the glass. Taller containers allow more room for root development. The water in the container should reach midway up the sweet potato. Keep the containers in a warm, shady place. Add lukewarm water to keep the level at the halfway mark. If you don't see any white roots emerging, or if the container water starts to smell after about 2 weeks, you'll have to discard it.

If the plant grows, you will see green stems that will develop ivy-like leaves. It will grow nice long vines for several months. Remember to keep water at the halfway mark in the container. When the vines start to die down, you can add them to your compost pile.

Create a display of vegetable greenery

This project is fun for children. Start with a bowl about 4 to 6 inches high. Uproot from your garden, or buy, some large carrots, some small beets with a little green growth on top, several radishes, and perhaps a few parsnips. Place the whole radishes and beets in the bowl. Cut off the top 2 inches of the carrots and parsnips and put these in the bowl, cut side down. Add pebbles to hold them in place. Add water until it reaches the halfway mark on the vegetables. Place your bowl in a bright site and wait for the foliage to grow. Keep the water at the halfway mark.

CARROT AND PARSNIP TOPS

Grow hyacinths in a glass

Hyacinth bulbs (*Hyacinthus*) are available in October or November. After a few months they'll provide fragrant blossoms. You will need a hyacinth glass to grow them in water. This is a container shaped like an hourglass. The bulb sits in the top and roots form at the base. Keep the roots covered with water. Put the bulbs in sterilized all-purpose potting soil in a pot. Cover with soil so just the tip is visible. Place in a cool site (40 to 50° F) for 6 to 8 weeks.

Trivia...

In ancient Greek mythology, Hyakinthos was the god of spring flowers. The god Apollo adored Hyakinthos, but killed him by accident. The hyacinth flower sprang up from the blood of the dead youth. The hyacinth is symbolic of sorrow, sadness, and resurrection.

Keep the soil slightly moist. When leaves appear, move the pot to a brighter site. When the flower buds begin to display color, put the pot in a sunny window at about 60° F. Do not overheat. When flowering is over, cut off faded flowers but keep the soil moist. Let the greenery die back and plant the bulbs outdoors in early spring.

HYACINTHS

Special projects for summer

OF COURSE, YOU'LL HAVE PLENTY *to do in the garden during the summer. Start in May, making sure your plants are kept as healthy as possible so they can resist insect pests that thrive in this season. If necessary, re-seed or re-sod the lawn. Plant shrubs and hedges that provide berries and shelter for birds. Plant your annual vegetables and flowers. During June, fertilize azaleas, camellias, and rhododendrons. This is also a good time to fertilize the lawn. July is for planting fall-flowering bulbs and for buying colorful perennials to liven up special garden sites. Read on for more fun ways to spend the summer months.*

Make pomander balls

Pomander balls have been used to scent closets for hundreds of years and they make super homemade gifts. The original pomanders had an apple base (*pomme* is the French word for "apple"). You can still make a pomander ball from a small, hard apple, but lemons, limes, or oranges are much longer lasting. If you have a citrus tree in your garden, you will have lots of fruit to use for this project, which will provide plenty of fun for the whole family. Children especially love to try making pomanders.

You'll need a fork, one or more containers of whole cloves, kitchen allspice, or ground cinnamon, and, of course, your citrus fruits. Poke shallow holes in the fruit with your fork. Use a random pattern of poking, rather than doing it in rows that could cause the lemon to break along the dotted line. Push a clove into each hole until the citrus is covered with cloves. Don't push too hard or the clove will disappear. You want it to stud the citrus exterior. The less citrus skin you can see, the better your pomander will look. When the cloves are in place, sprinkle the pomander ball with allspice or cinnamon. Poke a hairpin or bobby pin in the citrus center, leaving the rounded tip exposed so that you can pull it out and insert a ribbon or wire.

■ **Fragrant pomander balls** *make a pretty home-made gift for a friend – or even for yourself.*

The citrus should dry for at least 2 weeks in a dry, sunny spot. Turn the fruit occasionally, so the bottom gets some air, or place it on an elevated rack. The citrus will gradually shrink and become quite hard. This shrinkage holds the cloves in place. Insert a pretty ribbon, and use as a closet scent or as a holiday decoration. Some people cover their pomander balls with colorful netting, tying it with bright ribbon. Pomander balls will last for years.

Dry some herbs

On a warm afternoon, when the plants have not been recently watered, gather cut stems with leaves on them just before the flowers open. Place the cut stems, a bit apart from each other, on an elevated screen located in a shady, warm spot. Leave the stems and leaves on the screen until they're dry. Turn them from time to time to hasten drying.

■ **Dry flower** *bunches by tying them up and hanging them upside down.*

If you're drying more than one type of herb, label each group. Unless the weather is really humid, drying should take about 6 days. If the stem snaps easily, the herbs are dry and it's time to pick them. The flavor diminishes if you wait too long. Strip the leaves from the stems and store in a well-closed jar.

Dry some lavender

The best lavenders for drying are English lavender (*Lavendula angustifolia*), *L. intermedia*, and French lavender (*L. dentata*). For the best results, use the darkest-colored flowers you can find. Cut long spikes with pruning shears or a pair of scissors just as the blossoms are opening up. Remove all the leaves from the cut plant and hang the stems in loose bundles of about 12 stems, grouped together with a rubber band. The stems should be hung in a warm, dry, dark place – a garage is ideal. The flowers should dry out in about 2 weeks. When they have, strip them from the stems to use in *potpourri* and other fragrant crafts.

> **DEFINITION**
>
> *A potpourri is made up of dried flower petals and spices. But it also can contain sweet-smelling seeds, stems, and roots. Its scent comes from the aromatic oils found within each plant.*

LAVENDER

Dry some rose petals

On a hot, dry late afternoon, gather fully open roses in good condition. Select those with a really great fragrance, as they make the best potpourri. Old roses are particularly good for the job. Put a piece of screen on top of some blocks (an unused window screen is great). The screen should be raised about 2 to 3 inches off the ground. Sprinkle the petals singly, so that they don't touch each other, over the screen and let them dry for about 2 to 5 days, or until they are dry to the touch but not crumbly. Make sure the petals do not touch or the overlapping parts might develop mildew, which will ruin the scent. Other petals are dried in the same way.

> **INTERNET**
>
> **makestuff.com/ lavender_wand.html**
>
> *Visit this site for instructions on how to make pretty, sweet-smelling lavender decorations.*

Make your own potpourri

It's quite fun and inexpensive to make your own potpourri. First, find a wide-mouth half-gallon jar with a lid. These types of jars can be found at garage sales, thrift shops, and food wholesalers. If you can't locate a nice big jar, a smaller one will do.

Put in the jar about 1 cup each of dried lavender flowers and dried rose petals. Add ½ cup dried marjoram leaves and ¼ cup of dried leaves from two of the following: lemon balm (*Melissa officinalis*), lemon verbena (*Aloysia triphylla*), mint, orange, or rose-scented geranium (*Pelargonium graveolens*). You can also try concoctions with dried fragrant petals of carnation, chamomile, heliotrope, honeysuckle, lilac, lily-of-the-valley, mignonette, or tuberose. Add 1 tablespoon of dried orange peel, ½ teaspoon cloves, and ½ teaspoon cinnamon. You can substitute ½ teaspoon allspice or ½ teaspoon nutmeg for the cloves and cinnamon. Seal the jar for 4 to 6 weeks. Shake the jar well, and, if possible, stir the mixture just about every day. Shaking and stirring encourages good interaction between all the ingredients. This mixture will smell lovely for quite a while when placed in pretty, open containers.

INTERNET

frontiercoop.com/
aromatherapy/potpourri/
index.html

You'll find complete details about potpourri fragrance and how to make and use potpourri. This site provides potpourri history and lore, fragrance classifications, equipment, fragrant ornaments for any season, fragrant wreaths, skin allergy tests, and sources of essential oils used in perfume.

To make potpourri last a long time, many people add a fixative to their potpourri before letting it blend in the sealed jar.

A fixative absorbs the aromatic oils and slowly releases them. A common fixative is orris root, made from dried iris rhizomes.

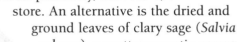

To add a fixative, put about 1 tablespoon in a half-gallon jar of potpourri. There are several other fixatives available, and you might want to inquire at a local pharmacy, craft store, or herbal store. An alternative is the dried and ground leaves of clary sage (*Salvia sclarea*), a pretty aromatic perennial for the garden. Or you can sprinkle dried pickling salt on your potpourri as a fixative. This is a non-iodized salt, which is available at some specialty groceries.

To keep ingredients for a potpourri all year round, separate the dried leaves and flowers in their own containers and keep them tightly sealed until you're ready to mix and place out in the household.

■ **Displays of potpourri** *cheer up the home in the winter months when fresh flowers are scarce.*

Autumn activities

WHEN FALL ARRIVES, *the gardener has a host of jobs. In August, it is time to spray unwanted weeds as necessary. You'll want to fertilize houseplants and prepare your garden beds for the next year in September. October means planting spring-blooming bulbs and seeding annual grasses. This is also the month when you should fertilize your flowering plants. If you aren't too busy keeping up with the falling leaves, here are other fun projects to try.*

Decorate your home with daffodils

Paper white or Soleil d'Or are exquisite, tiny white daffodils (*Narcissus*) that can be started indoors in water. The bulbs are usually available in fall, and will bloom within 2 months. Paper white has white petals surrounding a yellow center, and Soleil d'or is a golden color. Set bulbs about 1 inch apart in an attractive container about 5 inches deep. Surround the bulbs with small pebbles or colored gravel. These are available in nurseries or stores that sell tropical fish. About half of each bulb should be visible. Add water to the container until it covers about 1 inch of the bulb base. Put the container in a dark, cool site, at 50 to 65° F, checking on it from time to time to make sure it has enough water for root development.

In about 3 to 4 weeks, when the plants have developed a sturdy root system, put the pots in a sunny, warm site. These water-grown daffodils will never re-bloom indoors, but if you live in a relatively warm-winter area, let the foliage die back naturally and plant the bulbs outdoors after they have finished blooming.

Make some cornhusk dolls

If you've grown corn in your vegetable garden, you will have husks. If not, they are easy to obtain fresh at the supermarket when you buy corn, or dried at Mexican grocery stores where they are used to make tamales. You can also buy dry corn husks at craft stores. Cut off the crinkled portion at the base. Soak the husks in a pan of lukewarm water for 4 minutes to soften them, as they must be soft and pliable to be workable.

Take five husks, placing them one on top of the other. Fold this thick layer in half lengthwise. Wrap a rubber band around the top 1½ inches. Fold this short piece over, tucking the ends under the rubber band. This will be the doll's face. Take two of the smaller husks and roll them tightly. Place small rubber bands at each end of this roll, about ½ an inch from the ends. Put this between the husks so they protrude below the doll's face. The arms are now in place. Underneath them, place a rubber band to form the doll's waist. And now you have a girl doll that, if you want, you can dress up.

Create some apple dolls

After a few years, your apple tree will give you more apples than you need for cakes, pies, juice, and everyday munching. Experiment with making apple dolls. Making apple dolls is a true art form, and it takes experience to get the best results. But it all begins with the first apple.

If you don't have extra apples, buy several large red apples at the supermarket. Try different kinds if you want, to see what works best. Peel the apples, leaving just a little circle of skin at the top and bottom. Carve little holes where you want the eyes. To keep the apples from turning brown, squeeze lemon juice on them, making certain to cover well. You will have to hang the apples up to dry. Inserting a piece of rustproof wire, such as picture wire, through each apple from bottom to top gives you a hanging mechanism. Make a hanger-type loop at the top of the wire and knot the bottom. Place the drying apples in a cool, dark, draft-free site. Let them dry for about 3 weeks. Use white glue to add seeds, beads, or buttons for eyes. A red marker makes rosy cheeks. Cut a smiling mouth with a small pair of scissors and use a red marker or red felt pen to accentuate it. To keep the head shiny and well preserved, cover it with some glossy acrylic polymer coating from a craft store.

You can make the bodies out of just about any container. A plastic container works nicely and won't break. Small, empty, dish detergent bottles are a good size. All containers should be filled with sand. Push the holding wire into the container, then glue on the apple heads. You can make arms with pipe cleaners pushed through cuts in the container. Design clothing as you please and glue it to the container. Use cosmetic puffs or absorbent cotton to form hair.

Pretty placemats from autumn leaves

This project is fun and educational. Collect pretty colored autumn leaves of various shapes and place them, about 1 inch apart, in a single layer, between several sheets of newspaper. Change the paper after 24 hours. You can make multiple layers of leaves and newspaper, placing one on top the other. Put an old telephone book, board, or other heavy weight on top of the pile, and check that all areas are pressed down. Leave for about a month.

Cut a rectangle of clear contact paper about 10 by 14 inches. Peel the backing off carefully and lay it on a table with the sticky side up. Place the dried leaves carefully in a design of your choosing. Once they're placed they can't be moved, so you might make an image of the design before setting the leaves on the sticky paper. Cover your arrangement with white- or beige-colored paper, letting it stick to the contact paper. You now have a placemat or a decorative picture.

■ **Collect attractive** *leaves in early fall, before they dry and shrivel.*

Whiling away the winter

THE DARK DAYS OF WINTER *are a good time to get ready for the year ahead. As early as November you can start preparing your garden. This is a good time to prune your shrubs and to spray fruit trees for insect and disease prevention. You'll want to remove dead and diseased wood from your trees before the cold weather sets in. In December and January, start shopping! You can begin looking for bare-root roses and fruit trees at garden centers. In warm climates, it's a good idea to prune your rose bushes so they'll be pretty come blossom time. Browse through garden catalogs and buy some gift plants for the holidays.*

INTERNET

ag.ohio-state. edu/~ohioline/hyg- fact/1000/1248.html

Try this site for detailed instructions on how to get a poinsettia to re-bloom indoors a year after you have received it.

The holiday gardener

During the holiday season, there's a good chance you'll be giving and receiving some pretty gift plants. Although not all gift plants will thrive forever, some may last quite a while in your home, and a few may even do well if transplanted properly outdoors. Some of the traditional holiday gift plants have problems surviving long term because they've been forced to flower using severe commercial light alterations, way out of their normal schedule. It is difficult for the plant to recover from this shock, but not impossible.

Whether you are the giver or the recipient, you can keep holiday plants looking great with just a bit of simple care. The saucer-like containers underneath the colorful foil wrapping of most plants is often a bit shallow and might leak. Put a plate or other larger saucer under the plant package to protect your furniture and carpets. To prevent root rot, empty the saucer and the surrounding foil regularly. Gift plants you'll most likely be tending include azaleas (*Rhododendron*), Christmas cactus (*Schlumbergera buckleyi*), florist's cyclamen (*Cyclamen persicum*), Jerusalem cherry (*Solanum pseudocapsicum*), and poinsettias (*Euphorbia pulcherrima*).

Maintaining azaleas

There are evergreen and deciduous azaleas, but gift plants are more commonly the evergreens. With care, these are rather easy to place outside in rich, somewhat moist, well-drained soil. They like a semi-shady site outside. Indoors, give your gift plant plenty of bright light (but not direct sun), and keep it at a room temperature of about 65° F. Never let the plant's soil dry out, and avoid drafty sites. A warm draft for more than a few hours will cause almost total leaf drop and can kill the plant.

The gift plant may continue to flower for almost a month if you remove faded flowers promptly. Feed it with a liquid fertilizer for houseplants every 2 weeks if you intend to place it outdoors. When all the flowers are gone, acclimatize it outdoors in a sheltered site, and then plant it directly in soil.

The leaves of azaleas are poisonous. Don't let your kids or your pets chomp on them.

Keeping florist's cyclamen

Place the gift pot in a cool, well-lighted area, but not in direct sunlight. Do not let the plant touch a cold window glass. Keep the plant at a room temperature between 50 and 60° F, and keep the soil slightly moist. When watering, use lukewarm water and try to keep it off the leaves. With good care, the flowers won't completely fade until February.

I've had success placing the gift pot outdoors in a sheltered, lightly shaded spot until it acclimatizes, then transplanting carefully into very rich soil when the weather is consistently pleasant. Plant the cyclamen where the drainage is excellent, or the tuberous roots will rot.

The joys of Jerusalem cherry

Also called Christmas cherry and Winter cherry, the pretty scarlet berries of this plant are poisonous, as is every other part of the plant. Outdoors, it is an evergreen with white star-shaped flowers in the spring, followed later by the bright berries. It can slowly reach about 3 feet in height. Indoors, keep the plant in a cool, sunny site, at a temperature of about 50° F. If the room is warm or drafty, the leaves and fruit will quickly drop. If you want a challenge, dry and store their seeds until the spring, then put them in a mix of 50 percent sand and 50 percent peat moss. Keep them warm until they are about 3 inches high, then transplant them to a larger pot. Put outdoors in summer in a semi-shaded site, watering when the soil feels slightly dry, and fertilizing lightly.

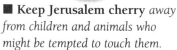

■ **Keep Jerusalem cherry** *away from children and animals who might be tempted to touch them.*

Poinsettia perfection

The most popular of Christmas plants, poinsettias can last for months indoors. Place your semi-tropical gift plant in a sunny site, preferably keeping it at a temperature between 60 and 75° F. Although you may need to place it near a window for the sunshine, keep the leaves from touching a cold window, as this will cause leaf damage.

Poinsettias are big water users. Keep your plant's soil just slightly moist at all times or the leaves will wilt and drop if it's too dry. Check the saucer under the pot, and if water is pooling there, drain it. Stagnant water will injure the plant's roots and take on an unpleasant odor. Eventually the leaves will turn yellow and drop. Indoors it is difficult to maintain a poinsettia so that it re-blooms the following year. While the red-flowered poinsettias are most common, there are also white, pink, yellowish, and speckled red and white varieties.

■ **Poinsettias will last** *well into the New Year if cared for properly. Try to place them away from vents that blow out heat, as these plants dislike drafts, be they warm or cold.*

Poinsettia flowers appear to be composed of the plant's bracts, or modified leaves, that resemble petals. But the actual flowers are the little yellow centers surrounded by the bracts.

Once the poinsettia fades, put it outdoors in a sheltered, sunny spot, keeping the soil moist. In spring, you can transplant it into prepared soil. Keep the soil moist and you may eventually have a 10-foot-high shrub. You can also make cuttings in late summer. Some people have a skin reaction to the sap, so it's best to wear gloves when handling poinsettias.

A simple summary

✔ There are still garden chores to be done in the winter and there is garden fun to be had throughout the year, both indoors and out.

✔ Many indoor gift plants can be transplanted outdoors after the flowers fade. Place them outside in a sheltered spot while still in their container. Water the plants as needed, and replant appropriately in the spring.

✔ You can use the plants you grow to make lovely personal gifts, such as handmade dolls and your own potpourri.

More resources

Books

I have more than 400 garden reference books, some quite antique. I love bookstores, the kind that have stacks of dusty books, because I often find a treasure with new tidbits of information, or a self-published book written by a devotee of this or that plant, or just something with scrumptious detail on a subject I love.

From my garden library, I have here compiled a list of the books I go to first when I have a garden question. Some of them are available in big modern bookstores or via the Internet, but others you must hunt for in independent bookstores, or in the stores adjoining botanical gardens across the country. It's so much fun – a learning adventure. Enjoy yourself!

Herbaceous Perennial Plants
by Allan M. Armitage, Varsity Press, Athens, GA, 1989.

House Plants for the Purple Thumb
by Maggie Baylis, 101 Productions, San Francisco, 1973.

A-Z Encyclopedia of Garden Plants
by Christopher Brickell and Judith Zuk, Eds., Dorling Kindersley Publishing, 1997.

A Gardener's Guide to Cacti & Succulents
by Peter Chapman and Margaret Martin, Salamander Books Ltd., London, 1988.

Sunset National Garden Book
by Suzanne N. Eyre, Ed., Sunset Books, Menlo Park, CA, 1997.

Pests of the Garden and Small Farm
by Mary Louise Flint, University of California, San Francisco, 1990.

Herbal Bounty, The Gentle Art of Herb Culture
by Steven Foster, Gibbs-Smith, Salt Lake City, UT, 1984.

Heirloom Garden,
by Jo Ann Gardner, Garden Way Publishing, Pownel, VT, 1992.

Potpourris and Other Fragrant Delights
by Jacqueline Heriteau, Penguin Books, New York, 1975.

Controlling Lawn and Garden Insects
by L. Patricia Kite, Ortho Books, Monsanto, CA, 1987.

100 Favorite Flowering Shrubs
by L. Patricia Kite, Metro Books, New York, 1999.

Ground Covers in the Landscape
by Emile Labadie, Sierra City Press, Sierra City, CA, 1983.

Lavender, Sweet Lavender
by Judith A. McLeod, Kangaroo Press, Australia, 1997.

Golden Gate Gardening
by Pam Peirce, Sasquatch Books, Seattle, WA, 1998.

Growing Fruit in Your Backyard
by Lee Reich, Macmillan Publishing, New York, 1996.

Propagation
by Alan Toogood, Stein & Day, New York, 1982.

Complete Handbook of Garden Plants
by Michael Wright, Facts on File, New York, 1984.

Directories of great gardens

American Gardens: A Traveler's Guide
Published by Brooklyn Botanical Garden
1000 Washington Avenue
Brooklyn, NY 11225
(718) 622-4433

Directory of Gardens in North America
Published by American Association
of Botanical Gardens and Arboreta
31 Longwood Road
Kennett Square, PA 19348
(610) 925-2500

Where on Earth: A Gardener's Guide to Specialty Plants in California
Published by AgAccess
603 4th St.
Davis, CA 95616
(916) 756-7177

Magazines for the gardener

It's almost too easy to find magazines devoted to gardening. Go to any large newsstand or bookstore, or look on the Internet at Home and Garden Magazines (www.agardenstore.com/magazines.html). A sampling of popular gardening magazines include:

American Homestyle & Gardening	Garden Design	Log Home Living
	Garden Gate	National Gardening
Better Homes & Gardens	Home	Organic Gardening
The English Garden	Horticulture	Sunset
Flower & Garden	House Home & Garden	This Old House

Regional magazines and special issues of *Woman's Day* and *Family Circle*, among others, also focus on the concerns of gardeners.

Gardening societies

African Violet Society of America
   2375 North St, Beaumont, TX 77702-1722
   avas@avsa.org

American Bamboo Society
   750 Krumkill Rd, Albany, NY 12203-5976
   www.bamboo.org

American Begonia Society
   157 Monument, Rio Dell, CA 95562-1617
   www.begonias.org

American Bonsai Society
   P.O. Box 1136, Puyallup, WA 98371-1136
   www.absbonsai.org

American Conifer Society
   P.O. Box 360, Keswick, VA 22947-0360
   ACSconifer@aol.com

American Daffodil Society
   1686 Greyfox Trails, Milford, OH 45150-1521, (513) 248-9137

American Hemerocallis Society (daylily)
   Dept. WWW, P.O. Box 10, Dexter, GA 31019
   gmercer@nlamerica.com

American Iris Society
   Marilyn Harlow, Dept. E, Membership Secretary, P.O. Box 55, Freedom, CA 95019
   www.irises.org

American Orchid Society
   6000 South Olive Ave,
   West Palm Beach, FL 33405
   www.orchidweb.org/

American Penstemon Society
   1569 S. Holland Ct, Lakewood, CO 80232

American Primrose Society
   Frederic Graff, Treasurer, 2630 W. Viewmont Way, W. Seattle, WA 98199-3019
   www.backyardgardener.com/aps.html

American Rose Society
   P.O. Box 30,000, Shreveport, LA 71130-0030
   www.ars@ars-hq.org

Cactus & Succulent Society of America
   Mindy Fusaro, CSSA Treasurer
   P.O. Box 2615, Pahrump, NV 89041-2615
   mpfusaro@pahrump.com

California Rare Fruit Growers (international organization)
   Fullerton Arboretum, CSUF, PO Box 6850, Fullerton, CA 92834-6850
   info@crfg.org

International Camellia Society
   P.O. Box 306, Clinton, NC 28328
   www.med-rz.uni-sb.de/med_fak/physiol2/camellia/home.htm

International Carnivorous Plant Society
Fullerton Arboretum, CSUF,
Fullerton, CA 92634
www.gardennet.com/InformationDirectory/
carnivorous

International Geranium Society
P.O. Box 92734, Pasadena, CA 91109-2734

International Palm Society
P.O. Box 1897, Lawrence, KS 66044-8897
www.palms.org

Lady Bird Johnson Wildflower Center
www.wildflower.org/

Mycological Society of America (Mushrooms, and
the like)
c/o Linda Hartwick, Allen Marketing
810 E. 10th St, Lawrence, KS 66044
www.erin.utoronto.ca/~w3msa/

National Chrysanthemum Society
NCS, 10107 Homar Pond Drive,
Fairfax Station, VA 22039-1650
www.mums.org

Native Plant Societies
www.acorn-online.com/hedge/h-socs.htm

North American Rock Garden Society
PO Box 67,
Millwood, NY 10546
www.nargs.org

Perennial Plant Association
3383 Schirtzinger Rd,
Hilliard, OH 43026
(614) 771-8431
ppa@perennialplant.org

Gardening on the Web

www.acorn-online.com/hedge/h-socs.htm
You'll find a state-by-state listing of addresses of
North American native plant societies.

www.ag.arizona.edu/pubs/garden/mg/fruit/care
This helpful site calls itself Fruit Trees: Planting and
Varieties. You'll get general information on all kinds of
fruit trees, including apple, apricot, cherry, fig, nectarine,
olive, peach, pear, plum, pomegranate, and quince.
Fertilization, thinning, pollination, irrigation, and
pruning are also discussed, with tips on named varieties.

www.ag.ohio-state.edu/~ohioline/hyg-fact/
1000/index.html
Ohio State University Extension has a large library of
horticulture fact sheets.

www.ag.usask.ca/cofa/departments/hort/
hortinfo/yards/landsca.html
The University of Saskatchewan College of Agriculture has
an extensive list of gardening articles. Check out this one
for help in choosing plants for home landscaping, including
advice on selecting shrubs and trees for a home garden.

www.ars.org
Visit this site to learn about the American Rose Society
(ARS). Founded in 1892, the non-profit ARS focuses on
the enjoyment, propagation, and promotion of roses. This
site provides an opportunity to have rose-related questions
answered by experts. You'll also find lists of events, local
societies, and membership information. It also has a list of
the best roses of the month, with details on each.

www.begonias.org
This American Begonia Society site contains projects, a
virtual greenhouse, library articles, book reviews, local
events and major shows, and information on how to join.

www.botanical.com
Botanical.com has information on many medicinal herbs.
On the home page, click on "word search," then type in
the name of the plant you want information about.

www.bulb.com
Site of the U.S. Netherlands Flower Bulb Information
Center, where you'll find plenty of facts about tulips and
other bulbs grown commercially in Holland.

www.colostate.edu/Depts/IPM/ento/j515.html
For more information on slugs, their history, habits, cultural controls, traps, barriers, and baits, click here.

www.daylilies.org
Visit this site of the American Hemerocallis Society. You'll learn about conventions, sources of daylilies, publications, and regional display gardens.

www.dlcwest.com/~createdforyou/lndscp1.html
The landscaping information page from Family Gardening offers suggestions on what questions to ask yourself and your local nursery expert when you're planning a garden, and gives advice on dealing with local suppliers and choosing plants.

dspace.dial.pipex.com/town/square/gf86/
The site of the Lawn Mower Museum in Southport, England. It displays the largest collection of vintage lawn mowers in the world, as well as toy lawn mowers and lawn mowers of the rich and famous.

ext.msstate.edu/pubs/pub456.htm
The Mississippi State University Extension Service offers advice on espaliers, including suggested trees, shrubs, and vines for espalier use, planting tips, espalier patterns, how to support espaliers, attachment devices, and training methodology.

www.frontiercoop.com/aromatherapy/potpourri/index.html
You'll find complete details about potpourri fragrance and how to make and use potpourri. This site provides potpourri history and lore, fragrance classifications, equipment, fragrant ornaments for any season, fragrant wreaths, skin allergy tests, and sources of essential oils used in perfume.

www.garden.com
This on-line magazine offers information about drip irrigation and soaker hoses, and more. There's also great shopping here, so you may want to hide your credit cards.

www.gardenguides.com/flowers/annuals/annuals.htm
Garden Guides' site on annual flowers discusses a very wide range of topics. Other areas of the same Web site look at perennials, bulbs, herbs, and vegetables.

www.gardenweb.com/directory/hsa/
Go to this address to find the Herb Society of America reference site. You'll find the society's history and purpose, membership information, a discussion of the herb of the month, a speaker's list, news of the many local societies, a calendar of events, meetings and conventions, seed exchange information, and publications, projects, and programs of interest.

www.gardenweb.com/glossary
This is the Garden Web Glossary of Botanical Terms, where you can look up more than 2,500 terms relating to botany, gardening, horticulture, and landscape architecture.

www.gourmetgarlicgardens.com/overview.htm
Click here for A Garlic Overview: if you like garlic, this is the site for you. There are good descriptions of the garden varieties available, history, folklore, harvesting information, cooking tips, growing tips, health benefits, garlic chemistry, reference books, on-line purchase catalogs, and how to braid. Lots of fun information!

www.graylab.ac.uk/usr/hodgkiss/bcss.html
Visit this site for a listing of national and international cactus and succulent societies that offer growing advice, as well as cutting exchange information.

www.guild.bham.ac.uk/bucv/tools.html
The Birmingham University Conservation Volunteers offer concise, practical information on all kinds of garden tools.

www.homeharvest.com/plantphpreference.htm
The University of Florida Cooperative Extension site has information about raising and lowering pH levels, and specific plant needs.

www.hummingbird.org/faq.htm
For questions and answers on hummingbirds in the garden, visit the Web site of the Hummingbird Society.

www.irises.org
The home page for the American Iris Society.

www.ivy.org
This site is brought to you by the American Ivy Society, a not-for-profit organization dedicated to ivy education and promotion. The site provides membership information, ivy care, ivy sources, and general ivy information.

www.lawninstitute.com/guide.html
Take a look at the Lawn Institute Homeowner's Resource Guide to a Beautiful Lawn, with explanations of grass types, seed selection, and how to plant and maintain a lawn.

main.tellink.net/~sues/
Learn all about how to turn your sugar maple sap into sweet syrup. This site includes an historical photo album, a cookbook, and a guest sugarer you can send questions to.

www.makestuff.com/lavender_wand.html
Visit this site for instructions on how to make pretty, sweet-smelling lavender decorations.

www.mc.edu/~adswww/
This is the home page for the American Daffodil Society.

www.mcvicker.com/hsscv/hsscv21.htm
Here you'll find information on deer and ideas for preventing them from damaging your garden.

www.mes.umn.edu/Documents/D/G/DG1108.html
Go to this site for information on raspberries for the home garden from the University of Minnesota. You'll find recommendations on local varieties, care, pruning, and diseases.

www.mes.umn.edu/Documents/D/G/DG1130.html
This site, Caring for Houseplants in Northern Climates, is affiliated with the University of Minnesota, a state where it gets very cold. You'll get basic instructions on lighting, water, temperature, humidity, nutrients, cleaning, and summer care.

www.msue.msu.edu/imp/mod03/master03.html
This address gets you into the Michigan State University Extension Home Horticulture database. It has information on hundreds of gardening topics.

www.naba.org
For a wealth of fascinating information on butterflies, how to attract them, and how to join a butterfly society, take a look at the site of the North American Butterfly Association.

www.naturalland.com/gv/ffg/sunflower.htm
You'll find three information-packed pages on sunflowers here, covering the plant's history, its growth habits, and uses. Planting tips, advice on harvesting, and details of where to find seeds are also given.

www.nhg.nrcs.usda.gov/ccs/Mulching.html
This site has easy-to-follow instructions on how to mulch, what to use, and the relative benefits of each type of mulch.

www.nps.gov/cherry
Visit this site to learn all about the cherry trees in Washington D.C., including the date of the annual Cherry Blossom Festival.

www.plantanswers.tamu.edu/fruit/fruit.html
Click here to learn how to grow all kinds of fruits. Information is provided by the Agricultural Extension of Texas A&M University. Although the information is targeted toward Texas, most of it is applicable nationwide.

www.rose.org
The home page of All-America Rose Selections, an association of rose growers dedicated to promoting garden roses. You'll find information on buying and growing roses, new hybrids, and rose history and symbolism.

www.sadako.com/pumpkin/growing.html
Go to this site for pumpkin-related activities, pumpkin links, pumpkin varieties, and for information on how to plant, care for, harvest, and store pumpkins.

www.stjamesparish.com
The gardeners at the St. James Parish in Louisiana provide practical information on repairing your old garden hose.

telework.ucdavis.edu/Propagation/Propagation12.htm #CuttingsPropagation
This is a lengthy and somewhat scientific, but excellent discussion on all types of plant propagation, including the most modern techniques used by commercial nurseries.

www.thegardenhelper.com
Search here for ideas on how to keep deer from the home garden, with a list of some plants that may be tried for varying degrees of deer resistance.

www.tpoint.net/neighbor/
The Gardening Launch Pad covers just about all you want to search out on gardens, or leads you to the information you require.

www.uidaho.edu/so-id/entomology/scale_insect_ and_mealybugs.htm
Look here for descriptions, photographs, and information about how to cope with scales and mealybugs.

www.wildhorses.com/compost.faq.html
You'll find frequently asked questions on compost here.

Catalogs for gardeners

Unless specified, catalogs listed here are of general interest. The inclusion of the following catalogs is for informational purposes only and does not serve as an endorsement of a particular vendor. There are many fine vendors that are not mentioned here.

Antique Rose Emporium
9300 Lueckemeyer Rd
Brenham,
TX 77833-6453
(800) 441-0002

Applesource (Apples)
1716 Apples Rd
Chapin, IL 62628
(800) 588-3854
www.applesource.com

Brent and Becky's Bulbs
7463 Heath Trail
Gloucester, VA 23061
(804) 693-3966
www.brentandbeckysbulbs.com

Brudy's Exotics
PO Box 820874
Houston, TX 77282-0874
(800) 926-7333
www.brudys-exotics.com

Burpee
W. Atlee Burpee & Co
Warminster, PA 18974
(800) 333-5808
www.burpee.com

Canyon Creek Nursery
3527 Dry Creek Road
Oroville, CA 95965
(530) 533-2166
johnccn@sunset.net

Cook's Garden
PO Box 5010
Hodges,
SC 29653-5010
(800) 457-9703
www.cooksgarden.com

Crystal Palace Perennials
(Water Garden)
PO Box 154
St. John, IN 46373
(219) 374-9419
www.crystalpalaceperennial.com

David Austin Roses Limited (Roses)
15393 Highway 64 West
Tyler, TX 75704
(903) 526-1800
www.davidaustinroses.com

Dixondale Farms (Onions)
PO Box 127
Carrizo Springs, TX 78834
(830) 876-2430

Dutch Gardens
PO Box 200
Adelphia, NJ 07710-0200
(800) 775-2852

Forest Farm
990 Tetherow Rd
Williams, OR 97544-9599
(541) 846-7269
(cost: $4 and well worth it)

Fungi Perfect
PO Box 7634, Olympia,
WA 98507
(800) 780-9126 (orders)
www.halcyon.com/mycomed/
fppage.html

Geraniaceae (Geraniums/
Pelargoniums)
122 Hillcrest Ave
Kentfield, CA 94904,
(415) 461-4168
www.freeyellow.com/members/
geraniaceae (cost: $4)

Gourmet Gardener
8650 College Blvd
Overland Park,
KS 66210
(913) 345-0490
www.gourmetgardener.com

Great Plant Company
PO Box 1041
New Hartford, CT
06057-9989
(800) 441-9788
www.greatplants.com

Gurney's Seed & Nursery Co.
110 Capital St
Yankton, SD 57079
(605) 665-1671
www.gurneys.com

Harmony Farm Supply
PO Box 460
Graton, CA 95444
(707) 823-9125
info@harmonyfarm.cm

Jackson & Perkins
1 Rose Lane
Medford, OR 97501
(800) 292-4769
www.jacksonandperkins.com

Johnny's Selected Seeds
1 Foss Hill Rd, RR 1
PO Box 2580
Albion, Maine 04910-9731
(207) 437-4301
www.johnnyseeds.com

K&L Cactus & Succulent Nursery
9500 Brook Ranch Rd E
Ione, CA 95640-9117
(209) 274-0360

Kactus Korrall
Route 1
PO Box 99D
Harwood, TX 78632
(210) 540-4521
www.kactus.com

Klehm Nursery (Peony specialists)
Rt 5, PO Box 197
South Barrington, IL
60010
(800) 553-3715
www.klehm.com

Lilypons Water Gardens
6800 Lilypons Rd
PO Box 10, Buckeystown,
MD 21717-0010
(800) 999-5459
www.lilypons.com (cost $5)

Mellinger's
2310 W. South Range Rd
North Lima, OH
44452-9731
(800) 321-7444
www.mellingers.com

Musser Forests, Inc
Dept S-99M
PO Box 340
Indiana, PA 15701-0340
(800) 643-8319
info@musserforests.com

Park Seed
1 Parkton Ave, Greenwood,
SC 29647-0001
(800) 845-3369
www.parkseed.com

Peaceful Valley Farm Supply
(Tools and supplies)
P.O. Box 2209, Grass Valley,
CA 95945. (530) 272-4759

Regan Nursery
4268 Decoto Road
Fremont, CA 94555
(800) 249-4680
www.regannursery.com

Rhapis Gardens Catalog (Palms
and the like)
P.O. Box 287
Gregory, TX 78359
(361) 643-2061
www.rhapisgardens.com/catalog/
(Online catalog only)

Roninger's Seed & Potato Co.
(Potatoes, onion, and garlic)
PO Box 307
Ellensburg, WA 98926
(509) 925-6025
www.irish-eyes.com (cost: $2)

Seeds of Change
PO Box 15700
Santa Fe, NM 87506-5700
(888) 762-7333
www.seedsofchange.com

Seeds of Distinction
PO Box 86, Station A
Etobicoke, Canada,
M9C 4V2
www.seedsofdistinction.com

Select Seeds (Antique flowers)
180 Stickney Hill Rd
Union, CT 06076
(800) 684-9310

Shady Oaks Nursery (Shade plants)
1101 S. State St
PO Box 7089
Waseca, MN 56093-0708
(800) 504-8006
www.shadyoaks.com (cost: $4)

Shepherd's Garden Seeds
30 Irene St
Torrington, CT 06790-6658
(800) 482-3638
www.shepherdseeds.com

Southern Exposure Seed Exchange
(Southern states specialist)
PO Box 170
Earlysville, VA 22936
(804) 973-4703
www.southernexposure.com

Territorial Seed Company
PO Box 157, Cottage
Grove, OR 97424-0061
(541) 942-9547
www.territorial-seed.com

Thompson & Morgan
PO Box 1308
Jackson, NJ 08527-0308
(800) 274-7333
www.thompson-morgan.com

Tomato Growers Supply Co.
PO Box 2237
Fort Myers, FL 33902
(888) 478-7333
www.tomatogrowers.com

Van Bourgondien Dutch Bulbs &
Perennials
245 Route 109
PO Box 1000
Babylon, NY 11702-9004
(800) 622-9959
www.dutchbulbs.com

Vermont Wildflower Farm
Reservation Center
Wildflower Lane
PO Box 1400
Louisiana, MO 63353-8400
(800) 424-1165
www.gardensolutions.com

Wayside Gardens
1 Garden Lane
Hodges, S.C. 29695-0001
(800) 845-1124
www.waysidegardens.com

White Flower Farm
PO Box 50
Litchfield, CT 06759-9952
(800) 503-9624
www.whiteflowerfarm.com

Wildseed Farms (Wildflowers)
425 Wildflower Hills, P.O.
Box 3000, Fredericksburg,
TX 78624-3000
(800) 848-0078
www.wildseedfarms.com

A simple glossary

Annual   A flowering plant that will grow, flower, make seeds, and die, all within the same year.

Anther   The portion of a flower at the tip of a stamen, containing pollen grains.

Anvil-type shears   A set of shears with a single cutting blade and a solid, non-cutting opposing part.

Arbor   An overhead trellis under which one can pass.

Arboretum   A tree garden.

Bare-root plant   A dormant plant sold with no soil mass around the roots.

Bicolor   A flower with two very distinct colors, each appearing once on a blossom.

Biennial   A plant that takes 2 years to complete a life cycle, growing from seed to leafy plant in the first year and flowering in the second year.

Bract   A group of modified leaves at the base of a flower.

Bud union   On a tree, the place where the trunk joins the roots.

Budwood   Strong young stems that have buds suitable for use in budding, whereby buds are inserted into cuts made in the bark of rooted cuttings.

Bulb   Bulbs are usually rounded, with a pointy tip, a round base, and an interior made of layers, similar to an onion. Mature bulbs – those that have been in the ground more than a season – reproduce by a dividing process within the parent bulb.

Cane   A long, slender branch that usually originates directly from a plant's roots.

Chilling requirement   The hours in which a plant must be cold during the winter months.

Corm   Corms are rounded, and are small to medium size and are solid all the way through. After a season, corms may produce cormlets around the parent corm. Each contains the ingredients to make a new plant exactly like the parent.

Crop rotation   To use a piece of land to grow a different plant than was grown there previously. Crops are rotated to discourage the likelihood of infestations by crop-specific insects and of crop-specific diseases.

Cultivar   A contraction of "cultivated variety." It's the progeny of a deliberate breeding effort which is known only in cultivation and reproduces plants with predictable, uniform characteristics.

Damping off   An incurable fungal disease also known as seed rot and seedling rot, whereby fungi residing in the soil attack and destroy young plants.

Deciduous   A plant that loses its leaves in the fall.

Dieback   The death of a shoot beginning at its tip, usually a result of disease or damage.

Double dig   To dig down about 2 feet rather than the usual 12 inches. Performed to provide roots with a greater amount of good quality soil.

Double flower   A flower that has three or more whorls of petals.

Drip line   An imaginary circular area around a tree based on where the tips of the outermost branches end and where rainwater normally drips.

Exfoliate   To come off in pieces, such as bark from a tree.

Fish emulsion   An organic product used to slowly release nitrogen to plants.

Flat   A long, wide container used in the sale of groundcover plants.

Fungicide   A pesticide designed for use against fungus.

Graft   The deliberate combination of two plants to create one plant, whereby a shoot of one plant is inserted into a slit in another plant.

Granule   The form of several gardening aids, particularly fertilizers and pesticides. Granules used in the garden are generally about the size of bath crystals.

Hardening off a plant   Making the plant a bit tougher so it can withstand cold, wind, or other outdoor natural weather conditions. You do this by gradually exposing it to the harsher outdoor environment.

Hardwood cutting   A cutting taken from mature wood, made in order to produce a new plant. Hardwood cuttings must be taken when plants are dormant.

Herb   The seeds, leaves, flowers, bark, roots, or other parts of any plant that is used for cosmetics, dyes, flavoring, fragrance, or health purposes.

Herbicide   A pesticide designed for use against weeds.

Hybridize   To cross or interbreed different plant varieties to produce a new plant, called a hybrid.

Insecticide   A pesticide for use against insects.

Invasive plant   A plant that grows aggressively, tending to take over the surrounding territory.

Nutrient   An element necessary for a plant's survival, such as nitrogen, potassium, and phosphorus.

Parasitoids   Organisms whose young develop in or on a pest insect, usually causing the pest insect's death.

Peat pots   Little pots made of pressed and dried peat moss. When you use them, you can place pot and plant directly into the garden soil for transplant, without damaging the root system.

Perennial   A flower that has roots that survive from year to year, sending out new growth in the spring.

Perennial grown as an annual   A perennial plant that has a very short life span, and that is usually replaced every year.

Pergola   An arbor covered by a roof or latticework on which vines grow.

Perlite   A soil component that is created from volcanic rock, and is slightly heavier than vermiculite. It is used to loosen heavy soil, and help oxygen and water reach plant roots.

Pesticide   A pest control mechanism. Insecticides, fungicides, and herbicides are all pesticides.

Pinch   To pick off the end bug of a twig or stem with the fingers in order to enhance growth.

Pinnate leaf   A leaf with little leaflets running along both sides of a main axis.

Plug   Cut-out section of good growing lawn inserted into prepared ground.

Pompom   A fully rounded flower.

Pot-bound   A potted plant with overgrown roots, also known as a root-bound plant.

Potpourri   Dried flower petals and spices kept in a jar. May also contain sweet-smelling seeds, stems, and roots.

Propagation   The deliberate creation of new plants from seed or other means.

Rhizome   A swollen section of an underground, horizontal plant stem. Roots grow from the underside of this stem, and plant buds develop on top of the stem.

Root hair   A small, tubular outgrowth from a growing root that absorbs water and nutrients dissolved in water.

Rototill   To dig a lawn in preparation for seeding. A rototiller's rotating tines dig into the ground as the mechanism is pushed. Also used to aerate, de-thatch, and to make special planting rows.

Runner   The trailing stem of a parent plant that generates a new, baby plant.

Semi-double flower   A flower with two or three whorls of petals.

Single flower   A flower with a single whorl of two to six petals.

Sod   Mature grass with roots set in good soil that is laid in large pieces to create a lawn.

Softwood cutting   A cutting from the stem of a perennial plant, made in order to produce a new plant.

Specimen plant   A single plant, usually medium-size or larger, which is placed so as to provide a focal point.

Spider   A double flower with long, tubular, graceful florets.

Spoon   A flower with florets that expand slightly into a spoon-shape at the end.

Sprig   Individual blades of grass set into the ground to create a lawn.

Stamen   A slim stalk inside a flower's petals that serves as a pedestal for the flower's pollen.

Succulent   A plant that stores water in its leaves, roots or stems. Generally easy to keep in very dry areas.

Sucker   A shoot springing below the ground, typically from a plant's roots, instead of from its stem.

Taproot   A strong center root that grows straight down into the soil.

Terrarium   A self-contained environment for animals or plants.

Thatch   A layer of dead roots and stems that builds up between growing grass and the soil.

Topiary   A tree or shrub clipped into an ornamental shape.

Trellis   A wooden frame with crossing strips, used to support climbing plants.

Tuber   A swollen, underground stem or root that stores buds for a new plant.

Umbel   A flower that sprouts from stalks spreading from a common center, similar to umbrella ribs.

Understock   A rooted cutting, usually from a plant with a hardy root system, that serves as the host plant for budwood.

Vegetative propagation   The creation of new plants from another plant, such as through stem cuttings, dividing, and grafting.

Vermiculite   A soil component that is created from mica, a mineral that has been heated, puffed up, and transformed into tiny, very lightweight chips that help retain soil air and water. It has no nutritional value for your plants.

Weed   Any plant that is growing where it's not wanted.

Index

Acknowledgments

Packagers acknowledgments

Cooling Brown would like to thank Margaret Doyle, Alison Bolus, and Corinne Asghar for their editorial assistance, and Barry Robson for illustrating the dogs, and bringing them so vividly to life.

Index
Patricia Coward.

Illustrators
Karen Cochrane, Martine Collings, Simone End, Will Giles, Sandra Pond, John Woodcock.

Picture credits

Clive Nichols Garden Pictures: 104 The Priory, Kemerton, Worcs.
The Garden Picture Library: 2 Howard Rice; 14-15 Ron Evans; 22 Henk Dijkman; 38 Mayer/Le Scanff; 48 Jane Legate; 72, 77 Mayer/Le Scanff; 86 Michael Howes; 102 Steven Wooster; 181 Mayer/Le Scanff; 234 Howard Rice; 239 Juliette Wade 249 John Glover; 254, 262 Howard Rice; 272 Erika Craddock; 283 Linda Burgess; 310 John Miller; 326 top Ron Sutherland; 378 Mark Bolton; 382 right Lorraine Pullin; 383 left Jane Legate.

Additional photography

Peter Anderson, Clive Boursnell, Deni Bown, Jonathan Buckley, Jane Burton, Andrew Butler, Eric Crichton, Geoff Dann, Andrew De Lory, Christine M. Douglas, Philip Dowell, Alistair Duncan, Andreas Einsiedel, Neil Fletcher, Frank Greenaway, Steve Gorton, Andrew Henley, Jacqui Hurst, Colin Keates, Dave King, Graham Kirk, Cyril Laubscher, John Miller, David Murray, Howard Rice, Bob Rundle, Karl Shone, Kim Taylor, Jerry Young, Juliette Wade, Matthew Ward, Juliette Watts, Steven Wooster.